The Politics of Writing Instruction

The Politics of Writing Instruction: Postsecondary

Edited by
RICHARD BULLOCK
and
JOHN TRIMBUR

General Editor
CHARLES SCHUSTER

BOYNTON/COOK PUBLISHERS
HEINEMANN
Portsmouth, NH

Boynton/Cook Publishers, Inc.
A Subsidiary of
Heinemann Educational Books, Inc.
361 Hanover Street   Portsmouth, NH 03801
Offices and agents throughout the world

Library of Congress Cataloging-in-Publication Data
The Politics of writing instruction: postsecondary/edited by Richard H. Bullock and
    John Trimbur: general editor, Charles I. Schuster.
        p.   cm.
    Includes bibliographical references.
    ISBN 0—86709—272—6
    1. English language — Rhetoric — Study and teaching — Political aspects.
    2. English philology — Study and teaching (Higher) — Political aspects.
    I. Bullock, Richard H.   II. Trimbur, John.   III. Schuster, Charles I.
PE1404.P58   1991
808'.042'0711—dc20   90—5217
                                                                CIP

Cover design by Wladislaw Finne
Designed by Vic Schwarz
Printed in the United States of America
91 92 93 94 95   10 9 8 7 6 5 4 3 2 1

To all those students — past,
present, and future —
whose encounters and struggles
with reading and writing
keep our job forever political.

Contents

Foreword

Draw enough breaths and you achieve seniority: damned if it hasn't happened to me. I surmise that I'm the oldest contributor to this volume, and while age guarantees neither wisdom nor even sense, it does marvelously extend the span of personal recall, and tempt the dotard to cash in on his one secure advantage. Not that memory is history, but perhaps the historians among you will grant these few memories some typicality.

1948: I took freshman composition, to the tune of Perrin and of eclectic readings from Shakespeare to Julian Huxley. I remember those, but remember *nothing* of Mr. Perrin's counsel about writing, or of my instructor's. It must have been the same counsel I got in high school: writing is correctness, topic sentences, organization, and the rest. Writing is writing. Anyhow, when in

1954: I taught my first section of composition (with no prior training, of course), I brought to my own students those same primitive truths, soon to be augmented by some lore about definition, assumptions, implications, and structures of argument, as well as some thoughts about tone, distance, metaphor, diction, and the like, drawn from the regnant New Criticism. Again, readings were the main thing, and I bet more of my students remember Sartre's *The Flies* and C. S. Lewis on pain than remember anything they learned about writing.

1961: My first full-time job, and a comp course that "did" Wordsworth, Keats, and Frost first semester and some novels the second, along with more of what wasn't, but might as well have been, Mr. Perrin's advice about writing. The tradition passed along from one generation to the next, of instructors who knew what sort of product students were supposed to make, but not how to enable them, instructors who had really meant to be teaching literature.

1965: We brought in linguistics. The horizons of discussion about composition had expanded mainly through the questioning of traditional grammar as a foundation for writing instruction. Descriptive linguistics had many advocates; *we* were among the first to try generative grammar. Still lots of literary readings; still the routine of a finished paper every week or two, promptly returned with comments and a grade.

1966: I became editor of *College English* and paid closer attention to the
national conversation about writing instruction. I began to hear about
(and pass the news on to *CE* readers) the open classroom, writing
without teachers, collaborative learning, students' rights to their own
language, the comp class as site of transgression and even liberation.

1975: My co-editor, Bill Coley, and I put together a collection of *CE*
articles on writing instruction, *Ideas for English 101*. In the preface we
wrote:

> In economic hard times, college students are less eager to break idols
> and more concerned to learn the skills which may (or may not) find them
> good jobs. Hard-pressed administrators and legislatures enforce this
> change in mood by demanding "accountability." Political reaction joins
> in thinning out the heady atmosphere of experiment.... With the
> slogan "back to basics" in their ears, teachers of freshman English may
> well feel now that their only option is to dust off the old handbooks and
> get cracking on punctuation and usage.

Yet now comes a book, in 1991, whose title calmly joins the word
"Politics" to the phrase "Writing Instruction," as if there were no disjunction
between those categories whose union had for so long been unthinkable,
and by 1975 was becoming hard to think, again. In eighteen papers by
respected professionals, many of them leaders in the field, not only the
word "politics" marks the distance of talk about writing now from such talk
a quarter of a century ago; the conversation has also naturalized talk about
(are you ready for a long list?) power, privilege, hierarchy, domination,
hegemony, inequality, injustice, oppression, alienation, resistance, subversion, empowerment, feminization, androcentrism, phallocentrism, class,
underclass, caste, production, social reproduction, consumption, cultural
capital, ideology, legitimation, contradiction, dialectic, and (gulp!) revolution. For another take on this phenomenon, check the "Works Cited,"
and see alien names like Althusser, Anderson, Aronowitz, Bakhtin, Beauvoir,
Bourdieu, Bowles and Gintis, Dinnerstein, Eagleton, Freire, Geertz,
Gilligan, Giroux, Gramsci, Hall, Heath, Moi, Wallerstein, and Williams,
commingling amiably with more domestic ones like Britton, Emig, Lauer,
and Shaughnessy. Furthermore, the essays are *not about* how to improve
the technique of writing instruction. They are about the social relations of
writing seen as inseparable from social relations writ large. Even allowing
that this volume does not speak from the workaday center — the "trenches" —
of the field, clearly something has happened to let the writers plant some
land mines there. Something has happened to disrupt or even explode our
self-conception.

What was it? Here are a few other dates, significant in my own chronicle
of change, but hardly personal:

1961: Freedom Rides
1964: Tonkin Gulf
1965: Watts
1967: Pentagon March
1968: MLA—along with the general rebellion, the first organized *feminist* uprising I had seen.

I won't dwell on the obvious—that the politicizing of comp responded to movements and events originating outside the university, in the traditional site of the political. They moved in, changed the terms in which we thought about our work, and provoked a "ruthless critique of all things existing," as someone once said. New students came in, too; and "student power." Black power and black studies came in. Women's liberation and women's studies came in. New and old male students had to make choices about the draft. (A landmark article by Peter Elbow in the November 1968 issue of *CE*, "A Method for Teaching Writing," brought his experience helping students apply for Conscientious Objector status over the divide and into the theory of comp.) Writing instructors didn't have to politicize the field, though some did: politics flowed into the classroom, and only then did we begin to notice that politics had always been there.

A genealogy for political comp would of course need to trace other lines of descent than the one from the 1960s movements. The tremendous expansion of universities, colleges, and community colleges in itself challenged old complacencies and routines, as it multiplied the number of writing classes. Then the collapse of the academic job market in 1969 created a reserve army of the unemployed, virtually guaranteeing the superexploitation of part-time faculty that Jim Slevin grimly surveys, and to which almost all the papers in this volume at least obliquely refer. Behind that story is a longer one of habituation to a two-class, lit-comp system, well documented and explained by Bob Connors. Surely the politicization of writing instruction must be in part understood as the insurgency of an underpaid, overworked, and disrespected occupational group. I would cite also the professionalization of that group, made feasible because its services were now in greater demand: career-oriented students thought writing a necessary skill, and a punctual literacy "crisis" stirred concern about writing among the wider public (see the papers by John Trimbur and Anne Ruggles Gere). With professionalization came more organizations, more meetings, more seminars, more journals—an arena within which the writing instructoriate could consolidate its anger as well as share discoveries about rhetoric.

I see all these determinations at work in shaping the politics expressed in this volume and endowing them with at least a marginal reputability—probably more than that—if not so centrist a position as some of the writers think. Anyhow, I welcome the growth of political comp, feel myself in alliance with the writers gathered here, and thank Richard Bullock, Charles Schuster, and John Trimbur for inviting me to join the conversation. Having done so first with speculations about how we came to be having it,

I turn now to other thoughts prompted by reading these essays; and a good, instructive, inspiriting, and infuriating read it has been.

Best get to the infuriating part, right now. Jim Slevin's account of working conditions, an account elegantly gendered in Susan Miller's essay, is like a grenade tossed into a rally. Stop, hold everything, we can't go on talking about subverting the dominant ideology and reinventing the curriculum until we face this disaster. As Jim puts it, none too rudely, the profession to which we belong "rests on, *is based on*, a foundation of despicable inequality." Yes. I could complement Jim's anecdote with a story about my own recent evaluation of an English department at another PhD-granting university, but what would the point be? I found just what he found; or a little worse, perhaps, since the TA stipend there is the same now as it was where Jim visited several years ago. Lots of overworked and underpaid people in endlessly deferred or dead-end careers help sustain the professional well-being that writers in this volume rightly associate with high theory, light teaching loads for stars, male and older-generation privilege, the ideology of great literature, and so on. That writing proletariat also enables us, the contributors to this volume, does it not? Would we have the free time to theorize the politics of writing instruction, imagine our way toward liberatory composition, and excoriate the two-class system in our field if we were in the other class?

Having stepped this close to the precipice of guilt, a sentiment of little use in thinking about economics, let me draw back and join the effort to understand this professional scandal. Jim Slevin sets aside the idea that exploitation of part-timers and graduate students owes to "economic problems beyond our control," and insists that those with power in and around our profession *"choose"* to maintain its two-class system. True, but not in circumstances of their own choosing, to paraphrase someone, again. Jim shows that the demographic argument for part-timers has been a cover, but I don't think he scans the market broadly enough to dismiss economic causes. Universities budget the resources they can get to create the product (academic credits and credentials) their students pay for; they have to compete for students; a reserve army of unemployed and semiemployed instructors is available. Q.E.D. At the average national rate for part-time instructors, Wesleyan's administration could staff my department's entire course offering with my salary alone, fire all the tenure-track faculty, save well over a million dollars a year, and thus put a thrifty end to the two-class system.

That few administrations make that sort of choice, in spite of its obvious appeal, owes to a variety of restraints. Among them are the need of most universities to preserve an image of reputability, and the success of the academic profession in linking institutional reputability to the employment of semiautonomous faculties and the support of research. If Wesleyan hired only part-timers, it would quickly slide into obscurity, no matter how well they taught. But why has the professionalization of "English" left so many of its aspirants outside the walls of security and independence it has built? The answer to that question comes clearer than before through Bob Connors' revealing history, as augmented by Jim Slevin's account of what happened in the 1970s and 1980s. (One of the pleasures of this book is the insight conferred on our disciplinary history by Connors, Trimbur, Newkirk, Herzberg, and others; no critical self-reflection without history, I say.) Almost from the start, the terms of our professional bargain ensured that writing instruction would be left on or beyond the margin, and the demographics and economics of the last two decades have only intensified a deeply inscribed pattern of neglect.

If I'm right, the reconception of our field called for by many in this volume will continue to run against the professional grain; and while the professionalization of comp itself along with public education and agitation may achieve some gains, I'm gloomy about the prospects unless the 1990s turn out to be another boom time, as atypical as were the 1960s according to Connors. That's no reason not to fight for what gains are within reach. Perhaps there is also hope in the internal subversions described by Louise Wetherbee Phelps and Toby Fulwiler. But I doubt that writing chauvinism and militancy will carry us far toward erasing the inequities that divide our community.

Beyond that, I think we should be wary about conflating those inequities with the broader injustice and irrationality that concern many of the present writers. Michael Holzman, Jim Berlin, John Trimbur, Susan Miller, Elizabeth Flynn, Victor Villanueva, and others chart structures and processes of capitalist patriarchy, locating within them the work that writing teachers do and the institutions and attitudes that make "common sense" of that work. This project of demystification sometimes says and sometimes takes it as a given that power and privilege in our society are wickedly maldistributed. Awareness of wasted lives and schematic disempowerment drives these explorations.

From that perspective, part-timers and grad students in English are on the edges of the professional-managerial class: some undergoing a long and dreary rite of passage into it, others perhaps seeing its door shut in their faces. But however lamentable the treatment of these people by universities and our profession, they have the cultural capital and class resiliency to make lives for themselves somewhere other than the ghetto, prison, or homeless shelter. Furthermore, it's not clear to me that inequality within our profession stands in more than a homological relation to systemic inequality in the U.S. and the world as a whole. If not, it could be misleading to conceptualize part-timers and TAs as an "underclass," or to let that term slide back and forth between them and the wretched of the earth. And as Susan Miller warns, some "intellectual and 'practical' moves toward equality for composition reproduce the hegemonic superstructure by implying that bourgeois social climbing and successful competition for intellectual 'clout' are legitimate signs of improvement." I hope we can enact professional solidarity without losing touch with the understanding that our profession itself (like all professions) is among other things an enclave moated against — and a set of finely tuned accommodations and responses to — circumambient injustice.

And here, I think, is the nub, the central knot of contradictions, for anyone interested in a liberatory politics of writing instruction. Injustice and exploitation are intrinsic, not aberrant. Capitalism creates and needs great inequality. It swallows up, and makes functional, inequalities like those of race and gender that already exist, using them both to feed a stratified labor market and to naturalize it (women's work, coolie labor, etc.) by attributing systemic unfairness to biological and therefore immutable differences. For more liberal minds, the educational system serves much the same naturalizing purpose. It allows people to imagine something called equal opportunity — never fully achieved but always in the making through a hundred initiatives and remedies — such that individual life chances are acceptably responsive to ability and effort.

As Michael Holzman notes, it is a "truism" that "the schools exist in order to reproduce the structure of society," and reproduction comprehends the ideologies that help make hegemony invisible, as well as the practices that constantly recreate and modify it. Holzman spells this out truly and mordantly for the ideology of literacy, as do many of the other writers here assembled for other dimensions of our social practice. How to make this knowledge inspiriting rather than paralyzing, for those working within this key apparatus of reproduction to criticize and subvert that which it is reproducing? This strikes me as the right question, though an uneasy and intractable one. Intractable, for one thing, because asked within an institution saturated with the ideal of opportunity and advancement. "Our current hegemony in the schools sanctions individual achievement.... How could a collectivity gathered for revolution be appealing to adolescents seeking access, after all?" asks Victor Villanueva. (From my own experience, it has a good bit more appeal to class-assured students where I regularly teach than to those I have taught at the local community college, usually the first in their families to get a whiff of access.) We help our students, particularly our writing students, in the most immediate and tangible way by equipping them to navigate the individualized market. The kind of help imagined by many of the present writers pulls in a different direction, toward critique and subversion of that market and its enormous superstructure (if the word may still be used) of supporting institutions — including our own.

To say the least, with John Trimbur: "imagination and political courage are required if literacy is to be re-presented as an intellectual resource against injustice...." Courage, in part because the effort entails demystification of our own work and our own privilege. And yet again, maybe not so much courage: Aren't we, most of us, tenured? Don't "they" pay us to teach critical thinking? Isn't much of our political practice (like the writing of these fearless words) comfortably housed within the discipline's reward system? Will I or my fellow contributors hesitate to add the titles of these essays to our résumés? Is the Pope Catholic? Is this hegemony, or what?

Think pragmatically or take local views, and there's much that can be done. Make evaluation of writing more collaborative, follow out the institutional logic of writing programs, infuse research with feminist thought, change the standards for tenure so that they respect what writing teachers do, change the dominant conceptions of composition and literature, and so on. I note with bemusement and empathy, not dismay, that nearly all the essays in this volume end with exhortations like these. How dependably the problem-solution format speaks through us when we undertake an assignment of this sort!

I see about five kinds of solutions in these essays, though some essays defy single classification. Try this rough scheme:

1. Nourish critical consciousness as we teach (Herzberg, Miller, Coles and Wall, Villanueva).
2. Work for a liberatory paradigm shift in "English" or literacy (Berlin, Flynn, Schwegler, Slevin, Phelps, Schuster, Fulwiler).
3. Create counterhegemonic institutions within school, or work to make school itself counterhegemonic (Holzman, Trimbur, Phelps, Bullock).
4. Work for job equity and solidarity within our profession (Connors, Newkirk, Miller, Slevin, Schuster).
5. Take our case to wider publics; educate and agitate (Donovan, Gere, Slevin).

I doubt that any of my colleagues would plump for a single solution to whatever it is, or would disparage the course set by others. But I hope to have suggested that "all of the above" is not a trouble-free program either; that tangles and contradictions abound; that hegemony mocks some of our best efforts.

Think globally, and none of the solutions proposed takes us far. It may be healthy to remind ourselves from time to time that we are only teachers and writers, not the massing army of social upheaval. There's an old habit, in the United States, of looking to the educational system for the cause or cure of every social crisis, a habit well analyzed by some of the writers herein. Let's not reenact a form of that habit by supposing that writing instructors might turn social reproduction on its head if only we theorize brilliantly enough, find the right Freirean pedagogy for North American college students; and work like demons. That way leads to burnout or paralysis: I share Villanueva's view that to get anywhere beyond reform "we must begin by acknowledging the unlikelihood of dramatic revolutionary change in the most immediate future." And to state the even-more-obvious: we can't move far in the liberatory direction beaconed by most of these essays until we are in sync with movements outside the universities and schools at least as coherent and forceful as movements of the late 1960s. No multiracial, feminist socialism in one profession, as someone else more or less said.

On the other hand, and to swing the rhetoric around to a different tack, we *are* teachers and writers: intellectuals. It's not nothing that in this little quadrant of academic life a scrappy pack of writing instructors and theorists has chosen to act as critical intellectuals, dissident intellectuals, disloyal intellectuals, and are reckoning how to use the means at hand in order to help the next generation find its own way of being critical, dissident, disloyal. This is not a revolutionary moment, but there will be a revolutionary moment in their lifetimes — you can say you heard it here. The defection of intellectuals is always a consequential stage in revolutionary process, though, of course, their defection may lead to no such outcome.

Revolution: what a quaint idea. The revolutions making news in the year of this writing are defections of quite another sort, from that which appropriated (and abused) the name of socialism. Some say socialism is dead and discredited. We're at "the end of history." But look around: not all that far around, no farther than the evening news. Hear about the devastation of rain forests, the riddling of the ozone layer, agribusiness's profligate dispersion of topsoil, the death of millions (soon to become tens and hundreds of millions) by starvation, the poisoning and depletion of waters, the depredations of AIDS and other epidemics, the brutalization of Latin America and Africa, genocide and death squads, the heedless waste of lives and cultures in our own rich, kind, gentle nation. Could there be a worse set of social arrangements than the one toward which Eastern and Central Europe now rush for securing a decent future on the planet? No social formation is permanent, least of all one that creates and feeds on such dominations. Capitalist patriarchy is dying too.

Our students may live to experience something worse. Or they may help make something better, something new that has as yet no name or plan. These night thoughts may seem remote from the politics of writing instruction, but I hope not; and I thank the present authors for pressing toward such connections.

Richard Ohmann

Preface

This book is the first in a series of volumes of original essays that will develop a political critique of writing instruction. In large part this project began as an expression of concern about the teaching of writing in American classrooms, from elementary school through graduate school. It began as a series of statements, observations, and questions raised by the members of the Commission on Composition, a deliberative body of NCTE comprised of teachers of writing representing the entire range of grade levels, elementary through college. In its annual discussions of "Trends and Issues" as well as its debates concerning the principles articulated in the 1984 Position Statement "Teaching Composition," the members of the Commission raised a number of significant concerns about the present health and future well-being of writing instruction. Some of those questions included: Who are we as a discipline, a profession? Can the teaching of writing be divorced from the social, political, cultural, and economic? What is the teaching of writing about? How are we bound by our historical practices, our rhetorical theories, our institutional definitions? Why is writing instruction a marginalized enterprise within so much of American education? And perhaps most important: How can we improve matters? What needs to be done to ensure that writing instruction—as a subject to be taught, researched, theorized, and problematized—assumes an appropriately powerful and valued place in American education?

The essays in this volume—which focuses exclusively on postsecondary education—address those subjects, pose more questions, and suggest at least some tentative answers. They tackle a wide range of perplexing issues: the role of literacy, the history of our field, public perceptions of writing instruction, the status of part-time composition instructors in English departments, the relations between composition and literary studies, tenure and promotion, writing assessment as institutional practice, writing across the curriculum, the impact of feminism and radical pedagogies, the implications of scientistic and positivist assumptions in the development of research in writing. We think these essays offer thoughtful, valuable, and at times troubling perspectives on our discipline. In a sense we are offering within this volume a general physical examination of the Rhetoric/Composition body circa 1990. And we are following through with a commitment made to the Commission on Composition—a commitment to produce one or more volumes of collected essays that speak to the varied concerns of writing specialists in American education.

In drawing together these particular voices within our profession, our concern as editors was not to put together a "representative" volume, whatever such a collection would look like. On the contrary, our desire was to develop a book around a modestly coherent set of principles, however difficult those principles are to articulate. We believe, for example, that the teaching of writing is unavoidably a political act. After all, there is no such thing as value-neutral teaching, certainly not value-neutral teaching of writing. As teachers, theorists, researchers, and historians have made clear, writing participates in a world of ideology and value. That many of those values remain invisible, in large part because they are so enmeshed within our culture as to seem "natural" to us, in no way diminishes their largely normative function. Writing is value-full, and all teaching built on and through a set of values is inherently and inevitably political.

We also unabashedly privilege certain practices in writing instruction over others. We prefer collaborative over atomized learning, critical and creative thinking over memorization and formulaic display, purposeful writing over exercises and drills. We prefer that writing be infused throughout an English curriculum, indeed throughout a multidisciplinary curriculum. We prefer a disciplinary perspective that makes its politics explicit so that all involved—from students and instructors to administrators and theorists—can make intelligent, knowledgeable, informed choices about their own actions. We prefer to conceive of rhetoric and composition as a multivoiced community, one in which all participants must be offered the opportunity to speak and be heard. We prefer that the teaching of writing, the research of writing, the theory of writing, and the administration of writing be valued as significant contributions within the life of English departments and educational institutions. Above all, we prefer to think of our efforts here as bringing us a step closer toward what Mina Shaughnessy called a "literate democracy."

As readers will quickly see, this set of principles is broad enough to incorporate a range of voices and politics under its aegis. We agree about a good deal concerning the politics of writing instruction, but there are differences, too—different versions of our collective history, different intellectual traditions that have influenced our teaching and research, different understandings about what we mean when we say that highly charged word "politics." We see our field defined not so much by governing paradigms and their periodic shifts as by an active and sustained conversation consisting of voices struggling to make our differences productive ones.

What this means, moreover, is that any book of this sort is necessarily an interim—and incomplete—report. Important voices remain outside the covers of this collection; subjects and issues of major significance go untreated here or are only faintly suggested. Some invited authors declined to participate; some for all their struggles fell short of our final deadline. We had a number of other essays and essayists that we would have liked to include. The material limits of a single volume and the pressure of time prevented us from extending the scope of this collection.

In fact, this shortcoming should become a virtue. Because teachers of writing at all levels have expressed so many different concerns, those of us involved with this project decided early on that we had too many issues to consider in one volume. As a result, a second volume is already under contract, *The Politics of Writing Instruction, K-12*, co-edited by Janet Emig and Joyce Armstrong Carroll. If these first two volumes succeed, we anticipate at least two further volumes: one to focus on two-year colleges and the other on minority education. Neither subject is adequately treated herein.

In drawing together the essays in this volume, we hoped to do more than simply provide a venue for splenetic venting. To express the legitimate rage and dissatisfaction that many writing-program faculty feel about inequitable funding decisions, unwarranted tenure and promotion denials, and the intellectual marginalization of composition within English departments and universities can be therapeutic; but we also hoped to achieve some larger purpose. First, we wanted to create some specific momentum toward change. We have no illusions that writing an essay about eliminating the exploitation of part-time composition lecturers, for example, will on its own achieve any results. What we hope this volume does achieve is the raising of consciousness among composition specialists, who will then initiate a wide-ranging discussion of these issues with their department colleagues, chairpersons, deans, associate deans, and divisional committee members. To further this end, we have exhorted the contributors to state their political and politicizing views, something difficult for many of us in academe. We hope the result is a book that can be shared widely and that will have some effect toward positive change.

Second, we wanted to create a book that would educate graduate students to the issues and challenges we all face in our discipline. The essays written for this volume articulate fundamental principles about what it means to profess writing as a career. Many of them offer specific recommendations for faculty, writing program administrators, English departments, and college programs. These are precisely the kinds of essays we think graduate students who comprise the future of our profession should read. We encourage and invite them to be part of the dialogue that we hope will be spurred by the publication of this book.

Finally, we wanted to draw attention to the subject of politics. It is a dangerous word, politics, for it implies partisanship, conflict, smoke-filled backrooms, shady dealings. Politicians cannot be trusted; departmental politics lead to bitter fights, broken friendships, and tenure denials. Politics is one of those dirty words that many think are best left unsaid. Academics in particular like to think of their work as apolitical: they generally prefer their research pure rather than applied. Our view is that politics drives curriculum, that we live within institutions that must continuously account for the political in order to maintain enrollments, budgets, public goodwill. Our view is that a genuine force for positive change in the ways and means by which writing is taught is possible only when we take stock of the

politics of writing instruction and begin to enter consciously and knowl-
edgeably into the political arena. This book is intended as a step in that
direction.

Richard Bullock
John Trimbur,
Co-editors

Charles I. Schuster,
General Editor

Acknowledgments

It is never possible to acknowledge all the people who have made a book possible, especially when the book emerges from multiple conversations and exchanges with colleagues, friends, students, and critics who share a vigorous and thoughtful interest in writing instruction. An accurate list of those to whom we are indebted would fill these pages, leaving no room for the essays. Clearly, however, we must acknowledge the particular contributions of the individuals represented in this volume. We thank them for their insights, their intellectual tenacity—and for their patience, which was tried and tested through successive and often contradictory editorial responses from the three of us. So, too, we wish to thank the members of the NCTE Commission on Composition, especially during those turbulent years from 1983 to 1987. For much of that time, this book was a mere glimmer in their political consciousness; their faith and commitment helped to keep this project alive.

We wish also to thank Bob Boynton and the fine staff at Heinemann-Boynton/Cook. Bob's belief in the project shored us up during those inevitable dark days when nothing seemed less likely than that this first volume would ever be completed. It is not possible for us fully to acknowledge his strong support, wise advice, and unflagging goodwill. Finally, we would like to acknowledge what a pleasure it has been for us to work together on this project. During the past two years, we have gotten to know one another—and our families—exceedingly well, at least through our frequent phone calls and frenzied correspondence, our sustained questioning and critiquing. We hope this volume reflects our sense of excitement and satisfaction; more important, we hope it contributes substantively to that disciplinary conversation out of which it is born.

1

Depoliticizing and Politicizing Composition Studies

JAMES F. SLEVIN

Georgetown University

I

Several years ago, I had occasion to serve as an outside evaluator of a writing program at a prominent eastern university that will remain nameless. I found a full-time faculty of around 30 members, each teaching a 2-2 load on the semester system; each had his or her own office in the campus's loveliest building. I also found a cadre of 59 graduate students, teaching two composition courses per semester, for a stipend (now taxable) of about $7,500. In addition to poverty-level wages, they were systematically prevented by these teaching duties from advancing toward their degrees; as a result, many of them had become permanent part-timers, in their seventh, eighth, and even ninth years of the graduate program. In some ways, by virtue of their temporal distance from their course work and from their dissertation director (who could help them find real jobs), they were moving backwards on a treadmill.

I also found a part-time faculty of 75, teaching a 3-2 load (that's right, the "part"-timers taught *more* courses than the full-timers). They were quartered, anywhere from three to six per office, in the basement of a building at least a quarter of a mile away from their full-time "colleagues." The best-paid part-time teacher, a woman (significantly, about 70 to 75 percent of them were women—a much higher ratio than among full-timers) with seven years experience at this school, received a salary that was less than 30 percent per course of that earned by an *entering* assistant professor.[1] No matter how well a part-timer taught, her pay was in no way determined by merit, and there had been no pay increments during the preceding three years. They received no fringe benefits, and were not eligible for financial support to attend conferences, much less engage in research. To make ends meet, most had to teach at other local schools, with some teaching as many as six courses per semester. They usually did not hear that they would be rehired—even those who had been there for years—until July or August, and they were obliged to follow a course syllabus

1

prepared by the composition director, with no opportunity to introduce their own material or pedagogical techniques. Except for those who had received their doctorates at this school, the part-timers knew only a few of the full-timers, and some part-timers knew none, except the director of composition. At this university, only four of the 30 full-time faculty *ever* taught composition.

I thought at the time that this was an exception, and while I now know it is different in degree, it is not different in kind from the condition of part-time composition faculty in this country. I begin with this anecdote about very specific practices — practices, as we shall see, that are pervasive and entrenched — to emphasize that the profession of "English Studies" is not simply a series of mental or discursive acts set apart from social, economic, political, and institutional structures.[2] It is my aim to describe some features of these structures, suggesting the difficulties they cause and some ways of responding to the "politics of composition" that they create. The most pertinent difficulties are economic, and to some degree social and political as well.

We should no longer hide from ourselves or from others that our profession, as it is now practiced in this country, rests on, *is based on*, a foundation of despicable inequality. I am referring primarily, though not only, to the use of part-time faculty to teach composition. I do not think we can consider this, any longer, simply an unfortunate consequence of bad times. It is something else entirely. I want to insist that this is a central feature — not an incidental feature — of the profession now. It is not a peripheral, temporary problem that is somehow going to go away by itself. We know, for example, that half the teachers at two-year colleges are part-time. We know that over one-quarter of the faculty at four-year colleges — one in four — is part-time, and that of those three full-time faculty it is almost certain that one will have only a temporary, non-tenure-track appointment.[3] And we know that even at our most distinguished departments, those 139 elite schools (6 percent of the total) offering the PhD), over half of those teaching are part-timers, TAs, and temporary appointments. Almost always, it is composition that gets taught by those faculty in the least privileged positions. As a consequence, it is in the vested interest of some to conceive of composition in ways that justify the marginal and exploited position of composition teachers.

It is simply the case that at many colleges and universities — indeed, far too many — the bulk of composition instruction is handled by part-time faculty — and often only by them. While undergraduate catalogs regularly speak with rapture of writing instruction's central contribution in preparing America's citizens and future leaders, such centrality is not apparent in the status of those who teach these courses. At best neglected, badly paid, with no hope of security, adjunct composition faculty serve their universities with a dedication that derives from their generous concern for their students and the intellectual excitement of the discipline they profess, despite the worst possible circumstances. The effects on the part-time faculty's morale, and inevitably on the quality of their teaching, undermine the central mission of the department and the university.

We are often told, however, that this policy, of relying on part-time, faculty to teach composition, is the result of economic problems beyond our control. Let's analyze this explanation, beginning with statistics from 1981.[4] In that year, of those earning humanities PhDs between 1960 and 1964, 93 percent had full-time academic appointments, nearly all of them, by now, tenured. For those earning their doctorates between 1969 and 1972, the comparable figure was 86 percent. But each year since 1977, only about 60 percent of those earning PhDs in English found full-time positions, and only about 40 percent found tenure-track appointments. The drop, then, was drastic, from 93 percent to 40 percent. And that figure of 40 percent includes many who recently have been denied tenure — or who might soon be denied tenure.

It is no coincidence that, beginning around 1974, we began to hear that enrollments in the late 1970s and 1980s were going to decrease drastically, so that postsecondary institutions simply could not afford to continue their tenure-track commitments when there would soon not be any students to teach. But, actually, things have not turned out this way at all. In fact, between 1974 and 1987, enrollments in colleges and universities have actually *increased*.[5] There is *no* evidence to suggest that things will get significantly worse in the future. And yet we continue to hear expressions of the same fantastic fears, justifying — without any basis in fact — a continued and in some cases increased use of part-time faculty.

It might be argued, however, that these figures do not bear on the teaching of the humanities, especially English, at four-year colleges. Here, it might seem, the situation is indeed bleak, requiring the expediency of part-time appointments. But a recent survey conducted by the Association of Departments of English (ADE) underscores just how unequal things are.[6] The ADE surveyed several hundred English departments (public and private, undergraduate and graduate) to determine the "condition" of English Studies. While departments differ considerably, a few generalizations can be made that show us that the study of literature and of writing is in a far healthier condition than many believe.

The ADE survey indicates, for example, that the English major is doing surprisingly well; only 20 percent of the institutions note a decline in the major, while in nearly twice as many (around 35 percent) the major has grown. (The other 45 percent are stable.) About 25 percent of the departments offering graduate English degrees report growth in their graduate programs in British and American literature, and nearly 70 percent of the graduate literature programs are doing either as well as or better than they were in the past three years.

But if literature programs are healthy, writing programs are by all accounts not just healthy but athletic. Here are some contrasts.

- While 35 percent of all English departments report a growth in the undergraduate English major, of those offering technical communication (roughly three out of every five departments) about 75 percent indicate a growth in this field, and only 8 percent report a decline. Significantly, at PhD-granting universities, presumably among the most distinguished institutions, 83 percent of those offering technical communication indicate a growth in their undergraduate technical writing program.
- While 25 percent of the graduate literature programs are enlarging, nearly 80 percent of those departments offering advanced degrees in rhetoric and over 85 percent offering advanced degrees in technical communication report growth in these areas. Significantly, these growth figures are *higher* (about 84 percent and 90 percent) at PhD departments.
- And while 31 percent of the graduate literature programs indicate decline, decline is reported in only 7 percent of the graduate technical writing programs and only 4 percent of the graduate rhetoric programs.

Briefly, then, about four out of every five writing programs, undergraduate and graduate, have grown in the past three years.

From the point of view of student enrollments, English departments are doing well, and writing programs significantly better: They constitute a boom industry. And yet the status of writing teachers is, with rare exception, dismal.

I belabor all of this only to reinforce the point: We are facing an enormous problem that will not go away simply by asserting that it should. Fully one-third of the "English professoriate" hold positions such as those as I have just described. That grand phrase, "English professoriate," seems almost ludicrous in such a context. The flourishing market for composition specialists (one out of every four advertised positions for the past five years) and the tenuring of composition directors (not far behind the percentage in other fields—68 percent vs. 82 percent), while encouraging in some respects, should not mislead us. These figures do not mean that part-time positions are being phased out and *replaced* by respectable appointments, but simply that composition programs function more harmoniously when headed by fairly secure colleagues whose professional complexion matches that of the staff. The French had at least some good ideas about how to run a colony.

The economic structure apparent in these statistics is both hidden and subtly reinforced by the English curriculum within which the work of writing instruction is inscribed. I will be talking about this curriculum not so much as a reality but as an interpretive document, a text, a piece of discourse. It is a discourse that functions as much to conceal as to describe, and it establishes an interpretive and evaluative code that governs how students understand and appreciate what it means to learn to read and write.

Since any writing program is set within the entire institution's program of studies, let me speak briefly about the latter before moving to the more specific case of composition. What are the discursive forms that constitute a curriculum? Primarily, there is the college catalog, which in our own time, and for at least one hundred years, manages to compartmentalize knowledge into various disciplines of study, compartments established and supported by powerful professional associations. Any departmental curriculum is a section of this collection, or a section of an anthology. Inserted within this collection of other texts, the English curriculum presents a fairly consistent set of features; there is a listing of requirements of various kinds, and then a listing of courses, beginning with the freshman level and moving on through more advanced courses, courses for the major, and in some places graduate courses. Everything here is hierarchical, with the hierarchy based on the principle of covering a body of literature that has been determined to merit our attention. The central point embodied in this arrangement is the privileging of canonical texts—the major authors and the general selection of white male masterpieces in the various courses that mark the "requirements" for the major or the graduate degree.

At the base of this curriculum, of course, are the vast majority of the courses English departments actually teach. But the curriculum—which tells us about courses but not *sections* of courses—consistently hides the extent of this base. MLA statistics indicate that roughly 70 percent of the postsecondary English classes or sections taught in this country are composition classes; in terms of number of sections, composition represents at least two-thirds of what we do as a profession. But the curriculum conceals these courses: They are all crammed within one or two different titles; one official description usually serves for all sections, even when the commitments of different teachers make for a quite diverse range of classes. These sections are usually and miraculously taught by that most ubiquitous of teachers, "Professor Staff"; often these are part-timers or graduate students, so they are never named in the higher curricular documents. Rather, they get named only in or on lower generic forms—the preregistration printout (occasionally) or the lowest form of all, the grade sheet, lowest because here even *students* get named. This is, truly, the bottom of the academic hierarchy.

The curriculum, then, communicates some important messages to students; it teaches students how to read the courses they enroll in and, to an extent, how to read the books and the writing that they do in those courses. It tells them what forms a coherent order and what doesn't, and to that extent what counts and what doesn't. By retaining as a central curricular focus the idea of coverage, based on a canon of works to be read, and by providing names of teachers or withholding them (that is, by signaling literature courses as "authored" and writing courses as "anonymous"), it enforces a way of thinking about ourselves and what we do.

II

Just as the curriculum can be seen to conceal immoral employment practices, so too there exists a powerful "conception" of English Studies that, it seems to me, functions as an ideological rationalization of all these inequalities. Indeed, this theoretical conception of the discipline endures, in part, because it so efficiently rationalizes the present state of employment and other practices that mark our departments. The growth in overall university enrollments and in English department enrollments offers no support for, indeed it contradicts, the claim that *economic necessity* requires the exploitation of so many marginal faculty. Academic institutions *choose* to do this, and they choose this practice primarily because they have other priorities but also because we let them get away with it. And we let them get away with it by endorsing and institutionalizing impoverished notions of composition and what it means to teach it. Without this reductive notion of composition to justify their actions, university administrators would have to face the shamefulness of their policies.

Within colleges and universities today, fields of inquiry commonly grouped together and designated "literature" and fields commonly grouped and designated "composition" are in fact often in very real intellectual conflict, for reasons we can easily identify. The fundamental subordination of teaching writing to teaching reading can be traced to competing attitudes toward language and history. By and large, those who locate themselves in the literature camp stress their concern with major texts and ways of reading these intrinsically important, autonomous, and for some "timeless" objects that demand sophisticated powers of analysis and synthesis. The importance of these texts, and the value of reading them, derive precisely from their separation from history and utility, from other discursive and nondiscursive practices and cultural formations. From that ethereal perspective, they consider the work of those in the compositon camp as impoverished in both its subject and the intellectual powers upon which it draws. As a result, those who do the work we generally include within the category of "composition" are seen as marginal to the real (as in "really important") work of English departments, at both the graduate and undergraduate levels. Those in composition are stained by their immersion in history, by a preoccupation with social practice, and by a concern with the uses of language that refuses to privilege canonical texts and forms. This conceptual framework seems absolutely indispensable in order to maintain the current economic structure of the profession. If we didn't have it, we'd have to invent it. But fortunately (for some), we do have it; it permeates the academy, even where we might expect to find it opposed.

For example, Terry Eagleton's remarks on the restoration of rhetoric as the core of English Studies, remarks quoted, perhaps, more often than they have been read, can serve as a case in point. He notes, in his peroration to *Literary Theory*, that

> I wish to recall literary criticism from certain fashionable, new-fangled ways of thinking it has been seduced by . . . and return it to the ancient paths which it has abandoned [that is, rhetoric]. . . .
>
> Rhetoric wanted to find out the most effective ways of pleading, persuading, and debating, and rhetoricians studied such devices in other people's language in order to use them more productively in their own. It was, as we would say today, a "creative" as well as a "critical" activity: the word "rhetoric" covers both the practice of effective discourse and the science of it. (206–207)

That seems to me a fine idea. But in the fifteen or so pages that Eagleton devotes to explaining this position, only one paragraph has anything to do with how writers compose — with the "creative" dimension of his rhetorical paideia. He in fact restricts his interest to how texts are received, not how they are produced. So he limits the notion of rhetoric in ways that many "rhetoricians" would not accept and which certainly ignore the best work in rhetoric and composition as most of us would understand it.[7]

There are similar tendencies in the work of other rhetoricians, many of whom are, ironically, important allies and significant defenders of composition study at their universities. Richard Lanham, for example, while using much of his *Literacy and the Survival of Humanism* to explain the importance of writing as the core of a new, post-Darwinian curriculum, claims that

> Much research in composition has been trivial and jejune, but even had it been better, it has often been of the wrong kind — namely research about pedagogy, about administration, about the delivery systems that socialize knowledge rather than the research endeavors that synthesize it. It is this threat of applied research which, as composition has grown, has sponsored so much fear and suspicion. (119)

While Lanham is often eloquent in his presentation of the importance of writing in the freshman/sophomore curriculum, he can also describe its teaching as something that "softens your brain" and "burns you out" (160). Unfortunately, he doesn't ask why such a course, especially one he considers central to the curriculum, necessarily has that effect. If it is because the teaching load is too heavy, then lower that load; if it is because the course is institutionally defined in that way,[8] then rethink the definition; but don't depreciate the kind of course it can be or the people who teach it.

Such views ultimately constitute *all* composition faculty, even those with full-time, tenure-track appointments, as something of an underclass. And so they get *treated* as an underclass, through an elaborately detailed set of norms that gives insufficient credit to, indeed discredits and therefore marginalizes, what they do. All this, too, is a political, social, and economic fact of our professional life.

Within this conceptual framework, those whose research interests specialize in composition are looked upon as "mere technicians," concerned with underprivileged modes of discourse and often with underprivileged students. They are in either case tied to history and society, and to the historical and social uses of language and education. They are also seen as lacking an established scholarly discipline and as concerned more with the practical problems of pedagogy than with the "higher and timeless intellectual pursuits" that mark the literary scholar's enterprise. There is distressingly little appreciation that the field of rhetoric and composition has its own body of scholarship; so, in many if not most departments, books and articles undertaking such research do not receive the credit they deserve, both when allocating "merit pay" and when deciding to tenure and promote.

Of course, if articles in *College English* and *CCC* are causing such alarm, composition *textbooks* are positively filling coronary wards with our humanistic elders. While in many disciplines this form of publication is highly derivative and secondary to the primary scholarship that alters "the field," good textbooks by composition specialists often constitute a primary way of communicating the results of extensive research. At the vast majority of institutions, such texts receive little recognition, no matter what their quality. Often they are not even considered because "their relevance extends only a few years," that is, because their historical immediacy is "impure" (too "applied") and their purpose tied too closely to social practice.[9]

III

The hierarchical arrangement of writing and literature is evident even at those schools where *everyone* teaches composition, where *all* faculty see their job as, in part, teaching students to write. The same vertical structure we see in the English curriculum and in staffing policies is evident in the structure and aims of individual courses, which can be microcosms of the profession.

Let me illustrate by turning to a description of two typical freshman-level English courses. The courses I have chosen fairly represent courses in which writing is integrated with the study of literature — but integrated in a hierarchical manner. I think that by looking closely at the logic of these descriptions, we can get a clear sense of what this hierarchy is, along with the assumptions on which it is grounded. Here's the first description:

The purpose of this course is to practice the close reading of poetry. We will concentrate our efforts on specific works of fine poets: Shakespeare (the Sonnets, *King Lear*, *The Tempest*), George Herbert (selected lyrics), Emily Dickinson (selected lyrics), William Carlos Williams (*Paterson*), Robert Lowell (*Life Studies*). The works chosen allow us to compare various forms (the sonnet, the lyric, the long poem, and the drama) and to ask questions about the changes that have occurred in poetic language from the 16th century to the present. Class participation is crucial. Written work will consist of five or six analytical papers.

In designing his course, "to practice the close reading of. . .specific works of fine poets," this teacher assumes several important things. First, these "works of fine poets" form a great tradition that constitutes, within all of literature, a privileged realm of study. Second, he presumes that we can understand changes in poetic language without reference to changes in the system of ordinary language. So poetic language has a special status and is essentially different from ordinary language. Third, literary works are autonomous aesthetic objects to be examined analytically. Finally, writing about literature seeks to communicate the knowledge gained from this analysis. In such close reading, in which analytical procedures are controlled by complicated comparative procedures, the student examines each work from a distance, guided less by the categories of his or her own experience than by those of period and genre (significantly, the categories, as we saw, that organize the curriculum).

Given this teacher's assumptions about literature, criticism, language, and learning, he intends writing assignments as exercises that serve to train the student to analyze. Because ordinary discourse is outside the special realm of literary objects with their unique poetic language, and because analysis precedes the communication of its discoveries, the learning of composition serves the understanding of critical analysis in much the same way that critical analysis serves the understanding of literature. Student discourse is entirely at the service of the texts studied, given little if any value in its own right. It is a mere exercise, through which the features of the texts chosen by the teacher will be more fully comprehended. The writing serves the analysis which serves, as Eliot commanded, the literary text.[10] This hierarchy is established by the privileged status of literature. More precisely, it is established by a theory — or rather a hypothesis — concerning the ahistorical nature of poetic language, its having its own self-enclosed development uncontaminated by history.

Here is the description of a second representative course:

An introduction to poetic and dramatic discourse as an essential way of representing and knowing reality. The course will involve detailed examination of important texts both from the traditional canon and from among those works (largely written by women and minorities) usually seen as outside the canon. Particular attention will be paid to structure, form, and prosody. The student's written assignments will include exercises both critical and creative.

In his concern with "structure, form, and prosody" and his concentration on "*important* texts" (the canonical and noncanonical forged into a *new* canon), this teacher seems to share at least some views implied in the previous description. But the hierarchy here is less conspicuous, more concealed. In his identification of poems and plays as "poetic and dramatic *discourse*"—discourse that is a way of "knowing reality"—he sees the literary work not as an *object* to be analyzed but as an *utterance* whose composing creates for the author, and whose interpretation brings to the reader, a genuine and reliable knowledge of experience. He is therefore concerned about, though not prepared to question or eliminate, distinctions between poetic and ordinary language. At one level, these discursive modes are similar, affording knowledge. He believes that doing exercises in both literary and nonliterary discourse constitutes an important way for students to learn. But by distinguishing between writing that is both "critical and creative," he reinforces the dichotomy he is elsewhere concerned to question; and, by characterizing student writing as "exercises," he suggests as well the radical differences between student writing and the writing studied.

I do not want to simplify the situation here, for these are courses that incorporate student writing in fairly serious ways; and I have no doubt that each of these instructors devotes considerable time and energy to the papers he receives. But they are courses that, however innocently, reproduce the vertical arrangement that marks our profession generally and that derives from the economic structure that so powerfully exploits substantial numbers of our colleagues.

IV

In the priorities accorded reading and writing in individual courses, in our curriculum, in our staffing policies, in our system of academic rewards, and in one very powerful and long-established conception of the discipline, we find the same hierarchical structure operating, based on fundamental oppositions that make extremely difficult our efforts to understand and treat literature and composition, and those who teach them, as equals.

It seems to me that teachers of writing, who relate the study of texts to the world of practice and the practical, who are interested in texts not only as they are but as they are produced, reproduced, and received by real writers and readers, can bring into being a radical reorganization of the professional hierarchy I have been discussing. The very concerns that locate us at the base or bottom of the prevailing power system—concerns with how texts are used by readers and writers in historical contexts—need to be elaborated, so that we can alter both the theory and practice of English studies. Our aim, then, should be not simply to resituate ourselves within institutions but, in doing so, to reconceive and reconstruct those institutions.[11] How *that* can be effected will require some elaboration, and a look into our past as a way of imagining such a future. It will involve work at all levels—pedagogy and faculty training, the undergraduate and graduate curriculum and faculty prerogatives, and political actions undertaken by our professional associations to alter the economic policies that underlie the current English apparatus.[12]

Richard Lloyd-Jones, in an article appearing in *The Future of Doctoral Studies*, formulates a paradigm for emerging rhetoric and composition programs that actually could serve as a compelling intellectual foundation for many of the reforms needed to subvert the prevailing hierarchies:

> [Such] programs engage the serious study of how language is generated in speech and writing and include a secondary emphasis on how instances of language are interpreted. Student writing and literary masterpieces and even oral exchanges are all proper objects of study. In these programs literary criticism is extended into rhetorical criticism and propaganda analysis. These scholars ease into area or cultural studies because they see all language in context. In short, their intellectual concerns are those of a department dealing in English language and literature even though the package may sometimes appear to be a bit trendy, the examples rather far from the canon, and the politics aggressively democratic.[13]

Unfortunately, Lloyd-Jones characterizes this conception as a latter-day "rationalization" of programs whose origins are decidedly neither intellectual nor, for that matter, very professional. And so he concludes that this kind of program is "thinly populated" and unlikely to serve as a center for the work of faculties.

Perhaps Lloyd-Jones's pessimism can be traced to his excessively modest estimate of the origins and intellectual foundations of rhetoric and composition programs. He traces these origins not to intellectual developments in the discipline or political developments in the profession, but rather to very practical needs in English departments for more coherent and better-managed writing programs. I think, however, that there is sufficient reason to question this view. Since the future of this field, and particularly the possibility of its full, transformative integration within our graduate and undergraduate programs, depends in part on how we conceive of these origins, it is crucial to question Lloyd-Jones's historical account. His seems to me an incomplete and blurred picture. By suggesting a gap between these programs' beginnings (depicted as little more than passive, practical responses to "open admissions" and other pressures) and what he considers merely contrived intellectual "rationalizations" that accompanied or soon followed their institution, his account ignores the very serious intellectual concerns that link the recent renewal of rhetoric and composition studies to simultaneous developments in literary studies and other disciplines. Indeed, I would suggest that it was rather the serious, though as yet un-"disciplined," theoretical interest in literary and rhetorical criticism and in cultural studies, not so "trendy" at the time, that led many directors of TAs, and many secure professors looking for new challenges, to take up their interest in composition in the first place. It was not solely—I doubt even primarily—their desire to help out around the department, though that they did, often contributing in astonishingly beneficial ways.

However dim the curricular and pedagogical implications at the moment of origin, intimations of such a conceptual framework are what *caused* "open admissions" and other "aggressively democratic" movements, which in turn accompanied not only the rise of Composition but the formation of much of post structuralist literary theory. These historical developments are intimately related, and the questions addressed several decades ago to certain forms of political domination and exclusion are now being addressed, within our discipline, to forms of intellectual domination and exclusion, though these latter questions have taken longer to find their way into the *New York Times*. The integrative paradigm that Lloyd-Jones dismisses as a mere "rationalization" of rhetoric and composition might more accurately be characterized as a recovery (or rediscovery) of original motives, a working out within the discipline of the implications of earlier, more conspicuously political and institutional transformational projects. And in doing this intellectual work, rhetoric and composition joins with other critical movements in contributing to the reformulation of English programs at all levels.

The writing movement in our own time has emerged from within this historical situation; the movement emerged, that is, as a form of educational and political resistance. It stood as an assertion that student and faculty commitments had to be freed from the institutionally established purposes to which they had been reduced. It addressed broad questions about the aims of education and the shape of various educational institutions — from the social institution we call the "classroom" to the general education curriculum to the nature of disciplines. It articulated both an uneasiness with current institutional structures and a desire for something different, both within and beyond the writing class. There was, of course, the usual degree of utopian fantasy and Rousseauvian rebelliousness about such claims. But they were, at the very least, the sorts of passion that energize reform.

The teachers at all levels who initiated this reform had a fire in their belly, not about student skills but about the nature of education itself, about the institutions that structure it, and about the students included in and excluded from those institutions. Given the particularly acute role that writing instruction and learning to write have historically played in the inherited aims and structures of education, the reconceptualizing of education quite understandably had as a focus the revitalizing of the teaching of writing. Intellectually, that reconceptualizing naturally took the form of a renewed interest in rhetorical and later cultural criticism. The past twenty-five years have witnessed the flowering of this intellectual field.

The catch phrases with which we are all familiar — writing to learn, writing as a way of thinking, writing as a way of knowing, writing as empowerment — are responses to a concern, not that students are incompetent or unprepared, but rather that they are often led to be uncaring — about ideas, about their own education, and often about other matters that transcend the more immediate interests of any particular classroom. This is perceived not as a condition unique to students who are poor or ill-served by their previous schooling but as a general condition of a generation. Concern with "access" and "empowerment" is finally a concern with students' alienation from the content and forms of their learning and their alienation from the institutions that are meant to encourage and enable that learning.

The key word here, alienation, applies as much to *faculty* as to students. What seems most striking about the evolution of writing programs is not what it tells us about students but what it tells us about faculty. It is a common theme of educational reformers, on both the right and left, that teachers are increasingly disengaged from their own labor, that they are discouraged by the circumstances of their work and alienated from the institutions which increasingly do little more than employ (as in use) them. In their formation as faculty projects, writing programs have enabled faculty to recover the kind of initiative that marked their originating sense of the vocation of teaching. Such programs reawakened and then nurtured the possibilities of initiative, the possibilities of being an active agent in the classroom and the school. These possibilities, more than "writing," account for the enthusiasm and vigor of teachers' participation in them. Because of the possibilities they afford teachers to act energetically and imaginatively *as educators*, and more particularly as educational leaders, writing programs have become the source of renewed commitments and a renewed sense of faculty engagement.

V

In sketching a way of understanding and so empowering composition programs, I do not mean to seem sanguine about the possibilities — more specifically, the agents — of change. What I have in mind depends on empowering faculty to effect change, partly through faculty-development programs that enable us to reach our colleagues and finally through greater economic and political empowerment for those exploited writing teachers to whom I referred in Part I. But significant change will require that we reach our future colleagues — those whose intellectual commitments and professional aims are being shaped by current graduate programs.

Our graduate students' education, constrained by the pressures of "specialization" and "coverage," does perhaps too little to prepare them to take responsibility for the wide range of undergraduate teaching responsibilities that so many departments will require of them. Moreover, the teaching opportunities we provide (opportunities that come too soon, demand too much, and occur in freshman courses that we have trivialized) only make matters worse. More needs to be done within current graduate programs to improve the preparation of future teachers. Students need the opportunity, through formal graduate course work, to set the work of English Studies in larger professional and theoretical contexts. My ultimate concern is to suggest that, as part of a professional degree program, the PhD curriculum should incorporate formal occasions not just for developing scholarship and improving teaching but also for inquiring about the profession of scholarship and teaching and about the institutions in which they occur.[14]

The last twenty years have witnessed a significant rise in graduate courses designed to prepare teachers. But, lacking the rigor and breadth of other graduate offerings, these courses have received only marginal status in most departments, and frequently bear no graduate credit. I am not advocating here simply the current "hands-on" teacher-training course, but a course that considers seriously an expanded definition of our discipline's teaching responsibilities. A graduate seminar preparing teachers to meet their dual responsibility, to integrate the teaching of reading and writing, would want to begin with a broad historical analysis of our discipline. It would consider our abandonment of "rhetoric" not simply as a mode of textual analysis but as a disciplined inquiry into how a writer or speaker constructs her discourse and makes its power felt. This revisionist history might trace how we have narrowed our concern to reading canonical works, to the detriment of our understanding of how those texts came to be and to be deemed worthy of our scrutiny. It would investigate not just how to teach writing but the history of writing instruction, including its role in socializing new student populations historically called "remedial." It would draw on the work of other disciplines (psychology, linguistics, and much of contemporary literary theory) as they contribute to our understanding of textual production. And it might even address the current preoccupation of nearly all humanistic disciplines with "discursive practices" by bringing to bear on this question major texts from the rhetorical tradition. Not simply a vehicle for teacher training but an arena for disciplined inquiry about the aims of English Studies and the meaning of liberal learning, this course would provide a crucial preparation for graduate students embarking on a new career.

Recent efforts (I am thinking particularly of Graff, Ohmann, Lentricchia, Fish) to situate scholarship and teaching within their institutional settings and larger historical contexts provide a solid framework for organizing such a seminar. This seminar could consider the origins of English Studies in relation not only to the system of departmental governance but also to the norm of specialization and the ideology of professionalism that rationalize it. It could examine historically how specific curricular arrangements were formed and how one's own theoretical inquiry into canonicity, periodization, genre, and authorship can be brought to bear in understanding and reconceiving those formations; how the profession's system of rewards and accompanying constraints (research expectations, teaching loads, evaluation procedures—about which graduate students know far too little) will affect their own commitments to scholarship; how their research will and will not contribute to their teaching, with at least some attention to how their own lives as writers can assist their teaching of writing. These hardly exhaust the possible topics of such seminars; others can easily be imagined. Whatever their specific syllabi, the aim would be to pose those questions that will empower graduate students as agents in reconceiving and shaping the institutions whose faculties they will join.

VI

This conception of our discipline and of our responsibilites to empower faculty and graduate students as agents of reform corresponds in important ways with the emerging political activism apparent in rhetoric and composition as a field. This activism is most evident in our increasing resistance to economic, curricular, professional, and intellectual forms of domination that mark the last twenty years of the academy's practices. Changes within the discipline will succeed, finally, only to the extent that the actions (curricular, pedagogical, and institutional) initiated by individual members of the profession are supported by professional associations like CCCC, MLA, and NCTE. The hiring practices, tenure and promotion procedures, and curricular inequalities noted above are not going to change simply because we alter our *ways of thinking* about rhetoric and composition as a discipline and writing instruction as a vocation, though they cannot change without these intellectual shifts. I wish to conclude by exploring one example of this professional activism.

The most serious instance of it so far has been the Wyoming Conference Resolution, which called upon English professional associations to act decisively to improve the conditions of those who teach composition. The resolution emerged from the 1986 Wyoming Conference on Freshman and Sophomore English, an annual event that draws approximately 200 participants.[15] Sent forward to the Conference on College Composition and Communication, the resolution was unanimously endorsed at the 1987 business meeting in Atlanta, and a committee was established (later known as the Committee on Professional Standards) to implement the resolution.

The committee had two charges. First, it was to prepare a "Statement of Standards and Principles for the Postsecondary Teaching of Writing"; after many revisions, the last of which was preceded by an open meeting for all CCCC members at the 1989 convention, this document was approved by the CCCC Executive Committee and issued as official CCCC policy in October 1989.[16] It called attention to the abuses I have discussed above, and urged fundamental reform in uncompromising terms. It asserted that writing courses should be staffed by permanent, full-time faculty, whose work should be recognized as the equal of all other fields; it insisted that the continuing misuse of graduate students and part-time faculty must be stopped and that where, for example, part-time faculty must be employed, their rights and rewards should be the equal of full-time faculty (in salary, fringe benefits, access to research and travel support, participation in departmental governance, etc.). It linked these changes to two principles. First, *quality education*, to which students have a right, depends on the quality of faculty, and so it urged that "the responsibility for the academy's most serious mission, helping students to develop their critical powers as readers and writers, should be vested in tenure-line faculty" (330). Second, the principle of *academic freedom* depends no less on such a commitment: "As the American Association of University Professors has affirmed, when institutions depend increasingly on faculty whose positions are tenuous and whose rights and privileges are unclear or nonexistent, those freedoms established as the right of full-time tenurable and tenured faculty are endangered" (330).

The committee's second charge was to explore how CCCC could engage in direct political action to alter the situation of writing teachers. The committee determined that the creation of standards, and even their wide dissemination (the statement was sent to over 10,000 college and university administrators and department chairs), would serve only to begin the kind of initiative necessary to effect change. That is, unlike previous efforts of this kind, the creation and publication of a document was considered only the beginning, not the end, of serious reform. So in its two years of deliberation, the committee laid the groundwork for continuing collaboration with major education and professional associations, all of which were involved in the process of drafting the CCCC statement. A few examples will illustrate the various forms this collaboration has taken.

1. All regional accrediting agencies (and their umbrella organization, the Council on Postsecondary Accreditation) have been alerted to the situation of writing teachers and encouraged both to incorporate our guidelines into their review procedures and to call on specialists in rhetoric and composition to participate in accreditation reviews. To that end, the names of distinguished scholars and teachers of rhetoric and composition have been forwarded to each of the regional accrediting agencies. In addition, the statement has been sent to all chairs of site teams and all English faculty who have served as site visitors.

2. Organizations that protect and support faculty rights (the American Association of University Professors, the American Federation of Teachers, the National Education Association) have been drawn in to support CCCC on this issue, and their resources are likely to be available to individual faculty seeking to make changes. In addition to providing direct advice on particular matters, these organizations have a wide collection of articles and position papers on issues concerning higher education, along with up-to-date information about salaries, working conditions, governance policies, and other matters useful when negotiating to improve the situation of teachers.

3. Education associations that represent higher education administrators (e.g., the American Council on Education, the Association of American Colleges, the American Association of Community and Junior Colleges) have assisted us in the dissemination of our statement to their members and have registered support for continuing to explore ways of effecting change together. Other English associations (like the MLA's Executive

Council) have endorsed our statement and urged its members to comply with our recommendations.[17]

This process of communication is central to the continuing work of the committee. For the next several years, CCCC members will be making presentations at the annual conventions of these various groups, just as representatives of these groups will be invited to address us. For the past several years, the issue has been addressed at special panels at the MLA, CCCC, and NCTE conventions, and the summer of 1990 saw all three ADE seminars (attended by up to 400 English department chairs) devote a plenary session and discussion group to the CCCC document. All of the major education associations have held or plan to hold workshops and panels at their conventions to consider the implications of the guidelines CCCC has developed.

Reform, finally, depends on the initiative of those most directly affected by the situation of writing instruction. What we can expect from other organizations is only support; if the situation of writing teachers is to be improved, it is our responsibility to initiate and sustain such efforts as these. CCCC has a special role in preparing and supporting its members for such leadership and in marshaling the continued support that our initiatives will need.

To that end, CCCC has authorized several new initiatives that will realize even more completely the aims of the Wyoming Resolution. It has established a caucus for all members interested in reforming the teaching of writing in accordance with the *Statement of Principles and Standards for Quality Education*. This caucus serves as a site for continuing discussion of major issues and as a way of exchanging information about successful strategies for change. Each CCCC convention will schedule special workshops to prepare individual CCCC members to implement the *Statement of Principles and Standards*. There will also be more specialized workshops and other kinds of training sessions to prepare CCCC members, identified as CCCC Regional Advisors, to facilitate change at institutions other than their own; they will assist faculty on nearby campuses in organizing to improve the situation of writing teachers and advise administrators about standards and models for acceptable professional practices. Similar workshops will prepare others from among the CCCC membership to undertake conflict resolution; so trained, and identified as CCCC Mediators, they will meet with parties involved in negotiating better practices on particular campuses, helping to resolve conflict. Finally, CCCC, through its Committee on Professional Standards, will continue to establish liaisons with representatives of other disciplines/organizations seeking to improve the conditions of faculty at postsecondary institutions and with businesses and business, law, and medical schools insofar as they support the improvement of writing instruction at the undergraduate level.

These professional initiatives constitute only one arena for reform;

another, perhaps more powerful arena is the general public. Through various media, those in positions to influence change must be made aware of the situation of writing teachers and the means necessary to improve it. State legislators, members of college/university boards of governors, parents of postsecondary students, and others need to learn that the quality of student education depends on precisely the kinds of reforms we have been proposing. Through various media, these groups must be reached, and in addition to increased efforts from CCCC/NCTE headquarters, individual CCCC members must assume responsibility for raising consciousness about these matters.

The energy necessary to address these massive problems and to persist in the effort to overcome them depends, in no small measure, on books like this one. Whatever else might be said about the "politics of writing instruction," our working together is crucial, and writing to one another is surely a part of that work. It is thoroughly consistent with the state of English Studies at this time to suggest that such a book, like Jefferson's Constitution, needs to be rethought every generation, and I would identify a generation loosely as every five years. The work I have sketched here has no foreseeable end; it will require vigilance and dedication of the kind we ordinarily associate with more conspicuously deserving social causes. That ours belongs in such a grouping might best be understood if I conclude with some remarks from the *Statement of Principles and Standards for the Postsecondary Teaching of Writing*:

> A democracy demands citizens who can read critically and write clearly and cogently. Developing students' powers as critical readers and writers demands in turn the highest quality of instruction. . . . Ultimately, every institution should extend to teachers of writing the same opportunities for professional advancement (e.g., tenure and promotion) and the same encouragement of intellectual achievement (e.g., support for research and reasonable teaching responsibilities) that they extend to all other faculty. As colleges have the right to expect of writing specialists the highest level of performance, so they have the obligation to extend the greatest possible support. To do less is to compromise writing instruction for future generations of American students.

That is a compromise we cannot in conscience entertain.

Notes

1. It is accurate to say that these figures reflect national patterns. According to Bettina Huber, in her article "English Salaries: Findings of the 1984–85 ADE Survey" (*ADE Bulletin*, 87, Fall 1987, p. 45), the mean salary for part-time faculty, per course, is $1710. This amounts to approximately 42 percent of the mean salary for all assistant professors, making the figure of 30 percent for *entering* assistant professors the likely national norm.

2. My information derives from the computer printouts that led to the "Report on the 1983–84 Survey of English Programs," an in-house report submitted by Bettina Huber to the MLA. These printouts were made available to members of the MLA's Commission on Writing and Literature, and I am grateful to the MLA for their cooperation in this research. Ms. Huber, with the assistance of Art Young, published a summary of her report in the *ADE Bulletin* (84, Fall 1986, 40–61). Additional information comes from the following sources:

— Bettina Huber, "English Salaries: Findings of the 1984–85 ADE Survey" (*ADE Bulletin* 87, Fall 1987, 40–49);

— Bettina Huber, Denise Pinney, David Laurence, and Denise Knight, "MLA Surveys of PhD Placement" (*ADE Bulletin* 92, Spring 1989, 43–50);

— Bettina Huber and David Laurence, "Report on the 1984–85 Survey of the English Sample" (*ADE Bulletin* 93, Fall 1989, 30–43).

3. These figures are developed from the information cited in the above footnote; they are also available in the "Statement of Principles and Standards for the Postsecondary Teaching of Writing," (*CCC* 40 October 1989, 329–336).

4. I am indebted to the MLA, and particularly to the work of Phyllis Franklin, David Laurence, and Robert Denhman, for these figures.

5. During this period, annual reports by AAUP published both in *Academe* and in the *Chronicle of Higher Education* indicate these increases in student enrollments.

6. The information presented here was made available through computer printouts provided by the *Language*. The comparisons between literature and writing programs developed below have not, until now, been published.

7. This argument is developed in greater detail in my article, "Genre Theory, Academic Discourse, and Writing Within Disciplines," published in *Audits of Meaning*, ed. Louise Z. Smith (Portsmouth, NH: Boynton/Cook-Heinemann, 1988, 3–16).

8. For a valuable critique of this practice generally, and with specific reference to UCLA, see Mike Rose, "The Language of Exclusion: Writing Instruction at the University," (*College English* 47 April 1985, 341–359).

9. In the "Report of the MLA Commission on Writing and Literature," published in *Profession 88* (New York: MLA, 1988), the Commission recommends four substantive areas of rhetoric and composition professional activity that deserve special consideration in tenure and promotion reviews. These activities include the publication of composition textbooks as a primary form of original research; collaborative research on articles and books that draw on diverse scholarly backgrounds and research orientations; professional activities such as workshops and seminars for faculty at all levels; and the particularly demanding administrative service that is often a regular part of a composition specialist's responsibilities.

10. T. S. Eliot, "The Function of Criticism," *Selected Essays* (London: Faber and Faber, 1932), 23–34.

11. The effort to redefine academic institutions marks the work of many areas of English Studies in our time — not just rhetoric and composition, but feminist studies, African-American studies, colonial and postcolonial discourse studies, and increasingly even American studies. What they have in common — and what might serve as a basis for a new order of English Studies — is both a concern with history and social contexts and, as well, a kind of activism, a merging of scholarly with activist work. They share a sense that the work of research and publication is

inseparable from the work of shaping institutional structures (the department, the university, forms of connection between the academy and the "outside" world, etc.). That these various fields might have solid reason to affiliate—in scholarly projects and in political action—is a recommendation that underlies much of what I have to say throughout this essay.

12. This phrase alludes to the work of Robert Scholes, particularly his important book, *Textual Power* (New Haven: Yale University Press, 1985), which begins with an analysis of the hierarchies within English Studies. I depart from him in my greater emphasis on institutional and economic and even political matters.

13. *The Future of Doctoral Studies in English*, eds. Andrea Lunsford, Helene Moglen, and James Slevin (New York: MLA, 1989, 19). This book includes many essays that support the position Lloyd-Jones articulates here and which give a central place to "rhetoric" as an organizing principle of English Studies.

14. For a more complete discussion of changes needed in our graduate program, see my article, "Conceptual Frameworks and Curricular Arrangements," *The Future of Doctoral Studies in English* (New York: MLA, 1989, 30—39). I would add that these suggestions apply as well to the retraining of current faculty; I am pointing here to the issues that, in my view, should ground rhetoric and composition as a field and that will aid us in reconceptualizing English Studies generally.

15. For a description of this process, see Frank Lentricchia, Sharon Crowley, and Linda Robertson, "Wyoming Resolution," *College English* 49 (March 1987, 74—80), and James Slevin and Linda Robertson, "The Status of Composition Faculty: Resolving Reforms," *Rhetoric Review* 5 (Spring 1987, 190—194).

16. *CCC* 40 (October 1989, 329—36).

17. A draft of the statement, along with a full description of the committee's contacts with these other organizations, was published in *CCC* 40 (February 1989, 61—72). The committee's work is more fully explained there and information about how to contact these associations is included. For additional information, especially about MLA/ADE involvement, see my article, "A Note on the Wyoming Resolution and ADE," *ADE Bulletin* 87 (Fall 1987, 50).

Works Cited

Eagleton, Terry. *Literary Theory: An Introduction*. Minneapolis: University of Minnesota Press, 1983.

Fish, Stanley. "Anti-Professionalism." *New Literary History* 17 (1985): 89—108.

———. "Profession Despise Thyself: Fear and Loathing in Literary Studies." *Critical Inquiry* 10 (1983): 349—64.

Graff, Gerald. *Professing Literature: An Institutional History*. Chicago: University of Chicago Press, 1987.

Huber, Bettina, and Art Young. "Report on the 1983—84 Survey of English Programs." *ADE Bulletin* 84 (Fall 1986): 40—61.

Huber, Bettina. "English Salaries: Findings of the 1984—85 ADE Survey." *ADE Bulletin* 87 (Fall 1987): 40—49.

Huber, Bettina, Denise Pinney, David Laurence, and Denise Knight. "MLA Surveys of PhD Placement." *ADE Bulletin* 92 (Spring 1989): 43—50.

Huber, Bettina, and David Laurence. "Report on the 1984—85 Survey of the English Sample." *ADE Bulletin* 93 (Fall 1989): 30—43.

Lanham, Richard. *Literacy and the Survival of Humanism*. New Haven: Yale University Press, 1983.

James F. Slevin 21

Lentricchia, Frank. *Criticism and Social Change*. Chicago: University of Chicago Press, 1983.

Lentricchia, Frank, Sharon Crowley, and Linda Robertson. "Wyoming Resolution." *College English* 49 (1987): 274–280.

Lloyd-Jones, Richard. "Doctoral Programs: Composition." *The Future of Doctoral Studies in English*. Eds. Andrea Lunsford, Helene Moglen, and James Slevin. New York: MLA, 1989, 15–20.

Lunsford, Andrea. Helene Moglen, and James Slevin, eds. *The Future of Doctoral Studies in English*. New York: MLA, 1989.

Ohmann, Richard. *English in America*. New York: Oxford University Press, 1976.

———. *The Politics of Letters*. Middletown: Wesleyan University Press, 1987.

Rose, Mike. "The Language of Exclusion: Writing Instruction at the University." *College English* 47 (1985): 341–359.

Scholes, Robert. *Textual Power: Literary Theory and the Teaching of English*. New Haven: Yale University Press, 1985.

Slevin, James, and Linda Robertson. "The Status of Composition Faculty: Resolving Reforms." *Rhetoric Review* 5 (1987): 190–94.

Slevin, James. "A Note on the Wyoming Resolution and ADE." *ADE Bulletin* 87 (1987): 50.

———. "Genre Theory, Academic Discourse, and Writing Within Disciplines." *Audits of Meaning*. Ed. Louise Z. Smith. Portsmouth: Boynton/Cook-Heinemann, 1988, 3–16.

———. "Conceptual Frameworks and Curricular Arrangements." *The Future of Doctoral Studies in English*. Eds. Andrea Lunsford, Helene Moglen, and James Slevin. New York: MLA, 1989, 30–39.

2

Rhetoric, Poetic, and Culture: Contested Boundaries in English Studies

JAMES A. BERLIN
Purdue University

To talk today of the politics of teaching writing is to talk of the politics of English Studies broadly conceived. Despite the frequent protests to the contrary, writing instruction after all is inescapably imbricated in the teaching of literature, even when literature is, as at the present, the dominant concern of those entrusted with managing language studies. As Kenneth Burke, Tzvetan Todorov, Charles Sears Baldwin, and I have argued, rhetoric and poetic have been explicitly conjoined in discussions of discourse throughout Western history. Their relation to each other has been variously formulated. At some historical moments — and perhaps most, as Jane Tompkins argues — rhetoric is the larger category, including poetry as one of its subdivisions. This configuration is not unexpected (except, of course, to the historically innocent) given the explicit focus of the rhetorical text on the management of political power — for example, as discussed in Plato, Aristotle, Cicero, Quintilian, Augustine, Wilson, and, more recently, Kenneth Burke. At other times, poetics is the master paradigm, including rhetoric as a minor subcategory within it, although this is almost exclusively a postromantic division, one designed to resist the actual lines of power in a society. The argument in this case is that the poet is superior to the rhetorician/politician — that is, more effective — precisely because he is outside the dominant power structures.

The ruling tendency in the English department since its inception some one hundred years ago has been closest to this latter position. As I have explicitly argued in my history of writing instruction and as Gerald Graff has tacitly indicated in his history of the English department (in which writing instruction is conspicuously absent), for English Studies all that is important and central in the study of discourse falls within the domains of literary texts and all that is unimportant and marginal is found in the realm of rhetoric. The result has been singular. Where previous generations of U.S. college students were prepared in the production of the political texts that would enable them to take their rightful place as leaders in their communities (see Guthrie, Halloran, as well as Berlin's *Nineteenth Century*), their descendants in this century have been as rigorously exercised in the apolitical, aesthetic interpretation of literary texts. The rhetorical text is then relegated to the limbo of freshman composition, a course offered only because of the alleged failure of the high school to do its job in what is now redesignated a "lower" level of study.

The explanation for this sharp departure can be found in examining the intersection of English Studies and the historical formations that encouraged it. My argument here is that changes in economic and social structures during the eighteenth and nineteenth centuries led to a new conception of the nature of poetic, a conception that defines the aesthetic experience in class terms and isolates it from other spheres of human activity, most explicitly the political and the scientific. I will call upon the work of Raymond Williams extensively in this discussion. This new division of the poetic and the rhetorical, the aesthetic and the political/scientific, I will then locate in the formation of major schools of literary criticism in the college English department in this century, relying on Graff's description of this development. Since Graff tacitly endorses the poetic/rhetoric relationship that Williams presents while denying its origins in social class, the empirical work of Pierre Bourdieu will be invoked in order to demonstrate the inscription of the poetic/rhetoric binary described by Williams and Graff in the very constitution of class relations in contemporary France.

I will conclude this historical analysis by considering the description of contemporary English Studies found in Robert Scholes's *Textual Power*, a work that responds to the current crisis in the English department's sense of professional purpose. While I do not plan to discuss the causes for the crisis, it is not difficult to see reason for concern in the recent decline of undergraduate and graduate majors in most departments as well as a corresponding loss of faculty positions. The Reagan administration's agenda for education reflected a narrow utilitarian insistence on career training in schools and colleges and a corresponding dismissal of the humanities as irrelevant. This conservative challenge from outside English Studies was matched by a critique from the left within as Marxists, post-Marxists, and poststructuralists questioned the disciplinary assumptions governing the field. Scholes's work represents one of the less radical of these internal responses, but a valuable one nonetheless. In it he both affirms the poetic/ rhetoric relationship described in the studies of Williams, Graff, and Bourdieu and presents a formulation for reinscribing it. That is, he offers a program for reconstituting the relationship institutionally prescribed in our treatment of poetic and rhetoric texts, a program that sees English Studies as reorganized under the rubric of cultural studies. I plan to use Scholes's contribution as a point of departure for considering an alternative reformulation of textual studies in the English department, this one more aggressive in acknowledging the intersections of power and language in the production and interpretation of discourse. In this explanation, I will argue that English Studies is entering a new moment in its development, a moment in which the received poetic/rhetoric relationship is being deconstructed and reformulated along lines that attempt to restore the recognition of the relations between discourse and politics.

The Historical Trajectory

The best comprehensive discussion of the historical events that led to the conception of the rhetoric/poetic relationship now inscribed in the English department is in Raymond Williams's *Marxism and Literature*. In the eighteenth century, Williams explains, the term *literature* "included all printed books. There was not necessary specialization to 'imaginative' works. Literature was still primarily reading ability and reading experience, and this included philosophy, history, and essays as well as poems" (47–48). Literature was thus little more than "a specialization of the area formerly categorized as *rhetoric* and *grammar*: a specialization to reading and...to the printed word and especially the book" (47). The nineteenth century, however, witnessed a significant change in the concept *literature*. Most important, literature "lost its earliest sense of reading ability and reading experience, and became an apparently objective category of printed works of a certain quality." Now literary quality is in the text, not the reader, and with this comes three related tendencies: "first, a shift from 'learning' to 'taste' or 'sensibility' as a criterion defining literary quality; second, an increasing specialization of literature to 'creative' or 'imaginative' works; third, a development of the concept of 'tradition' within national terms, resulting in the more effective definition of 'a national literature'" (48). Williams's explication of these is revealing.

First of all, the move from literature as learning in general to literature as taste or sensibility was marked by a shift in structure and site from the old scholarly profession based in the Church and in state universities— acknowledged by sharing classical languages — to the new scholarly profession defined in class terms. The new definition of literature accompanied the development of the bourgeoisie. This dawning class makes "taste" and "sensibility" characteristically bourgeois categories by seeing their class-determined experience of certain texts as objective qualities of the texts themselves. At the same time, the ability to experience subjectively these "objective" qualities is declared a sign of taste and sensibility, not class identification, so that the subjective experience is given objective status, made an inherent and universal, rather than a class-based and historical, feature of certain individuals. Criticism as it is today understood was a related development, shifting from learned commentary, "to the conscious exercise of 'taste,' 'sensibility,' and 'discrimination'" (49). Significantly, it marked the class-biased move to the consumption of printed works and away from their production. A certain notion of literary taste was now enforced by class membership, as indicated, for example, by references to the "reading public." This notion of taste created a set of complementary binary oppositions valorizing the subjective over the objective, the unconscious over the conscious, and the private over the public. It also insisted on the "immediate" and "lived" qualities of literary discourse, as distinct from the learned tradition of the old university. These class concepts were eventually taken over as the central element of the new disciplines of academic literary criticism, although added were "attempts to establish new abstractly objective criteria." Literary criticism was eventually "taken to be a natural definition of literary studies, themselves defined by the specializing category (printed works of a certain quality) of *literature*." Both *literature* and *criticism* in their modern senses then are the products "of a class specialization and control of a general social practice, and of a class limitation of the questions which it might raise" (49).

Second, the reservation of *literature* to the creative or imaginative was a response to the dehumanizing conditions of the new social order of industrial capitalism. The creative works of the imagination were now placed in opposition to all the horrors of social experience: "The practical specialization of work to the wage-labor production of commodities; of 'being' to 'work' in these terms; of language to the passing of 'rational' or 'informative' 'messages'; of social relations to functions within a systematic economic and political order: all these pressures and limits were challenged in the name of a full and liberating 'creativity'" (50). This is, of course, a development of the Romantic period in English literary history, the time when these binary contrasts were being inscribed in the parlance of the educated. Thus, literature is set against the inhuman realm of work in a cruel, exploitative economic order, an order in which the language of currency is rational and informative discourse. It was this mechanical discourse to which rhetoric was relegated, the world of practical affairs identified with the denial of all that was in the best interests of the individual. Significantly, the space for political discourse was thus obliterated since neither mechanistic science nor the aesthetic poetic were to address this dimension of experience (but more of this shortly). New terms that are now commonplaces for us, however, arose in connection with this semiotic: "art" moves from being a general human skill to that of the special realm of "imagination" and "sensibility"; "aesthetic" is no longer a general perception but a special part of the "artistic" and "beautiful"; the terms "fiction" and "myth" become marks of "imaginative truth," not fancies or lies. Art objects are seen as mythic and aesthetic, possessing qualities that appeal to taste and sensibility. Furthermore, it was these qualities that at first were to be extended to everyday life, and, later, when the destructiveness of capitalism reached everywhere, to be preserved from everyday life. In other words, the attempt to introduce the aesthetic into ordinary daily experience was declared impossible in a material and social world made ugly by the ruthless pursuit of profit. All that can be hoped for is to keep the aesthetic safe from this fallen realm, untainted by its corruption.

These elevated qualities of art were alternatively attributed "to the 'imaginative' dimension (access to a truth 'higher' or 'deeper' than 'scientific' or 'objective' or 'everyday' reality; a claim consciously substituting itself for the traditional claims of religion)," on the one hand, and "to the 'aesthetic' dimension ('beauties' of language or style)," on the other. There were also attempts to fuse the two, however, setting literary discourse against all other experience and discourse: "not only against 'science' and 'society' — the abstract and generalizing modes of other 'kinds' of experience — and not only against other kinds of writing — now in their turn specialized as 'discursive' or 'factual' — but, ironically, against much of 'literature' itself — 'bad' writing, 'popular' writing, 'mass culture'" (51). Thus was inaugurated the divisions between art and science, literature and politics, and high culture and low culture — in general the distinction between poetic and rhetoric. In the case of the two cultures, high literary culture was now defined by the new discipline of criticism, discriminating the important from the less important and unimportant, the critic becoming as necessary as the artist in making the authentically literary available for consumption. Once again, political discourse, the language of social arrangements, is relegated to the world of the fallen and unregenerate, the intractable realm of the rhetorical.

Related to this discriminatory function of criticism is the third element in the changing conception of the literary, the growth of national literature. Criticism called upon this national literature in exercising its cultural judgments, but not without transforming it: "The 'national literature' soon ceased to be a history and became a tradition. It was not, even theoretically, all that had been written or all kinds of writing. It was a selection which culminated in, and in a circular way defined, the 'literary values' which 'criticism was asserting.'" The result was the formation of a canon, "the absolute ratification of a limited and specializing consensual process. To oppose the terms of this ratification was to be 'against literature'" (52). To argue that discourse other than this narrowly defined literary category be taken seriously (either for consumption or for production, it should be added) was likewise to be hostile to the truly literary.

The Role of English Studies

Gerald Graff's discussions of the English department in the United States reveals the relevance of Williams's analysis to the present. In *Professing Literature: An Institutional History*, Graff clearly elucidates the manner in which successive schools of literary criticism in the U.S. university set themselves against the dehumanizing conditions of industrial capitalism. The evidence Graff presents, furthermore, indicates that most have embraced the binary oppositions that characterized the class-biased redefinition of literature described by Williams. This is seen vividly in the various charges leveled at those schools of criticism whose place is being usurped. Thus, Graff cites Edwin Greenlaw's 1931 list of accusations made by the New Critics against literary-historical research: "that it apes scientific method, that it is against ancient standards, that it is immersed in subjects of no possible use, that it destroys the ability to teach. It is neglectful of culture. It stifles creative art. It looks at facts rather than at the soul" (*Professing Literature* 248). A similar litany is in turn recited by Douglas Bush in his 1948 attack on New Criticism itself, as he denounces its "aloof intellectuality," its "avoidance of moral values," its "aping" of the scientific, and its treating criticism as "a circumscribed end in itself" (*Professing Literature* 248). Graff sums up the purport of the critiques leveled by one after another school of literary criticism at its predecessor: "scientism, preference for nit-picking analysis over direct experience of literature itself, and favoring the special interest of a professional coterie over the interests of the general readers and student" (*Professing Literature* 249). We can be sure, furthermore, that the "general reader" indicated is an abstraction that closely resembles the class-determined "reading public" of an earlier age. It is clear that all these charges were intended to show that the critical school being attacked was guilty of conflating the literary text with the marginalized discourse of rhetoric, the discourse of science and society. In other words, each of these charges mirrors the binary opposition in which the exalted discourse of canonized literary texts—the imaginary, the aesthetic, the disinterested appeal to private taste and sensibility—is opposed to the discourse of rhetorical texts—the scientific, objective, practical, and political, the interested appeals to the public intellect and reason.

Gerald Graff's discussion of literary criticism in the English department in *Literature Against Itself* also repeatedly demonstrates the institutionalization of these dichotomies. He cites with approval R. S. Crane's dismissal of New Criticism. The New Critic, explains Crane, "knows what the nature of 'poetic language' must be because he has begun by dividing all language into two opposing and incommensurable kinds—the language of 'logic' and the language of 'symbolism'—and then has deduced from this initial assumption that the 'symbolic' language of poetry must necessarily possess the contraries of all qualities commonly asserted of 'logical discourse'" (*Literature Against Itself* 178). The same opposition is found in Northrop Frye, of whom Graff says the following: "Over and over in successive works, Frye asserts that there are two orders of reality, an objective order in which we invest our beliefs, and a human order we impose on this order in order to give it meaning. The first order is that of nature or things as they are, dead, material, inhuman, and unavoidable; the second is the order of art, applied science, religion, culture, and civilization" (*Literature Against Itself* 182). The lifeless, meaningless material world is relegated to the language of logic, and the humanly significant realm of art is contained in the language of myth. Graff makes the point more strongly by explaining that the natural world in Frye's scheme is that domain "the wrong sorts of people put unquestioned faith in—positivists, moralists, social engineers, superpatriots, bureaucrats" (*Literature Against Itself* 185). Graff earlier in this work locates the same set of contrasts between culture and nature in I. A. Richards and later in Paul de Man, saying of the latter: "De Man, too, deduces the nature of literature by dividing all language into two opposing and incommensurable camps, but instead of dividing language into 'paradoxical' vs. 'steno-language,' de Man divides it into language that deconstructs itself by calling attention to its own fictiveness and undecidability, and language that presumes a naive confidence in its ontological authority" (*Literature Against Itself* 178). Graff's entire text is meant to demonstrate a set of binary oppositions inscribed in the institutional arrangement of literary studies: creation over representation; texts as open, indeterminate "invitation" against texts as determinate object; voyages into the unforeseen against boundaries and constraints; risk against docility and habit; truth as invention and fiction against truth as correspondence; meaning as "process" against meaning as "product" (*Literature Against Itself* 24).

Graff denies that these binaries are supported by class structure, arguing that this "thesis credits high culture and those who rule with a coherence of outlook neither any longer possesses. When the modernist revolution made Matthew Arnold's concept of culture seem outmoded, high culture lost what relative unity it may have had. A high culture which includes both Arnold and Artaud, Samuel Johnson and Samuel Beckett, has no ideological unity. As for those who rule, it is self-flattering but mistaken to think that these flexible pragmatists require high culture as means of justifying or consolidating their power" (*Literature Against Itself* 117). Graff's error, it seems to me, is in the assumption that the poetic/rhetoric binary must be explicitly invoked by all members of a class in supporting class divisions, his charge assuming a mechanistic base-superstructure model of cultural production. It is possible, however, that the poetic/rhetoric distinction can be used to reinforce class barriers by members of the academy who are unconscious of any political intention. They can do so, moreover, despite the disputes among themselves about the value of differing literary texts, since it is the response to the texts, not the texts themselves, that is important. It is here that the work of Pierre Bourdieu becomes instructive.

Bourdieu and the Uses of Culture

In *Distinction: A Social Critique of the Judgement of Taste*, Bourdieu reports the result of an empirical study in France of "the relationships between the universe of economic and social conditions and the universe of life-styles." His focus, as his title indicates, is on life-styles as they are imbricated in cultural pursuits. Bourdieu's intention is no less than "giving a scientific answer to the old question of Kant's critique of judgment, by seeking in the structure of social classes the basis of the systems of classification which structure perception of the social world and designate the objects of aesthetic enjoyment" (xiii—xiv). Bourdieu's work, by his own admission, is subversive since his study defines "the laws of academic or intellectual propriety which condemn as barbarous any attempt to treat culture, that present incarnation of the sacred, as an object of science" (xiii).

Bourdieu's study population consisted of men and women representing a full range of the social spectrum in terms of family background, education, and occupation. His method was to ask a series of questions about this population's responses to a variety of cultural experiences, experiences that included music, painting, photography, film, literature, and sports. It is perhaps not unexpected that Bourdieu's study confirmed previous findings "that all cultural practices (museum visits, concert-going, reading, etc.) and preferences in literature, painting, or music, are closely linked to educational level (measured by qualification or length of schooling) and secondarily to social origin" (1). It is remarkable, however, to discover that Bourdieu has located inscribed within French class relations the very same binary oppositions regarding culture that were described by Williams in his historical study and by Graff in his investigation of academic literary criticism in the United States.

Bourdieu discovered that a "work of art has meaning and interest only for someone who possesses the cultural competence, that is, the code into which it is encoded" (2). This code, furthermore, is always historically specific. At present it is constituted by a set of opposing terms that corresponds to the distinction between high culture and low culture and higher class and lower class. The first of these is the separation of form from function: "The primacy of the mode of representation over the object of representation demands categorically an attention to form which previous art only demanded conditionally" (3). The art that exists for itself, reproducing its own forms rather than the concrete objects of material existence, is here valorized. This means that the artist must be autonomous, free to create in accordance with his own program, not restricted to traditional devices or the external world. Bourdieu explains that it is the "'open work,' intrinsically and deliberately polysemic" that is to be preferred over that which lends itself to a small range of interpretation. As he explains, to "assert the autonomy of production is to give primacy to that of which the artist is master, i.e., forms, manners, style, rather than the 'subject,' the external referent, which involves subordination to function" (3). The capacity to enjoy the art that privileges creation over representation, the open text over the closed one, the unexpected and risky over the bounded and constrained, truth as invention over truth as correspondence (all binaries from Graff's scheme) involves a knowledge of the history of art since it is art objects of the past that serve as the referrents for this polysemic art. While this mastery can be acquired by intensive study, it is continuous and long contact with art objects that separates the highest orders from their educated imitators.

Bourdieu characterizes this disposition toward art objects the "pure gaze," a concept originating in the nineteenth century and appropriated in marking contemporary class distinctions. This response denies the continuity between art and life. Popular taste, he explains, is incapable of this pure gaze, preferring function to form, looking beyond the art object for its relation to actual material and social conditions—displaying a utilitarianism seen to be a part of the practical and political world. As Bourdieu explains, "working-class people expect every image to explicitly perform a function . . . and their judgments make reference, often explicitly, to the norms of morality or agreeableness. Whether rejecting or praising, the appreciation always has an ethical base" (5). The counter to this position is the intellectual response that perfers "the representation—literature, theater, painting— more than . . . the thing represented" (5). This involves, of course, a distancing from the necessities of natural and social experience, often resulting in the extension of the privatized aesthetic experience to all features of life: "the ability to apply the principles of a 'pure' aesthetic to the most everyday choices of everyday life, e.g., in cooking, clothing, or decoration, completely reversing the popular disposition which annexes aesthetics to ethics" (5). Thus, Bourdieu finds, for example, a statistical correspondence among class position, cultural practices, and eating habits.

Recalling for us Raymond Williams's language, Bourdieu sums up the disjunction between the disinterested cultural object that appeals to private taste and sensibility and the instrumental object that is concerned with the public, practical, and political: "The denial of lower, coarse, vulgar, venal, servile—in a word, natural—enjoyment, which constitutes the sacred sphere of culture, implies an affirmation of the superiority of those who can be satisfied with the sublimated, refined, disinterested, gratuitous, dis- tinguished pleasures forever closed to the profane. That is why art and cultural consumption are predisposed, consciously and deliberately or not, to fulfill a social function of legitimating social differences" (7). These social differences, furthermore, are conceived by Bourdieu in terms of cultural or human capital, the accomplishments of class and education serving as a medium of exchange in social relations that performs the function of money in economic relations. As indicated earlier, furthermore, the literary texts that form a part of cultural capital can change over time without jeopardizing class unity and the exchange process. It is the ways the texts are interpreted and used, not the texts themselves, that are important. Indeed, Bourdieu is himself mistaken in arguing for a particular version of the aesthetic as a constitutive element of the structure of social class. Aesthetic responses and the texts that evoke them are more accurately seen as appropriations in the service of class interests, reinforcing rather than creating differences more accurately attributed to economic and political categories.

Refiguring the Binary

In *Textual Power: Literary Theory and the Teaching of English*, Robert Scholes offers an illuminating summary of the results in English Studies of the historical and social developments charted here. Scholes argues that the "field of English is organized by two primary gestures of differentiation, dividing and re-dividing the field by binary opposition" (5). English departments "mark those texts labeled literature as good or important and dismiss those non-literary texts as beneath our notice" (5). Scholes sees this division as corresponding to the distinction between production and consumption, and, recalling Williams's analysis, asserts that consumption is privileged over production, "just as the larger culture privileges the consuming class over the producing class" (5). The nonliterary texts are relegated to the field of reading and the lower schools, since they lack both complication and disinterestedness: "But actual nonliterature is perceived as grounded in the realities of existence, where it is produced in response to personal or socioeconomic imperatives and therefore justifies itself functionally. By its very usefulness, its nonliterariness, it eludes our grasp. It can be read but not interpreted, because it supposedly lacks those secret-hidden-deeper meanings so dear to our pedagogic hearts" (6). The production of these nonliterary texts, furthermore, cannot be taught apart from the exigencies of real-life situations, so that the field of composition is regarded as a "pseudo-nonliterature," just as the attempt to teach creative writing in the academy is regarded as an effort to produce "pseudo-literature," the product of attempting to teach what cannot be taught. Finally, Scholes uses this governing scheme of oppositions to characterize English department practices along the same lines seen in Williams and Bourdieu: the division between sacred and profane texts, the division between the priestly class and the menial class, and the placing of beauty and truth against the utilitarian and commonplace.

Scholes's work is an intelligent and comprehensive attempt to address the destructively decisive oppositional categories on which practices in the college English department are based. His displacement and refiguring of them outlined in *Textual Power* is, however, less successful, although certainly provocative. Scholes invokes the deconstructive challenge to these practices from Paul de Man along with the objections from the left offered by Terry Eagleton and Fredric Jameson. He refuses to see texts as radically indeterminate and finally aesthetic as does the former while denying that they are as unremittingly political as does the latter. Instead, he argues for the multiple determination of texts depending on the semiotic codes — that is, cultural codes — that are located in them through the specific set of reading practices invoked in their consideration. In other words, texts can mean many things depending on the codes applied to them as well as the codes inscribed in them, the two acting dialogically. Their meanings are thus the product of an interactive process and are polysemic.

There are, however, a number of shortcomings in Scholes's method. The choice of interpretive strategies — the code preferred in a particular reading, whether political or aesthetic or historical, for example — seems arbitrary. No standard for choosing one in preference to another is suggested. This means that the political and the ethical become just one more set of choices, in no way to be recommended over any other. In short, there is in Scholes no concern for deciding among competing reading codes or, of equal importance, for integrating more than one of them. There is a fragmentation and an arbitrariness at the base of this system. In addition, Scholes's attempt to deconstruct the current rhetoric/poetic opposition and its invidious distinctions focuses exclusively on literary texts, once again reinforcing the conviction that they alone merit close analysis. Similarly, Scholes mentions nothing about the production of rhetorical texts — that is, the teaching of writing — assuming in the manner of those he opposes that learning to interpret literature will automatically teach students to master the methods of producing nonliterary discourse. Finally, there is in *Textual Power* a political timidity, a reluctance to explore fully the subversiveness of the charges leveled at the English department. Thus, any reference to the role that the practice of college English Studies plays in reinforcing the injustices of race, class, and gender bias is scrupulously avoided, even though it is not difficult to see that this is a part of Scholes's tacit agenda.

Williams, Bourdieu, and Scholes together point to certain conclusions about the current role of the English department in the larger social scheme. A literary studies based on the poetic/rhetoric bifurcation found in these departments serves the interest of a privileged managerial class while discriminating against those who are outside of this class. It does so, furthermore, through cruelly clandestine devices, refusing the political in the service of an aesthetic experience that implicitly reinforces discriminatory social divisions. All of this, furthermore, is occulted by its pretensions to disinterestedness. Thus, the English department's abhorrence of the rhetorical, of political and scientific texts, does far more than create a permanent underclass of department members whose putative role is the remediation of the poorly prepared. It more importantly works to exclude from the ranks of the privileged managerial class those students not socialized from birth in the ways of the aesthetic response, doing so by its influence on the materials and methods of reading and writing required for success in secondary schools, college admission tests, and the colleges themselves. Thus, the English department serves an important exclusionary function. It also mystifies the role it plays in precluding reading and writing practices that might address inequalities in the existing social order. In other words, by excluding reading practices that might discover the political unconscious of literary texts, and by refusing to take seriously the production and interpretation of rhetorical texts that address political matters, English Studies has served as a powerful conservative force, all the while insisting on its transcendence of the political. Thus, the college English department's insistence on the division of the literary and the nonliterary with its invidious dichotomies has served to entitle those already entitled and to disempower the disempowered, doing so in the name of the sacred literary text.

An Alternative Formulation

Scholes's analysis of English Studies is not the only recent assessment of English department practices (although it is certainly the most detailed in its criticisms and recommendations). These have come from a number of critics, including Eagleton, Jameson, Gayatri Chakravorty Spivak, Frank Lentricchia, Edward Said, Richard Ohmann, and Jonathan Culler. Here I would like to consider a formulation for reconceiving the rhetoric/poetic opposition that is being forwarded by those within rhetorical studies, the suspect side of the English Studies dyad. I wish to continue the discussions begun by Patricia Bizzell in "On the Possibility of a Unified Theory of Composition and Literature" and by John Trimbur in "Cultural Studies and Teaching Writing." Although I will not comment directly on their work, it serves as a rich context for my own. I wish here to organize my remarks around the formulation that I have been discussing under the rubric of social-epistemic rhetoric. As I have argued in "Rhetoric Programs after World War II: Ideology, Power, and Conflict," this rhetoric has acted as a counterpart to the calls from the literary theorists mentioned above for a reconstituted English Studies organized around a concept of cultural studies. Growing primarily out of the work of Kenneth Burke and, more recently, the Bakhtin circle, this rhetoric is one with these figures in addressing the challenges to traditional discourse study presented by Marxism and the poststructuralist linguistic turn as represented by Derrida and Foucault. Social-epistemic rhetoric most notably insists on examining all discourse within its historical context, examining the ways language serves as a mediator in the negotiation of individuals within their economic, social, political, and cultural moment. This rhetoric has accordingly begun with the reformulation of the divisive oppositions inscribed in the rhetoric/ poetic relationship occupying the center of English Studies, and I would like to devote the remainder of this discussion to considering this reformulation.

Epistemic rhetoric refuses to accept an inherent distinction between texts that are representational and texts that are creative. From this perspective, language in all its uses structures rather than simply records experience. Thus, language never acts as a simple referent to an eternal, extralinguistically verifiable thing in itself. It instead serves as a terministic screen to form and shape experience. All langauge use is inherently interpretive. All texts then become involved in invention, in the process of meaning formation. It is important to recognize, however, that this structuring of experience is never undertaken by a unified, coherent, and sovereign subject who can transcend language. No single person is in control of language: It is a social construction that shapes us as much as we shape it. In other words, language is a product of social relations and so is ineluctably involved in power and politics. Language indeed constitutes an arena in which ideological battles are continually fought. The different language practices of different social groups are inscribed with ideological prescriptions, interpretations of experience that reinforce conceptions of what really exists, what is really good, and what is politically possible. The discourse of any given group tacitly instructs its members in who they are and how they fit into this larger scheme, as well as in the very nature of the scheme itself. Thus, language practices enforce a set of ideological prescriptions regarding the nature of "reality": economic "realities" and the distribution of wealth; social and political "realities" regarding class, race, and gender and their relations to power; and cultural "realities" regarding the nature of representation or symbolic form in art, play, and other cultural experience. These ideological prescriptions, furthermore, are in continual conflict for hegemony, with the groups in ascendance calling on all of their resources of power to maintain dominance in the face of continual opposition and resistance. This conception of the constructive capacity of language thus completely negates the distinction between referential and creative discourse and the binary oppositions they have been made to enforce. All texts are formative in experience since all are involved in economic, social, political, and cultural considerations.

This leads to the denial of the opposition between the production and consumption of texts. Producing and consuming are both interpretations (as all language is interpretive) that require a knowledge of semiotic codes in which are inscribed a version of economic, social, and political predispositions. All language is interested, and the task of the rhetor as well as the poet, and the reader of the poet as well as the rhetor, is a working out of semiotic codes. These codes, furthermore, are never simply in the writer, or simply in the text, or simply in the reader. They always involve a dialectical relation of the three, a rhetorical relation in which writer, reader, text, and material conditions are simultaneously interacting with one another, doing so, furthermore, through the medium of the semiotic code, the linguistic center of experience. This encounter in language is never totally free since semiotic codes are themselves already interpretations. Thus, signifying practices of poetic as well as rhetoric are always historically conditioned, are always responses to the material and social formations of a particular moment.

This conception of the production and consumption of texts deconstructs and reformulates the contraries of the rhetoric/poetic relationship. The sharp oppositions between disinterested and interested, private and public, contemplative and creative, no longer hold up. There are no strictly disinterested uses of language since all signifying practices—both in writing and reading—are imbricated in ideological predispositions. We have seen, for example, how Bourdieu's study of cultural practices in France has shown the relationship of class and politics to aesthetic judgment. The private/public distinction is likewise broken down as we realize that language is a social device that is inherently public, that is social and communal. Individuals are indeed constituted by this public discourse, but, as the Bakhtin circle has insisted, each individual becomes a differentiated site of converging discourses that enables agency and change. The subject as discursive formation acts as well as reacts, the private and the public thus interacting dialectically. The private is neither totally separate from the public nor is it totally identical with it. And the distinction between action and contemplation likewise collapses as we recall that all texts are involved in politics and power—all tacitly or explicitly underwrite certain platforms of action. Finally, the distinction between high culture and low culture is seen to be, from this point of view, a validation of the class structure—a hierarchy of texts created from the perspective of a class interested in securing its own interests.

This perspective does not mean that all distinctions between rhetoric and poetic will be obliterated. It does mean the aesthetic cannot be regarded as a category functioning apart and beyond all other considerations. The historically determined aesthetic code is an essential element in literary production and interpretation, but it can function only in relation to other codes: It is never isolated and innocent. I have in mind here the sort of practice recommended by Bakhtin/Medvedev, who argue that literary study "is concerned with the concrete life of the literary work in the unity of the generating literary environment, the literary environment in the generating ideological environment, and the latter, finally, in the generating socioeconomic environment which permeates it" (27). All of us will continue to distinguish rhetoric and poetic, but we will do so on the basis of the writing and reading practices involved in each—the semiotic, culturally indicated codes appropriate to each. This will mean an end to the invidious valorization of the literary because of its rich organic complexity and its satisfaction of the aesthetic need, and the dismissal of the rhetorical because of its purported practicality and mechanical simplicity. Both are rich and complex in their expression of meaning and both are necessary in the continued health of a society. The work of English Studies will be to study the discursive practices involved in generating and interpreting both. The English classroom will then provide methods for revealing the semiotic codes enacted in the production and interpretation of texts, codes that cut across the aesthetic, the economic and political, and the philosophical and scientific, enabling students to engage critically in the variety of reading and writing practices required of them.

I realize that the scheme I have put forth to address the divisions in the English department and their relation to larger economic, social, political, and cultural formations will not be easily implemented. For many, surrendering the hierarchy of texts means surrendering considerable cultural capital, and this deserves some consideration.

As Immanuel Wallerstein has recently pointed out, university professors occupy a strategic place in the distribution of cultural capital. Wallerstein argues that historically the bourgeoisie is rarely satisfied with its status as bourgeoisie. Instead, it aspires to the cultural conditions of the aristocracy. Soon after its wealth is accumulated (usually with the second generation), the members of this class disengage from the direct management of their economic enterprises, living on rent, after the manner of an aristocracy. Those who take over the role of handling the quotidian tasks of making money are the salaried bourgeoisie, the managerial class. Most of this class can never hope to achieve bourgeois status because of the lack of capital: They are, after all, only wage earners — although well-paid wage earners. As a result, this group becomes concerned with accumulating cultural or human capital, the marks of the educated middle class, the educational certifications and accomplishments that distinguish this class from wage earners lower on the social scale. Cultural capital then becomes a commodity that can be passed on to this class's children in the form of dispositions and practices learned at home (for example, the aestheticizing of experience discovered by Bourdieu) and the certifications acquired through advanced education. The latter is secured through managing the educational system so that it favors their offspring — through class-biased achievement tests and entrance requirements, for example. In their conceptions of art and literature, furthermore, this managerial class emulates its aristocratic betters — that is, not the entrepreneurial class but those who have separated themselves from management in order to live a life of cultivation and leisure.

It is the role of English teachers to serve as the bankers, the keepers and dispensers, of certain portions of this cultural capital, their value to society being defined in terms of its investment and reproduction. Since this capital has been located almost exclusively in literary texts, it is small wonder that attempts to challenge the rhetoric/poetic binary on which the value of these texts resides is resisted. Surrendering this hierarchy of texts means questioning claims to preeminence and power both within and outside the classroom, challenging the very bases of professional self-respect. Changing English Studies along the lines here recommended then requires a reformulation of the very figuration of cultural capital on which our discipline is based. Understanding the stakes in the contest for those resisting change, however, will enable a more humanely intelligent strategy for new conceptions of the discipline, conceptions that will prepare our students to be better writers, better readers, and better citizens of a democratic society.

I want to thank Susan Carlton of Purdue and John Trimbur for helpful critiques of this essay.

Works Cited

Bakhtin, M. M., and P. N. Medvedev. *The Formal Method in Literary Scholarship.* Trans. Albert J. Wehrle. Cambridge: Harvard University Press, 1985.

Baldwin, Charles Sears. *Ancient Rhetoric and Poetic*. New York: Macmillan, 1924.

Berlin, James A. *Rhetoric and Reality: Writing Instruction in American Colleges, 1900–1985*. Carbondale: Southern Illinois University Press, 1987.

———. "Rhetoric Programs after World War II: Ideology, Power, and Conflict." In *Rhetoric and Ideology: Compositions and Criticisms of Power*. Ed. Charles Kneupper. Arlington, TX: Rhetoric Society of America, 1989.

———. *Writing Instruction in Nineteenth-Century American Colleges*. Carbondale: Southern Illinois University Press, 1984.

Bizzell, Patricia. "On the Possibility of a Unified Theory of Composition and Literature." *Rhetoric Review* 4.2 (1986): 174–180.

Bourdieu, Pierre. *Distinction: A Social Critique of the Judgement of Taste*. Trans. Richard Nice. Cambridge: Harvard University Press, 1984.

Burke, Kenneth. "Rhetoric, Poetics, and Philosophy." *Rhetoric, Philosophy, and Literature: An Exploration*. Ed. Don M. Burks. West Lafayette, IN: Purdue University Press, 1978.

Graff, Gerald. *Literature Against Itself: Literary Ideas in Modern Society*. Chicago: University of Chicago Press, 1979.

———. *Professing Literature: An Institutional History*. Chicago: University of Chicago Press, 1987.

Guthrie, Warren. "The Development of Rhetoric Theory in America, 1636–1850." *Speech Monographs* 13 (1946): 14–22; 14 (1947): 38–54; 15 (1948): 61–71; 16 (1949): 98–113; 18 (1951): 17–30.

Halloran, S. Michael. "Rhetoric in the American College Curriculum: The Decline of Public Discourse." *PRE/TEXT* 3 (1982): 245–269.

Scholes, Robert. *Textual Power: Literary Theory and the Teaching of English*. New Haven: Yale University Press, 1985.

Todorov, Tzvetan. *Symbolism and Interpretation*. Trans. Catherine Porter. Ithaca: Cornell University Press, 1982.

Tompkins, Jane P. "The Reader in History: The Changing Shape of Literary Response." *Reader-Response Criticism: From Formalism to Post-Structuralism*. Ed. Jane P. Tompkins. Baltimore: Johns Hopkins University Press, 1980.

Trimbur, John. "Cultural Studies and Teaching Writing." *Focuses* 1.2 (1988): 5–18.

Wallerstein, Immanuel. "The Bourgeois(ie) as Concept and Reality." *New Left Review* 167 (1988): 91–106.

Williams, Raymond. *Marxism and Literature*. Oxford: Oxford University Press, 1977.

3

The Feminization
of Composition

SUSAN MILLER
University of Utah

I realize that my title may unintentionally fail to frame my purpose, for it easily leads in two directions. "Feminization" calls to mind both positive new moves in composition to gender-balance research and teaching and negative associations with the actual "feminization" of a field that collects, like bugs in a web, women whose persistently marginalized status demands political action. But I have chosen this potentially slippery term precisely, to point a new reading of composition studies that places both the political action that we obviously need, and many new intellectual and practical movements toward gender balance in composition studies, against a prevailing negative cultural identity that "the feminization of composition" implies. Paradoxically, positive internal desires to gender-balance our field are contained by a negative, insistent external feminization in the phallocentric community where it was born. Much of the field's past, its continuing actual experience, and its usually overlooked but important symbolic associations result from a defining, specifically from a gendered, cultural call to identity.

By using the phrase "call to identity," I mean to bring to mind a group of related leftist political and feminist theories that explain identity formation as a result from a cultural context. Identities do not, in these views, result from the preexisting or essential qualities of a person, or of an area of social action, itself. Instead, they come into being through a cultural context of which we are already a part. This context is partially made up of a framework of assumptions and approaches, a superstructure, that places both individuals and certain kinds of social action in fairly well-enclosed cultural spaces, where they have names and identifiable discursive practices. These identifying spaces are hierarchically disposed, but cultural invitations to inhabit them are not simple edicts from on high. We tacitly accept these identities to maintain the superstructure that we live in, in a process of hegemonic consensus. The "low" is contained by its implied participation in a total system.

In regard to gender and the "low" situation of females, this reasoning emphasizes that categories of identity, or "subjectivities," map both individuals and groups (see Eagleton, "Subject" 95). For instance, a female may be constituted as "a mother," and therefore as a person who will sacrifice her personal separateness to attend to the frequent and private bodily needs of young children—elimination, cleanliness, and nurturance. But the culture also produces "motherhood," a symbolic domain that places a particular woman's self-sacrifice in an acceptable image of *the* Mother, a figure who occupies an idealized space of veneration. For many feminist theorists, it is well understood that no matter what range of individual biological, intellectual, social, economic, class, or other qualities people of the female sex may exhibit, this and other female identities (e.g., "wife," "whore," "girl") participate in similar cultural calls to "womanhood." This "hood" effectively cloaks differences to assure that females (and males) are socially identified by imaginary relations to their actual situations.

Many feminists also point out that within this process, the identity of the female person was specifically differentiated as "woman" to supplement, complement, oppose, and extend male identity. This separation of genders first organized cultures for their biological, economic, and social survival. A female's particularity or her ignorance of such category formation could not at first excuse her and has not later excused her from the cultural identity devised to ensure the continuity of traditions that regulate property, power, and status within and among communities.

I outline these theories and some of their corollaries because I want to argue that this view of lower-status female identity—including both its critique of dominance and submission and its view of historical requirements imposed for the sake of survival and tradition—is embodied by composition studies. A similar cultural call acting on composition has, that is, created the field's unentitled "place" in its surroundings and has limited both its old and its new self-definitions. This call and responses to it maintain the regular range of results that follow from the field's most common, as well as its most innovative, practices. Recent reactions to this call often attempt to overcome the field's feminization, but composition remains largely the distaff partner in a socially important "masculine" enterprise, the cultural maintenance of linguistic dispositions of power and enfranchisement.

To support this claim, I want to review "facts," a history, and relevant symbolic associations that negatively feminize composition, despite (and in concert with) some of our best efforts to overcome this identity. Making my case depends, I realize, on persuasively joining information we already know and accept about the status of composition to both a historical context and a larger symbolic domain that is usually preserved to explain purposes, practices, and status in more entitled cultural sites. We habitually, at least among ourselves, quote statistics and tell personal tales about the professional situation of the field and its members, but we rarely account for and evaluate these (quite accurate) perceptions from a theoretical perspective, to show how they arise from, and contribute to, the superstructure they maintain.

We can, then, begin uncovering the feminization of composition by reviewing some concrete bad news we already know. In fact, in the actual life-world of anyone who teaches English, the field is largely the province of women. As Sue Ellen Holbrook has so carefully shown in her essay "Women's Work," the sexual division of labor that characterizes all jobs has equally characterized composition. Holbrook points out that in decades when women have "risen" in the academy, at least in numbers, they have concurrently assumed lower ranks in subject areas associated with feminine pursuits—home economics, physical education, humanities, social sciences, and education. They have, on average, been paid 18 percent less than men; as late as 1986, they earned but 85 percent of what men in the humanities earned. In addition, women hold the part-time appointments in academic institutions. In 1976, women occupied 25 percent of full-time positions, but 38 percent of the part-time positions.

As we know, a large proportion of this part-time work force are housed in departments of English, where composition is usually taught. These paraprofessionals, to use Holbrook's term, occupy the lowest hierarchical status by virtue of their association with composition teaching itself, typically characterized as *elementary* teaching that is a *service* tied to *pedagogy* rather than theory (9). Holbrook estimates that two-thirds of all who teach composition are female. Two-thirds of the NCTE College section membership are women. In 1986, 65 percent of the program participants at the Conference on College Composition and Communication were female; in 1987, 58 percent were female. (In 1986, 45 percent of the participants at the MLA convention were female.)

Holbrook also points out that the gendered hierarchy these figures represent is repeated within composition as a sub-field of English Studies. In composition research, for instance, the hierarchy that subordinates women is maintained: Men appear to publish a greater percentage of articles submitted to *College English* (65 percent); books by men dominate in selective bibliographies (approximately 70 percent); male authors overwhelmingly dominate in "theoretical" (as against nurturant, pedagogical) publication categories (12−13). Holbrook's analyses of these demonstrable proportions and of the historical position of women as faculty in universities give her good grounds for inferring that "men develop knowledge and have higher status; women teach, applying knowledge and serving the needs of others, and have lower status" (7−8). Her inference is further supported by other concrete facts: according to her 1981 count of unambiguous first names, 71 percent of the members of the Association of Writing Program Administrators are men (13), and 73 percent of the programs Carol Hartzog described in her *Composition in the Academy* are administered by men who outrank the female majority of teachers they supervise (23).

These and other ways that the field of composition mirrors traditional "women's roles" are such normalized parts of our daily experience that we may overlook the seemingly contradictory self-images they force us to accept. That is, we are on the one hand so well persuaded that composition is, as Holbrook says, nonintellectual, pedagogical, service-oriented work that we hardly wonder that it is given over to women. We can, no matter how quickly we would deny our nobility in doing so, easily accept that composition is a field for "women and children," teachers and students whom we expect to be tentative about their commitments to "real" education, that which we (again, easily) assume will chronologically follow writing courses. But we also retain equally deep cultural images that thoroughly convince us that composition teaching is the "important" mission that English studies as a whole was constituted to perform. We see it as the locus for the best sense of the cultural literacy that is the imagined important mission of a university as a whole. Learning to read and write, we easily acknowledge, assures the continuation of our civilization. Our most "civilized" and powerful citizens—college graduates—must be confident, fluent producers and equally skilled analysts of discourse. But we are also accustomed to confessions that composition teaching, and composition research, are not something that "regular" (meaning powerful, entitled, male-coded, theoretical) faculty do. This apparent contradiction in the social text around composition studies deserves a great deal of attention, for it is here that the female identity of composition, clear in the facts I have just cited, becomes a larger "feminized" identity that is situated in a specific history that has its own cultural implications.

To get at this history, we can notice that the low status of composition (which is curiously seen as both the cause and the effect of the statistics Holbrook compiled) has always tied composition to "work" in a specific pairing with literary study, the "play" of English. As Richard Ohmann has pointed out, "Writing and Reading: Work and Leisure" describes the totality of English Studies (*Politics* 26–41). That is, the judgmental manual labor of composition opposes entitlements that females in the academy only rarely claim: relaxed mental contemplation, reflection, and most recently a more powerful "theory" of literary study. Consequently, to understand the well-established contradiction between the low-status and inverted female majorities in composition and its importance as "civilizing work," we need to look at the field's original and still most prevalent institutional position. It is the counterpart, the handmaiden, and low-order basement attached to vernacular literary study.

We can reasonably infer that this relationship is a product of the first disposition of composition instruction in new departments of English established in the late nineteenth century, both in England and in America. We have a great deal of historical evidence that the entirety of English, because it was comprised of vernacular language and literature, not the mystified classics, was at first associated with dilettantish, womanish images of belles lettres. It was, that is, letters for belles, identified as a "pink sunsets" tradition of teacups and limp wrists. But this symbolically gender-coded vernacular subject was also, in fact, taught by women in the mechanics and industrial institutes where its advanced courses first appeared, pointedly to address the imagined greater need for "civilizing" students in these institutions. Women taught English even in more elitist schools after its spread (Doyle 23). But not withstanding an elitist imprimatur, "English" was perceived as a "soft," not rigorous or difficult subject, an extension of the popular extracurriculum of polite learning into privileged educational institutions.

Nonetheless, English quite quickly assumed academic centrality, arguably because it was seen as a way to establish national unity among those who were not already entitled to a classical education, but who were being newly admitted to postprimary education. Terry Eagleton's *Literary Theory: An Introduction* argues forcefully that vernacular literature and language study became both the content and the idiom of the modern "parent" country because it included precisely the "poor man's classics," a nationalist substitute for religion. He cites George Gordon, an early professor of English at Oxford: "England is sick," Gordon said in his inaugural address, "and English literature must save it. The Churches (as I understand) having failed, and social remedies being slow, English literature has now a triple function, still, I suppose, to delight and instruct us, but also, and above all, to save our souls and heal the State" (quoted in Eagleton, *Literary Theory* 23). Lest we think this agenda supported only new British English studies, we must remember that similar ideas flourished even more readily in America. There they had been prepared for by an early Puritan morality that had led the *New England Primer* to rhyme "Thy life to mend/This book attend" (Tchudi 4—5). Lindley Murray's infamous *English Grammar, Adapted to the Different Classes of Learners* (1795) taught parsing to "discipline the mind" and to help students write "with propriety" (Tchudi 6). Arthur Appplebee, in *Tradition and Reform in the Teaching of English*, quotes one mid-nineteenth-century teacher/reformer who demonstrates American continuities of this tone in an equally moralistic and chauvinistic justification for vernacular literary study: "The first great aim in the literature course is a training for citizenship by a study of *national* ideals embodied in the writings of American authors, our *race* ideals as set forth by the great writers of Anglo-Saxon origin, our *universal* ideals as we find them in any great work of literary art" (my emphasis; Applebee 69).

Consequently, the entire complex of activities associated with "English" began its competition for a place among established academic subjects with a gendered, but blurred, spiritual identity. And this identity applied equally to the grammatical instruction that for Hegel was "the alphabet of the Spirit itself" (Graff 29). English originally had *actual* associations with a distaff, "soft" study of vernacular language and literature, which had formerly trained children of both sexes in the preliminaries to the rigorous classical education pursued further only by boys. But in establishing English Studies as a university-level discipline competing against the classics and against an equally plausible scientific center for the curriculum, promoters of English Studies asserted its *imagined*, or symbolic, manly associations with religious and nationalistic ideals.

Charles Eliot, the president of Harvard most often identified as the inspiration for the "new university" in which this blurred identity of English studies was to flourish in America, clarified how these contradictory associations were to become systematic practice in his 1869 inaugural address. There he announced that "English" would be the center of the new curriculum. This subject would ensure something like the unity that men educated in the earlier classical colleges had necessarily shared, despite the newly practical and more fragmented curriculum that characterized more "relevant" effort. But, Eliot qualified, this new Harvard education would be bestowed on two sorts of potential recipients—those already entitled, from "refined" homes, and the "new" student, the person whose hold on good character and correct values was only tentative, and who needed to receive both principles and a test (Douglas 129).

The principles—national, race, and universal—were to be learned in vernacular literary study. But the moral test, which would necessarily precede exposure to these principles, was the "test" of English composition. It became embodied only four years later, in both the well-documented Harvard Entrance Exam and "the" course in composition. This course was supervised by Adams Sherman Hill, the journalist and former classmate of Eliot's who was recruited to supervise it. It was thereby defined as a device for winnowing and sifting within the newly elevated, central, field of English. Composition was, then, established to be a place where Harvard could assure the worthiness, moral probity, and fitness of those who might otherwise slip through the newly woven net that would now take in additional, *but only tentatively entitled*, students. In this form, as Ohmann has said of its speedy national adoption, "it spread like kudzu" (33).

The actual establishment of university-level departments of English required a further professional implementation of this educational agenda, a "base" cooperating with this new superstructure. To inculcate literary principles, it was necessary to overcome the "nonserious," gender-coded, image of English by emphasizing its new departments' attachments to philology and to traditional methods of teaching classical language and literature, in order that the subject's work, and its professionals, would be perceived as "hard" (Graff 38). To compete against science and other subjects like traditional rhetoric, which had always been learned and taught in combative, exclusively male contexts, these departments had to overcome traditional, feminine, negative images of vernacular literary study. But they also had to implement Eliot's "test." To organize the discriminations and reassurances about social entitlement that Eliot's new vision of postsecondary curricula meant to maintain, the course in composition had to be a place to house those who studied and taught subjects that were now preliminary in a new sense. Divorced from the old college curriculum in classics, "composition" was defined for the first time as preliterary (or preprincipled), not as a part of rhetorical education for those already entitled eventually to "speak".

Even discounting the economic or survival needs that are often cited to explain composition's importance in the origins of English departments, composition conveniently, and precisely, contained within English the negative, nonserious connotations that the entire field might otherwise have had to combat. In mutuality with literary study, it enclosed those who might not "belong," even as it subsumed the soft, nonserious connotations of vernacular study. It became a place that the "best men" escape from, as we learn both from elaborate placement testing systems and from the frequency with which histories of English and of rhetoric describe Francis Child's release from teaching rhetoric courses at Harvard. But composition was nonetheless the symbolically essential way to verify the social and moral credentials of those admitted to the new university. Given an original societal demand in this cultural call to an identity for composition, we can explain the seeming contradiction between its status as women's work and its ceremonial cultural importance as the essence of an elegantly cooperative pair. Actual "woman's work" filled a necessary symbolic (and often actual) "basement" of literary studies in an easily understood process of identity formation.

The objects of this cooperation, composition students, of course have another subjectivity, or category of identity, that follows from the feminization I am describing. They took an entrance examination whose results were often made public to humiliate them, attended classes that enrolled one hundred or more students in their earliest, introductory exposure to "English," and were taught by ancillary help who were "supervised" rather than admitted to collegial academic freedom. The new pecking order in English departments connected these students to concrete manifestations of the "work" of composition described by Ohmann. For them and their teachers, composition was in fact, as it was in the newly established sustaining mythology of "English," work of a menial, backbreaking sort. "Daily themes" required daily writing and marking (Kitzhaber 169). But since the purpose of assigning these themes was to reveal the fitness of a new student "body"—the unentitled new student's spirit manifest in the physical surface of his language—this heavy, corrective workload was perfectly arranged to accomplish the introductory course's goals. This backbreaking (or more accurately, mind-boggling) work was fit, that is, for tentatively entitled employees of the academy, like women, just as the work of producing correct essays on inconsequential subjects was and remains with few exceptions a task for students whose verbal propriety is in question. It is work required of "new" students in any era, imposed on the majority who are taken to be only tentatively entitled to belong in higher education (Miller, Chapter 3).

But this new educational culture also supplied an acceptable covering mythology that accommodates both the work of composition teaching and its corrective treatment of students' linguistic bodies. Composition teaching, that is, took place in a historically well-established symbolic domain that invited cooperation with distasteful but necessary cultural work. The call to "work" was overlaid on already accepted religious images of grammatical correctness, Hegel's "alphabet of the Spirit." Just as the taxing demands of motherhood give mothers an imaginary relation to a venerable image of *the* Mother, the corrective task of dealing with writing by students who were now identified as only tentatively suitable for the social rewards of university enrollment provided its workers with a covering myth of the "English teacher." This particular cover story endows the composition teacher of whatever disposition; experience, or relation to status with qualities much like those of the mythologized mother; self-sacrifice, "dedication," "caring," and enormous capacities for untheorized attention to detail. But this figure is ambivalent. It also symbolizes authority, precision, and eternally validated, impeccable linguistic taste, qualities that prompt those who meet composition teachers to expect censure and disapproval.

As this duality suggests, composition teaching is not simply "motherhood," a service to father texts. The social identity of the composition teacher is intricately blurred, in a matrix of functions that we can understand through the instructive example of Freud's description of the "feminine," which was formed at about the same time that composition courses and their teaching first achieved presence in the new university. Despite the problematics feminists point out in his work, Freud's description of associations that contain ambivalently situated women can be seen as a reliable historical account of nineteenth-century sexual mythologies. His description of the Mother/Maid, a blurred dream figure whom he revised over time, suggests why our resistance to changes in the cultural image of composition teaching is so deep.

Freud first dreamed of his family nurse, a common member of the nineteenth-century bourgeois household, whom he later transformed into "mother." The nurse in his dream "initiated the young Freud in sexual matters" (Stallybrass and White 157). But later, in Freud's writing about "femininity," "the nurse has been displaced by the mother" (157). In various writings, Freud by turns associated seduction and bodily hygiene with motherhood and with the maid, at one time calling the maid the most intimate participant in his initiations and fantasies, and at another thinking of these matters in relation to perfect motherhood. In *The Politics and Poetics of Transgression*, Peter Stallybrass and Alloy White infer that because the nineteenth-century bourgeois family relegated child care to nurses, the maid both performed intimate educational functions and had power over the child. "Because of his size, his dependency, his fumbling attempts at language, his inability to control his bodily functions" (158), the child could be shamed and humiliated by the maid. But paradoxically, it is more developmentally "natural" to desire the mother than the maid, who is "hired help," so actual interactions with a nurse/maid might be fantasized as having occurred with the mother for whom the maid stood in.

It is fair to suggest that analogous symbolic blurrings still encode teachers of composition, even if we set aside comparisons between the "low" work of composition teaching and this representation of intimate work that at once corrects, educates, and seduces the young initiate. This analogy explains some otherwise troubling contradictions in the ways we habitually conceive of composition teachers, if nothing else. The bourgeois mother and maid, that is, each represent comfort and power, the contradictory endowments required of the service-oriented teacher of students who are, despite their actual maturity, sentimentalized as preeconomic, presexual, prepolitical children (Ohmann, English 149). The mother (a "pure" Victorian symbol) was the source Freud turned to for explanatory information about the maid. The mother was also, with the father, an authority. He displaced these associations of comfort and power onto the maid, but she was also given actual "dirty" work. Thus the maid was an ambivalently perceived site for dealing with low, unruly, even anarchic, desires and as yet uncontrolled personal development, the qualities of freshman writing highlighted in much composition pedagogy.

The Wolfman in Freud's writings developed great anxiety about his formal lessons in Latin, the public, formal, consequential language about which his comforting yet ambivalently perceived nursery maid knew nothing. The requirement, that is, to "'forget' the baby-talk of the body" (Stallybrass and White 166) created great ambivalence about his own body's functions, just as the process of forgoing "home" vernacular language for formal, publicly criticized English compositions displaces the vernacular linguistic confidence of most students. But the composition student is learning a "home," vernacular language *again*, as a formal system that now has public consequences, and is taught in that situation by the maid who is also a designated mother/power figure, not the new schoolmaster whom Wolfman encountered. Again, the cultural "importance" of composition is overlaid on its demeaned place in the family romance of English Studies.

Consequently, the potential identification between the low-status composition teacher and tentatively entitled "young" students creates yet another blurring. Students in their "practice" composition courses expect both infantile freedom from the embarrassment that the mother/power figure in the "real" family causes *and* those same embarrassments, in the form of corrections and information about propriety and "appropriateness" in a formerly familiar language. This at once comforting and powerful, but public and displaced, figure becomes a blurred point of transference for the student's anxieties over the maturation that inevitably accompanies developmental moves toward public language.

Consequently, the figure of a composition teacher is overloaded with symbolic as well as actual functions. These functions include the dual (or even triple) roles that are washed together in these teachers: the teacher is a nurse who cares for and tempts her young charge toward "adult" uses of language that will not "count" because they are, for now, engaged only with hired help; she is, no matter what her gender, the "mother" (tongue) that is an ideal/idol and can humiliate, regulate, and suppress the child's desires. But she is also the disciplinarian, not a father figure but a sadomasochistic Barbarella version of either mother or maid.

These are deeply held images, whose power is evident in their appearance as humorous stereotypes even among the people whose characteristics and practices contradict them. These images from nineteenth-century bourgeois culture had their own historical precedents, which ironically clarify the readily accepted view that the individual composition teacher is a culturally designated "initiator," similar to a temple priest or priestess who functions to pass along secret knowledge, but not to participate freely in a culture that depends on that knowledge. Strict regulations, similar to those devised to keep "hired help" in its place, prevent those who introduce the young to the culture's religious values and rites from leaving their particular and special status. These mediators between natural and regulated impulses are tied to vows, enclosed living spaces, and/or certain kinds of dress, the categories we might compare with composition teachers' self-sacrificing acceptance of work without time for contemplating its implications, their traditionally windowless offices, and the prissiness expected, at least in the past, in their personal presentations (Lerner 123–141).

This blurred initiating role, whether it is described as a religious/sexual initiation or as the groundwork now symbolically placed "under" an educated public's discursive practices, has been unstable in any context. Cultures never codified it even in ancient times, when socially separated *grammaticus* and *rhetor* competed, as Quintilian noted, over who should initiate students into rhetorical composition (*Institutes*, II.1). Consequently, the teacher of composition is assigned not only these roles, which might involve the initiating care, pedagogic seduction, and practice for adulthood provided by nurses in bourgeois homes. In addition, this teacher must withhold unquestioned acceptance, represent established means of discriminating among and evaluating students, and embody primary ideals/idols of language. This initiator, who traditionally has a great deal at stake in the model-correctness of his and her own language, must also *be* the goddess, *the* mother tongue, the discursive culture to which the student is introduced.

It might be countered that this complex call to identity contains any teacher of any introductory course claiming to initiate students into "essential" cultural knowledge. But the composition teacher consciously and unconsciously introduces students to the culture's discourse on *language*, which is always at one with action, emotion, and regulatory establishments. This teacher is always engaged in initiations into the textual fabric of society, and thus will always be in a particular and difficult relation to the superstructural regulation of that society. We see this difficulty daily, in the experience of those who are both demeaned by their continuing *ad hoc* relation to status, security, and financial rewards, yet are given overwhelming authority by students, institutions, and the public, who expect even the most inexperienced "English teacher" to criticize and correct them, even in settings entirely removed from the academy. In these and many other ways, the complexly feminized cultural call to identity imposed on teachers of composition is maintained, even after they themselves censure early mechanistic teaching and its obviously regulatory practices.

This censure signifies positive moves to redefine composition as a discipline, i.e., "composition studies" (see North 9–17), and to establish it as an academically equal partner in English departments. Such obvious, normal reactions from members of a marginalized culture unquestionably bode well for the fully theorized approach to writing and its instruction that could change the cultural expectation that its teachers be only initiating, service-oriented, self-sacrificing, practical people. But in view of the feminized identity I have established, the motives behind actions to "change" composition need cautious critiques. As statistics about who writes composition theory and who administers composition programs tell us, neither describing composition as a discipline nor asserting its equality has "worked" on the actually gender-coded professional circumstances of those who teach writing. These motives have not resulted in acknowledging the gender-coded call to identity that marks the field's cultural history, or in offering alternatives to the deep but blurred structures of identity I have described. Our continuing tacit cooperation with hegemonic superstructural values cannot be underestimated, nor can the hegemonic compromise that continues to constrain the field be "overcome," or "combated," with male-coded fortitude.

We have examples of such fortitude in attempts to follow the formative counterpart of composition, literary study, into an entrenched, privileged, "equal" academic position. The problem with such attempts at equality is that they contribute, no matter how inadvertently, to an improved status that continues the patriarchal hierarchy in which they begin. Despite their perfectly understandable motivations and the positive results for both the theory and practice they have created, "equalizing" privileges between composition and literature, or between composition and any other established field, signifies acceptance of values that ignore the beginnings and contradict the purposes of current composition teaching and research.

For instance, neoclassical histories of composition that insist on its intellectual continuity with ancient rhetoric create both a content and a form for composition history that should give us pause. These histories do not normally focus on composition as a discrete product of American discourse education, whose connection to rhetorical instruction was ruptured, not merely interrupted, by Francis Child's 1875 negotiated defection from Harvard's Boylston Chair of Rhetoric to concentrated literary research.

Nor do they consider other historical events, some of which I have described, in which the test-hungry National Committee of Ten, Eliot at
Harvard, and his henchman Adams Sherman Hill began a mechanistic,
corrective course without even honorific connections to rhetorical education. Neoclassical histories do not, that is, point out the hegemonic
significance of establishing a *freshman* writing course to winnow and sift
students in place of—not as a version of—traditionally later, upper-class
instruction for postgraduate public discourse.

In an otherwise admirable attempt to give composition a history and
thus allow it (as many have said of needed women's history) to participate
as an agent rather than an overlooked object in its own system of significance,
neoclassical histories inadvertently approve of traditional academic privileges
embedded in the fabric of hegemonic "traditions" and their overbearing
"common sense." Focusing on a limited "intellectual" history of composition
to the exclusion of its material circumstances implicitly places composition
in academic "Big" history, where it will accrue entitlements from "authority
and the ancients." But this tactic also sustains the hierarchies and privileging
mechanisms that those in the field complain of so often.

Similarly, inevitable desires to demonstrate that composition is a research
field have in some forms assumed that "research" must be empirical and
scientific. This attitude, by no means universal among composition researchers, values "hard" data, "rigorous" methods, and what are taken to be
generative "results" that will spawn further study. The intellectual contributions of this form of research are not at issue, but it is politically
important to notice that claims for its powerful, masculine academic position
imitate quite closely the "scientific" spirit that motivated and legitimized
literary New Criticism earlier in this century. The "purified" (ahistorical,
intransitive, theorized) "processes" of writers, and newly "objective," disinterested methods of studying them allow composition to claim, as literary
studies did under New Criticism, that it has an object of study and that it
can discover self-contained "meaning" in the act of writing apart from its
contexts—in the "act itself."

This particular way to code composition as academically male, like
neoclassical historicism, indicates a felt need to overcome its feminized
cultural identity. But displacing either the symbolically "soft" or the actually
marginalized status of the field and its female majority will not be accomplished by "combating" that identity, to achieve a success designed to
imitate the totalizing effects of New Criticism's reign. And neither research
that creates a male identity for composition studies nor historiography that
links it to a Big picture actually fulfills this disguised desire. Both, that is,
potentially alienate composition from consequential status among those
who have historically had all the "principles" endowed to English. One
adopts methods and vocabularies that ring false among many who already
resent "science" as a field with which they have always competed, and the
other focuses on a rhetorical educational history from which literary studies
purposefully sets about to estrange itself.

My reasoning implies, I know, that no movement from within composition studies could ever do more than reform the basic structure of its identity, and that we should all at this point perform the intellectual/sexual submission we were culturally called to, to "lie back and think of England." As Althusser (following Marx) wrote about the cooperation of seemingly "new" and "traditional" ideologies (before he acted out his personally held ideological privileges by murdering his wife), "every child knows that a social formation which did not reproduce the conditions of production at the same time as it [was] produced would not last a year" (quoted in Macdonnel 28). But going beyond Marx, he also argued that attempts to overcome what we take to be hierarchical dominance often sustain the hierarchy, the "means of production," in which ideologies install us. Althusser's argument clearly applies to specific "new" moves in composition like those with which I have taken issue. These and many other intellectual and "practical" moves toward equality for composition reproduce the hegemonic super-structure by implying that bourgeois social climbing and successful competition for intellectual "clout" are legitimate signs of improvement. Although they take many seemingly unrelated forms, they are *politically* unified attempts to become equal in, and to sustain, a hierarchy that their supporters often claim to be overturning.

Nonetheless, the negative feminization of composition need not last forever.

The field might, that is, enjoy a different, if not a "new," identity, precisely as a culturally designated space for political action. Composition studies has always had the process available to it that active feminists and African-Americans have employed to transform their marginalized cultures into sites were cultural superstructures and their privileging results are visibly put into question. Composition professionals can also uncover and describe what is at stake for larger cultural maintenance in the marginalized status of their field. By raising a different voice in an active conversation about the feminized actual, historical, and symbolic status of composition professionals and their students, we can, that is, begin to reveal existing counterhegemonic structures in the field's existing practices and intellectual positions. An *actually* improved status depends on openly consolidating the field's resistances to the cultural superstructure that first defined it.

My primary purpose has been to accomplish part of the first, conversational goal, but the second process of intellectual redefinition would re-represent the negatively "feminine" field as irrefutably counterhegemonic, not as a victim stuck in webs of compromise. For instance, composition might be redefined as a site culturally designated to teach *all* students, not an elite group. It therefore already is an encompassing site for empowering, not for repressing or "correcting," the discursive power of the majority. In addition, the field might highlight (as many have recently done) the status of its female majorities and the constructed marginal identity of its always "new" students. By drawing concrete attention to the ways in which political issues are played out in a contemporary academic situation that was first

constructed on antifeminist principles, it would ask neocolonial administrators to recognize, and to be accountable for, the political implications of
their enduring definitions of "composition" as the central institutional site
for colonizing and regulating otherwise questionable, nontraditional entrants
to the academy.

Other frequently noted characteristics of composition equally define it as
an already-designated place for counterhegemonic intellectual politics. The
field addresses writing-in-progress (and writing as process), not writing as
an immutable textual product. It thereby overtly claims that categories of
"high" and "low" texts are social, not essential, categories. "Good" writing,
as composition must define it, is the result of established cultural privileging
mechanisms, not of pure "taste." The field thus vividly demonstrates, in
practice and in theory, that a mixture of ideas, timing, entitlements, and
luck have designated some rather than others as "important" writer/
thinkers. The field's most productive methods of evaluation also judge
writing by situational rather than by universal standards, and thus insist on
the arbitrariness of evaluations and their relativity to particular power
structures. Additionally, the field's research opens rather than closes
borders among established fields, thereby arguing that making new knowledge is a shared rather than isolated process, a matter of cooperation rather
than of disciplined competition.

Each of these often stated but persistently unpoliticized practices and
insights in the field have positioned it to transform its negatively feminized
identity by engaging intellectual as well as practical political actions. As the
institutional site designated as a passive enclosure for "unauthorized" discourse, composition has simultaneously been designated as a marginalizing
power. But this enormous power to contain the discourse of the majority
can be, if its professionals wish to claim it, the strength that re-represents
the field's negative feminization. Composition is *also*, that is, an active
existing site for dismantling particularly troublesome versions of hegemonic
discursive "common sense" — particularly the exclusivity, humiliation, repression, and injustice hidden in nineteenth-century bourgeois moralities.

We have frequently translated these counterhegemonic implications of
the field's practices and intellectual positions into signs of an undifferen-
tiated "vitality" or "energy." But this abstract "energy" can be plugged into
interventions that would undo concrete political structures that have a
great deal at stake in negative images of composition teaching and the
writing of students. Composition is not, that is, a modern place to celebrate
a liberal "healthy pluralism" that reforms systems around it. It contains
active resistance to the exhausted social situations that produced both its
negative feminization and "traditions" that should have become cultural
embarrassments long ago. As Kristeva has said in resisting traditional
definitions of females, we can transform our own negative identity by
understanding the implications of composition as "that which is marginalized
by the patriarchal symbolic order" (quoted in Moi 166).

Works Cited

Applebee, Arthur. *Tradition and Reform in the Teaching of English: A History.* Urbana, IL: NCTE, 1974.

Douglas, Wallace. "Rhetoric for the Meritocracy." In Richard Ohmann, *English in America.* New York: Oxford University Press, 1976, 97–132.

Doyle, Brian. "The Hidden History of English Studies." In *Rereading English.* Ed. Peter Widdowson. New York: Methuen, 1982, 17–31.

Eagleton, Terry. "The Subject of Literature." *Cultural Critique*, No. 2 (Winter 1985–1986): 95–104.

———. *Literary Theory: An Introduction.* Minneapolis: University of Minnesota Press, 1983.

Graff, Gerald. *Professing Literature: An Instructional History.* Chicago: University of Chicago Press, 1987.

Hartzog, Carol. *Composition in the Academy: A Study of Writing Program Administration,* New York: MLA, 1987.

Holbrook, Sue Ellen. "Women's Work: The Feminizing of Composition." Unpublished ms. of 1988 presentation at CCCC, St. Louis, MO.

Kitzhaber, Albert. "Rhetoric in American Colleges: 1850–1900." Unpublished Diss. University of Washington, 1953.

Lerner, Gerda. "Veiling the Woman." In *The Creation of Patriarchy.* New York: Oxford University Press, 1986.

Macdonnel, Diane. *Theories of Discourse: An Introduction.* Oxford: Basil Blackwell, 1986.

Miller, Susan. *Textual Carnivals: The Politics of Composition.* Carbondale, IL: Southern Illinois University Press, 1991.

Moi, Toril. *Sexual/Textual Politics.* New York and London: Methuen, 1985.

North, Stephen. *The Making of Knowledge in Composition: Portrait of an Emerging Field.* Portsmouth, NH: Boynton/Cook, 1987.

Ohmann, Richard. *English in America.* New York: Oxford University Press, 1976.

———. "Writing and Reading: Work and Leisure." In *The Politics of Letters.* Middletown, CT: Wesleyan University Press, 1987. (Chapter 3).

Stallybrass, Peter, and Allon White. *The Politics and Poetics of Transgression.* Ithaca: Cornell University Press, 1986.

Tchudi, Stephen N. *Explorations in the Teaching of Secondary English: A Sourcebook for Experimental Teaching.* New York: Dodd, Mead, 1975.

4

Rhetoric in the Modern University: The Creation of an Underclass

ROBERT J. CONNORS
University of New Hampshire

Rhetoric as a college-level discipline entered the nineteenth century as one of the most respected fields in higher education. In touch with an intellectual and practical tradition more than two millennia old, yet revised and revitalized by recent theoretical advances, the professor of rhetoric in 1800 was a respected figure on his campus. His courses were subscribed, his opinions listened to, his guidance sought out by both students and administrators. A chair of rhetoric was a chair of power and honor, as it had been for 2500 years.

When, however, we look at the teacher of rhetoric a mere century later, what a sad change we find. Instead of being an honored and respected intellectual figure in community and campus, the rhetoric teacher of 1900 is increasingly marginalized, overworked, and ill-paid. Instead of being a senior professor, the rhetoric teacher is an instructor, or a graduate student. Instead of teaching a discipline rooted in millennia of tradition, he—or, increasingly, she—is teaching a congeries of theory and pedagogy less than forty years old. Rhetoric has changed in one hundred years from an academic desideratum to a grim apprenticeship, to be escaped as soon as practicable. Instead of being sought by students, rhetoric courses by the early twentieth century are despised and sneered at, and their teachers have fallen from the empyrean of named chairs to the status of permanent underclass— "composition teachers": oppressed, ill-used, and secretly despised. This is the story of that change.

The creation of the composition underclass cannot be understood without examining two essential changes that took place in America during the nineteenth and early twentieth century: First, the shift from the old-style undergraduate colleges, with their goals for limited and practical professional training, to a system of large universities based essentially on the German

55

model, with their rigorous intellectual and scientific tradition of graduate study. Second, the shift from oral to written discourse within rhetorical training, with its result an incredible rise in the amount of individual academic work that each teacher of rhetoric must do. This overwork, along with the increasing bureaucratization of the universities, allowed the formation of permanent low-status jobs in composition that were *not* filled by upwardly mobile scholars. Either of these changes by itself would have created conditions conducive to an academic underclass. Together, they guaranteed a powerful class system whose effects most of us are still living with today.

Structural Egalitarianism in the American College System

There is no concept of an underclass possible without its dialectical counterpart, an overclass. Such a class structure was not found in any organized institutional way in American undergraduate colleges as they were formed from 1636 onward. I do not, of course, mean to imply that there were no hierarchies in early American colleges; like any institutions, colleges operated as structures of power organized from the highest office—the president of the college—to the lowest—the student. But within the college structure, individuals were constantly shifting within these hierarchies. Students would become alumni; tutors would become professors; the professorship of logic might wax while that of mathematics waned. Within this ever-shifting structure of power and enterprise, however, there was no *continuing* group of institutionally marginalized people. There was no underclass.

American colleges of the pre-Civil War era were kept from evolving clear institutional classes by the relative simplicity of their organization, which usually consisted of a board of trustees, a president, and a faculty of professors and tutors. The president with the consent of the faculty, ran the day-to-day affairs of the college under the guidance of the board; very few colleges were so large that all administration could not be carried out personally.[1]

Part of the egalitarianism of college life is explained by the times. For better and for worse, the equality of condition proposed by Jeffersonian and Jacksonian democracy had an effect during the late eighteenth and early nineteenth centuries. With the casting away of monarchy, Americans demanded equality in the eyes of government and society, and from 1790 through 1840 the hierarchical impulse was under fire everywhere. If it never disappeared completely, the older class-based elitism at least made no institutional gains. Though American colleges were hardly egalitarian societies, they never evolved any permanent underclass largely because they never developed criteria for invidious class distinctions. Charles Nisbet, president of Dickinson College, found this lack of class distinction hard to bear: "Everything here is on a dead level," he wrote. "Our gentlemen are all of the first edition; few of them live in their father's house" (Morgan 66). The denominational background of many American schools, old and new, was Protestant, with all the distrust of hierarchy and essential antinomian impulse of Protestantism. As religious toleration and outright disinterest grew, even such traditionalist and religiously absolutist colleges as Yale softened their stances on election and preterition. Colleges came ever more to be on a "dead level."

The curriculum of the American college, based as it was in the classical tradition, also worked against specialization. Colleges through 1850 served as training grounds for the three essential professions needed by the young nation: doctors, lawyers, and ministers. Before that time, few colleges gave more than passing attention to mathematics, the natural sciences, or the modern languages. The older curriculum of Latin, Greek, Hebrew, rhetoric, philosophy, and logic, adapted from the English colleges, remained the center of college study. If the classical curriculum did not serve the professions as direct training, it was still considered necessary preparation for the continued course of "reading" or apprenticeship the student would carry on after graduation.

The classical curriculum was traditional, unitary, accepted, and well understood. It did not call for vast scholarship or for the concept of "advancing knowledge" through research. Indeed, it demanded only a relatively low level of subject specialization for teachers. It is not uncommon to see, in the vitae of early professors, specialties in rhetoric, then logic, then Hebrew; or chairs of natural philosophy, Greek, and belles lettres. Most professors could and did shift subjects, so in the classical course there never did grow up any subject-based hierarchy — or, indeed, any stable departmental system.

I do not wish to paint a utopian portrait of the old American college here. It was no paradise. Male-dominated, agonistic, seething with repressed contest and even hostility, it could be a hard environment. It did not develop much internal class system at least in part because such a small and select percentage of Americans attended it; colleges were a mark of an external class system. But for all the reasons mentioned, the college structure before the Civil War was in itself egalitarian in nature. There was no continuing structural underclass.

Then, within forty years, all that was to change, and a new institution, extremely hierarchical in structure, was born: the American university. Within the novel university structure, multiple hierarchies flourished, some fleeting but some endemic. The composition underclass as we now know it has proved to be one of the most durable legacies of the creation of the university system.

The German Influence on
American Higher Education

The American university is a unique institution, born by the grafting onto an English-based undergraduate college structure of a German-based system of graduate education and research degrees. The German university system as it existed in the nineteenth century was a completely research-oriented program of postgraduate study leading to a *Philosophiae Doctor*. It had no undergraduate component (this was taken up by the *gymnasium* systems) and was devoted to higher study and research rather than to any pedagogical end. The ideal of the German system was empirical scientific research; its real founders were such physical scientists as Leopold von Ranke and Hermann van Helmholtz and such physiological psychologists as Wilhelm Wundt. Painstaking analysis of particulars in the laboratory and the archive was the hallmark of the "German method," and to the traditions surrounding classical learning the Germans brought new methods and new interest in empirical scientific investigation. In such centers as Göttingen, Leipzig, Heidelberg, and Berlin, respected scholars and scientists were given support for expansive laboratories, small seminar classes of serious specialist students, and a highly developed system of professional publication.

As it evolved from the mid-eighteenth century through the nineteenth, the German university was the most advanced academic institution of its kind, and by 1800 Germany was attracting students from all over the world. Americans, always alert to important innovations, began to travel to Germany in great numbers after the settlement of the War of 1812 made foreign travel safe. A number of these young men found opportunities for higher study in Germany congenial, the exchange rate favorable, and the work itself exciting. In larger and larger numbers they began to go for masters degrees and ultimately for the PhD degrees that were not offered at all in their native country.

Between 1815 and 1915, estimates S. Willis Rudy, more than 10,000 Americans attended German universities for longer or shorter periods (165). They went to Germany as students, but they returned as scholars and evangelists of scholarship. Among these men (for they were all men) were such future American university presidents as Angell of Michigan, White of Cornell, Gilman, Dwight, and Porter of Yale, Eliot of Harvard, Folwell of Minnesota, Hall of Clark, and Barnard of Columbia. For these men, as for so many young Americans, Germany presented a new—and theretofore undreamed of—scholarly ideal. As Josiah Royce was to write later about those heady pre-Civil War days, young men gave vent to "positively passionate enthusiasm" for the German university:

> But in those days there was a generation that dreamed of nothing but the German University. England one passed by. It was understood not to be scholarly enough. France, too, was then neglected. German scholar-

ship was our master and our guide.... One went to Germany still a doubter as to the possibility of the theoretic life; one returned an idealist, devoted for the time to pure learning for learning's sake, ... burning for a chance to help to build the American University. (382–383)

Building the American University was exactly what these early enthusiasts for the German system had to do, and almost from the ground up. There simply was no tradition of organized research or serious graduate study in American colleges. The bachelor's degree, of course, was given, and most colleges also presented master's degrees, but these early master's degrees were primarily honorific; the criteria for earning them were usually little more than another year of residency and an informal thesis defense (Cordasco 16). There were, quite simply, no doctorates given in America before the Civil War, and no organized provision for a course of study leading to them.

The growing number of apostles of the German system began by the 1850s to work toward filling that lack. The American university, it was understood, could not generally be organized like German universities, offering only graduate courses.[2] The graduate divisions when they were founded would have to be piggybacked on existing undergraduate colleges. And, beginning in the late 1840s and gaining strength through the rest of the century, the university movement did create these novel hybrid institutions. At Harvard, Yale, Columbia, Princeton, Cornell, and the older state universities of the Midwest, graduate divisions were established. In 1850, there were only eight students officially identified as "graduate students" in the United States. Fifty years later, the Office of Education reported 5668 graduate students (Rudy 169). The first American PhD degree was granted by Yale in 1861, Penn granted its first in 1870, Harvard in 1873, Columbia in 1875, Princeton in 1879, Hopkins in 1879, and Brown in 1889 (Cordasco 16). By 1875 to 1879, American universities were granting an average of 32 doctorates a year, and in 1900 a record total of 382 PhDs were granted (Harmon 7). Within half a century, America had built a system of academic institutions that were generally admitted to be the best in the world; indeed, the influence of Germany itself declined markedly after 1900, as American universities were internationally perceived as better (Veysey 131).

The defining ideal of the American university, adapted directly from the German system so extravagantly admired by American academic travelers, was the idea of purely scholarly research. "Pure science," learning for the sake of increasing human knowledge, and not teaching or pedagogy, was the lesson carried home from Tübingen and Dresden:

For the devotee of scientific investigation, Germany opened up the vista of a new goal, then dramatized it by a process of initiation. The German laboratory and seminar offered these future American professors a novel mode of life, a private mode that turned them aside from the everyday world of society, politics, morality, and religion, even from the classroom itself, and removed them during most of their waking hours from their fellow men. (Veysey 133)

The ideals of this world in which disinterested research was the noblest of goals were intoxicating for many young Americans.

The importation of the German system of higher degrees and its conjoinment to the older American college led to distinct changes in the organization of the new institutions. Most obviously, they were made more complex. The order systems of president and faculty gave way increasingly after 1880 to the complex hierarchy of chancellors, presidents, provosts, deans, chairs, and full, associate, and assistant professors and instructors that we know today. The growth of this hierarchy was assisted by the importation of the German criterion for successful work: publication of results. The true researcher was expected, from his seminar papers through his dissertation (which was required in *every case* to be published) to show his worth as a scholar by disseminating his findings through a system of professional publication. And as soon as the university movement caught on—as it did with a vengeance through the 1870s and 1880s—the expected publication of research also provided the leaders of the new institutions with criteria for advancement within the hierarchy. Those who conducted and published their research were rewarded with promotions and tenure; they could "move up the ladder" from instructor through the ranks of professors.

This was quite a different world from the earlier college world and classical curriculum, with its emphasis on preprofessional generalism and "mental discipline." The PhD degree was from the beginning a Germanic "research" degree that contained no component (or even recognition) of undergraduate pedagogy. The traditional purposes of undergraduate college teachers were not at all those of the newer university professors, but the undergraduate and graduate faculties were forced to come together during the period from 1870 to 1900. In Germany this had been no problem, because university-trained professors sought positions themselves in universities, not in gymnasia. But American PhDs were expected to emerge from their hermetic research labors into an undergraduate teaching situation for which nothing in their training had prepared them.

Rhetoric in the Universities

Thus far I have been rapidly sketching in the background, and now I want to move directly to the case of rhetoric. Where did it fit into the burgeoning university movement, with its new degrees and its hierarchical research-based criteria?

The answer is that rhetoric did *not* fit in. It had no real place in the new universities, and its fall is exactly correlate with their rise. Here is why:

The Americans who traveled to Germany and returned to preach the gospel of the German university brought back with them not only the institutional dream, but a gathering shoal of actual German doctorates in the variety of subjects taught there. These new PhDs were in all of the fields that had evolved within the detail-oriented and empirical German tradition. Most central were degrees in the natural and applied sciences, especially chemistry, physics, biology, and mathematics. Just as important over the long run, however, were the "social sciences," as they were known: the range of subjects, drawn both from the humanities traditions and from newer positivist philosophy, that treated human actions and activity in limited contexts that allowed use of theoretical apparatus and laboratory methods. Prominent among these social sciences were the new physiological psychology pioneered by Wundt, the detail-based and statistical Germanic model of history writing, the new science of economics, and — most important for the future of English Studies — the new field of philological studies, which analyzed the development and structure of languages.

Americans brought back doctorates in all of these subjects from Germany *by the hundreds* between 1860 and 1885. And wherever a congregation of doctorates could be established, there was the germ of a university department: chemistry, physics, biology, botany, history, economics, psychology.

But what of rhetoric, which had been so important in the American college? Why were there no departments of rhetoric? The answer is simple. There were no departments of rhetoric because there were no German PhDs in rhetoric. There was, simply, no important German intellectual tradition of rhetoric active at all after around 1810, and thus there was no German field to export in the form of a PhD. Indeed, rhetoric as a field hardly existed in German universities.

In part, this German lack of interest in rhetoric can be ascribed to the nature of the field itself; it is overtly pragmatic and not easily accessible to empirical methods. Although there had been a very active German tradition in homiletic and neoclassical rhetorics as late as the 1780s, German publications in rhetoric sputtered and died very quickly after 1800. This decline of rhetoric must be inescapably linked with the rise of the German university system. Rhetoric is a field not easily made scientific, and thus it was not lifted with the other boats by the great positivist tide of German science in the period of 1780 to 1850. Just as important, however, was the essentially ethical (and, no doubt, political) condemnation of rhetoric made by German philosophers. Franz Theremin, writing in 1814, describes the German response to rhetoric:

> Finally, there are men — and men, too, highly distinguished for learning and science — who get a very low estimate upon eloquence, and would have nothing to do with it. For in their opinion, it is perfectly clear that its purpose is to excite the feelings, which is always useless, and sometimes even injurious. ... In their opinion, we should address the understand-

ing alone, and satisfy it by means of stringent arguments; all excitement of the feelings, and influencing of the will, were better omitted. (545)

Theremin also quotes Kant, who says in his *Critique of Judgment* that reading orations "is always accompanied with the disagreeable feeling of disapprobation toward a cunning art which understands how to move men like machines, to a judgment which, upon calm after-thought, must lose all its worth with them. Oratory, considered as the art of making use of the weaknesses of men . . . is worthy of no respect at all" (quoted in Theremin 55). This Lockean condemnation set the German tone toward rhetoric.

I do not wish to suggest here that no scholarly work was done in nineteenth-century Germany on rhetoric. Heinrich Schott's essentially pragmatic homiletic rhetoric texts (1807), Theremin's attempt to marry rhetoric and ethics in *Eloquence a Virtue* (1814), Richard Volkmann's classicist and historicist *Rhetorik* (1872), Friedrich Nietzsche's classically based *Lectures on Rhetoric* (1872–1873), and Wilhelm Wackernagel's belletristic *Poetik, Rhetorik, und Stilistik* (1873) all show that there was work done. But it was backward-looking or minor work (yes, even Nietzsche's), usually subordinated to philology, analytical philosophy, or classical historical study. As Nietzsche put it, "in recent times this art stands in some disrepute, and even when it is used, the best application to which it is put by our moderns is working short of dilettantism and crude empiricism" (Nietzsche 3).[3]

In comparison to the powerful German traditions in philosophy, science, and social science, work in rhetoric was insignificant and pitiful. And as a result, none of the Americans traveling to Germany for advanced degrees during the nineteenth century returned to purvey advanced study in rhetoric. They returned as social scientists, chemists, psychologists, mathematicians, philologists. None returned as rhetoricians.

Where did this leave rhetoric, as these newer men turned their enthusiastic hands toward creating the American university? In a rather curious place. Nearly all of the colleges upon which the new universities were engrafted had taught rhetoric from time immemorial; it could not be merely forgotten. Thousands of copies of Blair's *Lectures on Rhetoric and Belles-Lettres* poured from the presses each year prior to the Civil War, and this strong tradition could not be simply ignored. In addition, there were after 1875 increasingly loud calls for basic instruction in correct writing and speaking in colleges. Rhetoric teachers, who had very often been teaching writing as well as speaking since the 1820s, were asked to take on this task. So for both historical and culturally pragmatic reasons, rhetoric could not simply be jettisoned.

To the increasingly powerful acolytes of the German system, however, rhetoric was at best a suspect and unscientific study, one seemingly unredeemable by research, and at worst simply unscholarly drudge work. It could not be buried and it would not go away, but neither could it be saved as "real scholarship." And so rhetoric existed in universities between 1860 and 1900 as a curious relic of another time, stranger every year to the empirical and skeptical community of scholars that universities increasingly bred—an inexplicable survival: the vermiform appendix of the university structure.

Institutional Self-Reproduction and the Decline of Rhetoric

The anomalous place of rhetoric was reflected in the ways that American universities structured their gradually forming departments. Between 1860 and 1890, universities gave up their older system of generalist professors in favor of cadres of specialists, who were bureaucratically organized. The older college ideal of professors standing for "mental discipline" was replaced by a newer ethic of industriousness in specialized research. As Veysey sez, "The dominant characteristic of the new American universities was their ability to shelter specialized departments of knowledge. . . . In consequence, the old-time professor who was jack-of-all-disciplines rapidly disappeared from all but the bypassed small colleges" (142).

Within these new universities, filled with German- and gradually with American-trained PhDs, there were few figures to form separate departments of rhetoric. If we examine the foundations of university departments, we see departments of English Language, of English Literature, of Belles Lettres, of English and Belles Lettres, but rarely of rhetoric.[4] There was already some tradition of linguistically based study of English in American colleges during the 1850s, as Gerald Graff has shown in *Professing Literature* (37–42), and the newer philological research brought back from Germany was easier to add to "English" than to "Rhetoric." By conjoining the belletristic study rooted in Blair with the philological research coming from Germany, the modern English department got its start and was by 1880 chugging along.

In any bureaucracy, self-reproduction is necessary for institutional success and longevity. At this self-reproduction, the newly formed departments, including English, proved proficient. New graduate schools were founded in almost every year during the 1870s and 1880s, and soon new native PhDs were being sent into the world, charged by their teachers to be fruitful and multiply. The doctorate provided a convenient licensing structure for increasingly competitive graduate schools, and gradually, between 1880 and 1900, the PhD began to be seen as a sine qua non for prospective university (and even college) teachers.

It was this demand for doctorates that truly spelled the end for rhetoric as a discipline, because, as Graff and Veysey point out, English departments after 1885 were not equipped to reproduce any sort of nonliterary or nonphilological PhD candidates. Rhetoric after 1870 tended to be left in the hands of that curious transitional generation of non-PhDs that arrived at universities in the 1870s and 1880s and came to be especially associated with Harvard's English department. Such figures as John S. Hart, Erastus Haven, Edwin M. Hopkins, A. S. Hill, Barrett Wendell, Le Baron Briggs, G. P. Baker, Charles T. Copeland, Henry Frink, Henry S. Canby, and Hiram Corson all were involved deeply in attempting to create a new rhetoric of written communication during the period 1880 to 1910. Much of their pedagogical work became widely known, and their textbooks sold in the hundreds of thousands, but they had no PhDs, and they could not successfully reproduce themselves through the younger generations of graduate scholars they taught.[5] As this generation died off or became less active during the first two decades of the new century, no one stepped forward to fill their shoes.

We can also see (in the 1880s and 90s, before composition was completely identified as lower-level activity) very few PhDs who did important work in the field. Their situations are instructive. John Genung's career presents a thumbnail history of the times. Genung was a minister who was himself trained in the American oratorical tradition prior to going to Germany. He took his PhD in philology in Leipzig in 1881 and returned to America, where he was hired at Amherst College as a language instructor in 1882, became an associate professor of "rhetoric, oratory, and English literature" in 1884, a professor of "rhetoric and English Literature" in 1889, and a professor of "literature and Biblical interpretation" in 1906. When Genung first returned to the United States, bursting with his new knowledge, he attempted to graft the careful scholarship of Leipzig onto rhetorical issues, and seemed for a while to succeed. His 1886 textbook, *Practical Elements of Rhetoric*, was extremely influential. But as Genung attained seniority, he found rhetorical work exhausting. His own teaching and interest gravitated more toward literature and the Bible, and when he could, he left composition behind. For a PhD, what rhetoric was becoming after 1895 was too stony a field.

So nearly all PhDs, even those, like Genung, who were for historical or emotional reasons attached to rhetoric, left its theory and practice for the more enticing fields of literature or philology. There are a few great exceptions to this general rule, of course: C. S. Baldwin, PhD, Columbia 1894, whose rich scholarly work in historical rhetoric would pave the way for a generation of later scholars but who produced few disciples during his life; Lane Cooper, PhD, Leipzig 1901, who would later be responsible for helping to set up the powerful Cornell Speech department, which kept rhetoric alive by completely removing it from the orbit of English and composition for more than fifty years.[6]

The great figure, the really extraordinary naysayer and lonely giant in this drama was, however, Fred Newton Scott of Michigan. Scott tried, almost singlehandedly, to create at Michigan the sort of self-reproducing and serious scholarly organization for rhetoric that was being assembled for literature and philology elsewhere. For a quarter century, through sheer guts and brilliance, he succeeded in stemming the flood that had everywhere else inundated written rhetoric. With his own Michigan PhD, in 1889, from the Department of English and Rhetoric, Scott went on to build a departmental structure that could produce serious scholarship and scholars in rhetoric. He himself published voluminously, both books and articles. He was intensely active in professional organizations, first the MLA and then the fledgling NCTE. On his own campus, Scott used his growing influence (he was a full professor by 1901) to buck the national trend; he broke rhetoric out from English into separate and equal departmental status. His Department of Rhetoric, begun in 1903, was to last only two years after Scott's retirement due to illness in 1927, but during the 32 years from 1898 through 1930, Scott was to produce 149 master's degrees and 23 PhDs in rhetoric at Michigan (Shaw 562).

There was no place remotely like Michigan during Scott's time. Although his own degree was philological, he created a rhetoric curriculum at the doctoral level and produced his first rhetoric doctorate—Gertrude Buck— in 1898. His students would include famed journalists, essayists, fiction writers, even poets, as well as the composition and rhetoric scholars whose influence would be felt through the entire first half of the century. Joseph M. Thomas, T. E. Rankin, Karl Young, Charles C. Fries, Mary Yost, Helen Mahin, Sterling Leonard, Clarence Thorpe, Ruth Weeks, Marjorie Nicolson, and Edwin L. Miller all studied with Scott.

But it could not continue. As Wilfred Shaw—himself one of Scott's students—puts it in his survey of the University of Michigan, the Department of Rhetoric *was* F. N. Scott. His brilliance and charisma made it all possible. His doctoral students spread out into the world, but there were too few of them to make a difference, and the task was enormous. One by one, beginning with Gertrude Buck, they left composition and began to do literary work. Scott himself published more and more in literature and philology as the years went on. And when he retired in 1927, his department was within two years dissolved, the teachers and students folded back into the powerful and secure Department of English Language and Literature. Thus went the only serious attempt to create a rhetoric doctorate outside of speech departments. As far as written rhetoric—increasingly called composition—went, it was afterward to be found, and despised, in departments of English.

Outside of Fred Scott, there were no other PhDs championing rhetoric or moving to create departmental or graduate training structures. Philologists and literary specialists trained their own students to replace them, but rhetoricians did not possess the institutional structure to allow this. As the extremely active and respected transitional generation of composition generalists retired or died, they were not replaced. They were, instead, succeeded by the cadre of graduate assistants, low-level instructors, part-timers, and departmental fringe people who became the permanent composition underclass.

Teaching Conditions in Composition Courses

Composition came to be despised in part, as we have seen, because it could not boast the Germanically based scholarly cachet of philology or literary history. But this nonscholarly onus was not the only cause for the decline in the status of rhetoric teachers and their formation as an underclass. Some rhetoricians, after all, separated from English departments and built their own scholarly discipline of speech. It was within English departments that the underclass was formed, and it is to these emerging departmental structures that we must look for the conditions that gave rise to it.

Rhetoric had refused for reasons of tradition and history to disappear, as we have seen, although many of the emerging philological and literary scholars of the period from 1875 to 1900 devoutly wished it would. But though it would not be swept out, rhetoric was gradually transmogrified into "English Composition," a course based in writing rather than in speaking. The reasons for this transformation are complex, but we may trace the most important ones quickly.

In the 1860s, linguistic correctness came to be a cultural preoccupation in America with the onset of the great transatlantic usage debates between Henry Alford, G. W. Moon, Richard Gould, and others (Finegan 62—74). The educated classes in America were suddenly swept up in a wave of anxiety about the propriety of their speech and writing, and educational institutions responded to this anxiety. Harvard College instituted its first entrance examinations in written English in 1874, and to the horror of professors, parents, and the intellectual culture as a whole, more than half the students taking the exam failed it. Clearly something had to be done.

The Harvard exam and the continuing problems students had with it (and with the host of similar writing tests quickly set up by the many colleges that took Harvard for a model) created the first American college literacy crisis and the first experiments in required basic writing instruction on the college level. Adams S. Hill argued incessantly for a required freshman English course at Harvard: "Could the study [of writing] be taken up at the threshold of college life, the schools would be made to feel that their labors in this direction were going to tell upon a pupil's standing in college..." (12). In 1885, such a basic freshman course was offered. Very quickly, other colleges followed Harvard's lead, and mandatory freshman composition was the rule at most schools by the late 1880s. This highly symbolic response to a perception of threatening cultural conditions fit in neatly with the increasing demand for literate functionaries in business and industry. In addition, the idea that rhetoric was mainly written and private rather than oral and public allowed male teachers and students to accept the psychological demands of coeducation more easily, since few men wanted to compete or debate orally with women in any public forum.

For all these reasons, rhetoric became more and more oriented toward writing. We need now to examine more closely what went on in these new rhetoric courses after 1875. It was through these courses that composition came to be despised and the underclass came to exist. Its genesis there had to do with the nature of the composition work itself, and the conditions under which teachers were expected to do it. It was an initial failure to understand these classes, to realize what composition pedagogy demands of a teacher, that made a composition underclass inevitable.

American college classes from the Revolutionary period through the Civil War had typically been rather small, in part at least because the colleges themselves were small. At Bowdoin, a representative small American college, the graduating class averaged nine students per year from 1810 to 1815, 25 students from 1825 to 1830, and 50 students from 1845 to 1850. Yale was always the largest of the pre-Civil War colleges, and in 1855 Yale had only 472 students. Allowing for limited electives in sciences and modern languages, which became possible after 1800 at many colleges, the average size of the college course before 1860 was seldom larger than 40 or 50 students. Though we may today think that 40 students is a large class, professors of that period do not seem to have felt overwhelmed by their work. They had no publication demands and very simple service require-ments; they could devote most of their time to their students.

Rhetorical instruction before 1880 was often in both oral and written discourse, and we need to look more closely at these pedagogies. Oral discourse teaching relied on the same rhetorical principles that had been used for centuries in colleges: lecture for the theory, and forensics, orations, and debates for the practice. Note that these teaching techniques are not in any important way dependent on the numbers of students in a course. A lecture can be to 20 or 200 students; oral practice can be organized in groups or teams, and a teacher's comments on an oration may be heard and digested by all in a class. As the American colleges gradually enlarged, oral discourse teaching changed little in its presentation, and the demands it made on the teacher remained stable.

Writing instruction, however, did change radically. "As the meaning of the word rhetoric changes gradually in practical application," wrote C. S. Baldwin in 1894, "a corresponding change is taking place in the relation of the instructor to the individual student" (290). It was a change toward encouragement of student self-expression and toward much more individual-ized contact between teacher and student. "Instead of memorized literary criticism the courses in rhetoric deal largely in practice in self-expression," wrote Frances Lewis in 1902, "and the class-room work, once entirely recitation from a text-book, is now often on the laboratory plan. . . ." (15). The rise of "laboratory work" in composition, while pedagogically productive, meant a completely different set of demands was being placed on teachers. Writing, in comparison to oral rhetorical instruction, was seen to demand by its nature an essentially individualized pedagogy. Writing is an interior activity, and although techniques can be used to share writing among students, a primary transaction in any serious composition course came to be seen as between the student and the teacher. Each student came to be

seen as deserving a measurable individual chunk of the teacher's time and
energy. It might be much or it may be little, but it had to be there. This
inescapable demand, which came from the best-known teachers and schools
in America—and the related inability of teachers and administrators to
grasp its meaning in a changing college environment—led to the nightmare
of overwork that composition courses became.

At first the problem developed very slowly. During much of the first
half of the nineteenth century, college rhetoric classes were often devoted
to both writing and speaking. In addition, with small classes, professors
were able to give each student individual time without real hardship.
Nathaniel Hawthorne told of conferences he had over his themes at Bowdoin
College with the respected Samuel Newman, and Edward E. Hale reports
that during Edward T. Channing's long tenure as Boylston Professor of
Rhetoric at Harvard, "we had to write a theme for his examination once a
fortnight."

> The stuff which most of us wrote in those first themes was enough to
> make even optimistic angels weep.... But such as it was, we carried it
> in at three o'clock on alternate Friday afternoons.... You sat down in
> the recitation-room, and were called man by man, or boy by boy, in the
> order in which you came into the room; you therefore heard his criticism
> on each of your predecessors.... Everything was said with perfect
> kindness ... and if you had said a decent thing, or thought anything
> that was in the least above the mud, he was so sympathetic. Poor dear
> man! to read those acres of trash must have been dispiriting. (361)

Hale's comment in 1893 about the efforts of Edward Channing in 1840 is
instructive. Channing was much beloved by his students and taught written
rhetoric at Harvard from 1819 to 1851; he worked hard, but there is no
evidence that he was oppressed, or miserable with overwork. By 1851,
when he retired, Channing's largest course, the sophomore rhetoric course,
was probably no more than 60 students, up from approximately 35 in 1819,
when he was appointed. These were numbers that could allow a fortnightly
theme conference without hardship. And yet by 1893, Channing is pitied
by Hale, who continues his narrative thus: "Half a century afterwards,
when I was an overseer, the president of the time [Eliot] said to me, 'You
cannot get people to read themes for many years together.' I said, 'I thank
God every day of my life that Ned Channing was willing to read themes for
thirty-two years'" (361). We can see the change that has occurred between
1840 and 1890. From an honored professoriat, the Boylston Chair has
descended—even in the mind of the Harvard president—to the status of
an academic sweatshop, which wears out its people like ball bearings,
which then have to be replaced.

The reason for this change is simple: numbers of students.[7] Composition
courses of the latter nineteenth century became hells of overwork that

drove away all those teachers who were upwardly mobile and ground down those who were not. To understand how this happened, we must look more closely at the structures of courses as they evolved at colleges, especially in the 1880s and 1890s.

Numbers of Students in Composition Courses

American college courses under the classical curriculum were all required up until the 1820s. The Latin professor, for instance, would teach his Latin courses to the entire sophomore class, however large it was. Only with the beginnings of elective courses in the 1830s do we see the concept of splitting a class into several subgroups for specialized training. With the rise of the scientific schools, however, and the growing popularity of electives like the modern languages, such class splitting became more and more common. By the post-Civil War era, when the Germanic specialties began to be popular, many of the courses at most colleges were split courses.

The rise of the elective principle in colleges is usually closely associated with Charles W. Eliot, president of Harvard from 1869 to 1909. During Eliot's reign, Harvard became the uncontested collegiate and university model. It also completely revamped its curricular requirements, abandoning subject requirements for seniors in 1872, juniors in 1879, and sophomores in 1884. By 1894 the only required courses for freshmen were rhetoric and a modern language (Rudolph 294). And by 1897 the only required course at Harvard for any student was English A, Freshman Composition.

While the elective system did not take hold at *all* American colleges and universities, it was increasingly adopted throughout the country. Students might be expected to fulfill certain requirements for major departments, but after 1885 the old required curriculum was on the wane. Instead of a few professors teaching a very limited range of courses to entire college classes, American schools increasingly offered a larger number of highly trained and specialized professors teaching smaller courses open to a range of classes.

Except, of course, for rhetoric teachers.

Just as rhetoric as a discipline seemed to many Americans to hark back to the trivial tradition of the old English-based college, so the structure of the rhetoric course—and the freshman composition course based in rhetoric—seemed to hark back to the older whole-class-based college curriculum. The traditional sophomore rhetoric course and more absolutely the required freshman course were typically taught to an entire class, just as they always had been.

These were not, however, the classes of 20 or 40 or 60 students that had been common before the Civil War. The average size of the freshman class at Harvard was over 200 students by 1870, and by 1903 it had grown to more than 600. Even in smaller institutions growth was the rule, and by

1900 the enrollment of all of the most important state universities and nearly all of the influential Ivies was above 1,000 students.[8]

With these ever-larger numbers of students to serve and no class splitting or elective system to help ease their burden, rhetoric teachers were in a serious situation. The average freshman class was 200 or more students in many institutions, and these teachers were attempting to teach a course that required a certain amount of personal attention to each student. The expectation around the turn of the century was that each teacher would provide six to eight hours of personal conference to students for each two hours of class time (Hart 370). These teachers could not use mass recitations or simple tests. They had to read the writing of more students than was possible without real hardship.

What happened? They did it—or at least they tried hard. And the resulting overwork drove away any possibility that rhetoric as a field could attract the talented scholars who might have been able to forge it into a modern scholarly discipline despite its lack of Teutonic breeding.

We need only look at a few numbers to see what the rhetoric teachers of the late nineteenth century faced. At Harvard in 1892, Barrett Wendell read daily and fortnightly themes from 170 students—over 24,000 papers each year.[9] At Yale, one professor and one instructor were responsible for 250 composition students; the same was true at Iowa. At Wellesley, one professor and three assistants taught 600 students. At Minnesota one professor and three assistants taught 800 students in the Department of Rhetoric.[10] Fred Newton Scott of Michigan, writing in 1895, reported that

> I have read and re-read this year something over 3,000 essays, most of them written by a class of 216 students. . . . That the instructor should somehow lay hold of the student as an individual is, for composition work, simply indispensable. . . . But it must be borne in mind that in the larger universities the day of small and cosey classes is long past. Now the hungry generations tread us down. We hardly learn the names and faces of our hundreds of students before they break ranks and go their ways, and then we must resume our Sisyphyaean labors. (Payne 121–122)

However much we may today complain about our composition loads, these early teachers had a far worse situation to deal with. What is most amazing today, however, is the relative lack of direct complaint we hear from them. Barrett Wendell's tone in reporting his work with 170 students is cool and neutral: "It happens this year to be my duty to read [the daily themes] every day and to make some sort of note on them . . . of course, I must do it rather hastily. It is a matter of two or three hours a day" (660). These daily themes added immensely to the work of composition teachers at Harvard, but even the more standard weekly themes presented teachers with appalling overloads.[11] We have no complete or detailed information on teaching loads outside of such anecdotal references until the early part of the twentieth century. In 1909, however, the Central Division of the MLA (which was F. N. Scott's home base) voted to establish a committee to investigate the labor and cost of composition teaching at American colleges. Edwin M. Hopkins of the University of Kansas was appointed the chair of this committee, which began its labors in 1910 but did not complete them until 1913.

The Hopkins Report, as it was known, is a shocking indictment of the conditions and labor involved in teaching college composition. It is the more powerful for being written in a carefully understated tone. The Hopkins Committee based its report on nationwide surveys conducted between 1909 and 1913; these surveys were completed by around 20 percent of all American colleges. The results of the surveys were summarized by the committee in two pages; from that summary we may note the following as primary elements:

The average necessary duty of an English instructor according to the class and hour standards in effect was almost double (approximately 175 percent) that of an instructor in any of the other departments concerned. (20n)

The theme reading labor expected of a college freshman composition instructor is more than double (250 percent) that which can be carried on without undue physical strain. (20)

The results of the work are unsatisfactory and are the subject of general academic and public complaint. (21)

Conscientious and efficient teachers are brought to actual physical collapse and driven from the profession. (21)

The Hopkins Report did not produce these findings without basis; their surveys were rigorously tabulated. They found, for instance, that students were required to produce around 650 words each week on the average, that teachers could read around 2,200 word per hour, that teachers could read themes for only two hours at a stretch without strain, that the average number of composition students assigned to a teacher was 105, and that to read all of their students' work, writing teachers would need to spend thirty hours each week only on theme reading (20).

The Hopkins Report begins to give up some idea of why teachers — beginning as early as the 1890s — suddenly began to see rhetoric as drudgery and to desert it in large numbers. While teachers in other fields were dealing successfully with the larger numbers in their classes by evolving techniques of discussion and lecture, composition teachers were tied to the reading of thousands of themes. Thus could Charles Eliot lament his administrative difficulty in keeping composition instructors. Thus could a former writing teacher note in a letter, after having transferred to a different department, "I thank God I have been delivered from the bondage of theme-work into the glorious liberty of literature" (Carpenter et al. 329n). Thus could Hopkins quote the following pathetic lines from writing teachers queried about their status: "I have a better place in view," "I refuse to overwork, slighting my classes when necessary," "I have been trained for this work and can do nothing else, hence am helpless to change," "We hope for better things" (28). And thus, even Barrett Wendell's students could feel his lot was hard, writing, "How pitiful it must be for a man to peruse about 200 odd sermons every day, week after week, and, worst of all, like the shades in Hades, not be permitted to die" (C. H. Burdette, quoted in Newkirk).

Composition Teaching as
Ordeal and Apprenticeship

The terrible overwork to which rhetoric teachers were subjected was, for many of them, rendered supportable only by the hope that it would someday end, to be replaced by "the glorious liberty of literature." The conception of composition as an apprenticeship to the "real" work of literature had begun as early as the 1890s, when the use of graduate students as TAs first became widespread in universities. With these TAs at the bottom of the pole, the modern hierarchy of English departments was in place: TAs, instructors, assistant, associate, and full professors. And more and more, the teaching of rhetoric in college was detailed to the low ends of the scale, the hapless bottom feeders: TAs and instructors.

The appearance of this division of labor in the 1890s was coterminous with the gradual entrenchment of the freshman composition course in its modern form. As Edwin Hopkins put it in 1915, "The genesis of the present situation in English may be found in the change from memory training to laboratory training that was made perhaps thirty-five or forty years ago. When that change occurred, no attempt seems to have been made to ascertain the physical conditions necessary in the application of new methods, as is always done in business and scientific training" (115).

In order to understand the composition underclass as it developed in the 1890s, we must understand the psychology of the instructors who made it up. The PhD degree was less rigidly defined at that time than it is presently; a typical doctorate took only three years beyond bachelor's work to achieve, and the final year of doctoral study often coincided with the first year of an instructor's position. Teaching assistantships existed, but not in the numbers they now do, and the rank of instructor was typically where a young man started.[12] Since the PhD was an investigative or research degree which contained no rhetorical or pedagogical training, the young instructor emerged blinking from his isolate study into a world that was filled with alien work and dreadful drudgery.[13] "To the college instructor," said Franklin Snyder, "a section of English A has been, if not an actual symbol of academic serfdom like the iron collars of Gurth and Wamba, at least a badge of apprenticeship—something to be accepted as initially inevitable, but from which relief would come with the passing of time" (200).

It was early seen that the disparity between the work a young PhD was trained for and that he actually had to do was a serious problem. James Cox said in 1913 that "the PhD as at present conceived is not a teacher's degree but an investigator's degree. ... Very few can hope to make investigation a lifework and practically all are constrained to teach" (207), and the teaching work was nearly all composition. A questionnaire sent to English departments in 1915 showed that 39 schools required their new people to teach some form of freshman composition, while only eight allowed them to teach non-composition "junior-college literature" ("Report" 25). New instructors were regularly assigned three, four, or five sections of composition—sometimes while they were still attempting to finish their dissertations.

The results, predictably, of this situation, was that young instructors quickly came to hate rhetoric and composition with a passion that almost matched the feelings of their unfortunate charges. Lyle Spencer put the case tellingly in 1913 in a discussion worth quoting at length:

During the years of his training for teaching the instructor-to-be has not only been taught composition, but he has been led to regard the work as dull, uninteresting. He has been taught, if not by precept, certainly by example, that composition teaching is menial work, drudgery, a pursuit to be avoided. He has been taught to look forward to research work. The vision held before him has been that of scholarship. In his dreams he has seen himself the discoverer of the ur-*Hamlet*, of the lost version of *Love's Labour's Won*, or the other six books of the *Faerie Queene*—and the world rising up to call him blessed. Consequently he has looked forward to teaching anything but composition.

But when his last college day has closed and he is rudely awakened from his dreams, the only position open to him is composition, into which he is compelled to go for the bare necessity of a living. There he finds himself unprepared for the work, with no interest in it, and with the courses looming before him as so much drudgery. And though after three or four years he may have managed to read up and outline a fairly good series of courses, by that time promotion will have come to him and he will have passed on with the plaudit, "Well done, good and faithful servant"—and the work in composition will be given to another novice. And so through all the years the composition work continues in the hands of untrained men.

It is the calamity of our present-day composition teaching that our instructors are—the majority of them—not only without special training in their subject, but using the work merely as a stepping-stone for advancement. They do not expect to teach composition always; their interest is in other lines of work; and they either are only filling in, waiting for a man higher up—in Shakespeare or eighteenth-century literature or Middle English—to die, or else are teaching the subject only until they can get an assistant who will take what is regarded by them as the menial work. (In discussion following Greenough 118–119)

The composition overwork this forced on young instructors poisoned their whole relationship with teaching in general and with rhetoric in specific.

Thus, very early in the creation of the modern university system, was born the tradition—still, sadly, with us today—of graduate students and young faculty members "voting with their feet" against teaching composition and in favor of teaching literature. As J. M. Thomas (one of F. N. Scott's PhDs) said in 1916, the whole training of graduate students "has been such as to give them a notion that courses in composition are little more than a necessary evil" (453).

> This separation [between composition and literature] is made more pronounced by the feeling on the part of certain men that such utilitarian work is unworthy of their own high gifts, and that the training they have received, if it has not made them unfit for it, has at least fitted them for higher things.... In our colleges, at least, I feel that [the problem] springs in part from the fact that the older men confine their work to courses in literature, and that the courses in composition are generally taught by young men with no experience, or with very limited experience. Furthermore, they are put in charge of classes, and, without any sort of oversight or direction, or even competent advice, are left to work out their own destinies. In no other business in the world would such a waste of energy be tolerated. They are asked to learn to teach in the same way that boys used to learn to swim. They are thrown into deep water and are left to sink or to save themselves. There are a few who swim, there are a few more that manage to struggle out, they know not how, and forever after look with horror on composition. Many sink; a few are rescued by sympathetic friends, and never afterward venture out of the shallow but safer waters of courses in "literary appreciation." (456–457)

It is not hard to see why literary courses were so sought after and so completely safeguarded as their own by the senior professors. Then, as now, literary courses were easier to teach, drew more obviously on traditional graduate training, offered a lighter load, and could be shaped to the taste of the individual teacher.[14]

There is a great deal of evidence that the young aesthetically oriented, highly specialized students of literature and philology were exceedingly poor composition teachers, "inexperienced, unfitted by nature for the work, ill-trained, and sometimes, in addition, reluctant and disaffected," as an NCTE committee reported in 1918 ("Preliminary Report" 593). In his controversial "English and the PhD" of 1925, Harry T. Baker excoriated the influence of the degree in scathing terms:

> The missing characteristics of the fledgling Doctor of Philosophy are best shown by his often pathetic attempts to wrestle with the problem of teaching Freshman composition. Frequently he has to teach this for several years before being promoted to the delights of misrepresenting literature to undergraduates. Since his doctorate training and his natural temperament have not been largely concerned with the matter of good English he finds his work dull, and his pupils find it duller. The Freshman course in writing is the standing joke of American universities. The middle-aged doctors are not required to teach it, and the young ones teach it badly. (148)

Teaching, claimed Baker, was primarily a human problem, and PhDs were trained to investigate subjects, not teach students. Howard Savage in 1921 called the required composition course a "salvage dump for young doctors of philosophy, and especially for men and women of uncertain or negative qualifications" (439).

It was early realized that PhD training, though it was increasingly a necessary prerequisite for college training, often worked actively against effective teaching by inculcating arrogant and elitist attitudes in the "young doctors" being produced. Composition students would always be "impervious to learning of any kind ... young yokels that rush to the universities without thought of culture beyond that thin veneer necessary to get along with their fellow Babbitts" (486), as W. B. Gates sneered in 1929. This point is supported by a graduate student's comment on a freshman theme, quoted by V. T. Thayer in 1926: "'You should develop a grace of style and depth of comprehension. You need, too, to understand the aesthetic and spiritual values of the great masterpieces of the world's art, literary and pictorial'" (773). Here, clearly, is a gulf between teacher and student that boggles the mind.

The final indignity heaped on the rhetoric teacher after 1900 was the extremely poor pay given for teaching writing. Graduate teaching assistants during the first decade of the twentieth century did more composition work than any other sort, and their average yearly salaries lay in a range between $350 and $850 yearly, with the average around $650. By 1929, 34 percent of all colleges were using TAs to teach composition, and 47 percent of larger institutions relied on TAs regularly (Taylor 22). Instructors, who typically taught full time, did little better, averaging around $950 annually. Contrast these salaries with the annual salary of a full professor in 1907, which averaged over $2,300 (and was over $3,500 at many of the more prestigious universities) (Carnegie Report 42–45). By 1920 the average professor made $3,616, the average instructor $1,653. By 1929 the differential was $4,407 and $1,995. In general it remained true from 1900 through the

1930s that the instructor corps, which typically taught the same number of hours as the professorial, earned only 40 percent to 45 percent of what the professors earned (Boothe 12–13). In a study of teachers' salaries in 1932, Viva Boothe found that instructors were the only college-teaching rank to consistently run at a financial deficit; their combined expenditures ran to 103.4 percent of their meager salaries (122).[15]

And yet, though underpaid and disaffected, young PhDs took entry-level composition jobs in great numbers. They had little other choice; if they were to work at all, the entry-level jobs were the only ones available. To enter into business with the PhD was the only other alternative, and at least the composition teaching "kept the hand in" and kept the young teacher on a campus. But the "treadmill of freshman English," as Savage called it, was bitter drudgery for all who worked it. Out of this dreary grind the young PhD might eventually be promoted into "the glorious liberty of literature," but the composition grind would forever mark each English teacher. Rhetoric would always be, to each sufferer under a four-and-four teaching load, a wasteland of "small pay, smaller encouragement, and opportunities for adding to the sum of human knowledge smaller still" (440). They would escape if they could, and would despise and turn away from those who could not.

The Composition of the Underclass

Those instructors who remained teaching writing knew they could look forward to little better treatment—as long as they remained instructors, as long as they remained composition teachers. Though some members of this underclass were merely passing through, others chose, or were forced by circumstance, to remain. Who were these permanent members of the freshman composition staff and why were they willing to remain in the overworked underclass?

The answer to that question is complex and can be only provisionally sketched here. A part of the answer can be found in gender studies; it seems inescapably true that a disproportionate percentage of the instructor corps in composition has been women. After 1900, more and more women attended graduate school, and the statistics on their attendance vs. that of men are very telling. The following table tells the story:

year	# of male grad students	# of female grad students	# of male PhDs granted	# of female PhDs granted	# of male grad students per PhD	# of female grad students per PhD
1900	4112	1179	322	20	13	59
1910	6504	2866	365	44	18	65
1920	9837	5775	439	93	22	62
1930	29070	18185	1692	332	17	54

(from John 13–19)

What we see here is simple; there existed a very significant gap between the percentage of male graduate students who attained the PhD degree and the percentage of female graduate students. During the first three decades of the twentieth century, the differential was approximately three to one; where between 7 percent and 16 percent of men in graduate school would achieve a PhD within a decade, that figure never rose from between 3 percent and 5 percent for women.

What these figures mean, of course, is that, despite the rise in absolute numbers of women in graduate school and the absolute number of female PhDs, there were vastly larger percentages of uncompleted female than male PhDs. Women often ceased study after the master's degree or even before its attainment. Since after 1900 the PhD was almost absolutely necessary for promotion out of instructor rank (Stewart 250), most of these women, if they chose to remain in college teaching, were forced to settle into the rank of permanent instructor. And, indeed, Taylor's study in 1929 showed that of all composition instruction nationwide, 38 percent was being conducted by female instructors (22). This is certainly the highest percentage of female instruction found anywhere in colleges with the exception of the home economics departments.

That women were a disproportionate percentage of the composition staff was noted by Stith Thompson in 1930, discussing the Taylor Report. Thompson, by 1930, has become so mired to the existence of the underclass that he even asks whether it is not a good thing. "The pertinent question is raised as to whether a certain nucleus of rather permanent freshman composition teachers may be valuable, and this brings up the subject of women instructors—who do often seem to be willing to settle down to a life of efficient freshman teaching without any idea of going further in their academic career" (555).

Why were women willing to accept these conditions, and this pay? The answer is complex and can only be surmised. The academic culture as it existed from 1880 through the growth of the women's movement in our own time certainly did not encourage women PhDs, though it allowed them. Although, most women took their degrees in humanities fields— many in English—even in the humanities they had a hard time competing with men for the jobs given out by very real Old Boy networks. Many women chose to marry, and raising children was seen as the woman's job; full-time scholarly competition was difficult for active mothers of young children. Many women chose part-time work for the freedom it gave them in child raising. And in addition, the close-contact work of freshman composition, time-consuming though it is, seems to have been appealing to women in a way it was not to male PhDs.

For whatever reasons, the nurturing of younger college students through their required composition courses, while it never became an absolutely feminine activity, was work done on a permanent basis by many women, from World War I up through modern times. In 1962 we find Warner Rice echoing Stith Thompson's claim 32 years earlier: "We find, however, some students—especially young women—who are excellent teachers of lower-division English and who lack some of the interests or qualifications required for the PhD as it is traditionally given" (473). Even today, freshman staffs contain more female instructors than any other instructor corps on campuses.

The other permanent members of the underclass are the part-timers, who trade job status for the hours they desire, and the surplus PhDs, those unfortunates who make the long march only to find their achievement turned to dross by job-market conditions. As early as the 1920s their fates had been clear; indeed, except for an anomalous period during the 1960s, there seem always to have been more English doctorates than satisfactory tenure-line jobs, and this unhappy fact has stocked the composition underclass throughout the century. Oscar J. Campbell commented tellingly on it in 1939:

> The truth is that one of the most distressing products of the Freshman English machine is the academic proletariat that it has created. In the nature of the case, for the vast majority of those who begin their careers as section hands in Freshman English there is no future in the profession. They cannot hope for even moderate academic promotion. But, for all that, crowds of young men and women have been lured into the teaching of English by the great numbers of positions annually open at the bottom of the heap, and there they stick, contaminating one another with their discouragement and rebellion. I know of large departments of English in which no one has been promoted from an instructorship to an assistant professorship for over ten years. Instead, men from other institutions have been brought in over the heads of the wretched section hands. This process is natural—yes, inevitable—because the work of a Freshman English instructor does not fit him for the teaching of literature. So at the bottom of almost every large English department lies a kind of morass of unhappy, disillusioned men and women which poisons all its fairer regions. (181–182)

Although I do not share Campbell's tendency to blame the victims of institutional shortsightedness for damage to its "fairer regions," it is in the spirit of his pungent and still-true observations that I will close this essay. The composition underclass we have always with us, and many of the reasons for its inception still control its use and development today.

Rhetoric, although it has forced literary studies to recognize it as a legitimate scholarly specialty, still gets small respect at too many institutions. We do have our own PhDs now, and their number is growing, but thus far, too many rhetoric PhDs have been willing to blunt their own perceptions and act as the overseers of oppressive and pedagogically indefensible composition programs. There seems a curious ability to forget the despair that a four-and-four composition load can induce once one has fought free of the web via a rhetoric PhD. It is pretty to think that as younger PhDs in composition studies earn their way into positions of power in their departments, they will take active stands to better the lots of their confreres still toiling in the vineyards of heavy composition loads. The evidence thus far, however, points toward more jawboning than action.

Although the 200-student composition overloads of the past are mostly gone now, the overwork of composition teachers remains a key defining term in the problem of the underclass. It will remain a key problem unless distinctly addressed by rhetoricians, because composition teaching and literary teaching are not comparable in their demands on a teacher. This is hard to talk about, given the way our departments function. We must, however, come to terms with it somehow. *The fact is, as everyone knows who has taught both, that composition is harder and more energy-consuming than literature to teach well.* Literature teachers do not seek instructors to delegate composition instruction to only because literature has more cachet; literature is less work to teach. Because it is not required, attracts upperclass students, and has infinitely variable content, it is often more enjoyable to teach. And until English departments begin to address this reality — probably by creating some system of extra teaching credit for faculty who agree to teach writing courses — most tenure-line faculty members (in literature *and* in rhetoric) will continue to use the variety of stratagems and arguments long since developed to avoid teaching writing as much as they can. And the work will continue to fall to a structurally necessary underclass.

We have come a part of the way toward being able to deal with the class inequality that has been infecting English departments from a very early point. We have made rhetorical work respectable again as scholarship, after a century. Now it is the responsibility of all of us who study writing to struggle, both in scholarship and in the hard battles of pragmatic institutional politics, to *define* the task of teaching writing. We must let administrators, colleagues, and students know that composition can no longer be the poor relation of the "real" work of an English department, and that the permanent composition underclass will cease being a problem only when the work of teaching writing is put on a genuinely equal footing with the other work the department does. Unless and until teaching and studying writing can be made work the entire English faculty wants to share in, irresistible social forces will maintain the underclass and all of the unhappiness and poisonous inequality that have always followed in its train.

Notes

1. It might possibly be objected that the relation between the professors and the tutors in the college system constituted an institutional class system. Perhaps it was in the sense of a continuing organizational dichotomy; the professors were older, more highly trained, better paid than the tutors at early colleges. But these "class structures" were very different in several ways from those we know today. One great difference lay in the fact that tutors were not subject-specific teachers; they were assigned individual graduating classes — the class of 1799 or 1809 — rather than specific subjects like mathematics or rhetoric. The other difference lay in the

essentially nonacademic goals most tutors had. Typically they were young men just out of college, temporarily at loose ends, perhaps headed for a legal or ministerial career but not ready for the move. They did not plan to stay and did not. As Frederick Rudolph puts it, "The old tutor was in no sense an organization man — he was merely passing through" (163). They often stayed only a year or two before going onward in nonacademic life. Thus, although the tutorial positions were certainly inferior to professorial rank, tutors were not locked personally into perpetual organizational and professional inferiority.

2. The two great exceptions to this understanding were Johns Hopkins and Clark University, which were both founded as "pure" universities devoted to graduate research alone. Only later, under financial pressure, did both establish undergraduate divisions.

3. Nietzsche himself, when he offered his rhetoric lectures at Basel in 1873, could attract only two students, and his extended course of 1874 was canceled when no one signed up.

4. A few universities, such as Ohio State and Wisconsin, felt enough solidarity with the older discipline to initially found departments of Rhetoric and Belles Lettres, but such nomenclature disappeared rapidly after the 1890s (with the notable exception of Michigan's — or, rather, Fred Newton Scott's — Department of Rhetoric, founded in 1903).

5. The resources of their institutions and the directions of their colleagues combined to lead most of these generalists gradually away from compositon and toward literature, or drama, or administration. They also had to suffer the disdain of their more scholarly colleagues for any continuing affiliation with rhetoric. George Santayana scornfully referred to Copeland, the last great composition generalist at Harvard, as an "elocutionist" who provided a "spiritual debauch" for his students (Brown 125). By the time that such men as Copeland and Hopkins retired in the 1930s, they represented attitudes and techniques of teaching that were long gone from most campuses.

6. The history of the PhD degree in departments of speech is a fascinating one, but it cannot be told here. Essentially, speech departments were forced to bootstrap their own advanced degrees on specialites based in traditional degrees in English, classics, and philosophy. For a more complete coverage of this effort, see Corbett 5–11.

7. We must tread carefully through the minefield that is late-nineteenth-century educational statistics. There is no period for which statistics are as confusing and potentially misleading. Our two major sources, the Reports of the U.S. Commissioner of Education and those of the U.S. Office of Education, disagree sharply on many important numbers. It is not strange that numbers may turn untrustworthy when we consider the difficulty of defining such terms as "faculty," "student," and "degree" during the period from 1870–1900, when American universities were inventing and defining themselves.

What the statistics clearly do *not* show is a radical increase in the student/faculty ratio between 1870 and 1900. Here are some relevant numbers:

	1869–1870	1879–1880	1889–1890	1899–1900
Faculty#	5553	11522	15809	23868
Student#	52286	115817	156756	237592
Ratio	(9:4)	(10:1)	(9:9)	(9:9)

(Source: Harris 932. Harris's book contains a completely different set of statistics for these same realities on p. 924, gleaned from disparate sources and confusingly presented. I prefer these numbers, all drawn from the *Digest of Educational Statistics*, because they are more consistent with degree totals. "Lies, damned lies . . .")

The story told by these numbers is simple: The overall college student/faculty ratio remained almost exactly constant, at around ten students per faculty member, throughout this extremely important period. So we cannot claim that all college teachers were suddenly subject to dreadful overloads of students. Composition teachers, however, clearly were.

8. According to figures derived from Harris 936–939, the "average" undergraduate enrollment for the 30 most influential schools in the United States was 1,204 students by 1903.

9. For a fuller discussion of this issue, see Connors 39–41.

10. In the Department of Language and Literature, the same number of students were taught by three professors and three assistants. (See Payne for details.)

11. At Stanford, the professors voted to cancel the freshman composition course because they were "worn out with the drudgery of correcting freshman themes." "Had this salutary innovation not been accomplished, all the literary courses would have been swept away by the rapidly growing inundation of freshman themes, and all of our strength and courage would have been dissipated . . ." reported Melville B. Anderson in 1894. The composition course was turned over to two "approved teachers and to the various secondary schools," but Anderson reports that the department will hire more composition instructors because "it would be bad policy to allow any instructor to devote the whole of his attention to the work in English composition; for, however great a man's enthusiasm for such work may be, it is incident to human nature that no man can read themes efficiently for more than three hours at a stretch" (Payne 52).

12. This remained true until the 1960s. Earning the doctorate did not until the late 1960s automatically guarantee promotion to the professional ranks, which might come considerably later. See Archer 446–448.

13. There were a few practicum-style courses for new teachers at schools with "advanced" ideas. In 1912, Harvard began to offer English 67, a practicum-style course for new TAs, and by the mid-1920s, Donald L. Clark of Columbia was offering a course in composition pedagogy on the graduate level there. These were, however, rare cases. Most new TAs were given a textbook and some lore and shoved into the classroom to sink or swim. See Wyckoff 217.

14. We can hear the scorn in Thomas's voice as he describes the situation in 1916: "It is my personal opinion that the comparative ease of the task of teaching literature, of arousing enthusiam in regard to works that have a perennial charm, accounts as much as anything for the great attraction this field has for all young men entering upon the teaching of college English. There is on the contrary no field which so quickly searches out a man's weakness, which puts his ingenuity and resourcefulness to as keen a test, which really proves his ability as a teacher so quickly, as English composition" (456).

15. A sadly representative set of figures is found in Clifford Griffin's history of the University of Kansas. During severe budget cutbacks in 1933, all professors were forced to take salary reductions, and Griffin mentions several individuals' salary cuts. A chemistry professor was cut from $4,800 to $3,620. A history professor was cut from $4,500 to $3,425. And Edwin M. Hopkins of English, who was then in

his 43d year of composition teaching at KU, had his salary cut from $3,800 to $2,960. Thus thy wages, good and faithful servant.

Works Cited

Alden, Raymond, M. "Preparation for College English Teaching." *English Journal* 2 (1913): 344–356.

Archer, Jerome W. "Professional Career of the College English Teacher." *College English* 23 (1962): 445–469.

Baker, Harry T. "English and the Ph.D." *Educational Review* 69 (1925): 147–149.

Baldwin, C. S. "The Value of the Office-Hour in the Teaching of Rhetoric." *Educational Review* 8 (1894): 290–293.

Boothe, Viva. *Salaries and the Cost of Living in Twenty-Seven State Colleges and Universities, 1913–1932.* Columbus: Ohio State University Press, 1932.

Brown, Rollo W. *Harvard Yard in the Golden Age.* New York: Current Books, 1948.

Campbell, Oscar James. "The Failure of Freshman English." *English Journal* 28 (1939): 177–185.

Carpenter, George R., Franklin T. Baker, and Fred N. Scott. *The Teaching of English in the Elementary and Secondary School.* New York: Longman, 1903.

Connors, Robert J. "The Rhetoric of Mechanical Correctness." In *Only Connect.* Ed. Thomas Newkirk. Portsmouth, NH: Boynton/Cook, 1986, 27–58.

Corbett, Edward P. J. "The Cornell School of Rhetoric." *Rhetoric Review* 4 (1985): 4–15.

Cordasco, Francesco. *The Shaping of American Graduate Education.* Totowa, NJ: Rowman and Littlefield, 1973.

Cox, John H. "What Is the Best Preparation for the College Teacher of English?" *English Journal* 2 (1913): 207–214.

The Financial Status of the Professor in America and in Germany. New York: Carnegie Foundation, 1907.

Finegan, Edward. *Attitudes Toward English Usage: The History of a War of Words.* New York: Teachers College Press, 1980.

Gates, W. B. "In Defense of the PhD in English." *English Journal* 18 (1929): 482–487.

Graff, Gerald. *Professing Literature.* Chicago: University of Chicago Press, 1987.

Greenough, Chester Noyes. "An Experiment in the Training of Teachers of Composition for Work with College Freshmen." *English Journal* 2 (1913): 109–121.

Griffin, Clifford S. *The University of Kansas: A History.* Lawrence: University of Kansas Press, 1974.

Hale, Edward Everett. "My College Days." *Atlantic Monthly* 71 (1893): 355–363.

Harmon, Lindsey R. *A Century of Doctorates.* Washington, DC: National Academy of Sciences, 1978.

Harris, Seymour E. *A Statistical Portrait of Higher Education.* New York: McGraw-Hill, 1972.

Hart, Sophie Chantal. "English in the College." *School Review* 10 (1902): 364–373.

Hill, Adam S. "An Answer to the Cry for More English." In *Twenty Years of School and College English.* Cambridge: Harvard University, 1896.

Hopkins, Edwin M. "The Labor and Cost of Composition Teaching: The Present Conditions." *Proceedings of the NEA* (1912): 747–751.

—— "The Cost and Labor of English Teaching." *Proceedings of the NEA* (1915): 114–119.

—— *The Labor and Cost of the Teaching of English in Colleges and Secondary Schools with Especial Reference to English Composition.* Chicago: NCTE, 1923.

John, Walton C. *Graduate Study in Universities and Colleges in the United States.* Washington, DC: U.S. Government Printing Office, 1935.

Nietzsche, Friedrich. *Friedrich Nietzsche on Rhetoric and Language.* Ed. and Trans. Sander L. Gilman, Carole Blair, and David J. Parent. New York: Oxford University Press, 1989.

Lewis, Frances W. "The Qualifications of the English Teacher." *Education* (Steptember 1902): 15–26.

Morgan, James H. *Dickinson College: The History of One Hundred and Fifty Years 1783–1933.* Carlisle, PA: University Press, 1933.

Newkirk, Thomas. Personal research notes from Harvard archives. 1989.

Payne, William Morton, ed. *English in American Universities.* Boston: D. C. Heath, 1895.

"Preliminary Report of the Special Committee on Freshman English." *English Journal* 7 (1918): 592–99.

"Report of the Committee on the Preparation of College Teachers of English." *English Journal* 5 (1916): 20–32.

Rice, Warner G. "Teachers of College English: Preparation, Supply, and Demand." *College English* 23 (1962): 470–483.

Royce, Josiah. "Present Ideals of American University Life." *Scribner's Magazine* 10 (1891): 376–388.

Rudolph, Frederick. *The American College and University: A History.* New York: Knopf, 1962.

Rudy, S. Willis. "The 'Revolution' in American Higher Education—1865–1900." *Harvard Education Review* 21 (1951): 155–174.

Rutland, J. R. "Tendencies in the Administration of Freshman English." *English Journal* 12 (1923): 1–9.

Savage, Howard J. "Personnel for College Composition." *English Journal* 10 (1921): 439–449.

Shaw, Wilfred B. *The University of Michigan: An Encyclopedic Survey.* Ann Arbor: University of Michigan Press, 1951, vol. II.

Snyder, Franklyn B. "Twenty-Five Years of Trying to 'Teach' English." *English Journal* 24 (1935): 196–208.

Stewart, Charles A. "Appointment and Promotion of College Instructors." *Educational Review* 44 (1912): 249–256.

Taylor, Warner. *A National Survey of Conditions in Freshman English.* Madison: University of Wisconsin Research Bulletin No. 11, 1929.

Thayer, V. T. "The University as a Training School for College and University Teachers." *School and Society* 24 (1926): 773–779.

Theremin, Franz. *Eloquence a Virtue.* Trans. W. G. T. Shedd. Andover, MA: W. F. Draper, 1850.

Third Annual Report of the President and Treasurer. Carnegie Foundation for the Advancement of Teaching. Boston: D. B. Updike, 1908.

Thomas, J. M. "Training for Teaching Composition in Colleges." *English Journal* 5 (1916): 447–457.

Thompson, Stith. "A National Survey of Freshman English." *English Journal* 19 (1930): 553–557.

Veysey, Lawrence R. *The Emergence of the American University*. Chicago: University of Chicago Press, 1965.
Wendell, Barrett. "English Work in the Secondary Schools." *School Review* 1 (1893): 638–667.
Wykoff, George S. "On the Revision of PhD Requirements in English." *English Journal* 17 (1928): 213–220.

5

The Politics of Promotion

CHARLES I. SCHUSTER
University of Wisconsin — Milwaukee

Composition is a dangerous business, dangerous for reasons that I hope to make clearer in this essay. I don't intend by this statement that specialists in the area of rhetoric and composition are "dangerous" in any romantic sense. Those who profess writing and the teaching of writing are not swashbucklers or highwaymen; they are not the top guns of the academy. Quite the contrary, most rhetoricians, reflective of the discipline of English, believe in institutional values. They are conservatives — and conservators — in the tradition of Fred Newton Scott and John Dewey. Most love to teach and are profoundly committed to the pedagogical rewards that emerge from undergraduate and graduate writing classrooms. Many are schooled even as graduate students in the intricacies of administration and naturally are selected to administer programs in their own departments. Many of them are messianic about what they do, who they are, their talk laced with phrases about "empowerment" and "discourse communities," "enfranchisement" and "literacy." If they are revolutionary at all, it is in their zeal to promote writing as a fundamental activity of thinking and learning and to integrate it into all disciplines, *including* the study of literature. That such talk is "revolutionary" at all is part of the problem writing specialists face in their own institutions and their own departments.

English department faculty often view the writing program as the dark sister, the Maggie Tulliver of academe. The plight of such programs is that their faculty pervert the values of the establishment. Whereas most faculty in English find themselves awash in horror at the thought of teaching freshman composition, most members of the writing faculty choose to do so. Whereas most English faculty worship that critical entity known as "the book," with faculty prestige and salary depending entirely on publishing between hard covers, the discipline of rhetoric is driven like its sister, linguistics, by the article, the journal essay, the academic conference. Whereas most English faculty are at best disinterested administrators, most writing specialists are schooled in administration, quite literally, and take advantage of their expertise to develop curriculum and community support for their endeavors. Whereas many literature faculty define the classroom as an authoritarian field of inquiry in which professors maintain a privileged speaking role while students learn primarily through listening and imitating, composition faculty create collaborative classrooms and writing workshops, thereby undercutting the traditional professorial power structure. As a result of these differences, English department literary faculty often look upon their compositional brothers and sisters as incompetent, idiosyncratic, confused, valueless, untenurable. Thus the problem — a problem of perception, of value, of institutional pressures, of ideological difference.

Readings

This problem of writing within the academy, within its own home department, is strikingly reminiscent of a well-known parable that has much to say about social aspirations and class hegemony. I am thinking of George Orwell's *Animal Farm*, with its analysis of authoritarian and democratic class structures, its condemnation of communistic inequities. Most of the "characters" in *Animal Farm* are venal, weak, cynical, or cowardly, but one character in particular possesses considerable virtues: Boxer the horse. Boxer is a proletarian hero, like Stephen Blackpool in *Hard Times*, and he meets an equally unkind fate. Orwell describes Boxer as "an enormous beast, nearly eighteen hands high, and as strong as any two ordinary horses put together. A white stripe down his nose gave him a somewhat stupid appearance, and in fact he was not of first-rate intelligence but he was universally respected for his steadiness of character and tremendous powers of work" (4). It is Boxer, along with Snowball, who preserves the rule of the animals during the Battle of the Cowshed. It is Boxer who works tirelessly, selflessly for the farm. While all the animals (except the pigs, of course) work long days, Boxer also works part of each night as well, hauling stone for the mill, bringing grain into the barn. Ultimately, Boxer decides to work harder: "'From now onwards I shall get up a full hour earlier in the mornings'" (72). Inevitably, of course, his strength gives out, and Boxer collapses between the shafts of a cart while hauling a load of stone to the mill. Squealer, that most unctuous of pigs, claims that the workhorse is being sent to a fine hospital, but we know better. It is the knacker who comes and takes Boxer to the glue factory; the pigs spend the money earned from the sale on another case of whiskey for their nightly revels.

In the politics of English departments, composition specialists are like Boxer — not always, not inevitably, but often enough to give this analogy genuine force. This is not because they are forced into the role by pernicious chairpersons or scheming deans, although they are generally required to do more than their fair share of minding the farm. This is not because there is a national conspiracy against the discipline of rhetoric. Rather, one finds a complex ratio of motivations, circumstances, and historic inevitability. In characterizing Boxer, Orwell notes that the horse has two slogans: "'I will work harder' and 'Napoleon is always right,'" and that these two homilies were for the horse "a sufficient answer to all problems" (53). So it often is for specialists in writing. The Puritans of English departments, they generally believe both in the ethos of work and, less fortunately, in the beneficence of authority. Their zeal to teach and serve smothers that other extremely useful instinct: self-survival through the salvation of publishing. Too often they lack the pragmatic, hard-edged, usefully complicated, ironic intellectual footing of their colleagues who know that the system rewards a belief in self, not community. Too often they believe that hard work, and hard work alone, will be their salvation.

Composition specialists thus find the role of Boxer an easy one to play: it fits their psychology, their sense of mission, their tendency toward professional martyrdom, their work ethic. Like Boxer, they believe in "working harder." Like Boxer, they are committed to improving the condition of their farm and know that it is they—and no one else—who can accomplish this goal. They are quite often the responsibility bearers in an English department, the ones who care about undergraduate education, curricular reform, high school-college articulation. Moreover, English department faculty find it easy to let them assume this role of Boxer: Who else would choose to do all the work of teaching writing and administering freshman composition? (That is, after all, part of their "stupidity.") Who else is better equipped to administer composition programs, serve on college and university committees, direct the writing center? Isn't that their training? After all, that's why a composition specialist was hired in the first place—to haul the stone and get up an hour earlier every morning even if it means career death at the age of seven. And, secure in their knowledge that Napoleon is always right, that rewards follow responsibilities as surely as government always rules wisely, writing specialists follow their career track to its inevitable end.

Most of us know stories of composition colleagues denied promotion and tenure. Brought in to teach writing, they taught writing. Asked to administer freshman composition, they administered. Required to publish in their discipline, they placed essays in *College Composition and Communication, College English, Rhetoric Review, Freshman English News*—journals often scorned by departmental review committees. Numbers of them founded journals, initiated writing-across-the-curriculum programs, developed campuswide writing centers. Even so—even though they met their professional obligations and were liked and respected by their colleagues, chairpersons, and deans—they were still denied tenure and/or promotion. Many of the most famous faculty in rhetoric and composition have, at one time or another in their careers, received some such professional setback. To list them here would be to write a veritable *Who's Who* of composition.

The genius of Orwell's *Animal Farm* is its applicability to a wide array of governmental and bureaucratic operations. Given the hierarchies that inevitably exist within a department, a university, it is equally inevitable that some individual, some class of individuals will assume the role of Boxer. For the past several academic generations, rhetoric/composition has hauled the stone. For many years, this work was literally done by women: spouses, part-timers, faculty adjuncts. In many ways, it is indeed "women's work," for the teaching of writing demands that an instructor be nurturing as well as demanding. It demands a collaborative, collegial, interactive relationship between teacher and student that is currently identified with a "feminist" model of teaching as opposed to a "masculinist" model. The masculinist model privileges lecturing, competition, a Darwinian view of the classroom in which students must prove themselves capable or be eliminated; such an individualistic ideology is utterly inappropriate to teaching writing and, I would add, to most teaching altogether. Unfortunately, it is the masculinist model that predominates and carries prestige; the feminist model bespeaks a "service" role that most English faculty find abhorrent. (See Susan Miller's essay, "The Feminization of Composition," in this volume.)

If we extend this psychoanalytic, gender-based model further, we derive another useful "reading" of rhetoric within traditional English departments. If the specialty of writing represents the female principle, then literary criticism (New Criticism, Critical Theory, even Feminist Theory) is the father, the husband, the phallocentric principle. After all, most English departments are defined by literature and literary critical interests. In large part, these interests establish curricular programs; they hire and fire; they constitute executive committees, graduate policy committees, chair-persons. They wield the wand of power; they constitute the maypole around which most of us parade our obeisance. Married to these figures (and an uneasy marriage it is) are the writing faculty, dutiful wives who do much of the dirty work: teaching writing, reading myriad student essays, training TAs and lecturers, administering testing programs. That is the primary function of the composition wives: to maintain the house and raise the children, in this case the thousands of undergraduates who enroll in composition classes. Thus do they conspire in their own oppression.

In *The Daughter's Seduction*, Jane Gallop applies Freud's and Ernest Jones's insights on male/female relations to describe a model of desire. For Gallop, male/female relations are always a step apart because the male desires the woman, but the locus of the woman's desire is the children. Says Gallop: "The man wants to be with his woman; the woman stays 'for the sake of the children.' This is not a balanced, symmetrical dual relation, but one of three parties. The child is to the woman what the woman is to the man" (24). The lack of reciprocity creates unequal relations, hegemony, resentments, resistance.

To disrupt this power relation, the "woman," I believe, has several choices. She can forswear her love of the child, abandon the nurturant role of "mother," and enter into a love relation with the man. She can become the man, adopt a phallocentric mode of being, and in the process either shed the need for the male or subject him, make him "female," She can attempt androgyny, for herself and others — both male and female — and thus inscribe a sexless world or one that is polymorphically perverse. She can expunge the male presence from her society, through ideological or even physical means, and adopt a life of homosexuality. She can redefine sexuality and sexual power relations, move from "desire" to "sexuality," from active/ passive relations to one of mutuality and contiguity (Gallop 28–32). No matter which choice she takes, she (and her male lover) will likely need long-term counseling, made all the harder because he possesses no under-standing of her dilemma, no innate sympathy to serve as a spur to reform, and every reason to maintain the status quo. From his perspective the status quo is all he knows and all he needs to know: her role in life is after all a biologic imperative, as inevitable as hiring and firing composition faculty.

Part of the problem results from the inevitable hierarchic relations that obtain within the academy. University life is class life, almost feudal in its stipulation of working class and ruling class. Not only are professors at the top and students at the bottom, but such positioning also exists in relation to what we study, what we write and analyze. According to Nancy Comley and Robert Scholes, the discipline of English is characterized by binary oppositions based on "value": literature and nonliterature, imaginative ex-pression and expository writing, consumption (the reading of approved texts) and production (the writing of student essays). In such a pairing, it is the second of each of these terms that is subordinate, less valued, less rewarded. Within the college English classroom, Comley and Scholes describe a hierarchy of four levels of writing with literature at the top and "student compositions" at the bottom (see Emig 173). Thus those of us whose world is permeated with student writing are by definition among the expendable lower class; we are laborers, factory workers, piece workers. Such work may be necessary, but it is not important enough to reward with salary, benefits, and tenure. Often it is only in administration that one finds salvation; comp directors are sometimes seen as valuable—at least as long as they agree to run the writing program. As the dean of my previous university asked in 1984: "If we granted Charles Schuster tenure, what would he do in the English department once he no longer directed the composition program? What in the world *could* he do?" Like Boxer, I would have to be sent to the knacker as soon as I no longer hauled the stone.

As James Berlin has made clear, this kind of thinking has been character-istic of American university life for the past 75 to 100 years and is only just now beginning to change. It is a philosophy of education that has presumed that students must "learn" composition before graduating from high school, that "poetic" expression is privileged and "rhetorical" forms impoverished, that the teaching of writing is essentially a skills-based, form-based, error-based, handbook-based activity which assumes that writing is a mere tran-scription of thought, a basic activity like riding a bicycle that once learned is never forgotten (Berlin, chs. 2 and 3 in particular). Nor is this "philosophy of English" accidental; as Berlin states:

In tacitly supporting the impoverished notion of rhetoric found in the freshman writing course, academic literary critics have provided a constant reminder of their own claim to superiority and privilege, setting the range and versatility of their discipline against the barrenness of current-traditional rhetoric, the staple of the freshman course. (28)

The value of teaching literature is more self-evident: it extends the reach of culture and creates a shared sympathy and understanding of aesthetic objects. It develops multicultural awareness, unpacks the mind, makes us more sensitive to the imaginative powers of language. The value of teaching writing is inevitably suspect, as Trimbur, Miller, and others in this volume make clear, and thus must be contained within a basic-skills ideology. Such a view, of course, runs counter both to the two thousand year tradition of rhetoric within Western culture and to the view of most rhetoric and composition specialists that writing is constitutive to thinking and being (see Neel's excellent analysis, especially Ch. 6). The wonder is not that the discipline of writing is in such a sorry condition but that it is in any condition at all.

Writings

Only five years ago, this essay might have continued as an almost endless keening. But recent developments suggest a turning point in the relations between writing specialists and their departmental and university colleagues. The past 25 years have seen a resurgence of interest in composition, a dramatic revaluation of the fundamental importance of writing, a revitalized understanding of the institutional and disciplinary importance of rhetoric as a discipline. The Modern Language Association has created the Division of Teaching Writing and is beginning to attract specialists who are promoting interest in subjects rhetorical such as literacy, the essay, and discourse theory. Jobs for assistant professors specializing in writing and rhetoric abound; indeed, there are many more positions than qualified candidates to fill them. Although some rhetoricians have still been denied tenure and promotion, more of them have achieved those career goals and a small number have also been appointed to distinguished chairs (at the Universities of Mississippi and Connecticut and Texas Christian University to name just three). The number of registrants for the Conference on College Composition and Communication continues to climb, as does the number of scholarly journals and private and university presses demonstrating a significant commitment to publishing work in rhetoric and composition. Although work in "writing" is still difficult to publish, especially book-length projects, the situation is improved. More and more English departments are agreeing to allow writing specialists to publish work in their own refereed journals rather than requiring them to work by day in comp and then moonlight by publishing in lit. In large part, these positive developments reflect a general understanding that individuals specializing in that baggy discipline known variously as rhetoric, composition, and writing instruction can claim the right to work for promotion within their chosen field—even if evaluating that work remains a difficult problem for many departments and divisional committees.

Improvement notwithstanding, there are certain actions that I would recommend to produce a healthier climate for both specialists in rhetoric and the English departments they serve. Significant reforms are needed, all the harder to obtain because they must come about through a change of mind, a shift in the value structure. Unfortunately there is no reason for established and powerful faculty to foster reforms that will inevitably disrupt the pedagogy and politics of English departments, even if those changes have a positive effect on the discipline as a whole. Departments, like the institutions they serve, respond to new developments slowly and cautiously; fortunately, both history and what is being called "the literacy crisis" are creating an urgency toward reform. Without continued, positive change, English departments may well find themselves losing their composition programs and their student-credit-hour power base as writing specialists heed the advice of Maxine Hairston and form their own departments. Such a move, I think, would be unfortunate but it will also become inevitable unless the literature faculty achieve a genuine, productive relationship with their colleagues in rhetoric and writing. To forestall such a consequence— or others equally unfortunate—I think the discipline of English needs to transform itself in light of recent historical and disciplinary developments.

For example, English departments should strongly consider becoming departments of rhetoric—or departments of textual studies or departments of discourse. Jasper Neek, for example, celebrates the sophistic tradition of rhetoric and concludes that "for Isocrates, as well as for his teacher Gorgias and his predecessor Protagoras, rhetoric and writing belong at the center of the curriculum because rhetoric and writing are the ways to make choices in a world of probability" (211). Jonathan Culler believes that the essential focus of our attention should be "on two correlated networks of convention: writing as an institution and reading as an activity" (131). Although Culler is mainly interested in proposing structuralist poetics as "the theory of the practice of reading" (259), his emphasis on rhetoric and the constitutive importance of reading and writing echoes a similar argument that John Gerber made twenty years ago. Gerber, one of the original founders of the Conference on College Composition and Communication and one of the handful of great English department chairs during the 1960s and 1970s, argued that English departments had one goal: to train "our contemporaries to read and write" (20). Although modestly stated, this formulation describes the essential mission of English: how to read literary and rhetorical texts— and how to produce them. Such a reorientation does not require a name change; rather, it requires a sea change, a change of view. It requires that faculty concern themselves with how writers make meaning, with notions of textual production and interpretation, with the ways that culture shapes understanding by and through written discourses.

Graduate training in English departments should assume a leadership position in promoting this point of view. Of course, faculty create graduate programs and must believe in their own curriculum. I would hope that all faculty could subscribe to the description I have just offered. Whatever their differences, English faculty must conceive of our discipline broadly so as to include the analysis and production of poetry, novels, essays, film, business writing. Our responsibility as an English department faculty is to engage a whole variety of written discourses—from a freshman student essay to *King Lear*—in order to promote better reading and writing. Our graduate students must learn how to teach, conduct research, write, and reflect. They must become theoreticians of their own methodologies, self-reflective word processors, philosophers of language. Graduate training that reflects this definition will collapse the distinctions between "literature" and "writing instruction" and rehabilitate the discipline of English. In many cases, graduate training drives the department, and inevitably those graduate students become the future of our discipline.

Departments should sponsor faculty colloquia on the issues confronting our discipline. Department-specific, these colloquia might consider "the focus of our introductory literature course" or "improving the writing of our undergraduate English majors." I would urge departments to establish a "long-range planning committee" to think through such issues and promote productive debate among the various interests represented within the department. Such discussion is in the interests of all parties. As Stephen North has made clear, English departments have become "literary studies" departments in part by eliminating speech, theater, linguistics—that is, by so narrowing themselves as to become intolerant, fragile, irritable, and querulous. North argues that "in view of this stultifying homogeneity, composition, with its vital methodological diversity, constitutes new blood that English departments need very badly" (19). Clearly faculty in literary studies have at least as much to gain by such conversation and reform as those in writing.

Departments need to reevaluate teaching loads in regard to teaching composition. A typical literature class requires a faculty member to prepare lectures or discussions after reading (or rereading) a text; it usually requires little or no writing from the students. A typical composition class requires that a professor create a curriculum, assign writing (preferably two to three times a week), and respond to that writing thoughtfully. Rewarding as that work is, it is also constant and often overwhelming. Citing Richard Lloyd-Jones, Charles Altieri states that

> when the emphasis is on reading papers, the teacher approaches each composition as a human attempt at self-expression, looks for the writer's purpose, sees how well it is realized, and tries to help the person gain a

richer understanding of the issue and find better rhetorical strategies. Consider now the plight of someone teaching thirty or thirty-five students in a class, with three such sections in a quarter. This is more students than one would have in classes on simple skills like tennis. We know that fifteen can be taught well, but even forty-five in three classes for a quarter, to say nothing of every quarter, become a severe drain on the attention and sympathy a teacher can offer individual writers. (Literature teachers, in contrast, can attend to only a few chosen students who support their self-image.) (27)

As Altieri implies, composition faculty consider teaching literature like going on a paid vacation, the work load being so much lighter. If faculty trained in writing instruction are to teach composition—and most of them both need and want to do just that—then departments must provide them compensatory release time so they can pursue their own research and publication. In my view, a writing class should count at least as a double teaching load: If a typical load for a literature professor is six courses a year, then a professor of composition should teach only three.

Departments need to reevaluate the importance of teaching, particularly the importance of teaching undergraduate composition. To quote Charles Altieri once again:

The average regular faculty member (or, worse, the temporary staff member) who teaches composition faces a potentially rewarding task but must continually bear witness to the waste of human potential. Guilt and frustration vie with each other to suppress rage, until despair seems a state of relief and comfort. No wonder the self-delight of teaching literature becomes an alternative so enviable that the composition instructor only waits for the day when he or she can join the elite. Then the teacher can share the blind righteousness of colleagues in other disciplines as they glibly complain to classes of ten or fifteen that the students cannot express themselves. (27)

For Altieri, writing in *The ADE Bulletin*, the answer is for the ADE to "prepare and circulate to deans [I would add departmental chairs as well] a statement on qualifications for promotion and tenure in English departments. The statement must make clear what is distinctive about the teaching of writing and reading, and it must suggest, following the model of the class-size statement, that different kinds of institutions need different standards" (26). Such a statement is long overdue, and it should be reinforced by genuine departmental commitment to tenuring and promoting faculty who have demonstrated excellence in the teaching of reading and writing. Additionally, departments must recognize the contributions made by many writing faculty to the community; these faculty develop specialized courses for K-12 English teachers and create in-service programs, writing workshops, word-processing facilities, and other programs that strengthen that essential bond between public school and college English teachers. Except perhaps in the two percent of graduate English departments in America that place an exclusive premium on scholarly publication, such a valuation of teaching writing is essential.

Departments need to hire assistant professors in rhetoric and composition as colleagues and specialists, not as administrators and not as temporary staff members. No departments I know of would hire a beginning assistant professor of literature to chair the department or direct the graduate program. Yet these same departments choose freshly minted PhDs to direct writing centers and composition programs. Such a strategy undermines both the candidates and the programs they are asked to develop. Tenure and promotion confer equality, authority, power, influence. An untenured assistant professor who directs composition makes every decision with one eye glancing toward her senior colleagues and the other toward the dean. Moreover, administering a program drains away time best devoted to teaching, research, and publication. And it often makes enemies of certain colleagues, since the interests of a composition program inevitably conflict at certain points with those of the graduate or undergraduate literature programs. Departments should hire colleagues, not administrators. Writing specialists must define themselves—and be defined by their departmental peers—as colleagues in order to survive the tenure wars in their departments.

Departments should hire, whenever possible, at least one senior professor in the area of rhetoric and composition. Whenever I advise job candidates in rhetoric, my first suggestion is "go where a senior colleague will protect you." Departments need to hire at a senior level so that a representative of the writing interest will be free to speak, to serve, to vote, to support the growth and development of writing within the department and the university, and to protect assistant professors.

Finally, the most essential reform is to remind ourselves that reading and writing, literature and composition comprise a necessary and dialogic relation within every English department. I mean this in the most Bakhtinian of senses. A dialogic relation maintains the power of both terms; indeed, each constitutes the other even in their oppositeness. This sustained but delicate relation is akin to the Bakhtinian concept of *vzhivanie*, which Gary Morson and Caryl Emerson translate as "'live entering' or 'living into'" (10). "In *vzhivanie*," Morson and Emerson explain, "one enters another's place *while still maintaining one's own place*, one's own 'outsideness,' with respect to the other" (11). Disciplines live on one another's borders; this is particularly true of textual production and textual analysis, two complementary views of the same event.

Literature and composition are complements of each other; rather than oppositional they are appositional, each educating students to the reach and grasp of language. I have no doubt that future historians who assess the diminished power and influence of literary studies in America during the past twenty-five years will locate this failure at the disjuncture between the study of literary texts and the study of written production. This artificial distinction must be erased if the discipline of English Studies is to be healthy, and only a healthy discipline can incorporate difference by rewarding specialists in both reading and writing with tenure and promotion.

Works Cited

Altieri, Charles. "The ADE and Institutional Politics: The Examples of Tenure and Composition." *ADE Bulletin* 74 (Spring 1983): 24–27.

Berlin, James. *Rhetoric and Reality: Writing Instruction in American Colleges, 1900–1985.* Studies in Writing and Rhetoric. Carbondale: Southern Illinois University Press, 1987.

Culler, Jonathan. *Structuralist Poetics: Structuralism, Linguistics, and the Study of Literature.* London: Routledge & Kegan Paul, 1975.

Emig, Janet. *The Web of Meaning.* Portsmouth, NH: Boynton/Cook, 1983.

Gallop, Jane. *The Daughter's Seduction: Feminism and Psychoanalysis.* Ithaca: Cornell University Press, 1982.

Gerber, John C. "Suggestions for a Commonsense Reform of the English Curriculum." In *The Writing Teacher's Sourcebook.* Ed. Gary Tate and Edward Corbett. New York: Oxford University Press, 1981, 20–26.

Hairston, Maxine. "Breaking Our Bonds and Reaffirming Our Connections." *CCC* 36 (1985): 272–82.

Morson, Gary Saul, and Caryl Emerson, eds. *Rethinking Bakhtin: Extensions and Challenges.* Evanston, IL: Northwestern University Press, 1989.

Neel, Jasper, *Plato, Derrida, and Writing.* Carbondale: Southern Illinois University Press 1988.

North, Stephen M. "Research in Writing, Departments of English, and the Problem of Method." *ADE Bulletin* 88 (Winter 1987): 13–20.

Orwell, George. *Animal Farm.* New York: Harcourt, Brace and Co., 1946.

6

Composition and the Politics of the Curriculum

BRUCE HERZBERG
Bentley College

Curriculum as Ideology

What knowledge should an educated person have? This is the question that the curriculum is supposed to answer. A host of other questions are embedded in this initial one: What counts as knowledge? Do skills count as knowledge? What about attitudes and values? Who are the people who should have this knowledge? Whose responsibility is it to answer these questions and to provide education?

The curriculum represents a commitment to a set of values concerning the uses of culture and the uses of people. The curriculum declares what should be passed on to the future and what students should become. These are ideological issues, political commitments, and because of them the curriculum of a modern school is a battleground: The kinds of knowledge offered for study, the requirements for admission and certification, and the ends envisioned and achieved rarely reflect a consensus. More often, the curriculum is a package of contradictions. The curriculum, moreover, is not an independent entity within the school, and available knowledge is neither the only nor even the primary determinant of the curriculum.

Not long ago, when church and state were closely linked, the college curriculum served the churches and the ruling elite. The curriculum offered study in theology and tools of statecraft; it revered classical culture and preserved it by training students in its lore; and it embodied an epistemology that treated tradition and revelation as sources of knowledge. When this view of knowledge was challenged by the scientific and philosophical revolutions of the seventeenth century, the schools resisted, holding to a curriculum that reflected the ideology of the state-church power. The traditional curriculum was thus for years an implicit critique of the worth of scientific knowledge and a means of keeping the scientifically minded out of power. The curriculum changed only when social and political revolutions shifted the balance of power in society.

97

In our own time — that is, since the middle of the nineteenth century — the curriculum serves the new power team: state and business. Courses of study are named for jobs and professions, and the vast majority of degrees awarded are in fields like management, accounting, computers, agriculture, nursing, engineering, and so on. Needless to say, the epistemological preference in the curriculum has changed, as well as its ideological message. There is still a path to elite education, but the system serves mainly the professional and technical class.

The goal of the curriculum at any moment is to reproduce the culture valued by its sponsor, and why should this not be so? The first directive promulgated by the Deity in Genesis is "reproduce!" Surely the sponsor of education — family, church, guild, or government — would wish to reproduce itself, and with right. To identify the sponsor of education is to begin to answer the central questions about curricular politics. The sponsor's beliefs, traditions, rituals, values, skills, language, and desire for communal solidarity and continuity will in large part determine what counts as knowledge, who shall be educated, and so on. Reproduction is a fact of life — personal, political, and educational. Curriculum battles are not fought over reproduction itself; they are fought over what gets reproduced.

Education in Europe and the United States today reproduces a vast and rich culture, a long history of art, literature, and learning, a densely elaborated set of sciences, a political philosophy that values democracy, and institutions that reward individual achievement. This same culture also tends to devalue non-Western, nonwhite, nonmale, and working-class cultures. Schools tend to reproduce the existing social structure: the hierarchy of wealth and status, the alienated work pattern that sustains capitalism, the external discipline of labor, and the internalized profit goals of management, the consumer ideal, and much more.

The curriculum, then, is not a neutral medium for conveying knowledge, but a tool for controlling learning. It is not, to be sure, a perfect tool. Its power can be undermined and disrupted, by teachers, students, and other social institutions. It is always a site of ideological struggle — and it is not the only such site in the school (as the other essays in this volume show). The struggle to include and valorize nonwhite, non-Western, and women's cultures, for example, is not limited to the curriculum; it also goes on, sometimes more decisively, in decisions about hiring and tenure. The classroom, where students and teachers interact, is surely the most important place for ideological action. Here, the strictures of the curriculum may be followed, resisted, or ignored as the contradictions of the curriculum are played out. The curriculum is the context for classroom interaction: The overt curriculum tells what is to be taught and learned; the covert curriculum insinuates values and attitudes through the structure it gives to learning.

The forces that shape the curriculum inevitably affect the status of academic disciplines, as well as the configuration of knowledge that defines each discipline and the pedagogical methods each favors. The discipline of rhetoric and composition is no exception. Through its long history, rhetoric has inevitably served the reproductive goals of the curriculum, as it does today in its incarnation as composition or freshman English. Central to the classical curriculum, rhetoric taught the sons of the elite to value ancient oratory as the model of eloquence. Marginalized as a service course in the modern technological curriculum, composition teaches the children of the middle class to write clear and correct expository prose. But composition has also supported active resistance to social reproduction. Reproductive education tends to value the needs of society—that is, the needs of business and industry—over the personal development of the individual student. But many composition teachers question this ordering of values.

There are many reasons why composition teachers should be wary about the reproductive goals and strategies of the curriculum, but one particularly important reason is that the college composition course is at the boundary between public mass education and selective higher education. As mass education has expanded, college composition has been at the transition point, the point at which students from hitherto excluded social groups have the chance to enter college. The ability to use academic discourse is crucial to the success of "nontraditional" students, and composition teachers who have concerned themselves with their success are among the small number of college professors who find themselves confronting the contra- dictions of reproductive education. Freshman composition frequently serves as a curricular screen to filter out underprepared students admitted by the college. But composition may also offer a stepping-stone to academic skills and culture for these students. Indeed, the effort to address the problems of nontraditional students—students who are not already comfortable with the social, linguistic, and intellectual conventions of the academic world— is characteristic of many approaches to composition pedagogy. Composition teachers who wish to address the problems of socializing students into academic life have thus been led to ask whether reproductive education serves students themselves or some conception (whose?) of the larger social order and to wonder whether these goals are compatible or hopelessly contradictory.

In what follows, I will trace some steps in the formation of modern curricular ideology in Europe and the United States: the revolutionary eighteenth-century movement to create state-sponsored mass education; the emergence of a mass public school system in the United States in the nineteenth century; the changes that occurred in the colleges in the same period; and the way those changes affected the teaching of composition during the nineteenth and twentieth centuries. In the last section of the essay, I discuss the role of composition in strategies of reproduction and resistance.

Educational Reform in the Eighteenth Century

The desire and the right of the sponsor of education to reproduce itself through that education seems not only inevitable but necessary. But what about the desires and rights of the students themselves? In the eighteenth century, as the rights of individuals were articulated in political terms, educational reformers like Jean-Jacques Rousseau sought to shape a curriculum that respected individual rights. In the egalitarian curriculum imagined by the reformers, knowledge of many kinds, indeed of all kinds, would be offered; the light of reason would supplant religion, tradition, and entrenched interests in shaping curricular values; everyone would be educated, not just the sons of the aristocrats; and self-fulfillment would be the goal of education.

Who would be responsible for providing such an education? Who would support such a curriculum? It seemed certain to Rousseau and his contemporaries that the Jesuits, who controlled much of European education at the time, would not do so.

Anti-Jesuit feeling had been growing throughout Europe for many years, for the order seemed to embody every principle, every attitude, every idea opposed by the spirit of the Enlightenment, the spirit of Newton, Galileo, Bacon, Descartes, and Locke. In the Enlightenment, scientific investigation challenged revelation and tradition as the basis for knowledge. According to the new epistemology, knowledge comes from perception and reflection. Sense perception is a mere physical phenomenon, and perceptions are processed by the basic mental operations of memory and association, common to all people. If knowledge is based on the universal operations of perception and reflection, then it must be (as John Locke said) that all people are fundamentally equal. Inequalities are imposed, it would thus seem, by environment and education. It follows from this empirical approach to knowledge that democracy is the rational form of society and, further, that rationality demands freedom from a priori standards of truth. The curriculum of the Jesuit educational system was a continuing affront to these ideas. The syllogistic logic of scholasticism, based on the deduction of new truths from old, appeared to be totally discredited; the use of Latin as the language of instruction seemed anachronistic and elitist; and reliance on tradition and revelation as the sources of knowledge could be nothing but stubborn error. Moreover, epistemological skepticism joined with egalitarianism to produce the principle (and on some rare occasions the practice) of religious toleration. The militant Catholicism of the Jesuits, militantly embodied in education, was clearly intolerable to enlightened thinkers.

Reformers believed that education should be nationalized, secularized, and made universal and compulsory—for ignorance (as Descartes said) is the root of evil. The Jesuits, more devoted to their religion and their order than to the state, could not be trusted to educate the youth of the nation, says Louis-Rene de la Chalotais in his *Essay on National Education* (1763). La Chalotais defended the prerogatives of his country: "I venture to claim for the nation an education which depends only on the State, because it is essentially a matter for the State, because every nation has an inalienable right to instruct its members, because, in a word, the children of the State ought to be brought up by members of the State" (17). These sentiments were widely shared, for they appealed to advocates of nationalism, anti-clericalism, rationalism, and democracy. Indeed, in 1764, the Jesuits were expelled from France, victims of the Enlightenment. Even the Pope appeared to be enlightened: He abolished the Jesuit order entirely a few years after they were expelled from France.

Rousseau's Paradox Like La Chalotais and others, Rousseau believed that education needed to be nationalized as a positive act of liberation from the narrow curriculum and aims of the Church. Rousseau went farther, advocating universal education for children, not hitherto provided by the Church and not likely ever to be provided by private means. But Rousseau struggled with the implications of nationalization for the ends of education. Education, he believed, had two chief goals: first, to develop the powers of the individual, and second, to develop citizenship. There is something of a contradiction here, as Rousseau realized, for if the society that controlled education imparted its character to the system through citizenship education, then a truly liberating education for the individual could come only from a truly democratic state. There should, ideally, be no difference between self-fulfillment and citizenship. Thus, he concluded, education reform would have to follow the reform of society as a whole. In the meantime, students might be educated with an eye to individual development by fostering in them a critical view of citizenship and by leading them to test the ideas and habits promoted by social institutions against the dictates of their own reasons. Rousseau did not believe that education of this kind could of itself change society. It was simply an expedient. Society, he held, would have to be changed by other means.

In the meantime, the removal of the Jesuits in 1764 eliminated a considerable part of the French educational system. Some sort of national curriculum had to be established. Rousseau's ideas on education had wide currency, and in a remarkably short time they would dominate educational thinking. His emphasis on child psychology, for example, led educators to take account of the stages of intellectual and social development in designing curricula and developing pedagogical methods for elementary education. But there was considerable opposition to Rousseau's ideas, too. The Church was not gone, even if the Jesuits were, and the Church was not friendly toward the iconoclastic Rousseau. Nor was the government disposed to favor a scheme as revolutionary as the one he had proposed. The scheme for national education offered by La Chalotais in his anti-Jesuit screed was far less threatening.

La Chalotais stressed citizenship education, which should be guaranteed by an educational system that mirrored society and conduced to its best interests. Look again at the words of La Chalotais: the business about "inalienable rights" is disarmingly familiar, so note that La Chalotais is speaking of the rights of the State, not the rights of Man. The interests of the State dictate, in his view, that laborers should learn mechanical skills, but not reading and writing, which will just make them dissatisfied with their status. Relatively few people need advanced education, he says. To assure that the State's interests are observed, La Chalotais recommends that a Royal commission be appointed to settle the details of the curriculum and arrange for the writing and publication of standard textbooks in every subject and at every level. Faced for the first time with the questions of state-sponsored education, France and other nations favored the kind of approach offered by La Chalotais, one that displaced the frankly elitist classical curriculum while preserving traditional class distinctions.

The national curriculum was still on the agenda at the time of the French Revolution in 1789. Now, when the character of the state and the nature of state-sponsored education were both being debated, Rousseau's paradox was an immediate concern. Whose concerns were primary, those of the individual or those of the state? The individual-liberty faction fretted over the problem of how education for free individual development could be accommodated to citizenship education even under a democratic government if the interests of the state limited freedom at all, even to the extent of requiring schooling. Those who dogmatically equated liberty with the state's interests saw no problem here: children belonged to the state and owed it loyalty, which was to be inculcated through universal education. The practical solution that resulted from this debate was an uninspiring compromise: universal compulsory childhood education, centrally-produced textbooks, a basic standard curriculum that included civics, some attention to age-appropriate teaching, and greater independence for teachers.

Equal Opportunity A more interesting result of the education debate was the formulation by the Marquis de Condorcet, in 1792, of the principle of *equal opportunity* in education. It is clear, he asserts, that people are not equal, either in natural ability or in the circumstances of birth. The state cannot make people equal, but it should provide an education that will at minimum allow each citizen to act with some independence. Beyond that, each individual should have the chance to develop his or her (yes, her) natural abilities. Condorcet urges schools to teach positive knowledge and not deal with religion, politics, or morality. And he proposes an elaborate hierarchy of tuition-free schools with admission at each level based entirely on ability.

Equal opportunity appears to reconcile the contradiction between individual development and social reproduction—but only if the structure of society is benign. Condorcet believed in human perfectibility and hoped to see the creation of a truly revolutionary society in which natural differences would indeed be the only differences between people. But his hopes for the Revolution were to be disappointed. In France and throughout Europe, democratic movements failed and educational reform slowed to a crawl: monarchs, aristocrats, and established churches feared that education would lead to revolution and resisted attempts to extend state education to the "lower orders." When, in the late nineteenth century, universal education again appeared on state agendas, Condorcet's notion of equal opportunity would also reappear—this time, however, as a rationale for unequal education in an unequal society.

The University Curriculum The eighteenth century was a time of vigorous educational theorizing, but the reformers' schemes for curricular expansion and universal access to education did not come to fruition. Indeed, schooling in Europe changed very little during the century. Elementary education expanded somewhat to include more middle-class children, though the curriculum was limited to reading, writing, and religion. Grammar schools generally held to the classical curriculum, preparing students for the university by teaching Latin and Greek grammar. The "dissenting academies" sponsored by non-Anglican Protestant churches in England included training in agriculture and trades, but these schools were a rare exception to the rule.

In the universities, Enlightenment science and philosophy were forbidden. Only in Germany did the universities begin to share in the new spirit of inquiry by working to expand the curriculum and support research. Elsewhere, universities held fast to a curriculum that seemed—and indeed was—out-of-date and out of touch with contemporary ideas and needs. The great scientists and philosophers of the era were rarely associated with the universities, which seemed to be little more than relics of the Middle Ages.

The new knowledge of the Enlightenment spread through the efforts of private societies, which sponsored lectures and publications. Some of the societies came to be state-supported, a sign of the growing split between national needs and church-dominated education. Only rarely did new ideas penetrate the traditional curriculum. Change would come later, through the social pressures of the nineteenth century.

Democratic Education in the United States

In the United States, where the Revolution did not fail as it had in France, the potential for equal and equalizing democratic education seemed tremendous. The idea of equal opportunity was enthusiastically adopted in the creation of state school systems during the nineteenth century. In America, equal opportunity was promoted as the opportunity for equality: schools would be the route to progress, to civic virtue, to economic vitality, and to a universal aristocracy, with the universities as the training ground for the leaders of a democratic society.

The school system of the United States has been lauded in these terms since its inception. But "The Great School Legend," as Colin Greer calls it, has led historians of education to "mistake the rhetoric of good intentions for historical reality" (4). Despite masses of evidence to the contrary, American legislators, historians, and educators (including composition teachers) persist in believing that schools change social status. Only recently have a significant number of scholars accepted the apparent fact that, as

Herbert Gans says, "educational success follows upon economic success, and not the other way around" (Foreword in Greer, xiii). Where economic opportunities opened for poorer groups (e.g., for immigrant groups in the Northeast during periods of urban expansion), later generations in those groups could take advantage of schooling. But those subject to persistent economic discrimination, like blacks and the urban poor, have not been helped by the schools. The schools have generally failed to serve the interests of poor and working-class students. Rather, they have perpetuated class distinctions and reproduced the race, class, and gender discriminations found in culture and society. "America," says Greer, "is a very conservative society which likes to claim that it is devoted to equality and social change. It has a public school system designed to preserve that contradiction — by institutionalizing the rhetoric of change to preserve social status" (59).

Equal opportunity provides access to education but not necessarily education itself. Students for whom school represents an alien culture frequently fail or do poorly. For them, the myth of equal opportunity means that they lack the intrinsic ability to make it in a meritocracy. This negative certification proves to them, to the school, and to "society" that they do not deserve advancement. Moreover, educational success does not necessarily translate into economic success. Race, gender, and class background continue to be more important determinants of economic success than educational attainment. White men from the middle and upper classes, in other words, get the greatest benefit from their education. Finally, the class structure of the United States has not changed significantly during the past one hundred years despite a significant rise in the average educational level of the populace. If anything, the distribution of wealth has become less equitable during the twentieth century. The evident rise in status of some individuals and segments of the population hitherto excluded from the upper economic strata has contributed to the myth of equal opportunity without much affecting the distribution of inequality. As Rousseau recognized, education cannot change the nature of society. Giving citizens more education does not change the nature of work or the structure of the economy. Indeed, it appears that the nature of the economy determines the effects of education.

There was no Edenic period for American education. From the beginning, the goal of education for equality and individual fulfillment was an ideal not realized. The United States achieved much of what the French reformers dreamed of: by the mid-nineteenth century, American education was clearly moving toward a system of free, tax-supported, state-run, compulsory education. But the system's structure, curriculum, and effects were decisively shaped by the economic order: by the factory system, urbanization, and the corporate economy.

The development of state-run public schools in the United States was heavily promoted by the factory owners and the middle class, who quite explicitly wished to produce trained and obedient factory workers while providing a tax-supported system of secondary education for their own children. Under the factory system, wage labor became the source of income for most Americans, those who had been craftsmen and small farmers as well as new immigrants. Discipline and control were necessary for the smooth operation of factories, and schools were able to prepare people psychologically for such work. The elements of the overt curriculum—literacy and computational skills—may have had some value on the job. But for most workers and their employers, the overt curriculum was irrelevant. What mattered was the socializing effect of schooling—patience and submission to discipline—which are valued by employers and thus valuable to employees, who were encouraged to see these qualities as "application" and training in the "work ethic."

Public primary schools were for the most part readily accepted innovations, for they appeared to benefit people of all classes. But in many communities, workers and farmers resisted tax-based secondary schools because they saw little chance to benefit from them. Even if the wealthy paid most of the taxes, the workers would nonetheless be assessed for buildings, teachers, and supplies for schools that few of their children could hope to attend. This feeling of opposition conflicted with the hope that through education at least some of the sons of the working class could themselves become wealthy. The system, after all, appeared democratic. Those who excelled in school might continue on, though few in fact did. Education made class mobility possible for a few individuals, but for the working class as a body, education did not alter the status quo.

Toward the end of the nineteenth century, it appeared that one way to promote and equalize secondary education was through vocational schools. But as many workers realized and fledgling unions pointed out, vocational education expands the pool of skilled workers, creating an unemployment reserve that allows for greater wage control. And indeed, among the great promoters of elementary and vocational education were Rockefeller, Morgan, and the National Association of Manufacturers, who admitted that they sought not only skilled laborers but also the benefits of wage-inflation control (and, it may be added, the restraints of law and brute force when they were needed). Antonio Gramsci saw the dilemma clearly, predicting that the vocational schools proposed as part of Italy's educational reform would "crystallize social differences in Chinese complexity" (40).

The principle of equal opportunity seemed to call for a hierarchy of schools and curricula, just as Condorcet had proposed. The "equal opportunity" argument, of course, does not claim to create equality, but merely to allow everyone to rise to the highest level given "natural" ability. Equal opportunity was to offer a chance to overcome the inequities of birth and prejudice. No employer will overlook talent, the argument goes, to focus on race or class or gender, such prejudice being contrary to the more important profit motive. But the real function of the equal opportunity argument, given the actual effects of schooling, is to depoliticize the school and to defuse economic class conflict. The equal opportunity argument presents the curriculum, with its variety of practical and academic choices, as a ladder for climbing through the social strata, and suggests that natural ability or its absence accounts for one's place in the social order.

The elaborately stratified school system appears, too, to take the needs of the child into account, but it defines those needs almost exclusively in terms of job prospects. Both individual and national interests are purportedly served by preparing future workers with the skills and attitudes necessary for their jobs. The very inequality of school achievement serves a useful purpose in socialization, as Frank Freeman pointed out in 1924: "It is the business of the school to help the child acquire such an attitude toward the inequalities of life, whether in accomplishment or in reward, that he may adjust himself to its conditions with the least possible friction" (quoted in Bowles and Gintis 102).

Education cannot create equality, cultural or economic, in an unequal society. Modern schools have become a highly refined system for preserving the ideology of their new sponsor. During the nineteenth century, the national interest came to be identical to the interests of business for the United States and most European nations. Government-sponsored education was and still is education for the needs of business and industry. These needs are addressed by the hierarchy of schools, programs, and tracks from elementary grades to the university—which has become a part of the system of national-economic education.

College and National Education

Education has always reflected social status. Those who received the most education were those in the upper ranks of society, those with the leisure and resources required for advanced schooling. Liberal studies were, by definition, for those who were liberated from social and economic constraints. The liberal arts—defined by the medieval trivium (grammar, logic, rhetoric), the Renaissance quadrivium (history, music, mathematics, astronomy), and the Enlightenment subjects (modern language, philosophy, and science)—were the preserve of those who were already free, already citizens in the old sense of identifying their lot with the state's. The university, accessible only to those in this class, offered study that was of use to those who moved in the cosmopolitan sphere of politics and culture, or in the three professions, law, the clergy, and medicine.

During the eighteenth century, however, the university curriculum was under pressure from the same sources that had called for nationalization of the schools. The same charges made against the Jesuits in France could be and were justly made against the traditional universities of Europe. For the most part, as we have seen, the traditional universities resisted both the new philosophy and the politics it implied. Only government-sponsored reforms, such as those in Germany, and eventually the formation of colleges—

which sprang up on the margins of the universities and were later absorbed into them—forced the universities to admit the sciences, the vernacular, and their associated changes into the system.

Colleges in the United States were somewhat more progressive than European universities in admitting the new learning into the curriculum. The colonial colleges adhered to the classical curriculum, following the English model. But they were soon forced by student pressure and declining enrollments to experiment with science courses and even utilitarian subjects. Newer colleges opened after the Revolution readily mixed the old and new curricula, and the older schools soon followed. As colleges were founded through the new states, the curriculum reflected the concerns of the local constituency, which meant, by and large, an increase in agricultural, mechanical, and commercial subjects. Congress promoted science teaching in higher education as an aid to progress, and the Land Grant Act of 1862 stimulated the creation of colleges devoted to agricultural and mechanical studies.

The new subjects vied with the old for curricular space, but soon the colleges adopted the German model of departmentalization, adding the innovations of majors, electives, and tracks to solve the problem of curriculum packing. All of these developments sorted well with the American spirit of democracy and equality. Students could choose from a variety of courses, from the classical to the vocational. English replaced Latin as the language of instruction. The college degree created a technocratic class to rival the old aristocracy. (Many of the technocrats would send their sons to Harvard, demonstrating the power of "equal opportunity" to overcome the inequities of birth.) The university offered not one kind of study, the one considered the highest, but all kinds of study. Electives, departments, and majors changed the nature of the "course" of education from continuous study to a set of concurrent semester-long offerings. Courses were commodified: they could be "taken." And the variety of colleges—technical schools, business schools, junior colleges, and public universities—made college education more accessible to the population. A relatively small number of men and a much smaller number of women actually went to college, of course: In 1870, only 1.7 percent of the 18- to 21-year-old population was enrolled (Bowles and Gintis 201). And the prestigious universities kept the liberal arts at the center of the curriculum. Still, the changes in college education suggested openness to the democratic ideal, and soon enough, college enrollments would increase dramatically, with dramatic effects on the curriculum.

Rhetoric and Composition Repackaging the curriculum also affected the rhetoric-composition course. Rhetoric courses through most of the nineteenth century generally combined the eighteenth-century approaches of elocution, belles lettres, and psychology. These three approaches had already brought rhetoric into line with Enlightenment politics and philosophy. The first of these approaches, elocution, focused on effective delivery and proper pronunciation. Popular in Scotland, Ireland, and America, elocution promised to flatten dialects and teach people how to talk "proper" upper-class English. Elocution thus helped to break down the social barrier of linguistic discrimination between the upper and middle classes.

Belles lettres, the second approach to rhetoric, encompassed oratory, poetry, history, philosophy, and literary criticism—all branches of "fine writing," ancient and modern. Belletristic rhetoric was intellectually modern in combining a respectful attitude toward classical culture with increased regard for vernacular literature, and politically advanced in making a digest of high culture that could be used by the middle class. Belles lettres used literary examples to demonstrate both rhetorical and critical ideas, and students of belletristic rhetoric would write essays demonstrating their literary judgment.

Finally, the psychological theory of rhetoric explained the construction of rhetorical appeals in terms of appeals to particular mental "faculties," such as reason and imagination. This theory brought rhetoric into line with the chief philosophical currents of the age, including the notion that everyone was psychologically equal. In the nineteenth century, psychological rhetoric gave rise to the so-called "modes of discourse" on the theory that exposition, narration, description, and argument would be more effective if their special qualities were presented in isolation. These three theories made rhetoric the most modern of the old university disciplines. Many arguments against classical education were voiced during the nineteenth century, but rhetoric was rarely included in the attack. Indeed, rhetoric was closely associated with the needs of the new middle-class students of the expanded universities.

But the coalition of interests combined in the rhetoric course soon fell apart. Chairs of English literature appeared in Europe and the United States, and belles lettres moved to this new place in the curriculum. The rhetoric course now concentrated on speech and composition, relying more and more on prescriptive grammar, the sorry remains of scholastic logic, the modes of discourse, and new inventions like paragraph unity. In the early years of the twentieth century, speech went into a separate department, leaving rhetoric as the unwanted charge of the English department.

Rhetoric was defined by its fin de siècle proponents as the art of efficient communication, a suitable definition for a subject that emphasized correctness. Rhetoric, says Adams Sherman Hill in his *Principles of Rhetoric* (1878), is knowledge used as power. But rhetoric for Hill means, chiefly, correct expository writing, and the power he refers to is the power to make a living. As James Berlin puts it, the freshman composition course became, under Hill and the many like him, a course in business writing decorated with snippets of literature (*Writing Instruction* 63). In the new middle-class colleges, composition was a required course for freshmen, taught by assistant professors of English and graduate assistants. The emphasis in these courses was on expository writing. Persuasion, deemphasized in

Hill's book and its successors, came to be associated with oral performance and was relegated to the elocution course. The "current-traditional" model of composition teaching that was thus created in the last years of the nineteenth century was a necessity because of the large number of students and the constant turnover of new instructors who needed straightforward methods to teach a subject that they generally hoped to leave behind as soon as possible.

It Pays to Increase Your Word Power

Though much reduced in status and universally vilified as a stultifying wasteland, composition was nevertheless required for most freshmen. What purpose did this composition course serve in the college curriculum? For one thing, it straddled the two cultures of science and the humanities, opponents in the loudest internal curriculum battle in the university. Science was defended as the source of technological progress, guarantor of a rising standard of living, while the humanities were there to preserve the culture that would enliven the leisure hours of the technocrats. The composition course served as an introduction to both cultures, the scientific and humanistic. On the one hand, composition was a technical skill: writing could be described in terms of grammar and psychologically-justified modes of presentation, and it used logic as a way to ensure correct thinking. On the other hand, composition was illustrated by literature, which was presented as the exemplary form of descriptive, narrative, and even expository composition. Moreover, the composition course was amenable to a technical theory of curriculum-making that emerged at the end of the last century and has continued to affect curriculum work at all levels of education.

The technical theory of curriculum focuses on learning efficiency, relying on the methods of scientific psychology for measuring outcomes. This approach complements a view of education as skills development and problem solving in the service of technological progress. The technical approach to curriculum-making treated education as a form of manufacturing, fitting together interchangeable parts in an efficient sequence. Schools and college classroom buildings were even designed to look like factories (Jonas Clark Hall at Clark University was designed, I was told, to be converted into a shoe factory if the school failed).

In the technically-oriented curriculum, knowledge is treated as a neutral set of skills and facts, accessible, presumably, to anyone. Failure means the student's failure to apply himself to the task. Failure is therefore the student's responsibility. For college students at the turn of the century and the first decades of the twentieth century, this form of applied Calvinism was a test of the individual's pretensions to learning, and perhaps not an unreasonable test. After all, college promised a certain kind of success, and a certain kind of knowledge and skill was its price. Even so, this approach to teaching—especially in the public schools and in colleges later in the century—legitimates the traditional culture of the privileged classes by treating it as neutral fact, obtainable by mental labor regardless of socialization. To some extent, as we have already noted in the case of "equal opportunity" in public education, it is indeed possible to overcome socialization through mental labor. Such mental labor *is* a form of socialization, belated and sometimes painful, especially in its derogation of other forms of culture, social experience, language use, and even personal relations. The claim that education produced a meritocracy was "proved" by students who "transcended" their class origins, and the meritocracy reciprocally endorsed both the neutrality of school knowledge and the equal-opportunity claims of the school.

The "current-traditional" composition course embodies even today the aura of technical neutrality or objectivity. Studies of composition textbooks continue to find an overwhelming emphasis on correctness, the modes of discourse, and even old-style logic. The course's origin in the elite college curriculum is revealed in the literary and belletristic essays that illustrate the modes of discourse. The connection of this writing to a specific class culture is hidden by presenting the modes as ideal types of psychological universals. The message is that facts dictate culture, rather than the other way around. (E. D. Hirsch's theory of cultural literacy depends on the same notion, for he claims that access to social rewards, the development of creative habits of mind, and the formation of a unified society are functions of memorizing "facts.")

In the 1920s, the Progressive education movement offered another model of curriculum development, one that would result in a subjective rhetoric based on personal expression. The Progressive movement revived Rousseau's ideal of linking citizenship and individual education by treating the principles of democracy as a ground for a consistent view of personal development and social responsibility. Schools, in this view, should be workshops for democratic activity, in which students would find their own best interests coinciding with communal interests. The Progressives admitted that, in practice, personal needs were necessarily economic: The fully developed individual was one who could take a job, do it well, and thereby benefit society. With Rousseau's ideal, it seems, comes Rousseau's paradox, and though the Progressive movement could not escape the paradox, it did stimulate the articulation of ameliorative theories of education that challenged the positivism of the technocrats.

Knowledge is socially constructed in these new learner-centered theories, a function of the way that individuals interpret experience and communicate their understanding, sharing it with the community. The claim that knowledge is objective thus comes to seem an unacceptable imposition upon the individual. The Progressives defined this imposition as "ideological" in a purely negative sense, an appeal to a standard of meaning that is manufactured without the individual's participation or consent.

Many colleges responded to these ideas—identified sometimes as progressive and sometimes as liberal—by promoting "general" education. Technical education, specialization, and professionalization were well established in the curriculum. They were even described as "liberal," in the sense that liberation from material need was the bottom line for both the individual and civilization. Now seemed a good time, though, to revive education for personal needs and desires beyond mere economic security, to seek shared cultural experiences and values, to remember that culture (meaning high culture) needed to be preserved, and to promote openmindedness. Colleges reviewed their core curricula and distribution requirements, restoring them if they had been dropped in the elective craze.

In some colleges, usually the more elite ones, composition courses used creative writing, reflective essays, and autobiography as an alternative to the dominant model of expository writing. Students were to express their own meanings, to regard themselves as artists, to be original in thought and style. The literary models widely used in the expository course were more relevant in the expressive course, not only to the students, who were supposed to be stimulated (rather than cowed) by them, but also to the teachers, the graduate students, and assistant professors of English whose professional focus was on literary study.

Composition in the Modern Curriculum

For all the expansion of colleges in the United States, only a tiny percentage of the 18-to-21-year-old population attended college before World War II—about 12 percent in 1930, for example (Rudolph 210). College men were still the social, professional, and industrial elite. After the war, the proportion rose to about 20 percent (Bowles and Gintis 201). The new postwar student population was not very different from the old in the matter of choosing courses and majors, with vocational and preprofessional curricula outdistancing the arts. At the same time, however, graduate education expanded to receive the academic and professional elite. The technical rationale continued to dominate the undergraduate curriculum, including the composition course. Expository writing and grammar suited the generally practical goals of most colleges and their students. Except in a few elite colleges, the expressive writing course became a separate creative-writing course.

In the 1960s, personal writing revived as an expression of the political movements for civil rights, against the Bomb, and then against the Vietnam War. Once again, positivism (that is, the theory of objective knowledge) was opposed by an interpretive epistemology. People made meaning, and claims to the contrary were regarded as the means of oppression. Students in personal-writing courses would try to find their own voices, their own ways of seeing and understanding the world. To promote this search for authenticity was considered subversive teaching. It questioned authority, including the teacher's, even suggesting that students could learn to write without teachers.

Expressivism in composition promoted subjectivity as a form of opposition to both positivism and political oppression. Like the counterculture movement with which it was in many ways allied, expressivism saw no need for a deep analysis of society or politics. The badness of the established order was perfectly obvious. The goal was to make a positive change, to give individuals control over meanings, and to create a setting for democratic sharing of meanings. Deeply distrustful of politics and ideology as forms of anti-individual power, most expressivist teachers rejected the idea of collective resistance, and the political basis of the movement evaporated in the 1970s. James Berlin reflects bitterly that expressivism is "easily co-opted by the very capitalist forces it opposes. After all, this rhetoric can be used to reinforce the entrepreneurial virtues capitalism most values: individualism, private initiative, the confidence for risk-taking, the right to be contentious with authority" ("Rhetoric and Ideology" 487). In other areas of the curriculum, including education theory, the experience was much the same. Models of personal interpretation of knowledge turned on subjectivism, and political critique became merely implicit (Giroux).

Education in the 1960s also reacted to Sputnik. Science and mathematics became curricular priorities, well supported by grants and scholarships. In the public schools, tracking was part of the drive to promote achievement, preferably scientific, by the better students. Schools and colleges expanded their use of standardized tests in the effort to find and reward genius. But tracking and testing followed race and class lines, not surprisingly. Resources flowing to more affluent school districts led to a balkanization of schools along class lines. In 1967, Kenneth Clark complained that "American public schools have become significant instruments in the blocking of economic mobility and in the intensification of class distinctions" (quoted in Ciancanelli 195).

During the 1960s, IQ testing was touted as a way of measuring intelligence without respect to race or class. The results of IQ tests completely overshadowed sociological studies that confirmed Kenneth Clark's observation about classist schooling and offered instead psychological arguments for the genetic incapacity of blacks and the poor. IQ purported to explain in scientific terms why there were class lines and racial distinctions in school and economic achievement. Bolstered by this confirmation that natural ability was the only bar to success in society, equal-opportunity education and compensatory education appeared to be liberal triumphs. In addition, the object of educational research shifted from the school to the students, always a sign of the distance between the needs of society and the development of the individual.

It seemed only natural to turn cognitive testing into a tool for improving educational efficiency. Drawing on the scientific status of psychology, education research renewed its connection with the belief in objective knowledge. Psychological universals, once discovered, would guide curriculum design and assure appropriate attention to the student's needs. Like other student-centered movements, this one turned up a tremendous amount of information about the ways that students learn and focused attention on their needs. But applying this information to curriculum design had mixed results. On the one hand, teachers (or more precisely, teachers who had access to the necessary resources) could adapt their teaching methods to students' "learning styles," sometimes with striking results. On the other hand, psychological theories could, like the IQ results, suggest the incapacity of students to do certain kinds of work. Both results affected the cognitive study of the writing process.

Process became a byword in the 1970s. Writing teachers wished to validate the complex and messy process of false starts, dead ends, and revision that practiced writers took for granted, but which frequently dismayed students. Cognitivists naturally saw the process as mental. Similarly, the nineteenth-century psycho-rhetoricians had tried to align the modes of discourse with the mental faculties, though they focused on the reader rather than the writer. The connections between the two approaches are more than fortuitous: Both begin by assuming that there is a correspondence between the structures of the mind and of language. And both hope to end by describing the most effective way to match them together.

The universal model of the composing process sought by modern cognitivists also appears to neutralize social differences between students. The process takes precedence over the content; it is cognitive, not social, it relies on strategies, not cultural background or life experiences, and its proponents have claimed that it rises above politics. Like other objective methods, it treats failure as the student's responsibility, as mental incapacity or lack of effort (Bizzell). Once again, an equal chance and an equal method help to rationalize the claim that differences are only natural.

Mina Shaughnessy and others pointed to the possibility that students' writing problems weren't mental, but social. Shaughnessy was responding not to the still-young cognitive process approach, but to the experience of composition teachers in the open-admissions program at the City University system in New York during the early 1970s. At CUNY and other colleges with expanded admissions programs, a battle raged over the basic or remedial writing course. Should students get the economically productive (hence economically liberating) course in grammar and exposition or the politically hip (hence personally liberating) course in personal writing? Personal writing was attractive to many instructors who saw it as a way to interest students in what they wrote about, to generate writing without the additional impediment of academic subjects and styles. But in 1977, Shaughnessy said clearly what many teachers were feeling, that personal writing did not prepare students for success in college. Their authentic voices were not useful in any other part of the curriculum. A course that often helped middle-class students get some distance on the forms of their own socialization would actually impede students who were not similarly prepared for the college experience. Composition teachers who wished to help these students needed to help them cross the chasm between the cultural and linguistic forms they brought to college and those that counted for success in college.

Open admissions ended at CUNY in 1975, but at many state universities, at community colleges, and in a growing number of private colleges as well, the student population has expanded to include many black, Hispanic, working-class, and otherwise nontraditional students. As always, the success or failure of these students will not affect in any way the equal-opportunity argument that their very presence in college seems to support. Nor will their success in school necessarily translate into economic success: "Access to higher education," says John Beverley, "no longer guarantees youth from working-class backgrounds a higher income than that attained by their parents" (69). Reproductive education has shifted inexorably upward to the college level, with attendant stratification of schools and proletarianization of middle-management jobs (Bowles and Gintis 202–211). With about 40 percent of the college-aged population in attendance, college now has much the same role in the reproduction of labor that high school did in 1928 (Rudolph 212).

The change in the character of many colleges and the presence of so many nontraditional students represents a special challenge to composition teachers, who work on the boundary between the students' home culture and the academic culture with its potential (however small) for social and economic advancement. How can students be helped to succeed in school — which is, after all, what they want and what teachers are paid to do — without simply acquiescing to the school's reproductive purpose? Many composition teachers and theorists have turned for aid to the work of Brazilian educator Paulo Freire, who recommends education for critical consciousness — that is, learning to see and criticize economic and cultural contradictions. Learning to see these contradictions leads to an understanding of the dominant class language and culture without (ideally) being co-opted by it.

Two lines of explicitly political composition theory have tried to take Freire's advice. One is based on Freire's method of asking students to reflect upon their own experience in an effort to see how their attitudes and knowledge have been shaped by unexamined assumptions about society, culture, job experiences and expectations, and, mostly, previous schooling. What Freire calls "banking education" tends to correspond to the experience most students have had of schooling, namely, that they were treated as repositories of information on which they were expected to draw as needed. Freire's method calls upon students not only to critique the banking method and to explore its implications, but also to take responsibility for their own learning.

The other method is based on an attempt to demystify the conventions of academic discourse, to reveal, as explicitly as possible, the tacit assumptions that govern academic writing, in general and in each discipline. If students fail because they have not been socialized, through home experience and congenial schooling, to academic ways of thinking and using language, then it is imperative to show them how the system works. Writing is a form of social behavior as well as a complex system for manipulating knowledge, and the two functions are inseparable. The academic-discourse approach tries to make the operations of such a discourse visible and accessible, both for use and for critique.

Both methods hope to ease students' entry into the academic community, to empower students who might be filtered out by an objectified curriculum. If this were all, then these methods would be no more than efficient techniques for reproduction. But the goal, at least in theory, is to move from demystification to critical consciousness, to a more general awareness for students that knowledge is made by groups for their own purposes. The goal of critical consciousness makes it necessary to ask about the purposes of the knowledge in the curriculum, to bring into the rhetoric course itself the problems of differential socialization and learning, the rationalizations of equal opportunity, the premises of meritocracy, and the distance between education for individual fulfillment and for the requirements of society.

The critical-consciouness efforts in composition theory represent a way of articulating our current version of Rousseau's Paradox, of reflecting on the ideologies of the curriculum, and of resisting the current forms of social reproduction carried on by the school. Indeed, the critical-consciousness theories represent an important link between composition and the politics of the curriculum as a whole.

The distance between the culture represented by the traditional college curriculum and the culture of college students has been increasing. Many students are from working-class and minority families. Many are from middle-income families but have little connection to bourgeois culture—their extracurricular time is spent working, not in the drama club or even in sports. Most of them continue the trend of electing job-named courses of study that has characterized the last one hundred years of college expansion in the United States. But few of these students are going into the technocratic elite. Most will be workers in the postindustrial corporations, part of a "proletarianized" middle class. The colleges they attend are clearly part of nationalized education, serving purposes that secondary schools served not long ago. Colleges are more stratified, universities more internally tracked. Community colleges have become, in Stanley Aronowitz's words, little more than "masked unemployment" (87). Fewer and fewer of our students are the heirs to the traditional university culture or products of old-style bourgeois education. These are students for whom access to knowledge requires differential socialization and for whom a critical distance from a consumption-for-progress lifestyle can be liberating.

Yet college curricula and college professors are products of the elite part of the system. Humanities teachers, especially, may regard the arts as a refuge and decry the philistinism of their vocationally-oriented students. As John McDermott has cogently argued, "University professors as a group seem exceptionally uncritical of the limited value—and values—of a university education and the acculturation it represents." Students who come to share their values will, they believe, "be more sophisticated, more interested in good literature, more sensitive morally . . . These students will also be free of the more provincial ties of home, hometown, region, and class. In short, most academics take it as an article of faith that students benefit by exchanging their own culture for that of the university" (92).

Some students make this bargain and profit by it, as students have always done. But for an increasing number of others, the bargain is an equivocal one. McDermott argues that the traditional virtue of tolerance, essential for professionals and leaders, translates for most students into passive acceptance of the tyranny of a system that "impersonally" distributes credentials and rewards. Elite education, say Bowles and Gintis, is hardly appropriate in any case in colleges where 50 percent of the population will attend (206). College is becoming more like the public school system, providing job skills and appropriate attitudes for work. This development is quite clear in the rigid curricula of community colleges, business schools, rural state colleges, and vocational majors that combine skills with a liberal arts curriculum that still reflects the cultural milieu that served the professional goals of an earlier era in college life.

As composition teaching becomes professionalized and its professional agenda emerges, the composition class can become a critical site for reflecting on these problems. The profession has shown its desire to find, in expressive and communal theories of writing, a means of doing so. Composition teachers are already part of the effort to push the college curriculum to address the problem of the alienation of local culture by university culture. Critical consciousness has been and continues to be a goal of the profession. Composition theory has itself become an exercise in critical consciousness, drawing the hidden curriculum into the open and facing its consequences. The contradictions of the curriculum and the society it serves are becoming familiar as themes in composition courses. This is as it should be. Composition is relatively unprotected by "content" from the needs of students, and it behooves composition teachers and theorists to take a wide and enlightened definition of those needs and of the pressures that create them. This is a challenge that, to its credit, composition readily accepts.

Works Cited

Aronowitz, Stanley. *False Promises: The Shaping of American Working Class Consciousness.* New York: McGraw-Hill, 1973.

Berlin, James. "Rhetoric and Ideology in the Writing Class." *College English* 50 (September 1988): 477–494.

————. *Rhetoric and Reality: Writing Instruction in American Colleges, 1900–1985.* Carbondale: Southern Illinois University Press, 1987.

————. *Writing Instruction in Nineteenth-Century American Colleges.* Carbondale: Southern Illinois University Press, 1984.

Beverley, John. "Higher Education and Capitalist Crisis." *Socialist Review* 42 (1978): 67–91.

Bizzell, Patricia. "Cognition, Convention, and Certainty: What We Need to Know About Writing." *PRE/TEXT* 3 (1982): 213–243.

Bowles, Samuel, and Herbert Gintis. *Schooling in Capitalist America: Educational Reform and the Contradictions of Economic Life.* New York: Basic Books, 1976.

Boyd, William, and Edmund J. King. *The History of Western Education* (1921). 10th ed. New York: Barnes and Noble, 1972.

Ciancanelli, Penelope. "Politics and Public School Reform." In *U.S. Capitalism in Crisis.* Ed. Bruce Steinberg et al. New York: The Union for Radical Political Economics, 1978.

Freire, Paulo. *Education for Critical Consciousness.* New York: Seabury, 1973.

————. *Pedagogy of the Oppressed* (1968). Trans. Myra Bergman Ramos. New York: Seabury, 1970.

Giroux, Henry A. *Ideology, Culture, and the Process of Schooling.* Philadelphia: Temple University Press, 1981.

Gramsci, Antonio. *Selections from the Prison Notebooks.* Ed. and Trans. Quintin Hoare and Geoffrey N. Smith. New York: International, 1971.

Greer, Colin. *The Great School Legend: A Revisionist Interpretation of American Public Education.* New York: Basic Books, 1972.

La Chalotais, Louis-Rene de. *Essay on National Education* (1763). Trans. H. R. Clark. London: Arnold, 1934.

McDermott, John. "Campus Missionaries: The Laying on of Culture." In *Studies in Socialist Pedagogy.* Eds. Theodore M. Norton and Bertell Ollman. New York: Monthly Review Press, 1978.

Rousseau, Jean-Jacques. *Emile* (1762). Trans. Allan Bloom. New York: Basic Books, 1979.

————. *The Minor Educational Writings of Rousseau.* Trans. William Boyd. London: Blackie & Son, 1911.

————. *Rousseau on Education.* Trans. R. L. Archer. London: Arnold, 1912.

Rudolph, Frederick. *Curriculum: A History of the American Undergraduate Course of Study Since 1636.* San Francisco: Jossey-Bass, 1977.

Shaughnessy, Mina. *Errors and Expectations.* New York: Oxford University Press, 1977.

7

The Politics of Composition Research: The Conspiracy Against Experience

THOMAS NEWKIRK
University of New Hampshire

When I was in graduate school, one of my fellow students floated a possible dissertation topic to a Speech professor who taught the oral interpretation of literature. Wouldn't it be interesting, the student asked, to determine if oral interpretation improved students' attitudes toward literature? I remember the professor pausing. "Yes, I suppose. But if you find it doesn't help, please don't tell me."

How are we to read this professor's resistance? As the reflexive humanistic reaction to anything objective or numerical, an unwillingness to put cherished approaches to some external test? Or as the healthy skepticism of the practitioner who trusts her reading of her students? Is the response professional or unprofessional? How much should her own sense of her students' reactions count as "knowledge"? To explore these questions, it is necessary to tell a longer story.

This story (or my version of it) begins among the slag heaps of the steel plant in Bethlehem, Pennsylvania. The time is 1898, and because the Spanish-American War had begun, pig iron was suddenly valuable. Eighty thousand tons of it needed to be moved, and efficiency expert Frederick Winslow Taylor was asked to study the hauling operation. When he began his observations, each man hauled about 12 tons a day, but, after conducting a time study of these men, Taylor determined that this figure could be increased to 48 tons per day if the workers would follow the minutely detailed plan he devised. To test his plan, Taylor picked a Dutchman named Schmidt, an enthusiastic worker with seemingly boundless energy. Taylor recorded his initial conversation with Schmidt:

"Schmidt, are you a high-priced man?"
"Vell, I don't know vat you mean."

119

"Oh yes you do. What I want to know is whether you are a high-priced man or not."

"Vell, I don't know what you mean."

"Oh come now, you answer my questions. What I want to find out is whether you are a high-priced man or one of those cheap fellows here."

Taylor explained that a "high-priced man" could make $1.85 a day while the "cheap fellows" were making $1.15. Schmidt naturally wanted to know what a "high-priced man" must do. Taylor explained:

Well, if you are a high-priced man, you will do exactly as this man tells you tomorrow, from morning to night. When he tells you to pick up a pig and walk, you pick it up and walk, and when he tells you to sit down and rest, you sit down and rest. You do that right through the day. And what's more, no back talk. Do you understand that ... Now you come on to work tomorrow morning and I'll know before night whether you are a high-priced man. (quoted in Kakar 143–144)

This small experiment with Schmidt, one of the most famous in organizational management, illustrates one central principle of "Taylorism"—the separation of planning and execution of work. The hierarchical organizational chart that we know so well — with clear vertical lines of authority — represents one of Taylor's major contributions to organizational management. Up until Taylor's arrival at Bethlehem Steel, workers and foremen had considerable freedom to do their work as they saw fit. But, in choosing to be a "high-priced man," Schmidt gave up that freedom. Now he had to work to a script developed by a group of researchers who planned and evaluated his work. Schmidt became an automaton.

It didn't take long for educators to apply principles of industrial management to schooling. Administrators began seeing themselves as managers rather than educators. In 1916, Elwood Cubberly, noted Stanford educator, extended the metaphor to its logical conclusion:

Our schools are, in a sense, factories in which the raw products (children) are to be shaped and fashioned into the products to meet the various demands of life. The specifications for manufacturing come from the demands of 20th century civilization, and it is the business of schools to build students to the specifications laid down. (quoted in Callahan 152)

Students are the raw material—essentially inert—waiting to be "shaped." Teachers are the workers, like Schmidt, who carry out the plans of their superiors, those who make the specifications and outline procedures for meeting those specifications. The curriculum is a production plan—a grammar piece here, a Shakespeare piece here, a government piece here.

Unless everything is "covered" or put in place, the machine, obviously, will not run. (Who wants a machine with missing parts?) These specifications are set by a special class of technocrats or planners who oversee the work of teachers.

Not only is planning placed in the hands of this separate class, evaluation is also deemed too complex for the mere worker (teacher). Consequently, as Linda Darling-Hammond has noted, we have a virtual alphabet soup of accountability plans to evaluate instruction:

> Viewing teachers as semi-skilled, low-paid workers in the mass production of education, policy-makers have sought to change education, to improve it, by "teacher-proofing" it. Over the past decade we have seen the proliferation of elaborate accountability schemes that go by acronyms like MBO (management by objectives), PBBS (performance-based budgeting systems), CBE (competency based education), CBTE (competency based teacher education), and MCT (minimum competency testing). (209)

Because the teacher is often deemed unqualified to judge student progress, a 50-minute reading test is taken as more definitive than observations made over 180 school days.

Even practitioners come to doubt their capacity to make judgments. A friend of mine tells a story about a nurse on her first job. She was speaking to one of her patients, and as they were talking, she glanced over at the heart monitor, where she saw a flat, unmoving line. The nurse gasped, "This man is dead!"—*even as he was talking to her.* She habitually trusted the instrument even if it denied the evidence before her eyes. Central to Taylorism, then, is a denial of the value of the practitioner's experience. Schmidt was told to defer to the wisdom of the efficiency expert, just as the nurse was trained to defer to the monitor, just as the teacher defers to the standardized test.

While this conspiracy against experience was given impetus by the hierarchical organizational structures promoted by Taylor, it has longer roots than that. Plato's theory of knowledge minimizes the value of life experience, no place more elegantly than in the allegory of the cave and the shadows in *The Republic.* In this allegory, humans are chained in a cave so that they can only look forward; there is a fire behind them and between the fire and the prisoners, wood and stone figures are paraded so that they cast shadows on the wall in front of the prisoners, who accept these shadows as "real things." Only the philosopher has the capacity to break the chains, to turn and see the unreality of this shadow show, to go beyond the fire to the more dazzling light of the "intelligible region," and finally to bring this knowledge back to those trapped in the cave — even at the risk of persecution. The habits and actions of daily life — the shadows on the wall—distract humans from those things that are truly "real" and can best be perceived by the philosophers who would act as guardians in Plato's Republic.

Virtually all guides to educational research must reenact this allegory— they must begin by establishing the inadequacy of the more traditional sources of knowledge, what Clifford Geertz calls "local knowledge": custom, ritual, "common sense," and personal experience. In their 1936 textbook, Carter Good A. S. Barr, and Douglas Scates note that arguments from experience are subject to gross inaccuracies, among them:

1. argument from similar or limited number of instances
2. argument from positive instances and the neglect of negative instances
3. omission of evidence contrary to one's conclusions
4. erroneous conclusions due to prepossessions, preconceived ideas, and prejudices. (3)

The scientific method, by contrast, avoids "the treacherous verbalism of ordinary language" (14) and employs the more exact language of mathematics. It aims to be free from emotional bias, and, unlike accounts of personal experience, the scientific experiment is designed so that it can result in verified principles or scientific laws (23). Or, as George Mouly argued in his textbook on educational research: "Thus far we have developed a technology of material things; now we need to devote our efforts to an equally adequate technology of human living" (3).

And clearly, it was the controlled scientific experiment that was to create this "technology of human living." Case studies that focused on detailed observation were deemed inadequate for deriving generalizable principles (an astonishing claim, given Piaget's work, which was available after 1930). Mouly notes that case studies differ from experimentation because they allow more room for subjectivity and intuition—thus weakening the authority of any claims that might be made. But the primary criticism is the same one traditionally made against the value of experience itself— intensive studies of individuals are not likely to provide "any but the most tentative and crude generalizations" (355). The primary scientific value of case studies, according to Mouly, was "as a source of hypotheses to be verified by more rigorous investigation" (355).

While educational researchers like Mouly were undoubtedly sincere in arguing for the promise of science, his position also elevates the researcher class (as distinct from the teacher class) and provides a way for groups of researchers to claim disciplinary status—in Mouly's words "to assume their rightful place among their fellow scientists" (vi). But as Stephen North has noted, this move to professionalism necessitates an attack on one primary source of knowledge in teaching—"lore." Lore is primarily oral; it deals with practical problems; it draws on experience; and it is not subject to rigorous testing (teachers can nominate any idea that seems to work for them). Lore usually takes the form of a narrative; it is an account of trying an approach ("Last semester I had my students . . .").

If the efficacy of "lore" is not attacked, there are no grounds for establishing a class of researchers — a discipline — that sanctions knowledge. North claims that composition studies has attempted to move toward disciplinary status by claiming that reliance on lore has led to a crisis in instruction, one that can be remedied only by an infusion of knowledge created by nonpractitioner communities (scholars and researchers trained in specialized research methodologies). This attack, North claims, has worked:

> By 1980 . . . lore and Practitioner inquiry have been, for most official purposes, anyway, effectively discredited. It is now a second-class sort of knowledge, rapidly approaching the status of superstition — to be held or voiced only apologetically, with deference to the better, new knowledges. . . . (328)

Yet despite this seeming success, North claims that lore persists, absorbing and transforming this new knowledge much in the way a colonized people absorb the customs of the colonizers: ". . . lore is not the sort of thing that can be worn down, let alone eradicated. Not unlike a native religion in a conquered or colonized territory, persecution only seems to make it grow" (328–329).

Early composition researchers — like educational researchers in general — believed that controlled experimental research would provide answers to questions about the teaching of writing and would establish composition studies as a discipline. In *Research in Written Composition* Richard Braddock, Richard Lloyd-Jones, and Lowell Schoer listed questions that might guide researchers in composition. Among them were:

> What is the relative effectiveness of writing shorter and longer papers at various levels of maturity?
> Can a study of the newer types of linguistics help writers?
> Does the oral reading of rough drafts help the elementary school child strengthen "sentence sense"?
> What are the effects of various kinds and amounts of reading on the quality and kinds of writing a person does?
> Can formal study of rhetorical theory or of logic help the writer? (52–53)

Clearly, these questions were posed to encourage researchers to search out general principles of causation through the most powerful methodology available — the experimental design.

But even as these questions were being formulated, some proponents of experimental research were expressing frustration with the slow pace of progress. Donald Campbell and Julian Stanley lamented the "defections [of trained researchers] from experimentation to essay writing" (2). This defection was due to the failure of experimental techniques to live up to the unrealistic expectations of the "Thorndike era." Campbell and Stanley offer this more sober admonition:

> We must somehow inoculate young experimenters against this effect [the rejection of experimentation], and in general must justify experimentation on more pessimistic grounds—not as a panacea, but rather as the only available route to cumulative progress. We must instill in our students the expectation of tedium and disappointment and the duty of thorough persistence, by now so well achieved in the biological and physical sciences. We must expand our students' vow of poverty to include not only the willingness to accept poverty of finances, but also a poverty of experimental results. (3)

In the 1970s, as the focus of research in composition shifted to the writing processes, this impatience with experimental methods turned to a more profound skepticism—and rejection. Donald Graves argued that the decontextualized research report—where the act of teaching is a "treatment"—alienated the very teachers who were supposed to benefit from the research. Mischler criticized the positivistic assumptions upon which experimentation is based; meaning is contextual, and to "strip" the context, as experimental designs do, is to distort the phenomenon the researcher sets out to explain. Stephen North summarizes this disillusionment:

> For a long time, the method [experimentalism] and its practitioners have been regarded by the rest of the field—with a sense of comfort I think—as something of a sleeping giant, upon whose eventual waking Composition might pin its scientific hopes. Investigators have invoked it almost ritually, concluding their reports by looking ahead to the day when their tentative conclusions would be "subject to more rigorous and carefully controlled research," or words to that effect ... But well into the third decade now, the giant has barely stirred. The time may have come to begin wondering whether we haven't misread his quiescence all along—to wonder, in short, whether the giant is sleeping or dying. Or perhaps not a giant after all. (146)

In the remainder of this chapter I would like to explore three major responses to this crisis: one that denies it exists, one that attempts to view qualitative research (case studies and ethnographic studies) as compatible with traditional experimental research, and one that argues for the fundamental distinctiveness of qualitative research.

Denial

George Hillocks' *Research on Written Composition* might be viewed as a linear advance on the 1963 monograph of Braddock, Lloyd-Jones, and

Schoer. Hillocks surveyed over 2,000 studies and then conducted a detailed meta-analysis of 60 studies to determine the effectiveness of general modes of instruction (presentational, environmental, natural process, and individual) and of foci of instruction (grammar and mechanics, sentence combining, models, scales, free writing, inquiry). By aggregating studies and comparing the average gains (measured in standard deviations) of experimental and control groups, Hillocks is able to claim that environmental approaches — those with specific objectives and which engage students in specifiable processes — are "demonstrably more effective" (251) than approaches like "natural process" where there are only general objectives (e.g., fluency, voice), or "presentational," where students are far too passive (the relatively low performance by the individualized group is not explained).

Hillocks clearly believes that he is reestablishing experimental research as the arbiter of effectiveness in composition research. The supremacy of experimental methodology is evident in his dismissal of the case-study reports that Graves published as part of his study of young children's writing: "While narrative reporting on one child at a time makes for interesting reading, it provides little evidence that any one case is typical" (52). Hillocks even refers to the case studies published in the Research Update section of *Language Arts* as "research" in quotes.

Hillocks's assistant on this review of research, Peter Smagorinsky, has taken this position a step farther, arguing that the publications of Graves's 1979–1981 project should not be termed research at all. Echoing the traditional criticisms of experience in the early research manuals, Smagorinsky claims that Graves provides no negative evidence concerning his hypotheses and that the writing behaviors he observed may be open to different interpretations. Consequently, his work resembles "journalism" more than research:

> Before we can attribute (students' success) to solid research findings that describe general human behavior, we must test them under conditions that have better controls to rule out the many alternative explanations for performance of the children in Graves' study. (340)

This is, of course, the standard tag line. The sleeping giant will resolve the issue. But according to Hillocks, the giant has been hard at work.

Hillocks's meta-analysis has been criticized on a number of counts. Arthur Applebee, while agreeing with Hillocks's attempt to shift attention from the global "writing process" to more task-specific processes, criticizes the natural process/environmental distinction because the environmental approach draws heavily on techniques originally promoted by educators like Donald Murray, Janet Emig, and Peter Elbow — all people placed in the "natural process" category. In fact, the category "natural process" is depicted as such a passive form of instruction that it is a caricature of the positions of its so-called proponents.

But there are more fundamental questions from the practitioner standpoint. One of the great claims of experimental research is its generalizability. It is also the question a teacher naturally raises when any method is proposed—how does this idea apply to my teaching? Would this work for me? Paradoxically, Hillocks's studies may be weakest at the point where they are traditionally thought strongest. To accept the generalizability of these studies, the practitioner naturally wants to know what went on in the classrooms where the methods were used. It's hardly enough to know, for example, that models were used—how were they used? How were they selected? How were they introduced? How did the teacher conduct the discussion on the model? Research studies, however, are typically terse on these issues; the "treatment" is rarely described in enough detail for a teacher to visualize the actual instruction.

But the problem is even more serious. In his discussion of the 500 experiments, he notes that in fewer than 5 percent of these studies did the researcher present *any* evidence that the treatment was actually carried out as described. Such evidence was so infrequent that Hillocks could not insist upon it as a precondition for use in his meta-analysis. The teacher then might be excused for doubting that the complex issue of "using models" can be resolved by six studies (none of them published in a refereed research journal) that generally fail to provide classroom descriptions of how the models were used.

Another concern for the practitioner is the clear hierarchy of power in Hillocks's recommendation for the use of his results. He recommends that his conclusions can form the basis for "mandates" by local boards of education and promises that "boards which mandate the more effective instruction *and* which make funds available to teach teachers how to use it can expect higher levels of achievement in writing" (250). In other words, his methodology is so powerful that it can produce coercive knowledge, knowledge that compels action. Taylor's hierarchy is in place; the teacher must work to the directions of the researcher class.

Accommodation

Another response to the critique of experimentalism is—at least initially— more accommodating. Those arguing for accommodation often claim that the field of composition studies needs both observational (ethnographic and case studies) and the more traditional experimental studies. Moreover, these different research paradigms can be fruitfully integrated in a unified vision of composition research. The choice is not either/or. Often the tone of these appeals for disciplinary tolerance resembles that of a recess monitor addressing squabbling children:

Writing research is new and there is not much of it. It is not easy and there are, as yet, no magic keys to understanding it. Writing research needs to be varied without being unfocused, guided by theory without being dogmatic, progressive without being mindlessly trendy. (Bereiter and Scardamalia, 3)

Or, in Lauer and Asher's *Composition Research* we have this appeal:

An unfortunate and simplistic answer (to the problem of multimodality) would be to privilege one method of inquiry, valuing, for example, only knowledge that can be derived empirically. Another troublesome solution would be to encourage individuals to choose among the modes of inquiry, maintaining literacy in only one, an answer that would lead to parallel strands of inquiry. We contend that deliberate and interactive multimodality ... offers a richer opportunity for studying the complex domain of composition studies. (7)

At one level, it is impossible to disagree with this appeal for tolerance and cooperation among researchers working in different research paradigms. But it is also necessary to read the fine print — to understand the assumptions that underlie these appeals for multimodality.

One key test of this new tolerance for qualitative research is the status of the case study. And there's trouble from the start. Lauer and Asher claim that "qualitative descriptive research is often the first kind of empirical research done in fields that seek to identify the important aspects or variables of any phenomenon to be studied" (23). The justification for qualitative research, then, is that it can be preliminary to more rigorous and powerful experimental investigations. The case study's particular weakness is its inability to establish cause-effect relationships among variables:

It seldom has that kind of explicit power. It is instead, a design that, by close observation of natural conditions, helps researchers to identify new variables and questions for further research. (23)

Lauer and Asher similarly see ethnographic studies as seriously limited — although, of course, useful in suggesting "hypotheses for further study" (45). They note eleven problems in interpreting naturalistic research, all having to do with problems of human interpretation and selection of data. For example, researchers may fail to notice data that does not fit preconceptions; they may overemphasize novel data; they may lack access to key information or treat less reliable information equally with more reliable information; they may overgeneralize from a small sample or from one exceptional case. Then there is always the problem of replicability:

Researchers must be concerned about its replicability, its repeatability with the same results. Will the same variables be gleaned from new settings by other observers? Will the variables remain stable over time? Qualitative research has a limited ability to generalize to other samples, variables, and conditions like the one studied. (45)

Kantor, Kirby, and Goetz, while more optimistic about the future of ethnographic approaches, offer a pragmatic caution. It would be naive, they claim, not to recognize the necessity of justifying ethnographic approaches to "the educational research community" (302). To gain acceptance, researchers will need to establish that studies can achieve reliability and validity and that researchers are conducting "objective inquiries into language instruction" (302).

So the price of respectability comes high. The promises of tolerance and compatibility come with a catch. If the case study and ethnographic report are to be treated as research, they are still to be judged by the traditional standards of educational research — replicability, validity, objectivity, generalizability. To be accepted, researchers still must view a context as a set of variables, each of which can be separated and assigned a causative weight. To be accepted, the researcher must also accept positivistic assumptions about the existence "out there" of generalizable truths that transcend particular contexts, and they must view their own case study and ethnographic research as a preliminary sorting of variables so that other methodologies can be used to establish these truths. To be accepted, the researcher must, like the scientist, minimize the personal, interpretive nature of his or her own work. It's the cave and the shadows all over again.

Separation

A third reaction to the assault on experimentalism is to claim that ethnographic and case-study research works from fundamentally different assumptions about knowledge. From this perspective, attempts at accommodation obscure fundamental differences and fetter qualitative researchers with irrelevant requirements. Harste, Woodward, and Burke claim that ethnographic research is fundamentally incompatible with experimental research. They argue that the term "variable" reflects that positivist's belief that a complex event — learning to read in the classroom, for example — can be broken into component parts that can be isolated and studied:

Ethnography embodies an alternate world view. There are no such things as "variables." Rather, the things experimentalists call "variables" in an instance of language transact to form a new phenomenon, the subcomponents of which are not reducible. To "control" a component is to distort the relationships that occur, and in the process alter the event so that it is no longer an instance of what one was studying. (88)

Experimental research is weak where it is traditionally thought to be strong — in the capacity to generalize. If the isolation of variables distorts the event being studied, how can the study of "nonlanguage instances, where key aspects of the process (which we have yet to identify fully) are not allowed to transact, help us understand real language?" (89)

According to this view, one of the problems with early case-study research in composition was its attempt to assume the role prescribed by the traditional research paradigm. For example, Janet Emig concludes her pivotal study of 12th graders' composing with calls for further research that would replicate her study with larger samples. In doing so, she treats her case studies as representatives of the more general class of 12th graders and therefore must acknowledge the very preliminary nature of her conclusions and the need for a more extensive sample if this objective of generalization is to be met.

Such attempts to accommodate the traditional experimental paradigm stunt the growth of the case-study method. The power of this method is its capacity for particularization, for the creating of portraits of individual writers. Emig (understandably—this is the late 1960s after all) tried to straddle two paradigms. Lynn, her major case-study subject, is treated both as an individual and as a representative of the larger class of 12th-grade writers. North writes:

> The ... primary concern must be with the individual writer, whole and in depth, not the type—Lynn, and Tony, and Don Murray, not 12th-graders or unskilled writers, or professional writers. The larger image, the canonical theories, will evolve in due course. Let me try to make it axiomatic: To claim the authority that is rightfully and most usefully theirs clinicians need to recognize—indeed to revel in—the power of idiographic inquiry. (237)

North is similarly critical of the injunctions like those of Kantor, Kirby, and Goetz, which caution ethnographers to ensure validity and reliability in their studies. This, too, is seen as a crippling accommodation to the "educational research community." The task of the ethnographer is to make sense of an "imaginative universe"; it is a hermeneutical activity "like trying to read (in the sense of 'construct a reading of') a manuscript—foreign, faded, full of ellipses, incoherencies, suspicious emendations, and ten-dentious commentaries, but written not in conventionalized graphs of sound but in transcient examples of shaped behavior" (Geertz 232).

The researcher who chooses to embrace this new role—that of interpreter or reader—will need to face the traditional academic bias against the particular. As Linda Brodkey notes, "The academy has traditionally demon-strated a limited tolerance for lived experience, which it easily dismisses as 'anecdotes' or 'stories,' and in some quarters that intolerance is so great that any ethnographic narrative would be an affront to scholarly sensibilities" (41). According to Brodkey, ethnographic narratives "jeopardize the positivist campaign to deny everyone's lived experience, in the name of objectivity."

One obvious objection from the positivists would be the lack of generalizability of descriptive or observational studies. They would view an ethnographic study of a classroom or a case study of a special-needs student (e.g., Atwell, "a Special Writer at Work") as interesting but inert. There is no *internal* mechanism for generalization, no assurance that the student Atwell describes is typical of other special-needs students. But as readers, we perform this act of generalization—we determine if Atwell's Laura or Emig's Lynn resembles students we've seen. Are they plausible, fully developed, believable? Does the case study provide insight into the way these students write and think? Paradoxically, the case study gains generalizability through particularity—through the density of detail, the selection of incidents, and the narrative skill of the researcher. The researcher goes outward (toward generalizability) by going inward, by gathering and arranging such rich and varied information that the reader assents to the portrayal.

Another problem with traditional research concerns the supposed neutrality of the researcher in traditional studies, for the practitioner also asks—does this approach match what I believe, what I want for my students? If the ethnographic researcher openly assumes the role of narrator, these beliefs are revealed in the narration. Wayne Booth demonstrates how narration necessitates an acceptance by the reader of the author's evaluation of human behavior. He quotes Saul Bellow, who writes that "The intention of the writer . . . is to hold the reader to a sense of the weight of each action" (118). Our ability as readers to enter into this imaginative world of the writer is dependent upon our willingness to accept—at least provisionally—the scale of values of the author. Neutrality or objectivity—even if it were possible—impedes generalization because it disguises the value system that underlies the account.

In Atwell's case study, we see her own values vividly foregrounded when she describes her own misconceptions of special-education students:

> For a long time I looked at Boothbay's special ed students as walking packages of clinically defined disabilities. Batteries of tests administered by the school psychologist produced technical diagnoses I would not have dreamed of challenging—let alone reading. I didn't have to. Although I was the eighth-grade teacher, eighth-graders identified by the tests as language disabled did not come to me for English. They were tracked into the junior high resource room and the school's reading lab. There I assumed they received instruction designed to remedy their own particular disabilities. Each year I ignored the ghosts in my school, the eight or ten eighth-graders who never came to my room. ("a Special Writer at Work" 115)

There is nothing neutral about this passage. As readers, we confront an authorial presence and we vicariously participate in Atwell's rejection of this perspective on learning disabilities. The visibility of this perspective, the open invitation to enter a demarcated moral landscape, enhances the plausibility of Atwell's account.

Related to the issue of generalizability is the claim that ethnographies and case studies cannot produce cumulative knowledge. Clearly, ethnographies and case studies have not carried out their traditional role in this cumulative process—they have not indentified variables to be tested under more controlled conditions. Indeed, it is difficult to imagine a work like Heath's magisterial *Ways with Words* as a preliminary to experimental research. Instead, Heath's work has helped to initiate other ethnographies such as Taylor's study of literacy in the inner city and Fishman's study of Amish literacy. Graves's work with children's writing has helped initiate and guide the even more refined observational studies of Dyson, Hubbard, and others. The movement is more often horizontal or inward—rather than upward. As Geertz notes, "A study is an advance if it is more incisive—whatever that may mean—than those that preceded it—but it less stands on their shoulders than, challenged and challenging, runs by their sides" (244).

A third criticism of the ethnographic challenge to experimentalism is that it can lead to dogmatism and to the fragmentation of the field of composition studies. Bereiter and Scardamalia single out those holding a "holistic ideology" for their intolerance:

The main feature of this ideology is opposition to any research (or instruction) that deals with less than the full act of writing carried out under natural conditions. (21)

This ideology, they claim, confuses research methods with the ultimate purposes for which that research is conducted. While researchers would agree that the aim of research is to engage students in meaningful writing activities, this aim does not preclude studying students under laboratory conditions. "To hold strictly to a holistic ideology would mean giving up hope of understanding writing as a cognitive process" (21). Yet the Levels of Inquiry model they propose—which moves from observation as level 1 to more abstract and powerful methodologies with the highest being "Theory Embedded Experimentation" and "Simulation" (the building of precise models)—is only a slightly more elaborated version of the hierarchies that have traditionally devalued experience.

Linda Brodkey similarly claims that "it is not necessary for a field like composition studies to refuse to hear other stories in which others speak from different vantage points. . . ." (48). But her use of "story" to describe the work produced in other research traditions is significant. By calling these accounts—scholarly articles, research reports, and so on—"stories" she is arguing for an equality among them. The "story" is not at the bottom of a positivistic enterprise that privileges the "objective" research report.

Narratives are embedded in all academic discourse — even the most austere; each has conventions for telling that indicate to the writer what should be attended to and what should be ignored:

> Thus when Flower and Hayes claim and argue that "the process of writing is best understood as a set of distinctive thinking processes which writers orchestrate and organize during the act of composing (366)" readers might note, for instance, that this is a narrative stance and voice warranted by cognitive science, which is only one of the ways in which research might attempt to narrate the lived experience of writers. To choose this particular stance and voice is to relate the complexities of cognition rather than the social, political, and/or historical circumstances under which writers write. It is necessary for storytellers to suppress other stories. (48)

The model for Brodkey is not a hierarchy but a conversation.

Rather than devaluing the firsthand knowledge of teachers, these qualitative approaches validate that knowledge. The case study, in particular, might be viewed as an extension of the teacher's story ("Last semester I had this student . . ."). The more clinical case studies of Emig and Graves have spawned the teacher-written, classroom-based studies of Nancie Atwell, Carol Avery, Ellen Blackburn-Karelitz, Sue Bridge, and many others. Heinemann Educational Books has recently published two books devoted entirely to teacher accounts: Bissex and Bullock's *Seeing for Ourselves: Case Study Research by Teachers of Writing* and Julie Jensen's *Stories to Grow On*. Even Nancie Atwell's magnificently detailed *In the Middle* might be viewed as an extension of teacher talk — "Here's what's happening in my class . . ." All of these studies speak to what Bissex has identified as the key political question of educational research: "Who is empowered to see — to research, to know, and be known as an authority?" (17).

And, at root, this question has important implications for the status of women. The attempt by the academy to discredit experience, particularly in the area of child-rearing and education, is also an attempt to devalue the knowledge of those most intimately involved in raising and educating children — women. To erect Taylor — like levels of knowing — with experiential knowledge at the lowest level — perpetuates a patriarchal system where a separate class that is largely male (planners, researchers, theorists) presumes to test, sanction, or overrule that experiential knowledge. Even the familiar use of terms like "higher-order" and "lower-order" thinking tend to set up the analytic, the abstract, the distanced, and the objective ways of knowing as more worthy and rigorous than the narrative, the immediate, the empathetic, and the subjective.

One of the key metaphors in feminist studies of women's development is "silence." Adrienne Rich has written that "Where language and naming are power, silence is oppression, violence" (quoted in Belenky et al. 23). The silencing of teachers' voices — through devaluing the basis of their knowledge (experience) and their preferred means of relating that knowledge (narrative)—can also be seen as violence. In an address on motherhood, Rich urges the women to break the silence through a sharing of stories. For her references to motherhood we might substitute "teaching":

> I hope, and believe, that every woman in this room knows that on the subject of motherhood there are no experts. What we need, in any case, is not experts on our lives, but the opportunity and the validation to name and describe the truths of our lives, as we have known them. Whatever you hear from us [the speakers], remember that it is your own sense of urgency, your own memories, needs, questions, and hopes, your own painfully gathered knowledge of daughterhood and motherhood, which you must above all trust. Listen to us, then, as to four women who through certain kinds of luck, privilege, struggle, exceptional status, and at certain kinds of cost, have not only been able to live the experience of motherhood and daughterhood, but also to reflect and write on it. But listen even more closely to yourselves.
>
> What we all, collectively, have lived, as the daughters of women, as the mothers of children, is a tale far greater than any three or four of us can encompass: a tale only beginning to be told. (259–260)

In telling their tale, teachers need to recognize that the source of their authority comes from their intimate knowledge of the classroom and students, from intuitions honed by making thousands of judgments and observations of student work. It does not come through deference to expert opinion or through suppressing intuitive resources in favor of more distanced—and more academically respectable—means of observation. The opportunity will be lost if teachers fail to recognize the source of their strength and instead adopt the values of the hierarchical systems that have silenced them in the past.

Works Cited

Applebee, Arthur. "Problems in Process Approaches: Toward a Reconceptualization of Process Instruction." In *The Teaching of Writing: Eighty-fifth Yearbook of the National Society for the Study of Education*. Anthony Petrosky and David Bartholomae, eds. Chicago: University of Chicago Press, 1986.

Atwell, Nancie. *In the Middle: Writing, Reading, and Learning with Adolescents*. Portsmouth, NH: Boynton/Cook, 1987.

———. "A Special Writer at Work." In *Understanding Writing: Ways of Observing, Learning, and Teaching*. Thomas Newkirk and Nancie Atwell, eds. Portsmouth, NH: Heinemann, 1988.

Avery, Carol. "Lori 'Figures it Out': A Young Writer Learns to Read." In *Breaking Ground: Teachers Relate Reading and Writing in the Elementary School*.

Jane Hansen, Thomas Newkirk, and Donald Graves, eds. Portsmouth, NH: Heinemann, 1985.

Belenky, Mary, Blythe Clinchy, Nancy Rule, and Jill Tarule. *Women's Ways of Knowing: The Development of Self, Mind, and Voice*. New York: Basic Books, 1986.

Bereiter, Carl, and Marlene Scardamalia. "Levels of Inquiry in Writing Research." In *Research on Writing: Principles and Methods*, Peter Mosenthal, Lynne Tamor, and Sean Walmsley. New York: Longman, 1983.

Bissex, Glenda, and Richard Bullock, eds. *Seeing for Ourselves: Case Study Research by Teachers of Writing*. Portsmouth, NH: Heinemann, 1987.

Blackburn-Karelitz, Ellen. "The Rhythm of Writing Development." In *Understanding Writing: Ways of Observing, Learning, and Teaching*. Thomas Newkirk and Nancie Atwell, eds. Portsmouth, NH: Heinemann, 1982, 1988.

Booth, Wayne. *The Rhetoric of Fiction*. Chicago: University of Chicago Press, 1961.

Braddock, Richard, Richard Lloyd-Jones, and Lowell Schoer. *Research in Written Composition*. Urbana, IL: NCTE, 1963.

Bridge, Susan. "Squeezing from the Middle of the Tube." In *Understanding Writing: Ways of Observing, Learning, and Teaching* Thomas Newkirk and Nancie Atwell, eds. Portsmouth, NH: Heinemann, 1988.

Brodkey, Linda. "Writing Ethnographic Narratives." *Written Communication* 4 (1987): 25–50.

Callahan, Richard. *Education and the Cult of Efficiency*. Chicago: University of Chicago Press, 1962.

Campbell, Donald, and Julian Stanley. *Experimental and Quasi-experimental Designs for Research*. Boston: Houghton Mifflin, 1963.

Darling-Hammond. Linda. "Valuing Teachers: The Making of a Profession." *Teachers College Record*, 1985.

Dyson, Anne. "Negotiating among Multiple Worlds: The Space/Time Dimensions of Young Children's Composing." *Research in the Teaching of English* 22 (1988): 355–390.

Emig, Janet. *The Composing Process of 12th Graders*. NCTE Research Report No. 13. Urbana, IL: NCTE, 1971.

Fishman Andrea. *Amish Literacy: What and How It Means*. Portsmouth, NH: Heinemann, 1988.

Flower, Linda, and John Hayes. "A Cognitive Process Theory of Writing." CCC 32, (1981): 365–387.

Geertz, Clifford. "Thick Description: Toward an Interpretive Theory of Culture." In *Reclaiming the Imagination: Philosophical Perspectives for Writers and Teachers of Writing*. Ann Berthoff, ed. Portsmouth, NH: Boynton Cook, 1984.

Good, Carter, A. S. Barr, and Douglas Scates. *The Methodology of Educational Research*. New York: Appleton-Century, 1936.

Graves, Donald. "A New Look at Writing Research." In *Perspectives on Writing in Grades K–8*. Shirley Haley James, ed. Urbana, IL.: NCTE, 1980.

Harste, Jerome, Virginia Woodward, and Carolyn Burke. "Examining Our Assumptions: A Transactional View of Literacy and Learning." *Research in the Teaching of English* 18: 84–108.

Heath, Shirley. *Ways with Words: Language, Life, and Work in Communities and Classroom*. Cambridge: Cambridge University Press, 1983.

Hillocks, George. *Research on Written Composition: New Directions for Teaching.* Urbana, IL: National Conference on Research in English/ ERIC Clearinghouse on Reading and Communication Skills, 1986.

Hubbard, Ruth. *Authors of Pictures, Draughtsmen of Words.* Portsmouth, NH: Heinemann, 1989.

Jensen, Julie, ed. *Stories to Grow On: Demonstrations of Language Learning in K–8 Classrooms.* Portsmouth, NH: Heinemann, 1989.

Kakar, Sudhir. *Frederick Winslow Taylor: A Study in Personality and Innovation.* Cambridge, MA.: MIT Press, 1970.

Kantor, Kenneth, Dan Kirby, and Judith Goetz. "Research in Context: Ethnographic Studies in English Education." *Research in the Teaching of English* 15 (1981): 293–310.

Lauer, Janice, and J. William Asher. *Composition Research: Empirical Designs.* New York: Oxford University Press, 1988.

Mischler, Elliot. "Meaning in Context: Is There Any Other Kind?" *Harvard Educational Review* 49 (1979): 1–19.

Mouly, George. *The Science of Educational Research.* New York: American Book Company, 1963.

North, Stephen. *The Making of Knowledge in Composition: Portrait of an Emerging Field.* Portsmouth, NH: Boynton Cook, 1987.

Plato. *The Republic.* Trans. Desmond Lee. Harmondsworth, England: Penguin, 1955.

Rich, Adrienne. *On Lies, Secrets, and Silence: Selected Prose, 1966–78.* New York: Norton, 1979.

Smagorinsky, Peter. "Graves Revisited: A Look at the Methods and Conclusions of the New Hampshire Study." *Written Communication* 4 (1987): 331–342.

Taylor, Denny, and Catherine Dorsey-Gaines. *Growing Up Literate: Learning from Inner-city Families.* Portsmouth, NH: Heinemann, 1988.

8

Composition Studies from a Feminist Perspective

ELIZABETH A. FLYNN
Michigan Technological University

The contemporary feminist movement is now twenty years old. Not surprisingly, feminist scholars have recently begun the process of chronicling the history of the movement, focusing especially on its impact on a variety of academic disciplines.[1] In a field such as literary criticism and theory the impact of feminism has been unquestionably remarkable. Feminist literary scholars and critics began examining the impact of gender on the reading and writing of literature in the late 1960s and early 1970s in the form of articles[2]; their explorations soon took the form of books and journals. Today, numerous university presses have series coordinated by established feminist literary scholars, and feminist literary criticism and theory have become international in scope.[3] One measure of the impact of feminism on literary criticism and theory is its effect on male critics and theorists. A growing number of established male literary theorists—Wayne Booth, Jonathan Culler, and David Bleich, for instance—have "converted" to a feminist way of viewing literature and have declared their allegiance in statements that are surprisingly forthright.[4] Feminist literary criticism and theory are booming enterprises that show no signs of waning energy or commitment.

Unfortunately, there can be no chronicling of the impact of feminism on the field of composition studies because, until recently, the field has strangely resisted addressing women's issues. *College English* has published an occasional essay that looks at writing from a feminist perspective.[5] The major journal in the field, though, *College Composition and Communication*, until quite recently has published little more than a few scattered book reviews.[6] To my knowledge, only one book-length work addresses the topic, Cynthia L. Caywood and Gillian R. Overing's *Teaching Writing: Pedagogy, Gender, and Equity*.

In attempting to explain the absence of a feminist critique of composition, it will be useful to take a closer look at fields in which feminism has had a significant impact. Literary studies, as I have already indicated, as well as linguistics and speech communication, are good examples. The study of literature has always played an important role in the feminist movement. Major early feminist manifestos—Simone de Beauvoir's *The Second Sex* and Kate Millett's *Sexual Politics*, for instance—contain analyses of literature from a feminist perspective—critiques of phallic literature by males, for the most part. There was clearly a close association within feminist thought between a critique of patriarchal culture and a critique of the literary artifacts of that culture. At the same time, feminist literary critics were attempting to identify a tradition of female writers by reinstating the writings of lost or forgotten women authors and reinterpreting the work of canonical women writers so as to make visible their women-centeredness. Literature courses were among the earliest women's studies courses, and literary studies continues to enjoy privileged status within the women's movement, especially as the movement has been institutionalized within the academy. Indeed, the movement has been defined, in large part, by feminist literary scholars, theorists, and critics.

Linguistics and speech communication are fields in which a feminist perspective has also taken a strong hold. The influence of the feminist movement came somewhat later in these areas than it did in literary studies, the mid-1970s rather than the early 1970s. Still, a number of important works have focused on differences between the speaking behaviors of males and females.[7] Much of this work on differences between women's and men's speech is interdisciplinary, and it appears that feminist literary criticism and theory may have inspired at least some of it.[8]

In attempting to determine why feminism took root in fields such as literary studies, speech communication, and linguistics, but not in composition studies, it is necessary to examine the institutional structures in which these fields operate. Much of the work in literary studies and language studies had its origins in women's studies programs and women's studies courses that were developed in the 1970s and arose out of departments that had fairly well-established disciplinary bases. There were certainly no departments of composition studies at this time, and if there were composition specialists, they tended to be marginalized and isolated within English departments that saw themselves as having a loftier mission than the teaching of first-year English. In general, composition specialists were teaching lower-level courses or administering large, work-intensive programs.

My argument, I realize, rests on the assumption that the field of composition studies is quite new, postdating the fields mentioned above and even the contemporary feminist movement. I am making a strong and, I think, necessary distinction between rhetoric, an ancient discipline, and composition. Rhetoric is the parent discipline of composition studies, but the latter is an identifiable field with its own institutional structure and purposes. Serious problems arise if we conflate the two. James Berlin in *Rhetoric and Reality: Writing Instruction in American Colleges, 1900—1985*, for instance, identifies the "discipline" of college writing instruction as a development of the field of rhetoric, thereby denying composition studies an identity of its own. He discusses twentieth-century rhetoric in five phases, 1900 to 1920, 1920 to 1940, 1940 to 1960, and 1960 to 1975, reserving the period from 1975 to the present, what I would consider the period in which composition studies came into being, for a "postscript."

The unspoken argument would seem to be that composition studies is not new, not illegitimate — it has ancient origins, a respectable heritage, and unquestionably authoritative forefathers such as Aristotle, Plato, Cicero, Quintilian, and Kenneth Burke. Rhetoric is undeniably the parent discipline of composition studies, providing a body of scholarship that has profoundly influenced composition researchers and theorists. But composition studies has more specific concerns than does rhetoric, namely college-level writing in all its varieties including basic writing, first-year composition, advanced composition, technical communication, business writing, and writing in the disciplines. I would argue that work that would seem to transcend these boundaries — explorations of scientific discourse and writing in nonacademic settings, for instance — is related to the writing-across-the-curriculum movement broadly defined and would not be of interest to the composition community if it did not have some bearing on the teaching of writing on the college level.

The organization that sponsors the field's annual convention, the Conference on College Composition and Communication, came into existence in 1949 under the leadership of John Gerber when it became clear that college composition teachers had special needs that were not being addressed by the parent organization, the National Council of Teachers of English (Berlin, *Rhetoric and Reality* 105). *College Composition and Communication* and the Conference on College Composition and Communication provide the symbolic and actual anchor of the field of composition studies. It was not really until the late 1970s, though, that the organization and the subject had developed sufficiently to achieve an identifiable body of research and theory and a constituency sufficient to be characterized as a field. The 1979 CCCC conference had approximately 600 program participants. By 1980, the number of program participants had doubled to approximately 1200. During the 1980s, the field gained visibility as composition specialists arose, graduate programs began to emerge, and books such as Berlin's began to chronicle the field's history. We may have had writing programs in American colleges and universities prior to the late 1970s, and we may have had rhetorical treatises and rhetoric courses. We did not have an identifiable community of composition specialists, though, until the late 1970s and early 1980s, five to ten years after the emergence of the most recent feminist movement. Unlike literary studies, which was firmly established within the academy, composition studies was defining itself and attempting to defend its principles and practices. It was a new and vulnerable field uncertain of its identity or status.

One of the interesting characteristics of this new field, composition studies of the 1980s, is that it was clearly open to women. Berlin's discussion of the post-1975 era includes, of course, males such as Peter Elbow, Ken Macrorie, Donald Murray, William Coles, and Walker Gibson but also women such as Janet Emig, Patricia Bizzell, Lil Brannon, Lisa Ede, Andrea Lunsford, Lillian Bridwell-Bowles, Maxine Hairston, and Ann Berthoff. If several of these women, especially Emig, Lunsford, and Bridwell-Bowles, are now making explicit references to feminism in their work, their energies in the first part of the decade of the 1980s were devoted to defining and defending a field that had barely begun to recognize itself as such. The result was that the feminist critique of better-established fields such as history, anthropology, sociology, speech communication, and literary studies was never undertaken until quite recently within the field of composition studies.

Like all fields, composition studies is rooted in androcentric institutions and originated from androcentric disciplines. The most immediate influence on the present-day field, quite obviously, is the institution of the Conference on College Composition and Communication. As we might expect, the early chairs of the CCCC were men. Between 1949 and 1978 there were only four women chairs of the organization, three in the decade of the 1970s. The period from 1960 to 1975, which Berlin calls the "Renaissance of Rhetoric," was dominated almost entirely by men. The editors of *College Composition and Communication* during this period, Ken Macrorie (1962–1964) and William Irmscher (1965–1973), were males, as were the editors of *College English*, James E. Miller (1960–1966) and Richard Ohmann (1966–1978), and *Research in the Teaching of English*, Richard Braddock (1967–1972) and Alan Purves (1973–1978).

Caywood and Overing's *Teaching Writing: Pedagogy, Gender, and Equity* draws parallels between the process orientation of composition studies and the emphasis on process within contemporary feminist theory, thereby suggesting that the field is politically progressive. Close scrutiny of some process-oriented positions, though, reveals some incongruity with feminism. The work of Janet Emig would certainly seem to be progressive from a feminist perspective, for instance. But there is sometimes an emphasis in her research on the writer as an isolated individual divorced from social and political context.[9] And what about the work of Linda Flower? James Berlin in a recent exchange argues convincingly that she "uses protocol analysis to make universal generalizations about how all experienced and inexperienced writers compose, oblivious to such differences as race, class, and gender, as well as to the nature of the writing task undertaken" ("James Berlin Responds" 773). A process approach to the study of writing is not necessarily synonymous with female-centered epistemologies. Like other fields, composition studies is thoroughly androcentric.

Androcentrism

Feminist theory over the past twenty years has outlined the general characteristics of androcentrism and suggested ways in which it has influenced our ways of knowing in a variety of fields. Madeleine Grumet in *Bitter Milk: Women and Teaching*, for instance, discusses the androcentrism of our educational institutions, arguing that our schools imitate the spatial, temporal, and ritual order of industry and bureaucracy, indicating the complicity of both men and women in support of paternal authority (24–25). She says, "the paternal project of curriculum is to claim the child, to teach him or her to master the language, the rules, the games, and the names of the fathers" (21). Schools disrupt the maternal bond between mother and child. Drawing upon the work of Dorothy Dinnerstein, Nancy Chodorow, Carol Gilligan, and Mary Belenky et al., Grumet distinguishes between feminine and masculine epistemologies. Feminine ways of knowing are rooted in relatedness, in attempts to integrate the parts of their experience that the politics of gender, family, school, and science have separated (16). Masculine ways of knowing, in contrast, reduce preoedipal subject/object mutuality to postoedipal cause and effect (17). Grumet, in discussing Chodorow, says, "The male child who must repress his preoedipal identification with his mother negates it, banishing this primary object from his own conscious ego identity" (17). As a result, the male child's subjectivity, his maternal identification, and his objectivity, his sense of his mother as other, are alienated from one another (17). According to Grumet, fathers dominate communal activity and co-opt the word with the result that we have monologic epistemologies of cause and effect rather than dialogic ones—either/or constructions of truth and research models that denigrate the ambiguity and dialectical nature of human action to honor the "predictability and control of physical and mechanistic phenomena" (22).

David Bleich in *The Double Perspective*, also drawing on the work of feminists such as Gilligan, Chodorow, and Dinnerstein, outlines the characteristics of an androcentric world view: modalities of individualism, strong boundaries, adversarial attitudes, hierarchical thinking, and an interest in and respect for paradox (55). Female modes of thinking, according to Bleich, are characterized by modalities of relatedness and mutuality, indistinct boundaries, flexibility, and nonoppositional styles (57). Bleich argues convincingly that "until recently, the study of language has borne the usual social and epistemological marks of the masculine academy" (55). He sees that Noam Chomsky's concept of language, for instance, assumes the priority of the individual mind and is rooted in a biological conception of the nature and origin of mind and language (69). According to Bleich, Piaget, too, emphasizes the language user as an individual in isolation and describes language use as a mechanistic process (70). A cognitive view of language learning reflects an individualistic approach rather than a social approach. It emphasizes the separateness of the learner rather than her connectedness to others and to a particular social context.

Theories of language development and use that emphasize the rootedness of the language user in a social context, according to Bleich, are much more compatiable with a feminist world view than are theories that arise out of a cognitive perspective. He sees the work of L. S. Vygotsky and George

Herbert Mead as exemplifying this approach. Vygotsky sees language acquisition as both the internalization of social speech and the socialization of individual intelligence. Language is acquired through interaction, through dialectic. Mead places even more emphasis on the social dimensions of language acquisition, arguing that the social process of experience is prior to the existence of mind and explaining the origins of mind in terms of interaction among individuals within that process (50). Mutual or intersubjective knowledge is prior to the process of individuation. The individual acquires a self by internalizing others' conceptions of her (225).

According to Bleich, an "individualist identity," and hence a masculinist identity, pervades reading research and literary theory as well. The dominant masculinist models of reading presuppose an individual reader facing a single text and tend to ignore the variety of actual readings in a real-life context, presenting their own readings as if they were exemplary or fundamentally objective (17). Bleich also sees Derrida's work as having a highly individual focus and as reducing all of experience to textuality, thereby deemphasizing human agency and extralinguistic experience (54).

Neither Bleich nor Grumet is arguing from an essentialist position. They do not see that all females share a similar perspective regardless of their experience or cultural or historical situation. Rather, they see that males and females have, for the most part, had different experiences throughout history and hence have developed different interpretive perspectives. Grumet emphasizes women's roles as mothers, as the primary nurturers of children, and males as participants in the work force. These different experiences have resulted in different value structures, different world views. Males can take on the perspective of females and females can take on the perspective of males. More often than not, though, the male perspective prevails because positions of power and authority within society have been held by males rather than females. It is quite usual for women to think as men do but less usual for men to think as women do. Because cultures throughout history have been androcentric, women often identify with men and take on male ways of thinking and experiencing reality. Sometimes, though, men such as Vygotsky and Mead, mentioned above, gain enough critical distance from male modes to envision alternatives that complement feminist perspectives. Feminists such as Grumet and Bleich value female ways of knowing and behaving and call for an end to the domination of a single approach that devalues activities such as the nurturing of children and nonhierarchical ways of interacting.

To feminists, androcentrism is signaled by the exclusion of women's voices from whatever conversation is taking place and by a comfortable acceptance of the inclusion of only male voices, even if the content of the discussion is liberatory from a humanistic perspective. If women's special needs are ignored, the exploration can be said to be androcentric. Androcentrism is not synonymous with misogyny. It does not necessitate hatred of women or even a feeling of ill will toward women. It simply necessitates an ignorance of women's different epistemological perspective and of women's subordinate position in society. It is often difficult to recognize because it is so all-pervasive and so seemingly innocuous. Because of this, to identify androcentrism, feminists often resort—as I do—to counting the number of references an individual makes to women because it is often a good indicator of that individual's conscious awareness of women's issues.

Mary Daly claims that all enlightened individuals, males and females alike, have an obligation to fight against the oppression of women and for the elimination of patriarchal structures. If seemingly enlightened males or females do not play an active role in the struggle, they are working from androcentric assumptions and are actually, implicitly, contributing to the oppression of women. In *Beyond God the Father* she says, "the lack of explicit relevance of intellection to the fact of oppression in its precise forms, such as sexual hierarchy, is itself oppressive" (20). A feminist critique of composition studies necessitates at least two kinds of strategies: 1) the identification of androcentrism in all its varieties including the androcentrism of cognate fields; and 2) recuperation of those modes of thinking within the field that are compatible with a feminine epistemology, what I will call "femininism." Feminism is the conscious awareness of women's special perspectives and problems and the commitment to gender equity. Femininism is the use of feminine epistemological approaches, often unconsciously. The enterprise of critiquing the field from a feminist perspective is an ambitious one, impossible to complete in a single essay. My aim here is to initiate the process by demonstrating how these activities of identification and recuperation work. I'll begin the work of uncovering the androcentrism of the parent field of composition studies—rhetoric—and of recuperating the progressivism of two developments within composition studies, expressivism and Marxism.

Strategy #1—Identification of Androcentrism

A recent overview of modern-day rhetoric, *Contemporary Perspectives on Rhetoric*, written, by the way, by two females and a male, focuses on eight contemporary rhetoricians: I. A. Richards, Richard M. Weaver, Stephen Toulmin, Chaim Perelman, Ernesto Grassi, Kenneth Burke, Michel Foucault, and Juergen Habermas. Sonja and Karen Foss no doubt would have included women had there been any likely candidates since they consider themselves to be feminists.[10] Apparently, though, they could find none to include because the rhetorical tradition has been so male-centered. Foss, Foss, and Trapp define rhetoric as "the uniquely human ability to use symbols to communicate with one another" (11), hence their inclusion of a philosopher such as Foucault, who probably would not have considered himself a rhetorician. For the most part, though, the rhetoricians they discuss, especially Richards, Weaver, Toulmin, Perelman, and Burke, are neo-Aristotelians. Aristotle's *Rhetoric* is the ur-text for much contemporary rhetoric, a document that is both misogynist and androcentric. Aristotle says, for instance, "The virtues [excellences], and corresponding words, of a class that is naturally higher are more noble; those of a man, for example, are nobler than those of a women" (49).

It would not be difficult to demonstrate that all of the neo-Aristotelians who Foss, Foss, and Trapp discuss approach rhetoric from a male point of view. We might expect Perelman to be an exception since the co-author of *The New Rhetoric*, Lucia Olbrechts-Tyteca, is a woman and a former professor. Olbrechts-Tyteca's contribution to *The New Rhetoric* is unclear, though, as is her identity. Attempts to find out who she was and what she believed have, so far at least, proved to be unsuccessful.[11] *The New Rhetoric* is usually attributed to Perelman alone, and there is certainly not much evidence in the text itself of a female presence.

Contemporary rhetoricians, especially neo-Aristotelians, ground their conceptions of what communication is in the categories and concepts of classical rhetoric, the rhetoric of public debate, a realm traditionally reserved for men. Rhetoric was synonymous with argumentation, with attempting to persuade an audience. Classical rhetoricians focused on ways of discovering or inventing arguments, on strategies of persuasion such as appeals to reason, emotion, or ethics, on arrangement of arguments, and on kinds of arguments. Peter Dixon points out in *Rhetoric* that etymologically the rhetor is a public speaker and "His [sic] distinctive art is that of addressing courts of law and popular assemblies" (1). Rhetoric, then, is a discipline largely reserved for describing communication strategies associated with occupations traditionally reserved for men and agonistic attitudes traditionally associated with men. In ancient Greece, political discourse was reserved for a literate elite; slaves and women, for the most part, did not participate in argumentative exchanges.

It is not surprising, then, that classical rhetoric has a decidedly masculinist orientation and an emphasis on language that serves combative purposes. Walter Ong emphasizes the agonistic nature of rhetoric when he says, "Rhetoric retained much of the old oral feeling for thought and expression as basically agonistic and formulaic. . . . With its agonistic heritage, rhetorical teaching assumed that the aim of more or less all discourse was to prove or disprove a point, against some opposition" (110). He speaks of rhetoric as "antithetical," for the orator speaks in the face of implied adversaries (111), and of oratory's "deep agonistic roots" (111). According to Ong, the rhetorical tradition in the West has been related to the tendency among the Greeks to "maximize oppositions" in the mental and extramental world (111). Ong maintains that the rhetorical tradition with its agonistic roots was continued in the Latin schools of the seventeenth century, which aimed to prepare males for careers as clergymen, lawyers, physicians, and diplomats, whereas females entered the newer vernacular schools, which were considerably less influenced by the agonistic oratorical tradition (112).

What Ong's analysis suggests is that rhetoric does not examine communication processes that have other purposes—nurturing, comforting, caring,
consoling, explaining—more often associated with women and with the
domestic rather than the political realm.[12]

Contemporary rhetoric, I would argue, is androcentric because it ignores
women and women's issues and because it continues the rhetorical tradition
Ong identifies. The work of Kenneth Burke, for example, is a good example of
a rhetorician who focuses almost exclusively on the writing of males and
tends to describe patriarchal interpretive strategies and social structures as
if they were inevitable. Burke's work is important to consider from a
feminist perspective because he is the rhetorician who has certainly had
the greatest influence on composition studies. It is easy to forgive Kenneth
Burke his use of the generic "he" since his most important works predate
the feminist movement and since virtually no writing produced prior to
1970s, even that by feminists such as Simone de Beauvoir and Virginia
Woolf, uses gender-inclusive language. It is not easy to forgive his neglect
of women, though. The index to *A Grammar of Motives*, one of his most
influential works, lists references to 277 men and 3 women—St. Theresa,
Marianne Moore, and Josephine Miles.[13] The indexes to his other works
are much the same. Burke's intertextual references are overwhelming; he
has clearly read as widely as any contemporary intellectual. Unfortunately,
he seems to have read, for the most part, only male texts. He also seems to
accept the inevitability of women's subordination to men and to consider
women to be the "weaker" sex. He says in *The Rhetoric of Motives*, "The
hierarchic principle itself is inevitable in systematic thought. It is embodied in
the mere process of growth, which is synonymous with the class divisions
of youth and age, stronger and weaker, male and female, or the stages of
learning, from apprentice to journeyman or master" (141). Hierarchies,
according to Burke, will always be with us and have their "entrancements"
and "delights" (333); they are part of a "universal order," a chain, ladder, or
pyramid of "mounting worth" (333) with little possibility for movement to
the next hierarchical level. Burke has a decidedly male view of the world,
focusing on hierarchy, division, "logology," and paradox, ways of thinking
that Bleich associates with masculine epistemologies.

Stephen Toulmin carries on the agonistic tradition described by Ong. In
discussing the uses of argument, Toulmin chooses a model from the discipline
of jurisprudence. Arguments, according to Toulmin, can be compared with
lawsuits and the claims made in extralegal contexts with the claims made in
the courts (7). His aim in writing *The Uses of Argument* is to characterize
the "procedures and categories" used in arguing for and settling claims (7).
Later in the book, in discussing the layouts of arguments, Toulmin continues
this sense of argument as combat. A speaker or writer makes a "claim,"
which is then challenged by an opponent. The task of the arguer, then, is
to show that the claim is justifiable in the face of opposition. This involves

marshaling evidence—data and warrants—to support the claim. This evidence confers different degrees of "force" on the conclusions they justify (100).

Dale Spender observes in *Man Made Language* that rhetoric as it has traditionally been defined is a male-centered discipline. In discussing the work of Shirley Ardener, Spender observes that women are comfortable with the art of conversation, men with the art of persuasion, and that there is perhaps no easy transfer between these two arts (79). Spender says, "The concept of leadership, and all its concomitant attributes, is also inextricably linked with *public* discourse. Those who hold most sway, who are more influential, who are *dominant* are those who are sufficiently forceful to carry others along with them" (79).

Patrocinio P. Schweickart, in a paper entitled "Gender and Theories of Discourse," provides a feminist critique of contemporary rhetorical theory, emphasizing that theories of argumentation privilege rationality, and that rationality is considered to be a transcendent human faculty, transcending gender and sexuality (6). In actuality, though, according to Schweickart, the concept of rationality reflects a masculine subjectivity—"the notion of validity and reasonableness ... is abstracted from the intersubjectivity of man-to-man relations" (9). Argument theory, according to Schweickart, is characterized by individuation and a disjunction between affective and cognitive processes (10).

Schweickart suggests that a feminist theory of argument would focus on the interaction between speaker and listener. The nature of the reception of a piece of discourse would be as important as the nature of the production of that discourse. Schweickart rightly claims that although argument theory often pays some attention to considerations of audience, reception is almost always seen as a supplement to production and is almost always discussed from the vantage point of the speaker rather than that of the listener. Listening, though, is indispensable to speaking and has its own characteristics and responsibilities. A treatise on reception rather than argumentation could be rooted in feminist theories that emphasize the value of receptivity, caring, understanding, activities associated with a feminine rather than a masculine sensibility. Schweickart also demonstrates, though, that rhetoric has the potential for illuminating women's needs and concerns as language users if it is wedded to feminist theory.

Strategy #2—Recuperation of Femininism

As I have suggested elsewhere,[14] composition studies has, to an extent, feminized our conception of the nature of the composing process. It has done so because strong, politically progressive traditions have emerged as the field has developed. Two traditions are worth noting in this regard, that of less overtly politicized individuals such as James Britton and colleagues at the University of London, who recognize the social dimensions of language development and who call for a nurturing approach to the teaching of writing, and that of highly politicized individuals such as Richard Ohmann, who link their work directly to an analysis of advanced industrial capitalism and a critique of depoliticized approaches to composition studies. I will discuss these in turn.

If feminine approaches to language study are characterized by modalities of relatedness and mutuality, indistinct boundaries, flexibility, and non-oppositional styles, then the work of James Britton and colleagues is in some ways a feminine approach to composition studies. This is not to say the approach is a feminist one. *The Development of Writing Abilities* *(11−18)*, after all, uses the generic "he" and cites many more male writers than women writers. The works listed in the "References" section at the end of the book, for instance, include 98 by men, and 6 authored or co-authored by women. One of the authors of the book, though, is a woman, and at times the authors discuss research results in terms of "sex differences" (111). But more important, they reverse traditional hierarchies, valuing private expression over public display.

Britton et al. begin their book by discussing the limitations of a rhetorical approach to the problems they will address. They argue that the rhetorical categories of narration, description, exposition, and argument describe written products, not the processes employed to produce them, and tend to be prescriptive. They found psychological and linguistic studies in child development to be more useful than rhetoric in describing the processes involved in writing. Many of the individuals Britton et al. were influenced by were the same individuals Bleich identifies as having enlightened views about language development and use — Vygotsky and Mead, for instance.

Britton et al. speculate that the "intimate context" of expressive speech may be the matrix of the child's language development (140). Not surprisingly, they also posit that expressive writing is the matrix of the learner's development of writing abilities and thus is privileged in a way that trans-actional writing, writing in which the language user seeks to inform and persuade, is not. In privileging informal writing over formal writing, Britton and his colleagues are, in essence, privileging female ways of thinking over male modes, creating a place for intimacy and nurturance in other-wise product-oriented educational institutions. They are protecting the feminine — mothering — and fending off the dominance of the father.

The Marxist tradition within composition studies is exemplified by Richard Ohmann's classic text, *English in America.* Again, I am not arguing that the book is a feminist one. Ohmann has made reference to only slightly more women in the book than did Kenneth Burke in *A Grammar of Motives*: 17 as opposed to 347 references to men (or 4 percent as opposed to Burke's 1 percent). Also, it is not always apparent that Ohmann includes gender inequities when he discusses power imbalances. In discussing the extent to which textbooks have idealized argumentation, leaving out political factors, he says, "Argument divorced from power, money, social conflict, class, and consciousness is pseudo-argument" (158). He might have included gender in his list. He does use gender-neutral language, though, and does, at times, seem to be aware of women's issues and of the women's movement. He makes reference to Florence Howe's participation in the 1968 MLA revolt, for instance.[15]

English in America is valuable to feminists not because it overtly deals with feminist issues but because it provides a politicized critique of composition studies that can be extended to include gender considerations. Ohmann argues that the ideology that informs textbooks used in writing courses supports the tacit ideas of the dominant groups in society (159). Instruction in writing encourages docility and compliance rather than creativity and freedom. Composition textbooks work from a "crippled theory of where ideas come from and how they take hold" (155). They "envision no prior alignment of people and forces in society that cannot be overcome by a well-conducted argument" (155). They encourage students to produce alienated writing by advising them to begin with a topic and then derive a thesis.

According to Ohmann, teachers of composition, like teachers of literature, impart knowledge that has value to the technostructure. The economic system is decisive in determining the nature of the educational system and hence in determining what knowledge is and how it will be imparted in all fields including the teaching of writing. The main features of the economic system he blames for an alienated approach to composition instruction are private ownership and the "free" market (312). He sees that large corporations decide how people will live in our society, with the effect that individual choices are preferred over collective ones and convenience in the short run over survival in the long run (313). Only a radical alteration in the economic system will change the teaching of composition. Educational institutions need to be freed of a dependency on an economic system rooted in a dynamic of individualism, private ownership, and competition (330). Reformism is not enough because it tends to endorse the political and economic status quo (314).

The relationship between feminism and Marxism is complex; I do not intend to recount in detail the debates that have gone on over the past several decades. Suffice it to say that some feminists see that male domination over women rather than the economic system is the cause of the alienation women experience and that patriarchal oppression is present in all historical eras and all political and economic systems. Ohmann's solution, to substitute a socialist order for the present capitalistic one, would not necessarily address the issue of women's oppression.

Certainly, though, feminists, regardless of their commitment to Marxist ideology, would applaud Ohmann's recognition that composition studies, too often, has ignored political issues and described the composing process as if it took place in a political vacuum. Most of his claims about the limitations of our approaches to composition studies are useful in critiquing the field from a feminist perspective. Textbooks present writing as if the activity were socially neutral, as if it took place in a benevolent order where equality was both an ideal and a reality. Feminist research and theory suggest otherwise. Women often write, if they write at all, from a situation of powerlessness, marginality, alienation. Too frequently, their voices are silenced, their ideas ignored. To write with power, as some composition specialists urge, will take more than finding an authentic personal voice through freewriting and exchange of papers with peers. It will take a change in the social order, a shift in the balance of power. Writing with power and authority necessitates having power and authority, and while composition instructors can attempt to confer these on students, their attempts may be negated by forces beyond the classroom. Improved pedagogies by individual classroom instructors are not sufficient to bring about the conditions necessary to promote powerful writing by women students. Significant changes in the social and economic order must be made as well.

Conclusion

This essay is meant as a preliminary exploration of ways in which the field of composition studies resists or foreshadows a feminist approach to writing development and use. Quite obviously, there is considerably more to be said on the topic. I'd like here to suggest some directions future research might take. Manifestations of androcentrism or worse are everywhere. I've discussed only a few contemporary rhetoricians in this regard; the work of others, including classical rhetoricians, needs to be examined. The critique will no doubt yield more evidence of a generalized obliviousness to women's special ways of knowing and a valuing of agonistic approaches to language use. At the same time, we need to identify women rhetorical theorists and rhetors and to attempt to delineate a female rhetorical tradition.[16] This may necessitate expanding our conception of rhetoric to include philosophers such as Susanne Langer and literary theorists such as Louise Rosenblatt. It may also necessitate redefining rhetorical genres to include letters, diaries, and expressive essays.

We also need to look at the influence of positivism on composition studies. One way in which research on writing has gained legitimacy has been to emulate the assumptions and procedures of the hard sciences and the social sciences. The influence of the empirical orientation of scientific and social scientific disciplines has often been salutary. Too often, though, the influence has been positivistic rather than empirical, a privileging of detachment and objectivity over relatedness and subjectivity. Methods and procedures are presented as if they were value neutral when, in fact, they embody masculine values. The researcher is supposed to take on the persona of the objective reporter untainted by beliefs and values that arise out of personal experience. In reality, the researcher is buying into an entire system of beliefs and values that arise out of the collective experiences of males in privileged positions.

Feminist composition research would be engaged research, research that aims to correct the distortions resulting from androcentrism and to recuperate the suppressed perspectives of women writers, especially student writers. It would make use of nonpositivistic methods such as participant observation and interviews that encourage connectedness between researcher and subject and that invite transformation of the subject rather than mere detached analysis. And if it employed other empirical methods that necessitate greater detachment such as surveys, protocol analysis, and experiments, it would analyze the results of those approaches from a feminist perspective, bringing to bear feminist research and theory.[17]

The subfield of technical communication needs to be examined from a feminine perspective. The theories and research methodologies that are employed often arise out of the values of corporate culture and androcentric disciplines, classical and contemporary rhetoric. Even potentially enlightened research methodologies such as ethnographies and case studies too often leave unquestioned fundamental tenets of industrialism — hierarchy, the profit motive, and male domination. The growing body of work by feminist scholars on women's relationship to technology has had virtually no impact on work in technical communication. What is the role of the woman technical communicator in a corporate setting? Is the position alienating, or does it provide opportunities for transformation? How can the teaching of technical writing in colleges and universities be altered so as to make women's ways of interpreting reality central? Are collaborative modes of writing frequently employed in an industrial setting examples of feminine mutuality and respect or domination and control?

The critique of the field of composition studies and of subfields within it needs to be accompanied by recuperative work that identifies tendencies within the field that are compatible with feminism, or at least with femininism. David Bleich does an excellent job recuperating the feminine orientation of Shirley Brice Heath's *Ways with Words* in *The Double Perspective*. He finds that her work is valuable because it is committed and connected rather than objective and detached. She writes from the intensity of her lived experience. He finds the same qualities in the approach of Anne Sullivan, Helen Keller's teacher. A case could be made, as well, for the political progressivism of the work that Andrea Lunsford and Lisa Ede are doing on collaborative writing, for Marilyn Cooper's work on writing as social action, and for the growing body of work on literacy that calls our attention to the effects of race and ethnicity on language development. And there has always been an interest within the field in the use of gender-neutral language and guidelines for eliminating sexist language.

The field of composition studies is beginning to discover feminism. Janet Emig and Louise Phelps are co-editing a book tentatively entitled *Feminine*

Principles in Composition and Rhetoric. The 1989 Conference on College Composition and Communication took for its theme "Empowering Students and Ourselves in an Interdependent World" and included sessions on women's history, pedagogy, and values; how gender affects students' writing, reading, and small-group work; rhetoric and the women's suffrage movement; gender and research methodologies; and characteristics of women's writing. The *Journal of Advanced Composition* has done a special issue on "Gender, Culture, Ideology." We may be twenty years behind fields such as literary studies, linguistics, and speech communication, but we are beginning to catch up.

Notes

1. See Kramarae and Spender's *The Knowledge Explosion.*

2. Most of the articles in the May 1971 issue of *College English* were written at the request of the MLA Commission on Women and read at the Forum or in the Workshops on Women in the Profession during the 1970 Annual Meeting of the Modern Language Association. They are by such prominent feminists as Florence Howe, Elaine Showalter, Annis Pratt, Lillian S. Robinson, Sydney Kaplan, and Alleen Pace Nilsen.

3. Some university presses that have a series in women's studies include Southern Illinois University Press, the University of Illinois Press, The State University of New York Press, Columbia University Press, Cornell University Press, and Indiana University Press. There are many others. An example of an international journal is *Women's Studies International Forum* published by Pergamon Press.

4. See Bleich, *The Double Perspective*; Culler, *On Deconstruction*; and Booth, "Freedom of Interpretation: Bakhtin and the Challenge of Feminist Criticism."

5. Some examples are: Carol Carpenter, "Exercises to Combat Sexist Reading and Writing"; Thomas J. Farrell, "The Female and Male Modes of Rhetoric"; Margaret B. Pigott, "Sexist Roadblocks in Inventing, Focusing, and Writing."

6. Some examples are: Lallie Coy, "Review of *Woman as Writer*," (eds. Jeannette L. Weber and Joan Grumman, Houghton Mifflin, 1978) and Carol A. Huber, "Review of *Teaching Writing: Pedagogy, Gender, and Equity*," (eds. Cynthia L. Caywood and Gillian R. Overing, State University of New York Press, 1987).

7. Some examples are: Robin Lakoff's *Language and Woman's Place* (1975), Thorne and Henley's *Language and Sex: Difference and Dominance* (1975), Butturff and Epstein's, *Women's Language and Style* (1978), McConnell-Ginet, Borker, and Furman, *Woman and Language in Literature and Society* (1980), and Dale Spender's *Man Made Language* (1980). This work has continued in books such as Cheris Kramarae's *Women and Men Speaking: Frameworks for Analysis* (1981), Thorne, Kramarae, and Henley, *Language, Gender and Society* (1983), and Kramarae, Schulz, and O'Barr, *Language and Power* (1984).

8. The anthology *Women's Language and Style*, for instance, is a compilation of papers presented at the Conference on Language and Style sponsored by the Graduate Center—City University of New York in April 1977. Contributors include individuals in linguistics (Robin Lakoff and Sally McConnell-Ginet), and speech communication (Pamela Fishman and Francine Wattman Frank). Many, though,

are in literary studies (Nelly Furman, Carolyn Allen, Sydney Janet Kaplan, Annette Kolodny). We see the same interdisciplinary mix in *Women and Language in Literature and Society* (1980) edited by McConnell-Ginet (a linguist), Borker (an anthropologist), and Furman (a literary critic). The editors tell us in the preface that the book grew out of their association as colleagues in the Cornell Women's Studies Program. The book contains pieces by women in linguistics, speech communication, and anthropology, though 9 of the 21 contributors are in literary studies.

9. See my essay, "The Classroom as Interpretive Community."

10. I heard Sonja and Karen Foss deliver papers with a feminist orientation at the 1983 Speech Communication Association Convention.

11. The little information I have about Madame Olbrechts-Tyteca comes from a conversation with Jeanne Fahnestock at the Conference on College Composition and Communication in St. Louis in 1988. Lisa Ede was able to come up with little more for her talk on Olbrechts-Tyteca at the session of the Women Rhetoricians Interest Group at the 1989 CCCC.

12. For a discussion of agonistic rhetoric in the context of student writing see Susan Osborn, "Revisioning the Argument: An Exploratory Study of Some Rhetorical Strategies of Women Student Writers."

13. Actually, Burke not only mentions Marianne Moore in *A Grammar of Motives*, he devotes a section of the appendix to an analysis of her poetry (485–502).

14. See my "Composing as a Woman."

15. I should note that Ohmann was editor of *College English* when the 1971 issue devoted to women's concerns discussed above was published and so he contributed in an important way to the emergence of feminist literary criticism.

16. See Karlyn Kohrs Campbell's, *A Critical Study of Early Feminist Rhetoric* and *Key Texts of the Early Feminists*, Volumes 1 and 2 of *Man Cannot Speak for Her*. Campbell analyzes the speeches and writings of the nineteenth- and twentieth-century women's rights movement.

17. I discuss feminist research methods more fully in "Composing 'Composing as a Woman.'"

Works Cited

Belenky, Mary Field, et al. *Women's Ways of Knowing: The Development of Self, Voice, and Mind*. New York: Basic Books, 1986.

Berlin, James. "James Berlin Responds." *College English* 51 (November 1989): 770–777.

———. *Rhetoric and Reality: Writing Instruction in America Colleges, 1900–1985*. Carbondale: Southern Illinois University Press, 1987.

Bleich, David. *The Double Perspective: Language, Literacy, and Social Relations*. New York: Oxford University Press, 1988.

Booth, Wayne C. "Freedom of Interpretation: Bakhtin and the Challenge of Feminist Criticism." *Critical Inquiry* 9 (1983): 45–76.

Britton, James, Tony Burgess, Nancy Martin, Alex McLeod, and Harold Rosen. *The Development of Writing Abilities (11–18)*. London: Macmillan Education, 1975.

Burke, Kenneth. *A Grammar of Motives*. Berkeley: University of California Press, 1945.

————. *A Rhetoric of Motives*. Berkeley: University of California Press, 1969.

Butturff, Douglas, and Edmund L. Epstein. *Women's Language and Style*. Akron: E. L. Epstein, 1978.

Campbell, Karlyn Kohrs. *Man Cannot Speak for Her*, Vols. 1 and 2. Westport, CT: Greenwood Press, 1989.

Carpenter, Carol. "Exercises to Combat Sexist Reading and Writing." *College English* 43 (1981): 293–300.

Caywood, Cynthia L., and Gillian R. Overing. *Teaching Writing: Pedagogy, Gender, and Equity*. Albany: State University of New York Press, 1987.

Cooper, Lane. *The Rhetoric of Aristotle: An Expanded Translation with Supplementary Examples for Students of Composition and Public Speaking*. New York: Appleton-Century Crofts, 1932.

Coy, Lallie. "Review of *Woman as Writer*." Eds. Jeannette L. Weber and Joan Grumman. *CCC* 30 (February 1979): 94–95.

Culler, Jonathan. *On Deconstruction: Theory and Criticism after Structuralism*. Ithaca: Cornell University Press, 1982.

Daly, Mary. *Beyond God the Father: Toward a Philosophy of Women's Liberation*. Boston: Beacon Press, 1973.

de Beauvoir, Simone. *The Second Sex*. Trans. and Ed. H. M. Parshley. New York: Knopf, 1952.

Dinnerstein, Dorothy. *The Mermaid and the Minotaur*. New York: Harper and Row, 1976.

Dixon, Peter. *Rhetoric*. London: Methuen, 1971.

Ede, Lisa. "Lucia Olbrechts-Tyteca." Women Rhetoricians Interest Group. Conference on College Composition and Communication. Seattle, 1989.

Farrell, Thomas J. "The Female and Male Modes of Rhetoric." *College English* 40 (April 1979): 909–921.

Flynn, Elizabeth A. "The Classroom as Interpretive Community: Teaching Reader-Response Theory and Composition Theory to Preprofessional Undergraduates." In *Reorientations: Critical Theories and Pedagogies*. Eds. Bruce Henricksen and Thais Morgan. Urbana: University of Illinois Press, 1990 (193–215).

————. "Composing as a Woman." *CCC* 39 (December 1988): 423–435.

————. "Composing 'Composing as a Woman': A Perspective on Research." *CCC* 41 (February 1990): 83–89.

Foss, Sonja A., Karen A. Foss, and Robert Trapp. *Contemporary Perspectives on Rhetoric*. Prospect Heights, IL: Waveland Press, Inc., 1985.

Gilligan, Carol. *In a Different Voice: Psychological Theory and Women's Development*. Cambridge: Harvard University Press, 1982.

Grumet, Madeleine R. *Bitter Milk: Women and Teaching*. Amherst: University of Massachusetts Press, 1988.

Huber, Carol A. "Review of *Teaching Writing: Pedagogy, Gender and Equity*," eds. Cynthia L. Caywood and Gillian R. Overing. *CCC* 38 (October 1987): 355–366.

Kramarae, Cheris, Muriel Schulz, and William M. O'Barr. *Language and Power*. Beverley Hills: Sage, 1984.

————. *Women and Men Speaking: Frameworks for Analysis*. Rowley, MA: Newbury House, 1981.

Kramarae, Cheris, and Dale Spender, eds. *The Knowledge Explosion*. Elmsford, N.Y.: Pergamon, forthcoming.

Lakoff, Robin. *Language and Woman's Place*. New York: Harper and Row, 1975.

154   Composition Studies from a Feminist Perspective

McConnell-Ginet, Sally, Ruth Borker, and Nelly Furman. *Women and Language in Literature and Society*. New York: Praeger, 1980.

Millett, Kate. *Sexual Politics*. New York: Avon, 1970.

Ohmann, Richard. *English in America: A Radical View of the Profession*. New York: Oxford University Press, 1976.

Ong, Walter. *Orality and Literacy: The Technologizing of the Word*. London: Methuen, 1982.

Osborn, Susan. "Revisioning the Argument: An Exploratory Study of Some Rhetorical Strategies of Women Student Writers." *Praxis* (Spring/Summer 1987): 113–133.

Perelman, Chaim, and Lucia Olbrechts-Tyteca. *The New Rhetoric: A Treatise on Argumentation*. Notre Dame, IN: University of Notre Dame Press, 1969.

Pigott, Margaret B. "Sexist Roadblocks in Inventing, Focusing, and Writing." *College English* 48 (April 1981): 922–927.

Schweickart, Patrocinio P. "Gender and Theories of Discourse." Association of Departments of English Conference. Houghton, MI: 1987.

Spender, Dale. *Man Made Language*. London: Routledge and Kegan Paul, 1980.

Toulmin, Stephen. *The Uses of Argument*. Cambridge: Cambridge University Press, 1958.

Thorne, Barrie, and Nancy Henley, eds. *Language and Sex: Difference and Dominance*. Rowley, MA: Newbury House, 1975.

Thorne, Barrie, Cheris Kramarae, and Nancy Henley. *Language, Gender and Society*. Rowley, MA: Newbury House, 1983.

9

The Institutional Logic of Writing Programs: Catalyst, Laboratory, and Pattern for Change

LOUISE WETHERBEE PHELPS
Syracuse University

Writing Programs and English Departments: Changing the Question

Most often, the question of writing programs within academic institutions comes up in terms of their relationship to English departments. After arguing here that this formulation severely cramps our thinking, I will reframe the problem of writing programs in terms of their potential relationships to the whole system—the goals and structures of the educational institutions that house them. In this piece, my focus will be on writing programs as new educational philosophies and technologies that stress the system in salutary ways, acting as change agents within their institutions. I will suggest that the logical structure of writing programs makes them natural catalysts and laboratories for reform in higher education.

At a recent conference of writing program administrators, many speakers addressed issues related to the administrative location of writing programs, typically within departments of English: problems of budgeting, administrative authority, curricular control, faculty assignments, faculty rewards, and so on. Despite the advancement of composition as an academic discipline, commonly the hierarchies of English departments still control policy-making for writing programs and fail to appreciate them as intellectual enterprises grounded in theory and research (Commission on Writing and Literature). Among writing program administrators, the frustration of having responsibility without power remains an overwhelming preoccupation, displacing attention to conceptual issues like curriculum or evaluation (see Olson and Moxley on the limits of authority among writing directors).

These arguments about administrative autonomy for writing programs are inseparable from ongoing debates about the nature and viability of English studies, the present and potential connections between composition and literature, and the role of rhetoric as a unifying force (for a sampling of views, see Berlin; Clifford and Schilb; Horner; Irmscher; Phelps and Mailloux; and Winterowd). Each enterprise appeals to history and theory to anchor its case for institutional structures (political autonomy for composition, reorganization of English departments, control of graduate programs, and so on). Despite the complexity of the picture that various narratives and theories present, the argument returns obsessively to the "relationship," the gap, and the alternatives: literature/composition, rhetoric/ideology, identity/difference, separation/(re)unification. Above all, the paradigm is one of power—a dominant/subordinate relation and the promise—or threat—of its reversal (Johnson; Scholes 1–17).

In a 1985 address to the Conference on College Composition and Communication ("Breaking Our Bonds") Maxine Hairston challenged writing faculty to think the unthinkable: to consider walking out of English departments. She was recognizing that the growing intellectual and material strength of composition in the academy made this a viable possibility while continuing grievances made it defensible (see Robertson, Crowley, and Lentricchia). Yet many in composition remain extraordinarily reluctant to countenance "secession." Hairston's speech evoked cheers, but these were followed by a storm of criticism and renewed efforts to "bridge the gap" or refigure the relationship (see "Speculations" for Hairston's second thoughts; cf. Irmscher, Slevin, and Bartolomae). Meanwhile the literary establishment, going through its own revolution, began to take alarm at the possible disintegration of English. As some individuals in both literary studies and composition/rhetoric began to call for rapprochement, the Modern Language Association took a number of conciliatory steps. Initiatives include those reported by the Commission on Writing and Literature and the new ten-volume series of publications on research in composition and rhetoric recently announced by MLA.

Obviously, at both practical and intellectual levels, this love/hate schema powerfully organizes discussion and action on a very complex, politically charged set of conflicts, concerns, and possibilities related to composition in the academy.

Why, then, do I resist writing about it (or, rather, within it) here?

Because I think we are "stuck" in a classic trap of dualistic logic, feeding on images of conflict and violence (the bad marriage, the parent and rebellious adolescent, the victim and oppressor). As with all such polarities, we must find our way out of its impossible either/or choice or forever spin our wheels because it makes no sense to me for composition to seek a new role in the academy by assuming that English departments are more important to writing programs (even as enemy) than other possible partners, intellectual and institutional. And, finally, because I think that outside our own "academic village" this question is fundamentally boring, parochial, and essentially a matter of academic turf (I keep wondering uneasily what Charles Sykes, of *ProfScam* fame, would make of all this). I would like to get on to genuine questions about how writing programs can work within institutions to enhance education.

At Syracuse, establishment of a new writing program in 1987 presented a unique opportunity for breaking out of this impasse by creating a test case in which a writing program separated from its parent English department while leaving genuinely open the question of their subsequent relations. In a moment of grace, all sides agreed on a collaboratively produced "draft" charter for the new unit, with a clear agreement that it would serve as a general, revisable framework for evolutionary change.

This move has immediate tonal and rhetorical consequences for the original dilemma. The question shifts from the debate/choice framework to a provisional and experimental one ("What if we try this, what will happen?"). While the charter speaks of a "special relationship" between the new program and the Syracuse English department, it does not enforce a particular one but invites the political work that gives such a claim reality. In such rhetorical politics, relationships continue and evolve only when the parties have something at stake, something in common, something to offer, something to withhold, and some definition of their own identities that is not determined by the very "relationship" that is in question.

Quickly it becomes apparent that there is no single determinate "relationship" between writing and English — nor ever was. This term has concealed a multiplicity of relations — conflict, exploitation, paternalism, intellectual borrowings, parallel development, benign neglect, rivalry — between two groups with overlapping but different histories, disciplinary sources and influences, and contemporary agendas (Crowley and Phelps). Their problem is not to maintain a single relationship but to examine the densely textured ways in which their work converges and diverges; to negotiate seams, coalitions, alliances, principled disagreements, or simply mutual respect for separate concerns.

Much of what I have said so far parallels James Slevin's discusssion of the possible lateral connections across the boundaries between "composition" and "literature" based on common values, interests, and questions. He develops a critique focused on figuration, attacking the synecdoche of singular identity for English Studies: "Because synecdoche reifies into one stable 'identity' what is in fact a heterogeneous and ever-changing set of practices, we tend to think exclusively in terms of joining two separate and definable entities, 'literature' on the one hand and 'composition' on the other ... reduc[ing] the activities of scholars and teachers to membership in one or the other of two global entities, literature and composition. It thereby conceals the possibility of making, from among a great multiplicity of practices, connections that are more localized, specific, and *equal"* (547).

Slevin does not take his point to its logical conclusion, to recognize that the connections he exemplifies do not define or argue for "English Studies" or "English departments" in particular, but represent common themes in the humanities, social sciences, and even professional disciplines. (For instance, interest in the social contexts of writing connects composition to education, linguistics, anthropology, psychology, speech, and classics just as closely as it does to literary and cultural studies.) Without fully acknowledging it, Slevin has through his local, lateral strategy decentered the composition/literature bipolarity in favor of connections that necessarily place either group in relation to multiple "others" in the academy—and beyond.

Now I want to argue that this same revision of the original two-valued relationship, which Slevin accomplishes at a figurative level, takes place in institutional terms when a writing program separates from a department, freeing itself to recognize and advance affinities and practical connections with other academic units. A host of interesting institutional problems, issues, and relationships emerge that were hitherto obscured by its embeddedness in a departmental structure.

I am not concerned here with Syracuse as a model for institutionalizing writing programs, in or out of English departments. I agree with Hairston ("Speculations") that the political decisions locating writing in academic units must, at least for now, be local and institution-specific. What interests me is what happens—with respect to conceiving writing programs—when we bracket the "English" question, suspending it in order to pay attention to something else. The institutional arrangements at Syracuse are a form of bracketing, parallel to the intellectual strategy I am adopting in this essay. I hope thereby to reveal an institutional logic to writing programs, rooted in the structure of composition and rhetoric, that fortuitously matches the current needs for change in the academy.

Boldly done, separation of writing from an English department exposes previously submerged problems in a particularly pure and insistent form. Our program was deliberately set up to foreground those problems, refuse ad hoc solutions (such as had worked when the program was in English), and require creative, workable answers for the program to run at all. We are fortunate to work in a particularly open environment where such a gamble could succeed. But I shall not be speaking of solutions, only questions. My first point, then, is that many problems endemic to academic institutions (for example, rewarding teaching and service, planning workload for administrators, budgeting for nontraditional instruction, encouraging cross-disciplinary teaching and research efforts) become salient, lucid, and focused tasks in the context of defining the institutional logic of a writing program.

Further, although many writing programs within English departments develop relationships with academic units "across the curriculum," such relationships become much more visible when the writing program is an entity in itself, with its own faculty and administrative representatives forming working relationships with policy-making bodies and officials. No matter how a writing program is organized, it has major responsibilities to the students and curriculum of other academic units (in our case, through a sequence of required writing courses and pilot projects connecting writing to the disciplines). Furthermore, as an independent unit, the program begins to interact directly with nonacademic units like the library, computing services, space and facilities, and so on, bringing out and exploiting functional interdependencies, becoming an active player in negotiations for resources that were before subsumed — and neglected — within a departmental budget. (At Syracuse, the cost of the previous program was so buried within the English budget as to be unrecoverable.)

In the course of developing these relationships, an isomorphism begins to surface between the intellectual structure of composition and rhetoric, as a highly intertextual, multisourced discipline, and the unconventional ways it ties its teaching project to many different departments and colleges (in our case, both undergraduate and graduate). It becomes evident to other faculty that a writing program is acting out, through these linkages, philosophical and ethical principles strongly based in an intellectual tradition. Work with other faculty on curricular projects brings out intellectual affinities and renews historical relationships (e.g., between composition and speech communications, or rhetoric and philosophy, or writing and education). These interpersonal connections made initially for administrative and teaching purposes become routes to research discussions and collaboration.

These intrinsic features of writing programs become more valuable, as well as more visible, when writing and writing instruction are perceived as distributed, decentered functions tied into student learning and faculty teaching throughout the institution and throughout the undergraduate experience. Exactly how this is done differs greatly from one place to another, but the logic of writing programs calls for such a multiconnected, horizontally integrated organization. Further, this organization reflects, and when put into place furthers, the research mission of composition and rhetoric along with its need to access and translate for its own purposes an eclectic theoretical base in the studies of many disciplines. For example, the ability of composition researchers to study writing in academic and professional cultures depends on their entry to these cultures through the teaching routes created by writing programs.

The Match

Writing programs have developed inexorably toward cross-institutional operations, no matter what their departmental or extradepartmental base. In the form of Freshman English, writing instruction has long been one of the few common requirements for all students at a college or university. In that sense, writing has always been a broad feature of the undergraduate experience rather than a departmental specialty. Writing across the disciplines and writing centers are a natural extension of this mission, enhancing the institutional presence of writing programs and giving them an interdisciplinary intellectual dimension.

It is therefore of enormous significance to writing programs that the institutions housing them are in crisis. There is not really a single crisis, but many specific ones affecting different types of institutions, whose synergy and cumulative impact are finally drawing national attention to the state of higher education. These are some problem areas, for example: demographic changes in the applicant pool; dwindling resources; changing relationships to government and business; student preparation in the elementary and secondary schools; an influx of foreign graduate students; the incidence of drugs, rape, racism, and violence on campuses; and the need to replace most of the professoriate in the next twenty years. I will focus on the crisis of public confidence in undergraduate teaching, which exposes fundamental problems in the structure of higher education and calls for reexamination of the values and organization of the academy.

There is a growing literature of critiques and prescriptions for change in higher education. Two contrasting examples are the provocative muckraking of Charles Sykes in *ProfScam* and the benign, supportive recommendations of Ernest Boyer on behalf of the Carnegie Foundation. While they differ in tone as well as on the locus of responsibility (Sykes placing all blame on a selfish and irresponsible professoriate), they are in substantial agreement on many of the basic issues and problems.

One cluster of issues centers on teaching and the quality of the undergraduate experience. It is generally agreed that both have sunk to a shockingly low level in many schools, especially in the elite institutions. The root problem is that undergraduate teaching takes last place in higher education, after research and graduate study, sometimes even after big-time athletics, relations to corporations, or service to the state. This set of priorities has led to hypocrisy and cynicism about teaching, to a system in which publication is rewarded and good teaching punished. From this distortion flow many abuses, including such staples of American colleges as mass lecture classes, an incoherent curriculum, overreliance on poorly trained teaching assistants and underpaid part-timers, loss of collegiality, and inaccessibility of professors to undergraduates.

Sykes sketches out a history of this academic culture, beginning in the nineteenth century when American universities adopted the German ideal of the university as a center for research where the professor (certified by the new PhD degree) could contribute to the search for knowledge. It took most of the century for that shift in values to play itself out through the whole system of higher education, accelerating in the postwar period and especially in the nineteen-sixties with an influx of federal money that transferred power from local institutions to what Sykes calls the "academic villages": "the parallel, shadow universities that dominate the academic culture ... basically synonymous with the disciplines themselves" (21). With the sixties and their social conflicts and changes came the abandonment of general education as a curricular principle and what Sykes calls the "flight from teaching," with lower-division education in particular being turned over to teaching assistants, part-timers, and the "gypsies" — PhDs employed on a temporary basis.

Boyer paints a broader, more varied and subtle picture of the troubles of higher education, based on a study done by the Carnegie Foundation. In his account, the decline in undergraduate education both contributes to and follows from a pervasive disintegration of relationships within educational institutions and between them and other parts of society. "Cultural coherence has faded ... the very notion of commonalities seems strikingly inapplicable to the vigorous diversity of contemporary life. Within the academy itself, the fragmentation of knowledge, narrow departmentalism, and an intense vocationalism are ... the strongest characteristics of collegiate education" (7). He identifies eight "points of tension" in colleges that reflect an inability to find common ground and purpose and to resolve fundamental conflicts. As compared to Sykes's indictment, Boyer underplays the priority given to research as only one factor in the fragmentation, individualization, feudalization (the "academic villages"), and specialization that have torn the institutions apart. In this picture, the professor is a victim along with the student, as Sykes too implies in speaking of the lost "fellowship of scholars," replaced by turf fights, competition for grants, and the pursuit of tenure, promotion, and prestige — the currency of higher education.

Some of Boyer's points and observations are of special interest from the perspective of writing programs. He notes the discontinuity and incoherence of curriculum, not only within colleges but between schools and colleges. His chapter dealing with high school preparation puts particular stress on writing and reading, recommending better articulation and collaborative programs between the college and secondary levels. He agrees with Sykes that in college curricula diversity has become smorgasbord, and students have no guidance or principles to help them integrate their fragmented bits and pieces of knowledge. The students themselves are often passive learners focused on narrow career goals. The remedies Boyer proposes go beyond the notion of a common core, seeking to build three types of connections: across disciplines; between levels of the education system; and from the academy to the public world. He argues for an *integrated core*, inherently interdisciplinary and interdepartmental (including "language" as a major theme); an *enriched major* that requires students to put their own discipline in perspective with historical, social, and ethical questions; and an effort to *create community* through college-sponsored service programs. In each case, the remedy envisions a more active, independent learner fully engaged in the intellectual and social life of the institution and taking responsibility for understanding and contributing to the larger culture.

In discussing the issue of research and specialization, Boyer makes the important point that all professors, whether publishing researchers or not, should be "scholars," i.e., learners, and that they need to make their intellectual work accessible through various kinds of communication, participation, and dissemination, including both professional activities and innovative teaching projects. He also calls for faculty renewal through sabbaticals, faculty exchanges, grant programs that fund teaching experiments and curriculum planning, and other measures for supporting faculty members' intellectual growth. Finally, he recommends an appropriate balance between full-time and part-time faculty without, however, addressing adequately the issues of non-tenure-track faculty pay, conditions, and participation in university life.

For anyone who knows the history of writing programs, it is obvious that there is a close match between what they do, or try to do, and the needs for reform just outlined. This is not at all to say that writing programs are the panacea for the problems of undergraduate education, although I suspect some enthusiasts of "writing to learn" may think so. My claim is much more limited. First, I think that the concepts and goals of writing programs coincide in many respects with the emerging consensus about needed changes in undergraduate teaching and learning. Second, what one might call the metagoals of writing programs for creating working communities and multiplying connections across contexts make them a test case for studying and supporting such efforts. This is particularly the case because writing programs, in their emphasis on writing as a tool of thought, foster programmatic self-examination and thoughtful reflection about their own teaching projects and about the fundamental issues of college life. Third, the nontraditional organization of a writing program bears on institutional change in several ways. Writing programs carry out practical experiments with new administrative structures and roles along with nontraditional teaching formats; they co-develop or demonstrate such innovations to other faculty and academic units; they may stimulate changes in university procedures and structures to accommodate program needs. In the last respect, particularly, writing programs put a lot of pressure on universities to solve problems for them (problems that require solution if the programs are to survive, much less contribute to realizing institutional visions of change).

To make this case, I will first consider the principles motivating several writing programs and then generate an exemplary list of problems that writing programs pose for themselves or for their institutions.

The Principles and Challenges of Writing Programs

Jo-Ann Sipple begins her article on designing writing programs (writing across the curriculum) by noting that this movement addresses "a host of expectations around functional literacy, critical thinking, creativity, problem-solving strategies, reasoning skills, collaborative learning, and even faculty development" (444). Pointing out the need to articulate theoretical assumptions, she compares those of several colleges that have designed institution-wide writing programs. For example, Michigan Tech's program makes three assumptions drawn from James Britton's work: "'(1) Writing promotes learning, (2) writing is a complex developmental process, and (3) the universe of discourse includes a broad range of writing functions and audiences'" (Freisenger, quoted in Sipple 446–447). She cites Beaver College as using Kenneth Bruffee's theory of collaborative learning to implement the idea of community in the curriculum through peer readings of drafts and to incorporate writing into all teaching and learning. Her own college, Robert Morris, has been influenced by the work of Janet Emig, Elaine Maimon, and Richard Young, providing these premises: "(1) writing is a mode of learning; (2) each academic discipline that shapes the writing of its practitioners is driven by its own specialized procedures, conventions, and terminology in an interactive process between writing and learning; (3) writers can develop and apply defined sets of heuristics or writing strategies to help them think more effectively about the subject matter of their disciplines" (447). She goes on to point out that goals are more local, addressing the specific needs of an institution. For example, at Robert Morris, which has a business emphasis, the writing program helped faculty incorporate writing-to-learn strategies in the business disciplines in order for students to think and learn well in those disciplines. As outside evaluators pointed out, this purpose was indistinguishable from the goal of improving teaching generally.

These briefly stated principles only suggestively capture complex recognitions by the composition community of the relationships between writing and learning, self and society, commonality and difference, writing programs and the disciplines. The themes we would discover if we looked more closely at these programs, or at the theoretical discourse of composition and rhetoric, not only address the issues identified earlier in critiques of the academy, but actually negotiate the tensions we saw there. Those themes include, for example: 1) writing as a tool for students to become *active inquirers and learners*, countering the image of the professor as the privileged producer of knowledge; 2) general or *common* strategies and processes of literacy, applied and adapted for diverse rhetorical situations in deeply *different* discourse communities; 3) *collaborative work* using writing to solve problems, not only within writing classes but among colleagues, in curricular projects, research, and co-authorship (see Biddle and Fulwiler, for example); and 4) the patient, unglamorous effort to sustain shared tasks and to communicate through talk and text that builds community among the teachers and students of a writing program and across the territorial boundaries that divide institutions.

Many program statements express their goals for students' learning more clearly than their broad aims for institutional changes, either for strategic and practical reasons or because the intimate connection between the two has not yet become visible. Yet implicit in their own teaching goals is the hope of affecting for the better the attitudes and conditions of teaching and undergraduate life: by changing the way students approach learning in the disciplines; by working with colleagues redesigning their teaching, and through these interchanges giving teaching more value as intellectual work; by promoting other joint ventures including research and curricular experimentation; by demonstrating the possibility for faculty growth and renewal through cooperation. With luck and just the right conditions, writing programs can serve as catalysts for major institutional changes (Fulwiler and Young).

The establishment at Syracuse of a writing program with deliberately unspecified responsibilities to the whole university compelled us to articulate these institutional goals. A 1988 summary (written, incidentally, before I read either Sykes's or Boyer's books) states this as the program goal: "To use writing as a basis for reintegrating the often fragmented activities of thinkers and learners at a research university in terms of their common practices of inquiry and communication . . . [by creating] in the Writing Program a model intellectual community whose students, instructors, and researchers write, 'publish,' and work collaboratively with others at Syracuse to connect research, teaching, and learning across the contexts of the university." (For the full statement, see Appendix.)

Writing programs push the limits in more ways than I have yet accounted for. At Syracuse we have experienced this fact in a very concrete way, as step by step we tried to construct an unprecedented structure at the university. It becomes clear in this situation that redesigning writing instruction for such broad and unusual purposes necessitates change in virtually every aspect of program organization and support. In a favorable situation, where the institution wants the program to succeed, program development creates strong, positive pressures to solve these problems. Here is a sampling of such matters generalized from the Syracuse context, each a case where program needs have set constructive changes in motion. Our solutions are not the point (most are still highly experimental or partial); what matters is clear articulation of a problem. In this sense, writing programs are *heuristics for change* because they are inveterate problem-finders and problem-definers. As writing teachers know, recognizing and formulating a problem is a huge step toward generating creative solutions.

Problem: Writing programs need to be academic units, part of the intellectual mainstream, connected into the academic village structure. That means they need faculty of their own and a research component to their enterprise. Yet they are anomalous both within departments or as separate departments, because of their functions and programmatic structure. How can the institution define, and disciplines tolerate, an academic teaching-research unit that is not departmental?

Problem: Writing programs break down the conventional boundaries that distinguish sharply among teaching, research, and service; they value significant intellectual work by their faculty that cuts across these categories. How can the faculty reward system accommodate to this requirement, evaluating writing program faculty for tenure, promotion, and raises according to criteria appropriate to their assignments, the work of their discipline(s), and the goals of the program? How can their loads be adjusted to account for their work in curriculum development, professional development, teacher training, and so on?

Problem: Writing programs make unconventional use of space, for example in writing centers, tutoring in dorms, and computer clusters. They often need flexible, rearrangeable spaces. How can the institution modify its rigid concepts and categories of space to fit these needs?

Problem: Writing programs do not fit their teaching neatly into the time schedules and slots set up for conventional courses. Their teaching is not class by class, but *curricular*; it addresses the long-range development of students' literacy and intellectual potential. How can the institution budget and contract for teaching that is not tied to the day-to-day, semester, or year schedule? How can it take account of the developmental progress of writing skills and knowledge as opposed to incremental learning?

Problem: Writing programs have equipment needs that are not only unusual in the humanities (computer classrooms and labs, for example) but require special design of the equipment itself, the environment, and the services that support them. How will such needs be met—who will design the equipment, and how will it be paid for, housed, maintained, and supported with technical advice?

Problem: Writing programs require instructional budgeting arrangements that transcend the usual categories and institutional units, which are competitive and mutually exclusive. Once programs start developing new functions not accounted for by course credits and traditional instruction, including services and linkages to other units, they require not only new monies but new ways of calculating and planning costs and sources. How can the institution raise such monies and account for the collaborative, symbiotic nature of the writing program's pedagogical work?

Problem: Writing programs must solve the ethical and practical dilemmas of part-time instruction as well as teaching by inexperienced graduate students, often from disciplines other than composition. Writing programs cannot function without enriching the roles and opportunities of these teachers, who comprise the bulk of the faculty in many institutions, and must find ways to help them grow professionally and to reward them adequately. They must also establish an appropriate ratio and productive relationships among many different kinds of faculty and staff. How can an institution solve the thorny problem of part-time instruction fairly for all sides? How can it strike a balance between institutional and personal rights and requirements? How can it justify and manage the practice of using teaching assistants without exploiting graduate students or disadvantaging undergraduates? How can it account in its budgeting and employment structures for the many new nonteaching roles that such instructors begin to take on in a program that integrates teaching with inquiry, writing, and professional development?

Problem: Writing programs must develop entirely new evaluation systems to match their new goals for students, teachers, program, and impact on the institution and the profession. How can the writing program itself carry out this research on evaluation under constant scrutiny by the whole institution, given their typical constraints on time, budget, and intellectual resources? How can the institution support this rethinking of evaluation during a program's formative stages, while safeguarding the rights of students to quality education?

Problem: Writing programs must reach out to other parts of the educational system and make connections. How is this possible, given many other responsibilities, and how will the institution value these activities by faculty?

Problem: Writing programs are often dominated by women. Their organization and administration raise feminist issues about the academy's value system and power structure. Writing programs tend to imagine and experiment with organizational structures expressing different values and must make these practical and effective within the existing hierarchical, competitive systems of academic administration, even as they may hope to modify those systems over time. How will the writing program, and the institution, negotiate these tensions?

This selective list shows that the logic of writing programs (itself locally variant and subject to redefinition over time) poses many of the problems that confront higher education, and in a concrete form accessible to focused problem-solving. A writing program has the virtue of being relatively self-contained and collegiate (a face-to-face community, sharing space, engaged in common work), yet not isolated: its mission ties it into the administrative networks and the academic village structures that run collegiate institutions. Hence it is an ideal laboratory for conducting and disseminating the results of teaching-learning experiments and practical research, usually in small pilots. Such experimentation is often done in collaboration with other units. As Tom Peters points out, such "small starts" by problem-solving teams provide a flexible, adaptive mechanism for taking creative risks at low cost, in the contemporary condition of constant change ("thriving on chaos").

At the same time, a writing program can be a catalyst, an irritant or stimulant as well as a laboratory. It can push administrators and faculty toward genuine efforts to resolve long-standing problems that have been neglected. It can also discover problems that no one quite knew, or acknowledged, were there; invent new ones as a result of choosing new goals; or provide solutions that in turn generate new problems. Working with other units, it can function as a probe, a gadfly, a stimulus for thinking and planning, an organizer, a source of intellectual energy, a respondent, an assistant or co-planner, and so on. Many of its innovative practices, tried out on a small scale, can become patterns for others to try out or vary, with the advantage of precedent in breaking rules or showing the feasibility of unusual structures. Failures are just as important as successes for all these functions of writing programs — experimenting boldly, becoming a catalyst for others' innovations, constantly generating new patterns for instructional modes and collaboration (see Peters on "fast failures" and risk taking).

The most important contribution I think writing programs can make, though, with respect to higher education at large, is to exemplify the struggle to foster community in the face of the prevailing mood of skepticism, critique of all cultural institutions and their traditions, radical individualism, and loss of fellowship that troubles our colleges and universities. Certain features of writing programs often appear as disadvantages — for instance, their mix of part-time faculty, professorial faculty, and teaching assistants; their labor-intensiveness; or their "service" nature in relation to other departments or colleges — making their task both harder and easier. These features suggest the difficulty, but also the need and opportunity, for writing programs to coordinate the work of the three groups whose relationship has become so problematic: students, teachers without "researcher" status, and professors trained to "produce knowledge." Because their teaching conditions and approaches bring these groups into intimate propinquity (through small classes, mentorship of teachers, consulting or tutoring for students, faculty development and assistance, occupation of common space), mediated by a central curriculum or teaching project, writing programs have the rare opportunity to redefine that problematic relationship through concrete practices of community.

By fostering relations among these groups and engaging them all in critically examining processes of writing, learning, and teaching, writing programs can offer a different model of institutional change. Higher education began with a "heritage" model emphasizing transmission of cultural knowledge for general application by a citizen elite. It moved, following the German university, to a notion of the university as a research center staffed by specialists in knowledge production, with undergraduate education a hit-or-miss affair. Even at exclusively undergraduate colleges with a strong teaching ethic, this concept dominates the academic culture (Boyer 12−22). Many critics of higher education argue for return to the heritage model, often in a rather rigid mode (see Bloom; Hirsch; and Adler for some provocative critiques and proposals). Theorists in various fields of language, however, envision a third possibility, and writing programs experiment with it: reinterpreting research as learning, learning as research, and teaching as practicing and mediating both. From this perspective even assimilation of a heritage is a process of inquiry, and learners and teachers are each creative, critical thinkers in the same sense, though not the same modes, that professional scholars are. Inquiry and communication are the common (though highly diverse) activities that thematize colleges and universities as places where knowledge is produced, evaluated, applied, and shared.

Having tried to enlarge the conception of writing programs by placing them within an institutional rather than a departmental matrix, I want to end on a note of stringent modesty. I am wary of romanticizing writing programs as the new hero of education, embarked on crusades of moral liberation. Such views are naive and can become self-righteous and dogmatic if they claim that writing programs should solve every problem on anyone's intellectual and political agenda: liberate students from ideology and oppression, singlehandedly develop learners into critical thinkers, convert faculty in other fields to their educational philosophies, eliminate sexism and racism, transform the value system of the academy. It would be easy to leap from victim status to intellectual hubris and pedagogical imperialism, a caution well understood by pioneers in writing across the curriculum.

Among the factors that appropriately (and heuristically) constrain the design of writing programs are, for example, the size of the school; its traditions and sense of mission; fiscal realities (and the broader context of a national economy); students' preparation and their own goals for themselves; the available pool for selecting writing instructors and hiring professors; and the politics of literacy in an institution. To deal with the politics of literacy means removing the brackets that I placed strategically around the "English" question and coming to grips with it in the concrete instance, informed now by the larger context of institutional and cultural relationships. Locally, that means factoring into program planning the political and intellectual claims of other fields. It also means building up partnerships based on the common ground we share — and the productive differences. The relationship with English becomes a possible model for constructing such interdependencies and complementarities with other departments and disciplines.

In this spirit of modesty, I suggest that we see writing programs as an example of the rhetorical concept of kairos, of fitting into the historical and situational context. Rather than having all the answers, writing programs are asking the right questions at the right moment to contribute to reform in higer education. With luck, and propitious local circumstances, this situational fit enables writing programs to become a positive force for change by enacting their own logic: operating experimentally and hypothetically; nurturing a fragile sense of community in talk, text, and collaborative work; and seeking interdependencies where they can find them.

Appendix

Writing Program at
Summary of Program Goals 1988

Program Goal: To use writing as a basis for reintegrating the often fragmented activities of thinkers and learners at a research university, in terms of their common practices of inquiry and communication.

Method: To create in the Writing Program a model intellectual community whose students, instructors, and researchers write, "publish," and work collaboratively with others at Syracuse to connect research, teaching, and learning across the contexts of the university.

Program Theme: Reflective practice.

The Writing Program will:

- Help students use writing proactively to become designers and critical agents of their own education: to connect the parts of over-compartmentalized undergraduate or graduate experiences, strengthen them intellectually, and deepen engagement.
- Provide resources for students and other writers at the university to develop and refine their technical command and critical understanding of writing as a mode of rhetoric, especially within academic and professional cultures.
- Link undergraduate learning and teaching directly to graduate education, scholarly research, and professional practices, using writing to study and practice these reflectively as interdependent activities.
- Connect various liberal and professional knowledge practices and forms of rhetoric, in part by examining and respecting their differences.
- Support productive integrations and comparisons of writing with other symbolic tools, including nonverbal communication, and between writing and new technologies.

Works Cited

Adler, Mortimer J. *The Paideia Proposal: An Educational Manifesto.* New York: Macmillan, 1982.

Bartholomae, David. "Freshman English, Composition, and CCCC." *CCC* 40 (1989): 38–50.

Biddle, Arthur, and Toby Fulwiler. "The Community of Scholars in Our Own Backyard." *ADE Bulletin* 93 (1989): 17–21.

Bloom, Allan. *The Closing of the American Mind.* New York: Simon and Schuster, 1987.

Boyer, Ernest L. *College: The Undergraduate Experience in America.* New York: The Carnegie Foundation for the Advancement of Teaching, 1987.

Clifford, John, and John Schilb. "A Perspective on Eagleton's Revival of Rhetoric." *Rhetoric Review* 6 (1987): 22–31.

Commission on Writing and Literature. "Report of the Commission on Writing and Literature." *Profession '88.* New York: MLA, 1988.

Crowley, John, and Louise Wetherbee Phelps. "Two Views of a Special Relationship: A Letter." In *Sourcebook: A Guide to the Writing Program at Syracuse.* Eds. Lynn Briggs and Rob Faivre. Syracuse. The Writing Program, Syracuse University, 1989.

Fulwiler, Tobby, and Arthur Young, eds. *Language Connections: Writing and Reading Across the Curriculum.* Urbana, IL: NCTE, 1982.

Hairston, Maxine. "Breaking Our Bonds and Reaffirming Our Connections." *CCC* 36 (1985): 272–282.

———. "Some Speculations about the Future of Writing Programs." *WPA* 11 (1988): 9–16.

Hirsch, E. D., Jr. *Cultural Literacy: What Every American Needs to Know.* Boston: Houghton Mifflin, 1987.

Irmscher, William. "Finding a Comfortable Identity." *College English* 38 (1987): 81–87.

Johnson, Paula. "Writing Programs and the English Department." *Profession '80.* New York: MLA, 1980.

Olson, Gary A., and Joseph M. Moxley. "Directing Freshman Composition: The Limits of Authority." *CCC* 40 (1989): 51–60.

Peters, Tom. *Thriving on Chaos: Handbook for a Management Revolution.* New York: Knopf, 1987.

Phelps, Louise Wetherbee, and Steven Mailloux. "Rhetoric as an Organizing Term." MLA Convention. New Orleans, December 1988.

Raymond, James C. "Rhetoric: The Methodology of the Humanities." *College English* 44 (1982): 778–783.

Robertson, Linda R., Sharon Crowley, and Frank Lentricchia. "The Wyoming Conference Resolution Opposing Unfair Salaries and Working Conditions for Post-Secondary Teachers of Writing." *College English* 49 (1987): 274–280.

Scholes, Robert. *Textual Power: Literary Theory and the Teaching of English.* New Haven: Yale University Press, 1985.

Sipple, Jo-Ann. "A Planning Process for Building Writing-across-the-Curriculum Programs to Last." *Journal of Higher Education* 60 (1989): 444–457.

Slevin, James. "Connecting English Studies." *College English* 48 (1986): 543–550.

Sykes, Charles J. *ProfScam: Professors and the Demise of Higher Education.* Washington, DC: Regnery Gateway, 1988.

Winterowd, W. Ross. "The Purification of Literature and Rhetoric." *College English* (1987): 257–273.

10

Professing Composition in the Academic Marketplace

TIMOTHY R. DONOVAN
Northeastern University

Let me begin by recalling the familiar requiem for Willy Loman in Miller's *Death of a Salesman*: "Nobody dast blame this man. You don't understand: Willy was a salesman. And for a salesman, there is no rock bottom to the life. He don't put a bolt to a nut, he don't tell you the law or give you medicine. He's a man out there in the blue, riding on a smile and a shoeshine. And when they start not smiling back—that's an earthquake. And then you get yourself a couple of spots on your hat, and you're finished. Nobody dast blame this man. A salesman is got to dream, boy. It comes with the territory."

In a similar vein, the improvement of student writing in collegiate education has always seemed to me a worthwhile and inspiring challenge — a dream, it might even be called. For a number of years, this dream gained a modicum of reality while I was directing Northeastern's freshman composition program. But after gradually giving the program my own imprint and, seemingly, some development, the inevitable frustrations set in concerning the limits of introductory writing courses. Just what were we introducing our students to, I wondered, and were we preparing them enough in any case? I had in mind that perhaps a new program was needed at Northeastern, one that would provide some follow-up instruction at a more advanced level. I had no immediate model at hand, nor any clear idea of the best way to initiate one, yet in those flush times I guess anything seemed possible.

Indeed, the years since the 1970s have been a heady era for advocates of composition. More innovations, more programs, and certainly more careers have been made in the field than could possibly have been imagined earlier. This was also a time, it may be recalled, of the "literacy crisis," when it seemed that decades of consensus in education had eroded and standards had slipped until Johnny could not, among other things, write anymore. The popular press added to the clamor, especially in a now legendary *Newsweek* article in 1975. Around the country there were various

171

efforts to ameliorate the situation, such as workshops for teachers on writing. We ourselves at Northeastern responded with a national summer institute at Martha's Vineyard.

Ironically, it was during this period that I was asked to attend a meeting of a Faculty Senate committee concerned that the literacy crisis had reportedly surfaced on our own campus. It seems that complaints had been coming in from alumni and from employers about the writing ability of our graduates. Frankly, I wasn't sure that things were any different than they had always been, or at least any worse than at comparable institutions. But the committee, duly representative of various disciplines and departments, was pretty much ready to act. The moment seemed especially ripe for that advanced writing program I had been wanting.

Although the committee pondered various alternatives, including a proficiency test and remedial classes, it wisely concluded that all students should be required to take an additional writing course during their third year at the university. Upon authorization of the Faculty Senate and president, it was left to the English department, and ultimately to me, to implement the plan. I would now have my advanced composition program.

But what did I have, really? With freshman English you have an academic tradition, experienced teachers, and an established curriculum. With a new upper division program, however, you must make all that happen again but make it different, perhaps better, and definitely advanced. The charter handed to me I found to be exhilarating but somewhat intimidating, especially when I began to think about what thousands of students should now read and write and how I would set everything in motion.

Winning the right to tackle such a task also does not guarantee everyone's full attention, as any university administrator would know. Even a mandated program has to win its "niche," for whether starting up a genetic engineering company or revising the reading list in "Western Civ," institutions of higher learning are—and always have been—a marketplace for competing programs and ideas.[1] Understandably so, given the hundreds or even thousands of dollars spent in recruitment per student, and the fact that the current scramble for students promises to increase even more with the drop of college-age clientele. The array of different majors attracting them nationally numbers over 1100 (Amberg 531). Moreover, under the force of supply and demand, weaker programs are eclipsed by new ones every year, the latter sometimes surfacing only after a so-called raid on faculty at other institutions.

For financial support, faculty and students both rely on companies, agencies, and legislatures beyond the college gates. Contributions by industry now represent almost seven percent of the $13.4 billion spent by American universities on research, up from the less than three percent spent fifteen years ago (Gosselin 26). Higher education itself, in fact, is something of a big business, even a growth industry: at $124 billion in 1987–1988, it represented three percent of the nation's entire GNP

(Amberg 525). The federal government, too, is a major player in higher education. More than five billion dollars was awarded by the National Institutes of Health, for example, in grants and contracts for biomedical research, much of it conducted in university labs and facilities (Gosselin 26).[2]

Here I pause to surmise that probably few scholars, especially in the humanities, care much about this sort of business. It is, they might say, "not what I got my degree for." Indeed, it doesn't sound like their "calling," that priestly vocation to teaching and to research still motivating most of the professoriate (Smelsor 402). Fair enough, though most of them do appreciate that the bills must be paid and students encouraged to enroll. Most faculty also would resist the popular image of the college teacher, characterized by Renaissance scholar A. Bartlett Giamatti as "the innocent, a figure unfit for the rigors of what is still constantly called 'the real world,'" and, further, as a "rumpled child, fit to tend his grazing herd of adolescents across academic groves but totally lost before machines, money, and worldly temptation" (139). The late Giamatti himself, of course, spurned that image when, as president, he departed the groves of Yale for major league baseball, eventually to become its Commissioner.

My point is that writing specialists, too, sometimes have to be versatile, outward-looking academicians. Often we don't have the luxury of just keeping up with our field, for our particular (and some would say peculiar) garden stretches into other fields and toward the "real world" as well. Moreover, our professional success may be dependent on programmatic success rather than upon just the quality of our own teaching and scholarship. The life of the writing specialist thus entails a good deal of interaction with various deans, chairs, and committees; review of requirements, courses, instructors; agreement about responsibility, authority, and overall goals. In fact, it strikes me that there are few other academic areas — excepting perhaps mathematics — in which the necessity to work with individuals outside of one's own field is so manifest. (Can a proposal for "Biology Across the Curriculum," for example, even be imagined?)

Yet other faculty will not always be "smiling back" when mention is made of writing. Often it conjures up past frustrations with students and their inadequate papers. It's perhaps inevitable that faculty might regard writing (along with SAT scores) as the most visible and conclusive symbol of what's wrong with students these days. Privately they might even admit that it's just easier to ignore the problem altogether by giving the traditional lecture and a computer-scored test. Programs in writing, particularly for freshman, have consequently tended to be considered as insurance — though minimal coverage at that — against student illiteracy.

And who would "stoop to blame this sort of trifling ... or be lessened so" (as Browning's Duke asked) by providing such low-level instruction? At many universities, the answer is the adjunct instructor or graduate student. This practice raises another problem with the image conveyed by writing programs: Any institution looks favorably upon activities that enhance its prestige, and yet college writing programs are often seen as the end products of educational failure or a dereliction of duty in the lower grades. Freshman English, for example, has long been considered a vehicle for allowing students to either "catch up" or be "weeded out." The comments of James Freedman, president of Dartmouth, are, I think, indicative of this view: "Too many students arrive in college unable to do college-level math or writing. We do too much training at that level" (Cohen 9). Freedman worries that someone is going to ask, "Why are we paying $21,000 for that?" When such "training" is provided by part-time, untenured faculty, it is not likely to be touted around the university, much less showcased to parents and alumni.

Still, even if it's pedagogically effective, any program must be *cost-effective* to receive the ultimate institutional imprimatur: funding. Unfortunately, because writing instruction tends to be labor-intensive, the administration may regard it as a fiscal black hole. Class size and faculty loads are always prey in budget negotiations, and there is rarely enough money for every worthy area of teaching and research in the institution. Tempting indeed it must be just to have it announced that all students will henceforth report to the football stadium for composition lectures. In fact, with the number of degrees being awarded in the humanities declining, and given the historic divisions among arts and sciences faculty, it may be fortunate that composition garners as much support as it often does in some institutions.[3] The eminent critic and academic pundit Jacques Barzun captured this bias — and his own frustration — over forty years ago: "The crudest boor would not jog the elbow of a man pouring water into a beaker, and yet the operation is probably far less important than the search for the right word done by a motionless man with a vacant stare on his face" (304). And surely the single greatest cause of vacant stares on any campus is the writing program.

These various snares and delusions I mention only because they may be out there in the academic marketplace, awaiting anyone rushing in with the fervor of those who don't know what lies ahead. Simply put, not everyone buys into writing, much less the people and programs that deal with it. And though academic governance can truly be a mixed, shifting, and, to an outsider, even chaotic affair, there was never much doubt in my own mind that the implementation of our advanced writing program would ultimately be like writing itself: an act of persuasion. It was crucial, therefore, to know the audience. I was somewhat acquainted with people in the humanities, but the scientists, the engineers, pharmacists, therapists, nurses, as well as their main concerns, were relatively obscure to me. So I tramped off to (or phoned) various corners of the university to hear about typical students in diverse majors, the courses they were taking, and their reasons for being in school.

During that relatively brief period of investigation I learned more about my own institution than in all my previous years of service. What I also discovered was the notions of literacy at the advanced level were often as vague and slippery as at the freshman level. That, I presumed, was due partly to the nature of a modern university, that is, to the shift over the years from classical education, the increase in elective courses, the growth of professional disciplines, and perhaps the emergence of a multicultural student body. But whatever constitutes "literacy" at any level has certainly become a much more complex matter. As defined by Robert Pattison, literacy is a "mechanical ability with the technologies of language" as well as a "consciousness of language as a force in human affairs" (vii). But when implementing a writing curriculum, one has to ask just what "technologies" and what (not to mention whose) "human affairs."

Nowadays, of course, it's fashionable to speak of *many* literacies, including numerical, scientific, computer, and so forth; a syndicated financial writer has even spoken of *bargaining* literacy. The word has, in fact, very nearly lost its general meaning, with basic remnants surviving mostly in freshman English or liberal arts colleges as the principles of grammar and rhetoric useful in the affairs of the well rounded citizen/scholar. But the university curriculum today, which is so segmented and differentiated, seems to encourage the study of language technologies and human affairs in much more specialized ways. The recent success of some cross-curricular and professional writing programs demonstrates the obvious "force" writing has in the context of the academic or career specialty, generating information of immediate significance to the writer and providing practice in the rhetorical demands of such fields as law, medicine, technology, and business. Further, the body of research on writing in the disciplines and in the professions continues to increase. There is thus a great attraction, and justification, for promoting such writing at the undergraduate level, even at the risk of feeding into the careerism that is said to be burgeoning at campuses ranging from "the Sun Belt colleges to the universities in the Ivy League," according to Ernest Boyer (102).[4]

On the other hand, a backlash against what might be called the "marketplace mentality" of colleges and universities has been under way for several years now. Education, it is asserted, is being served up smorgasbord or cafeteria style, leading faculty to bemoan some startling gaps in their students' knowledge.[5] David Riesman, for example, remarks that "You could walk into Harvard Yard and find students who do not know who Theodore Dreiser or Thorstein Veblen were" (Cohen 9). Some complaints have become bestsellers, such as E. D. Hirsch's *Cultural Literacy* and Allan Bloom's *The Closing of the American Mind*. A recent report from the National Endowment for the Humanities is only the latest over the years to cite some parade of alarming statistics: 42 percent of graduating college seniors could not place the Civil War in the correct half-century; 58 percent did not know that Shakespeare wrote "The Tempest"; nor could 44 percent name the author of *Moby Dick*.

The result of this ongoing "fragmentation," Boyer observes, is that higher education is searching for "meaning in a world where diversity, not commonality, is the guiding vision" (3). One frequent solution has been the core curriculum. The NEH report, for example, titled "50 Hours: A Core Curriculum for College Students," proposes at least that many credit hours be earned by all students, regardless of major, in the foreign languages, world cultures, mathematics, and natural and social sciences. Such reforms often mention writing as playing some role in these requirements. Whether an essential core of knowledge actually exists, however, or whether mandating certain kinds and numbers of courses would yield it in any event, is something critics have questioned.

The same kind of debate may be reflected in the design of advanced composition programs: should writing be a common bond of the university; should it be compartmentalized through the disciplines; or should it be allowed, laissez-faire, to find its own level and location as needed? And getting a good reading on the nature and will of a university can often be difficult. Truth be told, perhaps many of us have imagined what it would be like if we ourselves had the license and wherewithal to put our own educational philosophy into full effect. I am reminded of Thoreau, for example, reacting to the stultifying classes he had endured at Harvard (Howarth 18). After graduation, he and his brother John founded The Concord Academy in 1839, a school that might today be termed "progressive," with the nearby town, woods, and rivers both the subject matter and classroom for its students. But like a good many such experiments, Thoreau's was ardently planned but short-lived. With his brother's health failing and his own writing production suffering because of the teaching workload (in particular he complained of having to spend so much time on student papers!), The Concord Academy closed down after just two years.

One's heroes may be Cardinal Newman, John Dewey, B. F. Skinner, or Thoreau himself, but no single writing program, no matter how artfully conceived in theory, could survive in practice without being adapted to the given institution. I would have to conclude, therefore, with deCastell and Luke that a "curriculum which is imposed, whether on individuals or entire cultures, cannot serve the same ends as one that is derived" (174). That is especially true when the full range of institutions is considered, such as the two-year or four-year school, those that are rural or urban, regional or national, selective or open-admissions, religious or nonsectarian, technical or liberal arts, and so on.

The program that we in fact evolved at Northeastern was not remarkably innovative, but that is not the story here. For the record, we are a large, urban university dominated by several rather independent professional colleges. The primary draw for students (besides the city of Boston) is "cooperative education," a system of six months of classes alternating with six months at a related job. Many students arrive with clear vocational goals. Ultimately, we decided that the best approach for us was to allow the academic marketplace to determine what writing students would do. Each college in the university was permitted to choose, from a menu offered by the English department, which course (or courses) it would propose for its own students. Not surprisingly, the more technical colleges signed on for Technical Writing; the business college opted for Business Writing; Arts and Sciences allowed a variety of courses; other colleges aligned a required major course with a writing workshop.

The entire program was phased in during a three-year period. Though there was some initial wariness, it was received favorably by most students taking the courses. We did stumble a bit here and there, running into some students unaccounted for, special exceptions that gave one pause, and schedules that defied logic. There was also the in-house matter of orienting instructors, developing guidelines, of imbuing the whole program with some degree of intellectual cohesion. And on more than a few occasions, I was saved from myself by the chair of English and a knowledgeable assistant. Never once, however, did I think that we had designed an ideal package, only that we had come up with something that was needed and, evidently, was delivered.

Perhaps somewhere there's a school at which all the students are busily churning out powerful prose in just about every class, where the very word *program* may seem alien. I am, however, quite certain of one thing: While it may never be popular to consider educational issues in terms of marketplace metaphors, unless we acknowledge that dreams must coexist with reality, then the dream of a better writing program will itself never become a reality. "A salesman is got to dream" all right, but as his son Biff remarked of Willy, "the man didn't know who he was." Now with the overriding issue of the 1990s likely to be accountability, writing programs, too, will have to account for what students learn, or don't learn. Individual faculty members can still accomplish a great deal in this regard, even in the gargantuan institution, but only if those individuals don't mind, or even thrive on, the give-and-take of the academic marketplace. The university needs us, but we need the university as well.

Notes

1. In this essay I use the phrase "academic marketplace" to mean the entire mission, governance, and operation of a college or university, although often it has more narrowly referred to the job market for professors. See, for example, Caplow and McGee.

2. Gosselin also reports that the U.S. Department of Health and Human Services became so concerned with the possibility that potential profits from medical research could corrupt the findings that it ruled investigators must disclose any financial interest they may have in research supported by public funds. The rule encountered a firestorm of protest from the scientific/academic community, and it was subsequently rescinded.

3. While the number of bachelor's degrees has increased in American universities by 88 percent from 1966 to 1986, according to Todorov, there was a 33 percent decrease in degrees awarded in the humanities (12).

4. Boyer notes that, in fact, about a third of all college students would actually drop out if their degree did not improve their chances for employment (102).

5. Though faculty dissatisfaction with the academic ability of students is endemic, it has apparently been on the increase in recent years. Amberg cites a Carnegie foundation survey of 1984 showing that, since 1976, there had been an 8 percent increase in dissatisfaction (527).

Works Cited

Amberg, Jay. "Higher (Priced) Education." *The American Scholar* 58 (1989): 521–532.

Barzun, Jaques. *Teacher in America*. Boston: Little Brown, 1945.

Bloom, Allan. *The Closing of the American Mind*. New York: Simon and Schuster, 1987.

Boyer, Ernest L. *College: The Undergraduate Experience in America*. New York: The Carnegie Foundation for the Advancement of Teaching, 1987.

Caplow, Theodore, and Reece J. McGee. *The Academic Marketplace*. New York: Basic Books, 1961.

Cohen, Muriel. "Worldly Shortages Beset the Ivory Tower." *Boston Globe* (9 Dec. 1989): 1, 9.

de Castell, Suzanne, and Allan Luke. "Defining 'Literacy' in North American Schools: Social and Historical Conditions and Consequences." *In Perspectives on Literacy*. Ed. Eugene Kintgen, Barry M. Kroll, and Mike Rose. Carbondale: Southern Illinois University Press, 1988, 159–174.

Dewey, John. *Experience and Education*. New York: Macmillan, 1979.

"50 Hours." National Endowment for the Humanities. Report in *U.S. News & World Report* (13 Nov 1989): 89.

Giammatti, A. Bartlett. "The American Teacher." In *The University and the Public Interest*. New York: Atheneum, 1981.

Gosselin, Peter G. "NIH Moves to Curb Industry-Science Ties." *Boston Globe* (6 Oct. 1989): 1, 26.

Hirsch, E. D., Jr. *Cultural Literacy: What Every American Needs to Know*. Boston: Houghton Mifflin, 1987.

Howarth, William, *The Book of Concord*. New York: Penguin, 1983.

Miller, Arthur. *Death of a Salesman*. New York: Viking, 1949.

Newman, John Henry. *The Idea of a University*. Garden City, NY: Image Books, 1959.

Pattison, Robert. *On Literacy: The Politics of the Word from Homer to the Age of Rock*. New York: Oxford University Press, 1982.

Skinner, B. F. *Walden Two*. New York: Macmillan, 1962.

Smelsor, Neil. "Epilogue: Social-Structural Dimensions of Higher Education." In *The American University*. Eds. Talcott Parsons and Gerald M. Platt. Cambridge: Harvard University Press, 1973, 389–422.

Todorov, Tzvetan. "The Core of the Humanities: Can the Center Hold?" *Current* (December 1989): 12–17.

11

The Quiet and Insistent Revolution: Writing Across the Curriculum

TOBY FULWILER
The University of Vermont

Movements become political to the extent that they ask institutions to make choices about goals, governance, methods, and the allocation of resources. What will have to change and why? Who will gain, who lose? How much will it cost? What will be the long-term effect? And how will we know it works? The movement identified as Writing Across the Curriculum (WAC) has become political, maybe even quietly revolutionary, as it asks educational institutions these questions.

In most cases, writing-across-the-curriculum programs did not start with political intentions. In the mid-1970s, at small schools and large, public as well as private, they were instituted to improve the general writing and learning abilities of college students. To do this, most programs focused on the primary movers and shakers of the academic curriculum, the college professors themselves, asking them to include more writing in all classes in all disciplines. The majority of academic courses, it was reasoned, already included a substantial set of required readings; few, however, included an equally substantial set of writing assignments.

However, asking historians, chemists, and engineers to help students improve their writing and learning ability has proved to be no simple matter. To effect real change in abilities as basic as writing and learning, these programs have asked, tacitly in most cases, that instructors alter as well their perceptions of other dimensions of the academic community: for example, 1) the role of language in learning, 2) their relationship to students in the classroom, 3) their interactions with colleagues in other disciplines, and 4) the nature of the academic institution itself. Intentionally or not, Writing Across the Curriculum has become an educational reform movement that asks hard, politically charged questions of the whole academic curriculum. This essay examines the nature of these political questions.

Premises

At first glance, the premises that underlie writing-across-the-curriculum programs seem more practical and pedagogical than political. That is, they sound like good, solid, reasonable, ideologically neutral ideas with some chance of helping teachers teach better and students learn better, while allowing educational institutions to conduct business as usual. John Dewey, for example, would surely approve of them all. But so would Paulo Freire. I might formulate these premises as follows:

1. Learners construct knowledge for themselves. Learning is not something that happens *to* learners, but something they make happen to and for themselves with the help of others. So, the more students write to themselves and talk with one another about what they are trying to learn, the more they own and take responsibility for their own education. And the less, by implication, they depend on the teacher to tell them what to think and know.

2. Learners learn best when they pose and solve meaningful problems for themselves. The best model for active, engaged learning probably comes from the students' world (home, street, and workplace), where real, everyday problems need to be solved, but where nobody has an instructor's manual or answer key. In other words, students will become more motivated, knowledgeable, skillful, and thoughtful when colleges and universities invite them "inside" to work on the real issues of the day. And, of course, to pose and solve such problems, students will necessarily use various modes of language.

3. Language is an instrument for learning. Learners read, write, talk, and listen to comprehend, understand, create, imagine, ask and answer questions, pose and solve problems, and in general to figure things out. They do all this with language all the time, in addition to using it to demonstrate to instructors that they *have* comprehended, understood, created, imagined and asked — which, of course, they do on tests and in term papers. As such, language — verbal, numerical, visual, musical — is the very center of the academic curriculum.

4. Language is an avenue to personal growth, social success, political power. People who speak and write persuasively in one or more languages are more likely to thrive in our culture than those who don't. In some instances, skill with spoken and written language means mastering the King's English; in other instances, it means being adept in a particular dialect community; in all instances, those who use language well are more likely to understand themselves and to influence and perhaps even govern others within their language communities. Educational communities that understand and support this premise provide curricula that are rich in language experiences for learners; those that understand and do not support this premise do not provide such experiences; some do not seem to understand this premise at all.

5. The faculty are the primary determiners of the way language is

perceived and used within academic institutions. Their beliefs, knowledge, skills, methods, and attitudes shape, to a large extent, how colleges operate and what they stand for. And what colleges stand for and teach shapes, in many instances, what students learn and stand for.

You will most likely notice that none of these premises is focused exclusively on writing. Instead, each treats language as a whole, complex, intertwined, mutually dependent symbolic network, not easily divisible into discrete entities, skills, achievements, or outcomes. However, the term "*writing* across the curriculum" caught on first because, of all the language modes, writing seemed to be the most easily misunderstood and abused in school curricula. A better term than "writing" would be "language and learning," but we'll dance with what brung us.

You will also notice that none of these particular premises focuses on the specialized writing of particular "discourse communities." Some WAC programs teach students the kind of reasoning and conventions required of specialists within particular disciplines, where history majors learn to write like historians, political-science majors like political scientists, and so on. In my view, those programs address an important but more specialized need than those that stress the language and learning connection as it functions *across* disciplinary boundaries—that is, which treats the academic community itself as a more generalized discourse community.

In articulating these premises to reasonable people who care about student learning, they sound pretty much like God, mother, and apple pie. However, if and when they are used as the basis for reformulating or restructuring academic programs, they begin to threaten business as usual. Why?

For one thing, WAC has given new meaning to the concept of faculty development. The interdisciplinary writing workshop was invented to transmit WAC ideas convincingly to college faculty. Such multiday workshops have been the most common method for introducing writing-across-the-curriculum ideas to college instructors (Knobloch and Brannon; Fulwiler, "Showing," "How Well"). At such workshops, instructors from a variety of disciplines explore the role of writing throughout the curriculum by sharing ideas and talking with one another, and by reading short articles by the likes of Peter Elbow, James Britton, Janet Emig, and Donald Murray. In addition—and more important—they do a substantial amount of writing themselves and examine what happens at various stages along the way—discovering, composing, revising, editing, sharing, and responding. In other words, most writing-across-the-curriculum programs begin with experiential learning for teachers to convince them to try more experiential learning with their students.

In addition, WAC programs address real deficiencies in college curricula with workable solutions. It seems clear that writing-across-the-curriculum programs develop at institutions of various sizes and missions because of perceived needs within their institutions (Huber and Young). They are most likely to be found at two- and four-year colleges with heavy teaching loads and large classes. They are less likely to be found—though no less needed—at huge research universities with large classes and equally high expectations for research and publication pressure. In many of these cases instructors have deliberately decreased the writing they require of students because writing assignments—as they conceive of them—take too much faculty reading and grading time. In some cases they want to do something about it; in other cases they do not.

At other institutions, with lighter teaching loads, smaller classes, and less research pressure, the need for more writing may take a different and even more insidious form: professors in the quantitative disciplines often find qualitative written expressions difficult to evaluate; professors in the humanities commonly believe it their duty to critique and correct everything their students write; professors in the sciences sometimes see little value in the verbal written exploration and speculation of undergraduates. A writing-across-the-curriculum program challenges all of these notions.

Finally, WAC programs cost somebody something. In economic terms, all instructional choices are political in one way or another: one decision reinforces the status quo, another challenges it, still another tries to ignore it. Consider, for example, that college instructors have only a limited amount of time and energy with which to teach each class. When they assign more writing, and when they use class time to talk about that writing, they take time and energy away from something else—lectures, discussions, quizzes—that they did before. When one teacher chooses to do this, it makes an individual difference in the quality of classroom education; when many teachers within the same curriculum make similar choices, it makes a political difference. The more students educate themselves through the active use of their own language, the more ownership they exert over what they learn, and the more they trust (own) their own perceptions. Students so educated are more likely to speak with their own authority within the academic community. When students learn (are allowed to learn? encouraged to learn?) that knowledge is not something received whole and memorized—or put in the bank (Freire)—but rather a construct that they themselves participate in making, the nature of so-called higher education changes (Bruffee). Let me conclude by looking at three necessary changes caused by strong WAC programs: 1) a faculty's relationship to students, 2) its relationship with one another, and 3) its relationship to the whole institution in which it operates.

Faculty-Student Relationships

Writing-across-the-curriculum classrooms change from places in which professors talk and students copy to places in which teachers and students together participate as partners in dialogue, as co-learners in asking questions, pursuing truth, constructing knowledge. The writing makes a difference, giving learners the time to focus, find, collect, organize, and rehearse ideas, allowing them stronger, more equal voices in their own learning. In other words, instructors who adopt the ideas promoted at writing-across-the-curriculum workshops change more than just their writing assignments: They change the nature of the classroom learning from individual, passive, and competitive to communal, active, and collaborative. Following are some of the practices that draw the students inside:

Expressive Writing Instructors who provide time in class for students to explore their own ideas and beliefs through informal (expressive) writing help students find their own voices, some of which will be antagonistic to the instructor's own agenda. In free and open classrooms, this is as it should be. Journal writing and freewriting—writing that the instructor will not grade or necessarily even read—are commonly explored topics at WAC workshops and become common practices at schools with WAC programs.

Open-Ended Assignments When students are invited to ask and answer their own questions (or pose and solve their own problems), they gain a powerful voice in determining their own curriculum—even within the disciplinary constraints that particular courses of instruction impose. Instructors who invite students to design the writing assignments, select research topics, and invent forms for reporting the results necessarily increase students' involvement, investment, and ownership in their learning.

Collaborative Learning Groups When students work together to pose and solve problems they best replicate the kind of learning that goes on in the world outside the academy—at home, on the streets, or within institutions. Real learning means that people put their heads together to both pose and solve problems. Instructors who give over class time for student-student meetings alter student-teacher relationships in important ways. Student ideas command center stage along with instructor ideas, and both are seen as legitimate and vital parts of the academic community. When students talk to one another in small groups, they take power and responsibility for their ideas and often work together as a group to support, refine, and defend those ideas—which strengthens, at the same time, their confidence and individual voices.

Real-World Writing Students are more easily engaged in writing tasks that seem real and useful; a regular workout with real-world tasks (case studies, hypothetical situations, letters to real editors, etc.) increases student motivation and strengthens their voices. That is, teachers who make assignments that deal with real-world problems *and* who provide real-world circumstances under which the work takes place continue to give students more power in determining and deciphering their curriculum. For example, instructors who provide opportunities for students to write rough drafts, to confer with teacher and classmates about the ideas in those drafts, and to write further in light of those comments invest school writing with an uncommon kind of authenticity. The audiences now include the students' peers as well as the teacher in a collaborative role. The resultant process by which the writing gets done is real, and students know that and are, again, allowed inside rather than kept outside.

Responses to Student Writing Responses recognized as honest yet friendly are most likely listened to by young writers. Instructors who respond to student writing with questions, approval, empathy, and suggestions — rather than commands, corrections, hostility, and grades — demonstrate to students that not all writing — nor by extension all student ideas — needs to be submitted for instructor approval, revision, or correction. The lesson here? That students must take responsibility for and make choices about their own ideas, writing, and learning. The reading of — rather than the evaluating of — writing demonstrates the collaborative and subjective nature of the making of meaning and knowledge.

Faculty Writing with Students This practice is commonly modeled by leaders at writing workshops and demonstrates to students that instructors are co-learners in their own classes; learning is never finished, not all wrapped up before the class starts. Students witness the process of their teachers still wrestling with and generating ideas related to the course of study, giving them more purpose in the pursuit of their own ideas. When students watch their teachers write with them, they feel like participants in a community of learners, which is quite different from being the subjects (objects?) of instruction. In addition, instructors who share their writing — warts and all — with their students subject themselves to some of the same risks of self-disclosure and potential ridicule that students must regularly take; it is a leveling process, giving instructors — as well as students — only as much authority as their current written ideas warrant.

Faculty-Faculty Relationships

Writing workshops, by their very nature, introduce faculty to one another in settings that neutralize traditional university hierarchies and cut across both disciplinary and college lines. It is common for participants to express, sometime during the first day of a workshop, that this is the first or the best experience they've ever had in sharing ideas with colleagues across the curriculum. In the process, workshop participants often find social and intellectual connections with one another that suggest further work and mutual exploration after the workshop is over. In other words, one of the outcomes of writing workshops is the generation of a true community of scholars, often at odds with normal university categories, compartments, and channels, a community of scholars generating new possibilities for collaborating rather than competing with one another in the generation of knowledge.

Expanding the Canon One of the central conventions of writing work-shops is the serious consideration they give to student writing. Formal student papers are collaboratively examined to find out *what is right* as well as what is deficient. Informal writing, such as that found in student journals, is looked at for evidence of cognitive activity rather than stylistic or grammatical correctness. When workshop leaders treat seriously the texts that previously many instructors have only criticized or rejected, they begin to make room for new voices in the traditional textual canon—which includes the sciences and social sciences as well as the humanities and fine arts (Hairston).

Collaborative Publication When faculty meet one another at workshops, it is not uncommon for them to embark on mutually beneficial publication projects (Maimon; Fulwiler and Young). For one thing, most workshops model the positive benefits of collaborating on a piece of writing—either by co-writing, sharing, or writers' receiving peer responses. For another, people who share ideas often find that they have more ideas in common than not and find something about which to write. Finally, and commonly, participants are encouraged to see their own writing in a more positive light than they may be accustomed to—resulting in the courage to try to publish more. This latter is especially important for college faculty who have not published much in their academic careers. Co-writing, in fact, is one of the best, easiest, and most common ways for neophytes to break into academic print—and workshops commonly provide faculty with the means and courage to do so. Being able to publish their work in some avenue of the academic community is akin to finding and owning their own voices in that community, making them more likely to become stronger political players in the academic power game.

Interdisciplinary Scholarship When faculty talk, write, and research together, they are more likely to dismantle the needlessly sharp disciplinary barriers that separate one view of knowledge from another. Writing workshops attended by faculty from a variety of disciplines make it more likely that interdisciplinary research and publication will result in the university community. In addition, the act of writing itself is an integrating mechanism, asking authors to make their ideas clear to audiences beyond themselves—an idea also promoted at writing workshops. In a number of college settings, the writing workshops have provided the impetus and ideas for cross-departmental, cross-college, and cross-disciplinary scholarship (McCarthy and Walvoord).

Pedagogical Research Faculty who take seriously the idea that writing promotes better learning often want to find out whether or not the learning really is better in their own classes (Thaiss). Consequently, a number of research studies have now emerged as a result of teachers asking—and trying to answer—questions about their teaching (Young and Fulwiler). In many blue-ribbon institutions, such research has been traditionally and strictly the province of professors in the schools of education. Writing across the curriculum is changing that, making such classroom-based, pedagogical research a legitimate activity for professors in any discipline. Knowledge so generated is bound to have a positive effect on the nature of teaching, learning, and community at the institutions where it takes place.

Faculty-Institution Relationships

Institutions that encourage and nourish WAC programs may find themselves changed in ways for which they did not bargain. If faculty and students locate more egalitarian and open ways of approaching learning, the institution itself may follow.

Balance The degree to which teachers ask for more student writing across the curriculum may be the degree to which they bring in fewer research dollars or spend fewer hours pursuing their own specialized research. I believe that research and scholarship are essential functions of the modern college or university—at least where course loads make room for such professional activities. But writing-across-the-curriculum programs argue, first and foremost, for balance. They argue that teachers should, indeed, spend more time on their teaching—at least more thoughtful time, sharing teacher voices and values with students and using writing to help accomplish that.

A Language-Centered Curriculum The net result of admitting more writing into the whole curriculum is a tilt toward a multidimensional, more decentralized, less authoritarian curriculum. An institution encouraging its faculty to pay attention to qualitative measures of student learning—which writing necessarily is—will pay less attention to more simplistic objective measures of learning. It is also more likely to pay similar attention to subjective expression and exploration in other areas of institutional measurement and achievement, perhaps even more time in creative teacher-student projects and less in strictly esoteric, isolationist research activities.

An Empathetic Curriculum The degree to which teachers admit more student writing in their course of study is the degree with which they begin to empathize with younger learners, champion their voices, and question the necessity of absolute and often arbitrary standards of performance and behavior. An empathetic curriculum is a student-centered curriculum and, as a result, a more politically egalitarian one.

Altered Reward Structures In many colleges and universities, teachers who pay more attention to assigning and responding to student writing spend more time on their teaching—especially in generating more dialogue between themselves and their students—than instructors who communicate with their students primarily through objective tests. However, the current reward structure at many institutions does not favor increased attention to teaching, a condition leading to further debates about the goals of higher education and the allotment of resources. More faculty attention to student writing and learning in the curriculum may challenge the publish-or-perish principle of tenure and promotion as well as the impersonal modes of student evaluation that currently dominate so many of our institutions of higher learning.

Writing-across-the-curriculum programs ask all participants in the learning community to use language thoughtfully, to shape and extend their ideas and voices. They do so quietly but insistently, believing that the

degree to which students find and trust their voices is the degree to which
they — minority and middle class alike — influence and help direct our society.
Higher education is passive and stuffy by habit, not intention. I don't buy
conspiracy theories ("It's dangerous to teach them to think!"), but I do
believe in the inertia of institutions, the deadliest enemy of change, reform,
and revolution. Writing Across the Curriculum creates change because it
addresses simultaneously the inertia of student, faculty, and institution
alike. It starts from within, with ideas from without, and addresses the real
teacher in all of us — which is why we entered education in the first place.

Works Cited

Berthoff, Ann E. *Forming Thinking Writing: The Composing Imagination.* Rochelle
Park, NJ.: Hayden, 1981.

Britton, James, Tony Burgess, Nancy Martin, Alex McLeod, and Harold Rosen.
The Development of Writing Abilities 11—18. London: Macmillan, 1975.

Britton, James. *Prospect and Retrospect,* Ed. G. M. Pradl. Portsmouth, NH:
Boynton/Cook, 1982.

Bruffee, Kenneth. "Collaborative Learning and the 'Conversation of Mankind'"
College English 46:7 (November 1984): 635—652.

Elbow, Peter. *Writing Without Teachers.* New York: Oxford University Press,
1973.

Emig, Janet. "Writing as a Mode of Learning," *CCC* 28:2 (May 1977): 122—28.

Freire, Paulo. *Pedagogy of the Oppressed.* New York: Herder and Herder, 1970.

Fulwiler, Toby. "How Well Does Writing Across the Curriculum Work?" *College
English* 46 (February 1984): 113—125.

————. "Showing, Not Telling, at a Writing Workshop." *College English* 43 (January
1981): 55—53.

Fulwiler, Toby, and Art Young, eds. *Language Connections.* Urbana, IL: NCTE,
1982.

Gere, Anne Ruggles, ed. *Roots in the Sawdust: Writing to Learn Across the
Disciplines.* Urbana, IL: NCTE, 1985.

Hairston, Maxine. "The Winds of Change: Thomas Kuhn and the Revolution in
Teaching of Writing," *CCC* 33 (February 1982): 76—88.

Huber, Bettina, and Art Young. "Report on the 1983—84 Survey of the English
Sample," *ADE Bulletin* 84 (Fall 1986): 45—46.

Knoblauch, C. H. and Lil Brannon. "Writing as Learning Through the Curriculum."
College English 45 (September 1983): 465—474.

Maimon, Elaine, Gerald Belcher, Gail Hern, Barbara Nodine, and Finbar
O'Connor. *Writing in the Arts and Sciences,* Cambridge, MA: Winthrop, 1981.

McCarthy, Lucille Parkinson, and Barbara E. Walvoord. "Models for Collaborative
Research in Writing Across the Curriculum." *Strengthening Programs for Writing
Across the Curriculum.* Ed. S. McLeod. San Francisco: Jossey Bass, 1989.

Murray, Donald. "The Maker's Eye: Revising Your Own Manuscripts." In *Learning
by Teaching,* Portsmouth, NH: Boynton/Cook, 1982, 68—72.

Thaiss, Christopher, ed. *Writing to Learn: Essays and Reflections by College
Teachers Across the Curriculum.* The George Mason Faculty Writing Program,
Fairfax, VA: George Mason University, 1982.

Young, Art and Toby Fulwiler. *Writing Across the Disciplines: Research into
Practice.* Portsmouth, NH. Boynton/Cook, 1986.

12

Autonomy and Community in the Evaluation of Writing

RICHARD BULLOCK
Wright State University

In red: *Your thesis is provocative and interesting, and you develop your argument well. Unfortunately, this essay does not conform to the assignment, so I have no choice but to fail it.*
Or, in pencil: *This essay has a lot of good ideas, but I'm not satisfied. You don't develop any of them as well as you could, take them as far as you need to to answer the reader's questions.*

These comments, the likes of which I've written on students' essays and received on my own, exemplify in different ways a central tension in writing evaluation: the potential conflict between our students' individual achievements and the demands of the classroom, the writing program, the curriculum, the community. We see our students as individuals and believe this to be good; their writing results from an idiosyncratic process, their ideas represent novel solutions to the problems posed by the writing task, they each deserve our individual attention in the classroom and in conference. We try to assess their writing in terms of its success in achieving the writer's aims in writing it, rather than — as was done in the bad old days — judging its worth by comparing it to some mythical, perfect essay we kept in our heads but "seldom brought into scrutiny" (Brown 119).

And yet. We ask all the students in our classes to do certain assignments, to write certain kinds of essays. We assign grades on 4-point, 12-point, or some administratively simple scale, sorting our students, finally, into a limited number of boxes: "A" student, "C" student, "F" student, "Withdrawn" student. As individual teachers, we create a class that by definition has coherence as a social unit, that demands group behaviors that are well defined and very restricted, that requires conformity — and that demands assessment of the student not as an individual but as a member of this group. Indeed, we follow our culture's demands for control over our students and their writing by establishing such a system and by reserving the power of evaluation to ourselves. In this essay, I will explore what it means for ourselves and our students to accede to this demand; how this accession leads to conflict between our philosophies and our pedagogies; and how we might lessen — or, indeed, eliminate — the tensions between our beliefs about writing, its teaching and evaluation, and the demands our culture places upon us.

Coach and Judge in the Writing Classroom

Peter Elbow has described this tension in terms of the conflict between teacher as coach and teacher as judge. The coach nurtures the individual and tries to develop that individual's potential; the judge assesses the individual's work in relation to "an obligation to knowledge and society" (327). This conflict in roles, Elbow concedes, cannot be resolved. One can only attempt to split oneself as radically as possible between the two roles, setting up the judging criteria as explicitly as possible so that the rest of one's time may be spent coaching — as if the teacher were both judge and defense attorney, at once watching impassively from the bench, twirling the gavel, weighing the evidence with a disinterested and impartial eye; and feverishly admonishing the jury while (like television attorney Ben Matlock) helping the defendant establish the best case possible.

The coaching role itself makes evaluation collaborative between student writer and teacher. As Rexford Brown notes, evaluation of a draft that will then be revised takes on the character of the interaction between a master and an apprentice: "The product being evaluated — perhaps even the person being evaluated — changes in the course of the evaluation. When the director works with the actor, when the dance master works with the dancer, when the woodworker stands by the apprentice at the lathe, learning and evaluation fuse" (118). Judging, on the other hand, backs away from this complicity in and shared responsibility for the emerging piece of writing to a more detached assessment of the product — what is finally turned in.

The flaw in Elbow's analogy and in my discussion of it so far, though, is that it assumes that the classroom exists in isolation, in the same way that Matlock's courtroom exists only as a set in a studio. It ignores the programmatic, institutional, disciplinary, and cultural communities of which each individual classroom, its students, and its teacher are part. When I teach, I embody a complex web of roles, expectations, and constraints that make my autonomy in the classroom an illusion; when I coach, I coach according to accepted rules, and coach my students toward culturally defined and proscribed ends; when I judge, I bring to my judgment a wealth of criteria, definitions, biases, and tastes that spring not only from my own considerable powers as an individual but also from my upbringing, my training, and my social, political, economic, and cultural surroundings.

That's the problem. As a coach or judge working in isolation, I'm flawed. I filter what I think are the demands of my school and its writing program (along with the demands of my position, my culture, my history, etc.)

through my own sensibility, and most of the time I'm only imperfectly reliable. In large-scale writing assessment (of which more later) that problem of individual idiosyncracy is ostensibly acknowledged and dealt with through intensive training sessions and multiple readers. In law, the same problem is addressed through similar means: If Matlock thinks his judge has messed up, he can appeal. That appeal will be looked at by panels of judges as it goes up the ladder of courts, so that his case will receive multiple readings in search of a fair verdict. In the isolated classroom, however, appeal is often impossible, as there is no one to appeal to and no obvious structure in which to pursue an appeal. The illusion of autonomy serves to "protect" the teacher from second-guessing and helps reinforce the myth of the teacher's objectivity as well as her power over her students.

Jay Parini rightly notes that "knowledge is always 'biased', and that the mask of objectivity hides every form of prejudice" (B1). As teachers (coaches and evaluators), we try to be disinterested judges only of the text's success in realizing its writer's intentions, but we know we're not disinterested every time we pick up a student essay denying the Holocaust or suggesting that genocide may be an appropriate response to a country's problems (and we do pick them up). We're not entirely sympathetic coaches when we advise a student to clarify her thesis or alter her tone; we're coaching students to become better writers of the sort of writing they're likely to be judged on (by no doubt less sympathetic judges) once they're no longer in our classes. Coach or judge, we don't teach in a vacuum.

We shouldn't evaluate in a vacuum either. Although large-scale writing assessment takes place in a rigidly constricted form, since in such readings the goal is agreement and suppression of idiosyncratic readings rather than conversation and consensus, what gives large-scale writing assessment its power should characterize classroom writing evaluation: it should be conducted collaboratively, teachers working together to evaluate their students' writing. For teachers, this sort of assessment should take place in the context not only of the individual classroom (which shapes the students' writing and exerts powerful influences on their processes and products) but of the school's writing program and the discipline of composition studies. In practice, that means that some student writing should be evaluated by several teachers teaching in the same program who understand not only the particular classroom conditions under which the writing was produced and the programmatic tenets informing the syllabus, but also the theories and concepts on which their instruction is based. In practice, that means that writing teachers must understand theories and procedures governing the evaluation of writing. They must talk regularly with one another about what they do (and not just by relating "war stories"). They must relinquish the odd "privacy" of the classroom by visiting one another's classes. In short, they must give up complete autonomy over their students' grades.

This is an important point: Evaluation cannot take place in a vacuum, but most teachers of writing are asked to evaluate writing in isolation from one another, without proper training in writing evaluation, and without the support of commonly accepted disciplinary standards and values. This isolation reflects the marginal status of most writing teachers and serves to perpetuate their marginality while protecting (or seeming to protect) the existing university structure. When they are working in isolation, the competence of marginal instructors can be called into question without reference to norms of behavior (indeed, they may be simply "not rehired" without explanation); at the same time, that isolation protects the system from needing to justify the use of underprepared instructors, since determining their effectiveness is very difficult. The implications for the classroom of such a situation are serious. Without shared values, writing assessment is doomed to subjectivity. Without proper training of its practitioners, it is doomed to quirkiness. And without community, evaluators cannot know whether their standards as coaches or judges are in fact *standards*, or are merely consistent within their own minds.

As things exist now, grading is largely an exercise in solipsism, and our classes reflect this in the way that all teaching is in some way "to the test." If our grading of students is private—and therefore not very reliable, the work only of our own minds and criteria (even if we think we're conforming to some external standards)—our instruction, geared toward the attainment of the goals embodied in those criteria, is equally private. The result is the solipsistic classroom, isolated from "the community of scholars" of which it is a part and, ironically, defended on the grounds of expertise and academic freedom. Until very recently in English, the attainment of professional expertise (in literature studies) brought with it escape from the writing classroom, which was left to those whose expertise was grounded in experience, not professional training. Academic freedom was intended to protect scholarly endeavors, not the work of untrained craftsmen who until recently did not do research.

Isolation, Collaboration, and Power

As we move to professionalize the teaching of writing, then, and as teachers of writing reshape their roles as teachers and researchers (see Bullock; and Goswami and Stillman), we need to acknowledge the special nature of teaching and assessing writing. The model of the isolated teacher in the classroom with the closed door cannot work for us, because our profession advances collaboratively—as the MLA has acknowledged (in its "Report of the Commission on Writing and Literature" 73). Our assessment of our students cannot rest on a single reading by an isolated teacher, either: through collaborative grading, multiple readers, the use of portfolios, and other means, our students deserve the benefits of shared expert evaluation, which improves not only our assessment but the rest of our teaching as well.

A collaborative teaching stance has overt political implications. The norm for college teaching is generally one of ignorance: For the most part, I don't know what my colleagues do in their classrooms, I don't talk with them much, if at all, about pedagogical issues, and I participate in the institutional assumption (even if I don't believe it) that anyone who is tenured is by definition an adequate, if not excellent, teacher. This is a useful stance for the privileged members of the academy, just as the isolation of writing teachers I spoke of earlier is useful. By and large, it dampens potentially threatening criticism of individual faculty members (what are you going to do with a tenured full professor who's a lousy teacher if you find him?); it creates an unspoken complicity within the professoriat akin to that of other professionals who, entrusted with policing their own, more often cover up "fallen" members of their ranks, perpetuating the myth of their collective competence (see, for instance, the literature surrounding "the love doctor," James Burt, or the fate of "whistleblowers" in the biological sciences, the government, or the military); and it facilitates the maintenance of research and scholarship as the only true goals of a professorial career, since teaching is difficult to assess, idiosyncratic, and finally to be left for assessment mostly to the impressions of students in the course.

Collaboration changes all that. When I read another instructor's students' drafts and she reads mine, we engage in a conversation about the emerging text that may contain disagreements and contradictions. The student should see from these differing interpretations that readings are multiply suggestive, that the teacher cannot be "objective," let alone the infallible judge—the writing can be discussed and responded to, but not definitively critiqued. The teacher cannot be trusted, finally; responsibility for revision must lie not with the instructor but with the student.

When I grade another instructor's students' essays and she grades mine, we have to talk. Our talking involves articulating for each other our criteria, our standards, our tastes, our biases as they apply to each student's essay. When we disagree, and we will, we must work out a hierarchy of our criteria: Which impression is more accurate in terms of the grade to be applied, more useful to the student? To what extent should our reading be colored by knowledge of the student as an individual? Our talking also has programmatic and professional effects: We are forced to lay out in public to another, equally "professional" writing instructor our pedagogy and, if we are part of a writing program, how our pedagogy fits into the program—or where the program does not fit our students' needs. In other words, implicit in this self-revelation and conversation is a critique not only of our own teaching but of the context in which it takes place, and its fruitfulness does not lie in coming to agreement. As Miles Myers observes, "discrepancy can lead to a fruitful dialogue about our underlying assumptions about teaching good writing as well as about its evaluation" (32). Collaborative activities for students acknowledge that "the production of meaning in written language itself is a social or collaborative process" (Trimbur 100) and further complicate the evaluation process by producing multiply authored texts; collaborative evaluation activities by teachers of writing extend that acknowledgment to reading, grading, and teaching writing.

In practice, collaborative responding and grading help deflate the illusion of power under which teachers often operate. Teachers initially resist any practice that appears to diminish their autonomy and power in the classroom. As Brown observes in noting the persistence of instruction in grammar and mechanics because they provide ways of cowing non-English teachers, "You do not give up power like that even when you are flying high; much less are you likely to when you are besieged" (122). By maintaining that illusion of power, though, teachers isolate themselves from one another and from power of a greater sort. Several essays in this volume address the problem of the writing teacher's status — or lack of same — in the university. Part of the reason for teachers' lack of status and lack of power lies in their willingness to participate in a system that grants them seemingly unlimited power in one arena, the classroom, while rendering them powerless and subservient in the larger arenas of the English department and the university as a whole and that maintains this system in large part by isolating teachers from one another. Once teachers begin to discuss their students' essays and their teaching practices with one another, however, they challenge the received notions of the role of pedagogy in the university (as something not worth talking about) and by extension assert the value of teaching as a vital part of the university's reason for being.

Writing Instruction and "Reality"

And then. All this talk about dialogue and collaboration has a nice, humanistic ring to it, but no matter how well we justify to ourselves the value of sharing and working together, we have to deal with the university faculty, university administrators, and employers who demand that we demonstrate our rigor and "standards" (which are usually assumed to be too low). Humanistic arguments about helping students define themselves (Myers 32) or about teaching "clear thinking in language" (Murray, *A Writer* 241) are likely to fall on deaf ears in the face of complaints that "Our students can't write — and this after two semesters of freshman English!"

In recent years these complaints, along with those of others who have complained that students leaving high school cannot write either, have led to a proliferation of large-scale assessments of writing: placement tests, exit tests, "junior rising" tests, and competency tests, all of which serve in one way or another to sort students according to their writing ability, to act as gates through which students may or may not pass, and to send the clear message that teachers cannot be trusted. The issues involved in these tests have been thoroughly and usefully explored; see, for instance, the essays in Greenberg, Wiener, and Donovan; Faigley, Cherry, Joliffe, and Skinner; White; and Bizzell's review of all three books, along with Beard and

McNabb and *Notes from the National Testing Network in Writing*. Suffice it to say that any project to assess individual students' writing abilities, over time or in a single instance, is fraught with philosophical, ethical, and methodological peril.

The basis of this peril lies in the premises governing writing instruction, themselves problematic, and their conflict with the premises governing testing. As James Berlin outlines them, the two major theories underlying composition teaching during the twentieth century have been the current-traditional and expressionist. The current-traditional or positivist school bases instruction on the premise that "the certain existence of the material world is indisputable. . . . When the individual is freed from the biases of language, society, or history, the senses provide the mental faculties with a clear and distinct image of the world" (52–53). There is a reality independent of our ability to express it in language. On the other hand, the expressionist theory, as propounded by Ken Macrorie, William Coles, Jr., and others, begins with the Platonic view that "Truth is . . . discovered through an internal apprehension, a private vision of a world that transcends the physical" (Berlin 53). There is, again, a reality that does not depend on language for its expression, but the reality is within each individual. For the positivist, reality is public, *out there*, and language is primarily a means for "transmitting truth" (52); for the expressionist, reality is private, ultimately inexpressible, and "to present truth language must rely on original metaphors in order to capture what is unique in each personal vision" (55).

Philosopher Richard Rorty sees the positivist-expressionist split as basic: According to him, the tradition of philosophical inquiry since Plato has been an "attempt to fuse the public and the private . . . to unite a striving for perfection [of the self] with a sense of community" (xiii). This quest, though, is an impossible one, for both self-oriented and community-oriented philosophies have begun with the premise that either the self or reality has an "intrinsic" nature that is "out there waiting to be known" (11). This idea leads to a problem with our conception of language: How well does language represent that intrinsic nature? Is it a *medium*, of expression of the true self or of representation of the true reality? This definition assumes that language "is somehow a unity, a third thing which stands in some determinate relation with two other unities—the self and reality." If language is a medium, the underlying assumption is that "there are nonlinguistic things called 'meanings' which it is the task of language to express, as well as the idea that there are nonlinguistic things called 'facts' which it is the task of language to represent" (13). What if, though, language is not a medium at all? What if, as Rorty, following Wittgenstein, argues, language is a *tool*? As tools, languages—or, more properly, vocabularies—are sets of words and structures that we use to cope with various situations. They have no intrinsic nature; they develop—evolve—to meet specific needs.[1] Like other tools, vocabularies are adequate to the task at hand or they are not. If a vocabulary is no longer adequate to the task—in the way, for instance, that current-traditional vocabularies with their emphasis on form and style and inattention to invention proved inadequate to the expression of the concepts of writing-process pedagogy—then, by trial and error, "somebody . . . proceeds to invent a new vocabulary" (12). In fact, then, vocabularies are the product of chance, contingency, natural selection: "Our language and our culture are as much a contingency, as much a result of thousands of small mutations finding niches (and millions of others finding no niches) as are the orchids and the anthropoids" (16).

This way of describing language also implies a conception of the nature of reality, and that conception holds that we are our vocabularies. In other words, we cannot know any transcendent self or external reality that is not defined by our vocabularies. Rorty explains:

> The very idea that the world or the self has an intrinsic nature—one which the physicist or the poet may have glimpsed—is a remnant of the idea that the world is a divine creation, the work of someone who had something in mind, who Himself spoke some language in which He described His own project. Only if we have some such picture in mind, some picture of the universe as either itself a person or as created by a person, can we make sense of the idea that the world has an "intrinsic nature." For the cash value of that phrase is just that some vocabularies are better representations of the world than others, as opposed to being better tools for dealing with the world for one or another purpose. (21)

Our vocabularies define and constitute our worlds and also our selves, a truth first articulated by Freud. Freud's delving into the details of his subjects' lives demonstrated that each of us is shaped by those details, which, unconsciously, we turn into metaphors that define our lives. Freud "thinks that only if we catch hold of some crucial idiosyncratic contingencies in our past shall we be able to make something worthwhile out of ourselves, to create present selves whom we can respect. . . . He suggested that we praise ourselves by weaving idiosyncratic narratives—case histories, as it were—of our success in self-creation, our ability to break free from an idionsyncratic past." We recreate ourselves by understanding and overcoming our pasts, and we do this by verbalizing; specifically, by creating narrative and metaphors that redescribe every aspect of life—those "crucial idiosyncratic contingencies"—and so redefine our self-identity (34–37).[2]

Rorty considers this redefining of the individual a process of "de-divinizing" and suggests that the thrust of philosophical, psychoanalytical, and literary thought in the twentieth century has been toward de-divinizing the individual and the world. "The strategy is the same in all these cases," he writes. "It is to substitute a tissue of contingent relations, a web which stretches backward and forward through past and future time, for a formed, unified, present, self-contained substance, something capable of being seen steadily and whole" (41). This principle of the incomplete, impossible-to-pin-down, contingent web has informed composition studies through such diverse principles as Ann E. Berthoff's that "learning to write is a matter of learning to tolerate ambiguity, of learning that the making of meaning is a dialectical process determined by perspective and context" (71) and Donald Murray's declaration that "A piece of writing is never finished" (*Learning* 71). Indeed, Berlin demonstrates that current composition teaching bases its pedagogy on a denial of a stable reality existing independently of language and language users: "For the New Rhetoric truth is impossible without language since it is language that embodies and generates truth" (56). The world, this web of relations, is composed, and composed of language; we use language as the tool with which we construct our world and ourselves.

Although in this world individuals need to make selves for themselves through "the always incomplete, yet sometimes heroic, reweaving of such a web" (Rorty 43), the individual self is not alone. In this world, people will "derive the meanings of their lives from . . . other finite, mortal, contingently existing human beings" (45). Morality, then, is "the voice of ourselves as members of a community, speakers of a common language" (59).

In other words, we're all in this together; there is no priesthood, either of religion or of science, to order our behavior or judge its results. Even so, though, this is not a nihilistic or meaningless world. Although we have no responsibility to a stable, preexisting reality, truth, or God, we have a responsibility to others, just as we have a responsibility to ourselves. And this twofold responsibility, which cannot be unified as the Romantics and Platonists thought, leads to direct ethical and political consequences. Most baldly, in a society governed by these principles, "the point of social organization is to let everybody have a chance at self-creation to the best of his or her abilities, and . . . that goal requires, besides peace and wealth, the standard 'bourgeois freedoms'" (84).

Self-Creation, Portfolios, and Individual Students

How does that definition of the "ideal liberal society" mesh with writing instruction and writing evaluation? The part about letting everybody have a continuing, perpetual opportunity to redefine and recreate themselves relates well to current pedagogical practice, which usually acknowledges writers' needs to create meaning that is personal to themselves through writing. In a world governed by contingency, however, the creation of meaning through language takes on new meaning: An accurate paraphrase of Forster in this world might be, "How do I know who I am until I see what I say?" We create our selves through language. And if our selves are webs of contingencies, stretching backward and forward in time, we create our selves through narratives. In this light, the use of collected drafts and portfolios of writing represent the most appropriate method of evaluation because they provide an implicit narrative of the progressive development of a piece of writing or of several pieces in the sequence of a writing course. Read in this way, the successive drafts form the basis of a story, the story of the writer's journey through episodes of writing and learning (and, following the work of James Britton and Linda Flower, the writer's journey from self-creation and expression to preparation of the resulting text for sharing with a community).

Conversely, the isolated single draft testifies to the conceptions Rorty denies: It presents us with purported evidence of something called "writing ability" that somehow differs from the writer's performance on any particular writing task. Like the stable self and stable reality, this "writing ability" is nonlinguistic, potentially able to be described in words that represent its underlying truth, and measurable in terms separable from its possessor. In the classroom or in the testing room, this model denies individuality and particularity in favor of a "true" abstraction. As Herbert Kohl notes, standardized tests generally "are constructed to create a hierarchy of success and failure rather than to determine the competency of individuals.... Through trial and error a test is built so that the results will conform to a normal curve of achievement. This implies that some students must be expected to fail; that a certain amount of failure is normal." And, he continues, "Failure is no big thing except in the lives of individuals" (16–17). A test that is expected to fail a certain percentage of those who take it denies to that percentage by fiat the opportunity to succeed; it is "a distinctly undemocratic notion" (Kohl 17).

Like other positivist ways of dealing with "reality," testing denies individuality; it exists to sort groups into predefined categories of ability or performance. As such, standardized testing (by essay or optical-scanner form) acts as an extension of the automaton principle as Tom Newkirk outlines it in this volume. The individual is evaluated not as an agent but as a reactor—she doesn't exist meaningfully until "prompted" into action by others. In placement-test settings, before a new class of freshmen arrives on campus we think of them as faceless, abstract, "essentially inert" (Newkirk). These students come to life only in the testing room and only in a restricted and predetermined way: by producing writing in response to our prompt. Their efforts are then read only to permit them to be sorted into categories, which are themselves abstract ("basic" or "remedial" on one extreme, "honors" on the other) and economically driven (the number of seats available in the various courses is usually determined before any testing takes place, again predetermining the results of the sorting). Placement testing, competency testing, the ETS, the ACT, and other large-scale testers assume that there is some external standard, something called "writing ability" that can be measured in individuals and compared across large populations, rather than seeing these students as "webs of contingency," individual and unique, with their own stories to tell (and retell).

As I have noted, this concept of the individual defined by the vocabularies she uses fits easily with current composition theory. More specifically,

Joseph Harris, synthesizing and extending recent work by David Bartholomae, Patricia Bizzell, and Raymond Williams, notes that "Social theories of reading and writing have helped to deconstruct the myth of the autonomous essential self." Further, he argues, the idea of community is just as mythical and plural, that it "allows for both consensus and conflict, and . . . holds room for ourselves, our disciplinary colleagues, our university coworkers, *and* our students" (20). Rorty's version of this contingent, constructivist social setting is his liberal society, to which it is central that truth is "what comes to be believed in the course of free and open encounters" (68) and, consequently, "that in respect to words as opposed to deeds, persuasion as opposed to force, anything goes" (51−52). In such a society, the fact that "anything goes" precludes the restriction of students' writing efforts and privileges the individual student. Allowing these students to tell the stories of their writing through multiple-draft submissions and portfolios at all levels (as SUNY−Stony Brook [Camp and Belanoff], the University of Minnesota [Anson], and schools across the country are demonstrating can be done) makes the evaluation of their writing consistent with our teaching and with the principles of freedom, including the freedom to be judged on terms consistent with one's community and personal history, rather than on some externally imposed, reductive standard.

Then Who Judges?

The question we're left with, though, is the need for such judging to go on at all. Throughout this essay I have tacitly accepted the premise that teachers must evaluate students. But if, as I have just argued, writing is a way by which our students redefine themselves in the web of contingencies we call the world, if they are as much as part of the community as anyone else, then how do we draw a line, in the testing room or in the classroom, separating them (the evaluated) from us (the evaluators)?

Elbow argues from standards set by society and the discipline:

We are invited to stay true to the inherent standards of what we teach, whether or not that stance fits the particular students before us. We have a responsibility to society—that is, to our discipline, our college or university, and to other learning communities of which we are members— to see that the students we certify really understand or can do what we teach, to see that the grades and credits and degrees we give really have the meaning or currency they are supposed to have. (328)

The concept of "inherent standards" is already incompatible with my argument so far, and further is largely mythical, as the old ploy of distributing a student essay to a roomful of teachers to evaluate, knowing that they will give the essay every grade possible, demonstrates; but an equally serious problem is the assumption that we in the academy know what society wants. George O. Klemp, a researcher in human-resource management, rightly acknowledges that university education is geared toward the acquisition of knowledge. However, according to Klemp. "Our most consistent finding has been that the amount of formal knowledge one acquires about a content area is generally unrelated to superior performance in an occupation." Rather, exceptional performance in "a wide variety of occupations" depends on cognitive skills, defined as evaluative thinking, conceptualization, and systematic thinking; interpersonal abilities, including the ability to influence others, be sensitive, and network or develop useful relationships; and intrapersonal factors, including confidence, initiative, and persistence (37–40)—little of which is taught in college and little of which is nurtured by evaluation. "Society" turns out to be a poor arbiter of academic standards, if occupational success is an indicator.

The solution, it seems to me, is to invite students to participate in the evaluation of their work, negotiating with one another and with their instructors in an open exchange, acting as full members of the classroom and university community. In such a class much would change. The authors of texts would be in a position to defend their efforts, to express their standards for self-evaluation in a social arena peopled by readers of varying ability who could temper the individual's self-image with communally developed standards. The student writer would learn in the process the differences between writing as an act of self-creation and writing with responsibility for readers; far more than the writer-based/reader-based distinction defined by Linda Flower and John Hays, this distinction would clarify the ethical and political implications of the act of writing in a world in which the writing serves to create the writer, who must then place herself in the social world of other writers and readers who are also struggling to create themselves. In such a situation no one is privileged; no one person may with impunity act as Evaluator.

The benefits of building a writing class and its evaluation around such shared responsibility and collaboration are many. The difficulties of the traditional gate-keeping role described by Elbow would be alleviated; the discredited Platonism of the grading system and its implicit measuring of students against a mythical perfection would be dropped; our schools' endorsement in its practices of conceptions of reality and the self that contradict what is taught in their classrooms would be diminished, if not eliminated; and students' exclusion from the conversation that constitutes and defines the human community would disappear. Students would develop evaluative thinking and interpersonal abilities as they discussed their portfolios with peers and instructors. Through being partners in evaluation, rather than victims of it, they would develop confidence, persistence, and initiative while learning to self-evaluate, the toughest job faced by any writer. While grades might continue to be given and assessments of student achievement made in this truly collaborative situation, the distinctions among coach and apprentice, judge and judged would become subsumed in respectful, negotiated conversation in which learning and evaluation — as in apprenticeship days — would once again fuse.

Notes

1. Rorty acknowledges the limits of this analogy by noting that "the craftsman typically knows what job he needs to do before picking or inventing tools with which to do it. By contrast ... [language] is a tool for doing something which could not have been envisaged prior to the development of a particular set of descriptions, those which it itself helps to provide" (13).

2. Freud's concept of our need to recreate ourselves through language is echoed in Bakhtin's statement that language "lies on the borderline between oneself and the other. The word in language is half someone else's. It becomes 'one's own' only when the speaker populates it with his own intentions, his own accent, when he appropriates the word, adapting it to his own semantic and expressive intention. Prior to this moment of appropriation, the world does not exist in a neutral and personal language ... but rather it exists in other people's mouths, in other people's contexts, serving other people's intentions: it is from there that one must take the word and make it one's own" (quoted in Ede 11).

Works Cited

Anson, Chris, Lillian Bridwell-Bowles, and Robert Brown, Jr. "Portfolio Assessment Across the Curriculum: Early Conflicts." Minneapolis, MN: 6th Annual Conference on Writing Assessment, April 16, 1988.

Beard, John, and Scott McNabb, eds. *Testing in the English Language Arts: Uses and Abuses*. Rochester, MI: Michigan Council of Teachers of English, 1985.

Berlin, James A. "Contemporary Composition: The Major Pedagogical Theories." *College English* 44 (1982): 765–777. Rpt. *The Writing Teacher's Sourcebook*. Ed. Gary Tate and Edward P. J. Corbett. 2nd Ed. New York: Oxford University Press, 1988, 47–59.

Berthoff, Ann E. *The Making of Meaning*. Portsmouth, NH: Boynton/Cook, 1981.

Bizzell, Patricia. "Review: What Can We Know, What Must We Do, What May We Hope: Writing Assessment." *College English* 49 (1987): 575–584.

Britton, James. *The Development of Writing Abilities 11–18*. London: Macmillan, 1975.

Brown, Rexford. "Evaluation and Learning." In *The Teaching of Writing: 85th Yearbook of the National Society for the Study of Education, Part II*. Ed. Anthony R. Petrosky and David Bartholome. Chicago: NSSE, 1986, 114–130.

Bullock, Richard H. "A Quiet Revolution: The Power of Teacher Research." *Seeing for Ourselves: Case Study Research by Teachers of Writing*. Ed. Glenda L. Bissex and Richard H. Bullock. Portsmouth, NH: Heinemann, 1987, 21–27.

Camp, Roberta, and Patricia Belanoff. "Portfolios as Proficiency Tests." *Notes from the National Testing Network in Writing* 7 (1987): 8.

Ede, Lisa. "Writing as a Social Process: A Theoretical Foundation for Writing Centers?" *Writing Center Journal* 9 (1989): 3–13.

Elbow, Peter. "Embracing Contraries in the Teaching Process." *College English* 45 (1983): 327–339.

Faigley, Lester, Roger D. Cherry, David A. Joliffe, and Anna M. Skinner. *Assessing Writers' Knowledge and Processes of Composing.* Norwood, NJ: Ablex, 1985.

Flower, Linda. "Writer-Based Prose: A Cognitive Basis for Problems in Writing." *College English* 41 (1979): 19—37.

Goswami, Dixie, and Peter R. Stillman. *Reclaiming the Classroom: Teacher Research as an Agency for Change.* Portsmouth, NH: Boynton/Cook, 1987.

Greenberg, Karen, L., Harvey, S. Wiener, and Richard A. Donovan. *Writing Assessment: Issues and Strategies.* New York: Longman, 1986.

Harris, Joseph. "The Idea of Community in the Study of Writing." *CCC* 40 (1989): 11—22.

Klemp, George O. "The Meaning of Success: A View from Outside the Academy." *Liberal Education* 74 (1988): 37—41.

Kohl, Herbert. *Basic Skills: A Plan for Your Child, A Program for All Children.* Toronto: Bantam, 1984.

Myers, Miles. "Classroom Research and Writing Assessment." *Notes from the National Testing Network in Writing* 8 (1988): 32.

Murray, Donald M. *A. Writer Teaches Writing.* 2nd ed. Boston: Houghton Mifflin, 1985.

————. *Learning by Teaching.* Portsmouth, NH: Boynton/Cook, 1982.

Newkirk, Thomas. "The Politics of Writing Research: Or the Conspiracy Against Experience." In *The Politics of Writing Instruction: Postsecondary.* Ed. Richard Bullock and John Trimbur. Portsmouth, NH: Boynton/Cook, 1991.

Parini, Jay. "Academic Conservatives Who Decry 'Politicization' Show Staggering Naïveté About Their Own Biases." *Chronicle of Higher Education* 7 (December 1988): B1—2.

"Report of the Commission on Writing and Literature." In *Profession '88.* New York: MLA, 1988, 70—76.

Rorty, Richard. *Contingency, Irony, and Solidarity.* Cambridge: Cambridge University Press, 1989.

Trimbur, John. "Collaborative Learning and Teaching Writing." In *Perspectives on Research and Scholarship in Composition.* Eds. Ben W. McClelland and Timothy W. Donovan. New York: MLA, 1986, 87—109.

White, Edward M. *Teaching and Assessing Writing: Recent Advances in Understanding, Evaluating, and Improving Student Performance.* San Francisco: Jossey-Bass, 1986.

13

The Politics of
Reading Student Papers

ROBERT A. SCHWEGLER
University of Rhode Island

In the year following my father's death, my mother sorted through the cartons in the basement of their home and began sending me envelopes filled with sepia-toned photographs of great aunts and great uncles. Among these was a carefully posed picture of a group of men standing by a horse-drawn merchant's wagon, some in suits, others with the open collars and rolled-up sleeves of workingmen from the early 1900s. The stiff poses of the men convey a sense of awkward pride and dignity. The wagon, looking newly painted and hitched to a well-groomed horse, announces in shiny letters the wares of "Schwegler & Levea—Greengrocers."

My father's drive to succeed, his willingness to work at two jobs —teacher and pharmacist—stemmed in part from the threat of poverty that came at age twelve when my grandfather died. But the feelings of fear and loss that drove my father had other roots as well, beginning with the threat to social status posed by the bankruptcy of the greengrocer business, my grandfather's subsequent injury while working as a laborer at the Pierce Arrow plant, and his physical decline and death.

At least this is how I received the story as a child and a teenager, sensing with it my father's pain and accepting the framework of values: a desire for material achievement and security as well as a sense that social (class) identity is both essential and fragile.

As I read student papers, I am especially moved by stories of loss or threats to the writer's social identity or economic security. I value as well the efforts of a student who struggles for grades and praise not as steps toward a career or even as validations of the writer's efforts but for their message of belonging and security: "Yes, this is how an educated person writes. You are one of us, a college student, a member of this social class." I enjoy, of course, an accomplished student essay that goes beyond formulas to blend personal voice with skillful use of rhetorical strategies. But I am also drawn to the paper whose struggles with academic diction and awkward but ambitious phrasing seem to whisper frantically, "I can do it. Let me stay!"

Other teacher/readers, I suspect, respond likewise to the values embodied in student papers and composing behaviors. Some may be drawn to particular images and values they encounter in narratives of growing up. Or they may perceive special force and pertinence in arguments about pornography or gun control congruent with their own outlooks while exhibiting a sharp critical awareness of the reasoning in papers supporting positions they oppose.

At the same time, it is difficult for most instructors to conceive of a positive role for responses conveying their moral, social, or political attitudes. In his anatomy of the possible roles for readers of student texts, Alan Purves leaves little room among categories such as "common reader," "editor," and "critic" for the instructor who interacts with the values in a paper or who acknowledges to students that her perception of a text's meaning is conditioned by her social, cultural, or political concerns. While some of the most influential discussions of response and evaluation have encouraged teachers to provide "genuine personal reactions" (Knoblauch and Brannon 132) to student texts, they have at the same time viewed the teacher/reader as a "sounding board" whose job is to identify authorial meaning and intent and report on the "communicative effectiveness" of a text (Brannon and Knoblauch 166; also Sommers).

Despite acknowledgments that reading is an active, or transactive, process (Probst; Griffin), discussions of response and evaluation have continued to focus primarily on textual meaning. The content of readers' responses — specifically the values that permeate teacher/readers' reactions and help constitute the mental texts they create as part of the transaction of reading — has been largely ignored. Lacking any clear role for value-laden responses, most instructors have tried to suppress or displace them, lumping them with other inappropriate kinds of comments: those that "perpetuate archaic modes of expression, propagandize for a particular style, or coerce agreement with a sociopolitical attitude" (Sloan 35).

Like many other composition instructors, I, too, have feared that value-laden responses will lead me to be partial or to impose some ideological "ideal text" on student essays. Thus, in reading and evaluating student papers, I have often relied on formal criteria: coherence, evidence, thesis statements, stylistic clarity, and correctness. I have tried to guide my personal responses to reflect "community" standards, sometimes unconsciously echoing the language of textbooks. Detailed assignments, grading sheets, and peer evaluation guided by comment sheets have also put distance between my social and political values and the comments I make on student writing. When possible, I have tried to make my commentary direct and personal, but also to remain in the role of an "assistant in the student's effort to make meaning" (Probst 74), focusing on authorial intention and negotiating with the student over the effectiveness of particular choices in form or content.

These techniques are familiar and useful elements of contemporary pedagogy. Yet they also can be, and often are, part of an elaborate set of strategies instructors employ to suppress or displace value-laden and political readings of student papers by putting the locus of evaluation outside the individual reader, situating it instead either in the text itself or in a supposedly community-wide set of standards expressed either in formal terms (thesis statement, clarity, logic) or in the responses of a putative "average reader." What we must remember, however, is that none of us can escape our personal histories as readers of texts. To the extent that our histories and our selves are socially constructed, all readings of student papers must be in some measure political and value laden. So, too, are the relationships we establish with students. In leaving the political dimensions of reading and teaching unacknowledged, we do not banish them; instead, we conceal them, often moving them beyond both recognition and control so that they can undermine teaching and learning.

Three sets of professional practices and assumptions have encouraged composition instructors to suppress value-laden responses to student writing and ignore the political dimensions of their reading and teaching practices:

1. the belief that reading and evaluation of student papers ought to be objective,
2. simplistic models of the cognitive process of evaluation, and
3. some often unexamined but widely held paradigms governing the relationship of teacher/readers and student/writers.

I would like to examine the implications of these assumptions and offer in their place perspectives incorporating the inevitable social and ideological grounding of response and evaluation into the act of composition teaching.

Objective/Subjective

During this century, composition teachers have generally viewed the reading and evaluating of student papers as, ideally, an objective rather than subjective process. Of course, few have argued that it can ever be objective in a technical sense, since different readers cannot be counted on to give identical scores to a text. Nonetheless, objectivity has been a goal in two informal senses, that is, in tying evaluation to the features of the text (the object) and not the reader's responses to it, and in trying to create uniformity among readers' perceptions and judgments.

The act of reading student papers has thus been often conceptualized as the identification of textual or content features assumed to be marks of writing quality to the exclusion of readers' responses to ideas, values, and stylistic force. Moreover, the role of the reader has been conceptualized as that of a representative of the standards of a larger audience, perhaps as embodying the tastes of the general educated readership for expository essays or the discourse preferences of a specific interpretive community.

Hence the reader of student writing has been defined as an authoritative reader (a generalized or decontextualized subject) and not as an individual respondent.

In the first half of the century, research and pedagogy emphasized the use of grading scales and commentary cards that focused primarily on the formal features of texts and attempted to make the teacher's job of grading papers easier while at the same time eliminating inequality (or unreliability) in grading (Gere, "Empirical Research" 115–118). In the second half of the century, driven in part by the need for interrater reliability in research and in large-scale assessments and in part by a recognition that both untrained and trained readers relying on grading scales varied widely in judgments of papers (Gere, "Empirical Research" 115–116; Diederich), attention shifted to readers, specifically to methods such as holistic scoring, as ways of eliminating reader bias and achieving regularity (reliability) in response (Hillocks 100–102; Gere "Empirical Research" 117–118).

Neither grading scales nor holistic scoring attempts to make the individual reader disappear. After all, it is the reader who applies the scale or generates a holistic score. Nonetheless, the reader—the responding subject—is in both cases assumed to be of less importance than the text and to be in need of control. As Anne Gere puts it, "The interaction between reader and writer, the context in which the writing is produced, and the textual representation created by the reader are subsumed by pervasive attention which focuses on the written text and emphasizes reader consensus in response to this text" ("Written Composition" 47).

These developments have run parallel to the rise and dominance of formalist literary criticism, characterized by an emphasis on form, on determinate meaning, and on the decontextualization of interpretive reading, as well as by a hostility to reader-response approaches and a flight from the social and political implications of texts. It would be foolish, therefore, to ascribe the struggle for objectivity in reading and evaluation simply to forces in composition research and pedagogy. And there are certainly laudable motives in the struggle to achieve some sort of "objectivity"—a desire for fairness, a fear of undue partiality, and the search for a reliable method of scoring to counter arguments for indirect, multiple-choice assessments of writing ability (White; Odell). Nonetheless, these motives are often mingled with an excessive suspicion of subjectivity in interpretation and assessment along with a belief in the determinate meaning of texts and its centrality in reading. One may speculate as well on the extent to which the tendency of instructors to impose ideal texts of their own on student work (Brannon and Knoblauch) derives from the assumption that there are universal, objective standards that can be used to judge the quality of writing.

The following summary comment on a student paper illustrates how response strategies centered on formal elements and employing a distanced, authoritarian "teacher role" (Fuller) can displace personal reactions and values. Anson offers these comments as an example of a "dualistic" response style, fitting them into a classification derived from William Perry's developmental and epistemological scheme. I have borrowed the example as a way of suggesting that phenomena we have grown used to discussing in psychological terms may also be analyzed within social or political frames.

Overall, the paper shows sensitivity and understanding. What the paper does not have is a coherent paragraph organization and composition. This is unfortunate because it mars the effectiveness of what has been for you clearly a painful but educative experience. Try to organize your thoughts in terms of paragraphs that explore and describe *one* thought at a time. It would also have helped if you had established a "theme" (simply an overall controlling idea) for the paper in the opening paragraph. The paper also has an awkward, contradictory and repetitive sentence. You make a free use of contractions that are much too casual and not used in formal writing, you have clauses in the same sentences that contradict each other, and you make the same statament several times without adding anything substantial to what you have already said ("I knew I had made the right decision" is an example). So, overall I would say, in the future exercise more caution in planning your paper and more control in writing clearer, more precise and effective sentences. (Anson, "Response" 347)

The only time "I" appears in this passage to denote the respondent is in the final sentence, directed to future writing activities. In the opening sentence, however, the instructor's personal responses to the paper's ideas, values, and rhetorical force appear to be displaced onto the paper itself by being treated as attributes of the text ("the paper shows sensitivity and understanding") rather than as evaluations offered by the reader (e.g., "I found your treatment of the subject sensitive and filled with understanding"). A student might assume, therefore, that if "sensitivity and understanding" are qualities of the text, they should be apparent to any competent reader, though the forms of expression might need to be corrected and polished. Pedagogically, however, it is far more important for a student to recognize that "sensitivity and understanding" are qualities a reader has perceived — that they are responses to the text. Such recognitions may well foster a rhetorical and flexible awareness of audience, a perspective that characterizes the thinking of successful student writers (Roth).

Formalist strategies of reading and response have been effectively criticized for their failure to attend to student texts as meaningful communicative events (Gere, "Written Composition"). In analyzing the instructor's comment cited above, for example, Chris M. Anson observes,

What stands out here is [the instructor's] cursory *response* to [the student's] writing as a reflection of a human being coming to terms with her commitments. The *meaning* of [her] text . . . suddenly fades from view, and the assignment becomes a kind of rhetorical trick simply to get [her] to reveal her practices in paragraph structuring and adherence to the conventions of "formal" discourse. Whatever beliefs [the student] has developed about the world, she may begin to think that the written language, in the rigidity implied by [the instructor's] constraints on organization and development, is not the medium through which to explore them. ("Response" 347)

Such approaches have also been criticized for their negative effects on student writing and their imposition of a teacher's authority over texts that rightfully belong to the student/writer (Sommers; Brannon and Knoblauch).

Still, even those who call for readings that pay attention to the meaning of student texts or for "ordinary" rather than "teacherly" readings (Fuller) seem unwilling to endorse responses that are individual, subjective, and value-laden, preferring instead some form of displacement like, "I believe most readers would find your arguments here unsettling or unconvincing because of the lack of evidence." Or a primarily positive focus. "I can really share the anguish and frustration of the victim's parents here." They draw back from a reaction like

I think you ought to know that I get really distressed when people try to convince me that capital punishment is good because it will save money (just as you argue here). I feel that this argument ignores the fact that living, breathing people are going to die. I suppose I might find this argument easier to accept if you explained that the money saved would enable the government to do some really good things, such as helping homeless families, but even then I'm not sure how convinced I would be. I don't want to put too much pressure on you here or to seem too closed-minded, but I also want to let you know that I'm a bit of a tough audience in this matter.

In encouraging teachers to leave control in the hands of student/writers and to refrain from imposing their Ideal Texts on students' efforts, Brannon and Knoblauch envision for teacher/readers only a limited, reactive involvement in questions of meaning. The instructor's role is to recognize the intended meanings in a student's text and to report on how satisfactorily they are conveyed, thereby initiating negotiation over "ways to bring actual effect as closely in line with a desired intention as possible" (162). In this arrangement, ideas and values are created by and belong to the writer, not the reader; "negotiation" is limited primarily to matters of form and expression. Even Thomas Newkirk's call for "a dialectical encounter between teacher and student" (328) stops well short of envisioning the teacher/reader's response as offering an antithesis to the student's thesis, though

Newkirk does attempt to delineate an active role for readers in the "constant interplay between audience and intention" (329).

What are the causes of this hesitation between acknowledging the primacy of meaning and accepting a teacher/reader's subjective constructions of meaning or of responses making plain an instructor's social or personal biases; moral or political positions; or even reactions like boredom, sympathy, or irritation? We ought not underestimate the continuing force of formalist approaches to reading and literary criticism, especially what Stanley Fish identifies as the "formalist assumption . . . that subjectivity is an ever present danger and that any critical procedure must include a mechanism for holding it in check" (9). Even more likely explanations, I think, are that we hesitate to remove the tacit restraints that now limit response because of our experiences with authoritarian approaches to reading and evaluation and because we are aware that the imbalance of power in instruction can give a teacher's comments coercive force.

Nonetheless, once we recognize the extent to which we are constituted as reading subjects by the social and interpretive communities we inhabit, we ought to be able to deal directly with the lingering fear that subjectivity leads to chaos; to unstructured, incoherent responses; or to the expression of idiosyncratic biases. We might see, for example, that subjective response need not be authoritarian. I sometimes use a paper entitled "A Two-Foot Hole or a Two-Inch Hole?" in evaluation workshops. The paper argues in graphic terms for allowing police to use heavier-caliber weapons that are more likely to cause disabling injuries that halt the flight of criminals and are also less likely to cause ricochets that harm bystanders. Those instructors who wish to express disapproval of the author's arguments or the values implied by them generally take one of two paths. Some reveal their distaste briefly but then focus on formal aspects of the paper. This approach tells a student little about how to respond to the concerns of her audience other than by working on the formal elements of the text and encourages her to view the teacher as a somewhat mysterious, disapproving, and authoritative other. On the other hand, a few instructors respond with comments like, "I find this statement and the examples that follow upsetting because . . . ," thus providing a context in values and perceptions for their responses. This approach gives the student information she can use to restructure, re-contextualize, or simply enhance her arguments, and it encourages her to view the teacher as a reasoning and reasonable respondent.

The authoritarian or coercive force of a teacher's comments depends, as I will argue later, on the relationships of power and responsibility established between teacher/readers and student/writers. When conflicts (or agreements) between a student's values and those of an instructor are acknowledged or explained, they can be valuable for learning. Unacknowledged or unexplained reactions still shape reading and evaluation, but they have the power to distort learning.

Cognition and Evaluation

I am not suggesting that every comment on a student paper or every remark in a conference be grounded in questions of value. Rhetorical strategies and stylistic matters are certainly important subjects for discussion. Sometimes students are best served by a reader who acts as a sounding board, other times by one who functions as a helpful editor. We can choose, however, to make value-laden responses — to foreground them — because they are always available. Our readings are never neutral: they are always, inevitably ideological and political — at least to some extent — and we can choose to foreground or suppress this aspect.

Despite widespread recognition that reading is an active, constructive process, the cognitive process of evaluation has been assumed to be simple and straightforward, concerned primarily with form and authorial intent. Even sophisticated discussions of assessment rest on an assumed model of judgment similar to that outlined in a popular textbook:

> Evaluation of a literary piece, as for any other creative endeavor, is meaningful only when based somehow on the answers to three questions: (1) What was the author's purpose? (2) How successfully was it fulfilled? (3) How worthwhile was it? ... Many things are written and published that succeed very well in carrying out the author's intent — but are simply not worthwhile. (Decker and Schwegler 449)

Though in answering question 2 ("How successfully was it fulfilled?") the teacher/reader might be assumed to be participating in an act of evaluation, she does so only in a limited sense, estimating a correlation between intention and accomplishment, and excluding questions of value and ideology. Such an exclusion is apparent in the formulation offered by Brannon and Knoblauch:

> And when evaluation is undertaken, as a last step in the process we propose, the standards invoked do not have to do with fixed preconceptions about form or content as stipulated by some Ideal Text. Instead, they relate to communicative effectiveness as an experienced reader assesses it in a particular writing situation. The standards of communicative effectiveness are how well the writer's choices achieve stated or implied purposes given the needs and expectations of an intended audience. If the evaluator finds the writer's choices to be *plausible* (as opposed to "correct") all of the time, the grade for that writing is higher than if the choices occasionally or frequently create uncertainties that cause failures in communication. (166)

Implicit in both these typical discussions is a view of reading, especially of student papers, as a two-part operation consisting of interpretation (including an estimate of communicative effectiveness) followed at times by judgments of value. Though estimates of communicative effectiveness are certainly evaluations, this rough model absorbs them into the process of understanding, which is assumed to be nonpolitical in the sense that it does not rely on social or moral criteria or draw to any great extent on the reader's personal experience and attitudes. Judgments of value are presumed to be more or less separate from the act of interpretation. The role of an individual reader's values in such judgments is downplayed because she is encouraged to adopt the role of a reader whose social situation and outlook are most favorable to the intended purposes of the text.

This model reenacts a fact/value split that guided literary criticism and scholarship for much of this century, though it has recently been subjected to trenchant criticism (Smith 5–15). One particularly clear statement of the fact/value distinction is E. D. Hirsch's sharp differentiation between, on one hand, acts of understanding and interpretation directed to textual meaning (including attention to the relationship of intention and accomplishment) and, on the other hand, judgments of a text's significance as it relates to readers' values as well as events, personalities, and other texts. Moreover, the assumption that a reader can arrive at estimates of communicative effectiveness more or less independently of her values, preconceptions, and social situatedness in turn implies a view of reading as a linear process of meaning transferral.

At first glance, contemporary discussions of writing and response may seem to have abandoned these models of reading and evaluation in favor of social, interactive perspectives paralleling developments in reception theory, poststructuralist thought, and reading theory (Harker). Deborah Brandt, for example, argues that both comprehension and composition take place in actual or projected social contexts. A similar concern for context and interaction is apparent in an increasing focus on the process of teacher-student negotiation during revision (Onore) and in calls for greater attention to "dialectic encounter" in the relationship of teacher/readers and student/writers (Newkirk 328).

Nonetheless, Louise Phelps's observation that "theories of teacher response lag behind" the recent shift in rhetorical theory to an emphasis on "activity in context" (61–62) is accurate. For example, Martin Nystrand's discussions of the social nature of writing and reading skirt questions about the roles of values and ideology and concentrate instead on identifying the conditions for clear, meaningful communication (Nystrand, "Social-Interactive"; *Structure*; "Sharing"). Chris M. Anson's discussion of the role of ideology in response to student writing is more promising, though his view of the values involved in response is restricted to "instructional ideologies": "the teacher[s'] values, beliefs, and models of learning . . . their awareness of student development and intellectual style, their knowledge of educational theory and research or their exposure to a variety of instructional modes and techniques" ("Response" 354). What we need, then, is a model of the cognitive process of reading and evaluating—with special emphasis on response to student texts—that makes plain the extent to which the process is grounded in personal, social, and cultural ideology and experience. Such a model can also serve to remind us that as instructors we do not have the choice of making our readings of student texts ideological or non-ideological. The choice rather concerns which elements of the experience to foreground in our responses and to acknowledge as we arrive at an evaluation.

Elsewhere (Schwegler) I have described in detail some of the components of a model of the cognitive process of reading and evaluating student papers that is built on contemporary reading and rhetorical theory (van Dijk and Kintsch). The discussion that follows highlights the socially and culturally grounded elements of the process. Central to this alternate perspective are two assumptions designed to replace those that lie behind traditional views of reading and evaluation. In place of the assumption that reading to understand and estimate communicative effectiveness and reading to respond to values and evaluate are different and separable tasks, the new perspective assumes that all acts of reading are simultaneously acts of understanding, interpretation, evaluation, and response to values. In place of the assumption that it is primarily the features and information in the text and not the reader's knowledge, values, or interpretive strategies that shape reader response and judgment, the new approach assumes that response and judgment are shaped by the reader's knowledge; ideology (personal, social, cultural); social situation; and interpretive strategies (often shaped themselves by social and cultural ideology and class [Bourdieu]) as well as by textual features and content. From this perspective, then, the reading of student papers and acts of response and evaluation are prob-lematic, socially situated processes taking place at all times within the value frameworks (ideologies) of the teacher/reader.

When an instructor begins reading a student paper, she draws cues from it or the context and blends these with background knowledge (stored in schema) to arrive at an initial estimate of the text's purposes and design. Most instructors are aware, of course, of the role of expectations in evalu-ation of the formal or generic qualities of texts, especially insofar as a writer's understanding of generic constraints and skill in employing them can contribute to the communicative effectiveness of a text: "Because you are trying to get readers to agree with your point of view you ought to state your thesis early in the paper." Because genres are cultural conventions, they also entail social and ideological expectations based on readers' associ-ations of a genre with a particular discourse setting (Couture 79—85). When a text confirms expectations for organization and broad logical relationships, as in the case of a report in a technical writing class that embodies the teacher's (or textbook's) conception of the finished product, then the values entailed in matters of genre often are not apparent to the person reading and evaluating. But when a text departs from generic expectations, as in the case of feminist literary criticism that employs personal narrative rather than expository patterning, it may pose a direct challenge to the reader's ideological expectations. And when a text clearly mishandles generic conventions, readers may question not only the writer's skill, but also maturity (in the case of student writers), understanding of the social setting, or failure to appreciate the cultural and social background of the intended audience.

More important than matters of genre, however, are those features of discourse addressed by the term *register*. *Register* refers to the "meaning potential" of reader-writer-text interactions: "the range of meanings and structures typically associated with a particular setting" (Kucer 325). The register of a discourse type or setting includes its "characteristic vocabulary, sentence structures, organizational patterns, modes of interpersonal expression, or logical patterns of reasoning and evidence" (Bernhardt 191). As M. A. K. Halliday points out (111), registers are manifested in language, but are themselves social and ideological structures, not linguistic forms. Thus, a student paper on a controversial issue will likely elicit in an instructor's mind knowledge of generally accepted ways of formulating the issue and similar issues; an understanding of the appropriate discourse styles and strategies; and an awareness of how other texts have addressed the issue, especially those with cultural and social importance.

The following opening paragraph from a student essay is probably conventional enough to prompt little personal moral response from an experienced composition instructor:

There are many solutions to the drug problems of junior high and high schools, one of which is not mandatory drug testing. Because of the numerous opposers and conflicting viewpoints it is difficult to find a universal solution. I believe that a more probable solution rests in the education of students, rather than in disciplinary action.

The context of production, the manner of topicalization, and the style identify this paragraph as part of a student essay. Inscribed in the register for such texts is a set of hierarchical social relationships identifying the relative power and status of reader and writer. Thus, simply by deciding to read a text as a student paper, an instructor becomes socially (and ideologically) situated with regard to it, though her own values may of course determine the way she evaluates departures from or adherence to the constraints of the register. And by the same token, the student writer of the paragraph above acknowledges his inferior status in the phrase "the numerous opposers and conflicting viewpoints," an attempt to incorporate the language of the teacher and the textbook: "opposition," "opposing points of view." While some students respond with defiance to the constraints of the student register (Freedman, "Registers" 342), the majority take on willingly the tasks of the novice, one of which is to employ the technical language of the field—of chemistry, or of literary criticism, or in this case, of composition. But this writer's failure to employ the language in the correct form or in a manner we might recognize as characteristic of the "best students" or "most accomplished writers" marks him as a novice or perhaps (I would argue) as an outsider who does not quite understand the stylistic mores and the special language of the discourse setting.

To draw on Pierre Bourdieu, we might say that the student acknowledges the value of "educational capital" but reveals through the false note of a word like "opposers" that he is still not fully competent at the game of discourse that certifies its attainment (see Bourdieu 65–70). Indeed, I would argue that the factors of class; of monetary, cultural, and educational capital; of power and hierarchy that Bourdieu sees as determining judgments about and the distribution of cultural goods (including written discourse) are manifested in the expectations that constitute registers. At the same time, how a particular instructor responds to conflicts between her expectations and the register of a student text—with helpful advice or with brusque, negative comments—is likely to depend on a number of things, including the instructor's view of the social role of education.

Even a common and seemingly neutral assignment such as "Prepare an essay analyzing the point of view in 'A Rose for Emily'" entails expectations whose ideological grounding becomes evident when a paper fails to fulfill them. Consider, for example, a student paper that opens with these statements:

> In William Faulkner's short story "A Rose for Emily," he uses a narrator in the first person to help convey the main idea behind the story, which is one of loneliness, something almost everyone can relate to. When I first read the story, I couldn't understand why the author would spend so much time describing a strange old lady. Then I looked at our textbook and I started thinking that maybe he was illustrating the theme of "Complexities of Love" which I think is very important.

Responses such as "high schoolish," "unsophisticated," "uncritical," or even "ignorant" and "childish" are likely to occur to an instructor, to be suppressed, perhaps, in favor of pedagogically oriented responses designed to help the student think and write critically about the story. But both sets of responses—the directly evaluative and the corrective—may be viewed as reactions to the way the act of analysis has been defined, as ethical rather than aesthetic or formalist, and to the manner of expression, which does not display the language or the stance expected in academic literary study, even at a novice level. As Bourdieu has demonstrated (11–96), there is generally a strong correlation between superior social status and formalist, decontextualized approaches to art, on one hand, and between ethical approaches and lower social status. I would contend that these relationships, reproduced in the forms of expectations for novice critical discourse, can lead to responses like "uncritical" and "unsophisticated." The hostility with which some instructors greet departures from the norms for student literary analysis ("This student barely knows how to read, much less write a good critical paper") suggests that in violating expectations, a student may also be perceived as calling into question the value of the cultural and educational capital that constitutes the teacher's authority.

A clash of registers in the reading and evaluation of student texts is therefore likely to be more than a case of differing expectations for style of expression. Conflicts between registers involve differing conceptions of the task, the context, and reader-text-writer relationships, conceptions that are part of the frameworks of social and cultural values — ideological networks — that underlie all acts of reading and writing (Belsey; Macdonell).

Ideology, broadly defined as "The conscious or unconscious beliefs, habits, and social practices of a particular society" (McCormick, Waller, and Flower 285) and including personal beliefs and attitudes, also plays an important role in the next stage of reading, the attempt to build a coherent mental representation of a text's meaning. Working within a scaffold of expectations for a particular text, a reader tries to build a coherent mental image of its meanings and purposes using cues and information from the text as well as inferences from prior knowledge. Inference serves to fill in those many elements of the representation not explicitly detailed in the text. Perceptions of coherence and incoherence in student papers as well as judgments of the adequacy of detail and support can vary according to the assumptions and knowledge of the teacher/reader. So too can estimates of a paper's focus, development, and organization.

Register and the social relationships it manifests also play an important role in the mental images instructors create of student authors. Barritt Stock, and Clark have noted the tendency of readers of placement exams to create mental images of the authors as prospective students and to frame their responses to the text in terms of these images. In examining think-aloud protocols of composition instructors reading student papers, I have noted that readers often draw information from the text and from prior experience with student writers to create images of what might be called "inferred authors." These images take several forms:

Author as student   This is the type of student that you hope you have one of in every class, I have one this semester who I had before and she wrote a paper interestingly very similar to this.

Author as strategist   Again the um details that the student has chosen tell me that they do understand the material, they researched it well.

I don't know if this student really, really remembers Mammy, too young for Jolson. I suspect not but if this person could have used uh *Bartlett's Familiar Quotations*, I suspect.

Author as individual (personal characteristics and attitudes)   I am saying *she* all the way through, that may be sexism, this may be a man. But it's written like what I would think a woman, a woman's writing would be.

Instructors sometimes use an inferred author—or the inferred traits and attitudes of a known author—as part of value judgments, comparing, for example, the supposed maturity or critical ability of the student to those of other students. Most often, however, inferring an author is a strategy that enables teacher/readers to view a text as a communicative, social act, something produced by a writer to share thoughts with a reader. This not only places a discourse in a social context but also encourages readers to respond to and evaluate it as a moral and social act.

Paradigms

As I have argued, differing views of the role of the teacher in evaluation and response can lead to either foregrounding or repressing questions of value. Views of the teacher's role as authoritative, authoritarian, and pre-scriptive have dominated traditional approaches to composition instruction and have led to an emphasis on form (Purves; Knoblauch and Brannon; Fuller). Contemporary approaches that view the teacher as a general reader or a writing coach have placed more emphasis on a paper's content and message. Cognitive models may either disguise or highlight the inevitable contributions of ideology. Moreover, the paradigms we employ to con-ceptualize the relations between teacher/readers and student/writers in a composition class are political. First, they guide the distribution and exercise of power in the classroom society. Second, they reproduce in various ways the relationships that characterize the larger societies to which we and our students belong. Complex and shifting though these paradigms are, they do at the same time form some relatively clear patterns. To identify these, it may be helpful to view the classroom writing situation as consisting of three primary components—writer, reader, and text—each varying in authority. In addition, it is helpful to regard the relationship of writer, text, and reader in the classroom as one form of the broader relationship among producers, cultural goods, and consumers, similar to that linking, for example, authors, novels, and readers, though it may feel uncomfortable to apply economic and political language to what most of us experience as a personal and "humanistic" relationships.

In taking this approach, I am drawing on the concept of "overdetermi-nation," which suggests that the relationships within any segment of a society are shaped by the multiple effects (interaction) of the relationships in the rest of the society so that no social entity can be considered indepen-dent of others (Resnick and Wolff 1–25). And I am also making use of Louis Althusser's observation that one of the main functions of education (and of other institutions such as the legal system, the family, and the communications industry) is "reproduction of the relations of production" (146) as they exist in the practices and dominant ideology of a society. This is not to say that teaching practices simply replicate or blindly inculcate the characteristic relationships and attitudes of management and workers, for example, or of professionals and administrators in a particular social and economic system, though they may do this. As Althusser and others have pointed out, education is a relatively autonomous site at which the dominant ideology in a society or culture comes into contact and struggles with competing ideologies (Althusser; Macdonel 33—36). And it is a site where the participants may accept, refuse, or struggle to change the roles offered to them by a society and culture (Macdonel 39—40).

To put these concepts in more familiar terms, a composition class offers a number of roles, some reflecting widely accepted attitudes (teacher as authority, student as learner), others reflecting different degrees of disagreement with or rebellion against typical teacher-student relationships (teacher as writing coach; teacher as fellow writer). To take on a role is to be constituted as a subject by it and to step into relationships of authority and power that may reflect a dominant ideology or resistance to it. Most composition instructors are likely to recognize the various roles they and their students can perform (Purves; Horvath). Most are also likely to admit that struggle is a regular part of writing classes, whether it be over the need to revise, the proper response to an essay, the appropriate grade for a paper, etc. What many fail to recognize, however, are the political dimensions of these roles and struggles, and the extent to which they enact power relationships and can become avenues for repression or for growth and change.

In a traditional composition classroom, the instructor specifies the nature of the text to be produced by creating a detailed assignment, choosing specific models, focusing class discussion, responding to student writing, etc. A student's role is to understand the task and to reproduce its specifications in a paper while adding "value" to the product in the form of style, content, and insight. Though such an arrangement leaves open some power for students as creators of a text, most authority accrues to the instructor, who functions both as a reader of the text and as its writer.

It is arrangements of this sort that Brannon and Knoblauch have in mind when they criticize writing instruction that imposes on a student writer an instructor's vision of an "Ideal Text" and in so doing usurps the writer's text and intentions. Such relationships are not limited to composition courses in which the instructor imposes a particular rhetorical pattern on student writing. It can apply as well to a literature course in which students must enact a strict thesis and support structure. Or to a writing-across-the-curriculum course with a different formal requirement.

Teaching that centers power in the expectations and responses of a teacher/reader can be considered authoritarian even when it attempts to encourage and reward critical thinking and even when it aims to empower students by helping them master the discourses of various academic disciplines. This pattern centralizes power in ways similar to the worker-management relationships that characterize much industrial production in our society and the hierarchical patterns found in many companies and government agencies.

Students in authoritarian classes frequently complain that they are re-quired to write the paper the instructor wants and that, despite talk about "learning to think critically" and "expressing your ideas clearly and fully," their real task is to "psych out the instructor." At the same time, their instructors may complain about the lack of real critical thinking in student essays or wonder why these essays are simply "manicured corpses" devoid of imagination and insight. While instructors may sometimes be correct in pointing to lack of critical thinking ability, psychological immaturity, or appropriate background knowledge as the cause of problems in writing, I suspect that these explanations often have a repressive function. They encourage us to view a conflict or struggle as a problem. They make students rather than the power structure the locus of the problem. And they provide grounds for ignoring signs of defiance: boredom, cynical adherence to trite formats, cheating, and other reactions characteristic of settings in which one's efforts are undervalued or not valued at all.

In contrast, the paradigm of "ownership" or "rights" that dominates contemporary discussions of evaluation and response (Brannon and Knoblauch; Onore; Phelps) transfers considerable authority to student writers. Proponents of this approach argue that a shift of authority from teacher/reader to student/writer is necessary because

As long as judgments of what may be "better" or "worse"—that is, of what constitutes improvement in writing—remain the province of teachers alone, then the writer cannot fully and authentically engage in choice making and problem solving. And without the authority to make choices, the writer can never understand how central are the con-sequences of any meaning-making activity in writing. (Onore 231–232).

Within this paradigm, the authority of the instructor as reader is greatly reduced, especially when peer groups and collaborative learning are employed in ways that make students not only the writers but also the primary readers of the texts produced in a course. Though this arrangement may seem radical, it nonetheless reflects and reproduces some of the dominant relationships of power and production in contemporary American society.

Under the "student ownership" or "rights" paradigm, an instructor retains ultimate responsibility for initiating student writing, but the emphasis on revision and on formative responses to successive drafts serves to shift authority to the writer. The importance of the initial assignment lessens as a student discovers, with the aid of her instructor, her "real" intentions for the text. The language commonly used to describe this process emphasizes the importance of student control over the evolving text and stigmatizes forms of response and evaluation that appropriate students' texts (Sommers).

In one form, this approach casts teachers first in the role of listeners—to the students' texts and to the students as readers and evaluators of their own texts—and then as questioners whose responses help students pay attention to the effectiveness with which a text conveys meaning (Murray). In another form, the instructor responds as a "real" reader, concerned primarily with what the author has to say, not with identifying errors (Fuller).

The relationship of writer and reader(s) is viewed as one of "negotiation," not, as the term might suggest, between parties with differing interests and values, but between parties who agree on the primacy of the writer's meanings and have also agreed to cooperate on refining the meanings and their expression: "a process of negotiation, where writer and peers or writer and teacher (or tutor) work together to consider, and if possible to enhance, the relationship between intention and effect" (Brannon and Knoblauch 163). Recent expressions of the paradigm have tried to allow readers a more active role and to move toward a dialectical view of negotiation without abandoning the primacy of the writer's rights in a text:

> In arguing for a process pedagogy, we are arguing at the very least for a writer's right to his own texts and not so subsidiarily for the right of the classroom community to interpret and feed meanings back to the writer. Paradoxically, while a focus on meaning-making requires individual ownership of a text, it simultaneously requires that a writer negotiate with that community his or her intended meanings so that neither pure idiosyncrasy nor tyranny results. (Onore 232)

Paradox is probably an appropriate word for this position since it tries to maintain "ownership" or "right" as a governing concept without modifying it in response to the competing concept also acknowledged as central, the "right" of readers to assert their perceptions of a text's meaning.

Use of "ownership" and "right" as metaphors for a particular approach to response and evaluation rests on the assumption that private property— including the rights to intellectual and cultural property—is a dominant value in our society. Thomas Newkirk is correct in pointing out that metaphors used to discuss the relationship of reader and writer within this paradigm "echo private property and contractual law" (328). At the same time, however, the projected relationships of production in the classroom under this paradigm do not seem to be reflections of the dominant conditions of production in the society in quite the straightforward manner of those predicated by the authoritarian paradigm, though they may well be reflections of the complicated processes of cultural production in our society.

What I am suggesting is that the "ownership" paradigm reflects a certain confusion over the most effective conditions for production—industrial as well as cultural—and over the proper roles for labor and management, producer and consumer, teacher and student. In both practice and theory, this approach to writing instruction is less satisfactory than it might seem at first. For example, one of the clearest impressions left by Sarah Freedman's detailed study of response to student writing in two classrooms is the extent to which all writing activities are shaped by the teachers' values despite the teachers' obvious respect for students' ownership of texts: "As with Peterson['s class], every activity in Glass's classroom is informed by her philosophy of teaching writing. Thus, assignments, whole-class discussion, and peer-group work address collectively her hopes for her students' cognitive and academic growth" (*Response* 133). It seems likely, then, that though pedagogies based on this paradigm may lead to an improvement in student writing, they do so only through a superficial transfer of authority.

It makes little sense to criticize this approach as superficial and ameliorative rather than radical, however, for the benefits of even a limited transfer of authority over writing are plain in the reports from practitioners (see Anson, *Writing*). A more serious criticism is that in both theory and practice, this approach involves unresolvable contradictions and repressions that undermine it.

To limit the role and authority of the teacher/reader to that of a "soundingboard" (Brannon and Knoblauch) is to risk suppressing the value-laden, ideological, socially situated responses that constitute constructive reading, thereby making the reader a mere adjunct to the act of writing. On the other hand, to recognize reading as a meaning-making act and acknowledge the authority of the teacher/reader, while maintaining the primacy of student rights over a text, is to create a paradox, consisting of two separate rather than contingent authorities:

> To a degree, the student owns his or her paper, but the paper is *intended* for others in the way property isn't; and so, to a degree, the writing is also owned by its readers. No one (I hope) condones the practice condemned by Knoblauch and Brannon in which students must guess at some Platonic text that exists in the teacher's imagination. But by the same token, the expectations of the teacher, the course, and the academy must interact with the intentions of the student. Intention, in other words, cannot be an absolute, a "God-term." (Newkirk 329)

This contradiction can be overcome if both instructors and students are willing to play "paradoxical roles," at once asserting their own authority and recognizing the authority of the other, a process that takes place through negotiation (Newkirk; Onore). Negotiation, however, deals with differing perceptions of meaning and judgments of the effectiveness of expression, differences that can be resolved by focusing on a common goal: the articulation and development of the writer's intention. Negotiation, that is, involves a willingness on the part of teachers and students to alter their perspectives and, I would add, a willingness on the part of both to ignore contrasting values whose examination might heighten their differences.

Much of what this paradigm has to offer to composition instruction is laudable. What I find most remarkable about the various discussions of it, however, is the lack of recognition that reader-writer contacts can (and often should) lead to a sharpening of differences (or conflict) between values and ideologies, or perhaps to the strengthening and extension of mutual beliefs. By restricting the process of negotiation to creating agreement, the current practice of negotiation excludes possibilities for articulating questions of value, for identifying agreements and disagreements, and for productive conflict that encourages change.

These exclusions point to the outlines for a third paradigm of teacher/reader-student/writer relationships, one that encourages the foregrounding of values and ideology in response and evaluation while focusing on reader-writer differences as occasions for growth and change. According to this perspective, the classroom is a site of struggle between the legitimate authority of both readers and writers, their contrasting positions in the educational hierarchy, and their respective values. Seen in this way, the act of reading and responding to student papers reproduces the struggles that characterize our evolving society: conflicts over modes of industrial production and exchange; changes in ethnic and cultural patterns; questions of educational and social structure; issues of race, gender, and class.

By assuming that the interaction of values and ideologies, not simply the communication of meaning and information, is an important purpose for writing and reading, teachers and students in composition classes can view each other as contingent rather than hierarchial authorities. To do so is to acknowledge the ways in which production and consumption can be said to "produce" each other (Holub 126). That is, this paradigm offers a way to regard writers and readers as standing in a dialectical relationship, with neither having priority. This paradigm differs from the other two not so much in the recognition of a dialectical relationship but in its refusal to grant priority to either and in its belief that this dialectic ought to be characterized by struggle and conflict as well as by cooperation.

When the authorities of readers and writers are treated as contingent, writing becomes the inevitable product of their interaction — and the quality of this product becomes the focus of attention. This is especially true when both the writing and response deal with questions of value or involve differences in ideology. In a composition class following this paradigm, interchanges of reader and writer are made accessible to critical examination and become sites for struggle and change.

Admittedly, the power of teachers is greater than that of students, so to speak of contingent authorities is not to envision equal power. The relationships of power within American education and society sharply limit the extent to which authority can be effectively redistributed in any classroom. In addition, a teacher's knowledge, skill, and experience relative to that of students often creates an imbalance in authority. Nonetheless, teachers can use their authority to create significant roles for both writers and readers. They can choose to foreground rather than suppress questions of value and

ideology. Susan Wells, for example, argues that even a course as instrumental in aim and as closely tied to the dominant power relationships as a
technical writing course can be conducted in a manner that directs critical
attention to the social relations inscribed in discourse, thereby opening
possibilities for empowerment and change.

Instructors can also structure the occasions for writing in ways that give
authority to students. Open topics allow for some transfer of control,
though they are often variations on a theme established by an instructor.
Encouraging students to redefine a writing task in consultation with the
teacher is a further step, especially if the instructor is willing to voice
disagreements or misgivings while being open to reasoned persuasion.
Open or writer-generated assignments can be effective as well when they
call for consultation between student(s) and instructor and when the instructor's opinions are not given undue weight. Collections of readings in
cultural or media studies and the methods of analysis used in these fields
offer other ways to foreground ideology. Moreover, depending on how they
are employed, traditional collections such as argument readers and thematic
literature anthologies provide similar opportunities. So, too, do case-study
projects and simulation exercises. In all cases, however, the choice of
materials and activities should be open to challenge from students.

The potential for difference, struggle, and student criticism in all these
approaches is essential, both because it can lead to growth and change and
because it can set limits on the authority of the teacher/reader. Moreover,
though they represent a new paradigm, none of these strategies is difficult
to implement in a contemporary composition class. In contrast, it is much
harder to envision a language and procedures for evaluations grounded in
value. One problem is that we have been trained to regard these judgments as
inherently suspect and unfair. Another problem is that there is no readily
available body of lore to provide practical strategies.

The language of marginal and summative commentary we have learned
from handbooks, our teachers, and teacher training is predominantly
formalist and often implicitly authoritarian. To escape the constraints of this
language, those who argue for readings that focus on a writer's intentions
have begun demonstrating what form appropriate responses might take:
"Are you saying that it doesn't really matter? Do you believe that?" "I can't
tell whether your purpose here is just to make someone feel better or
really to argue that all colleges are alike and that going or not going is an
unimportant decision: in either case, do you really believe your statement?"
(Knoblauch and Brannon 127–128). A similar effort is necessary for responses
to the quality of ideas, the depth and persistence of reasoning, the patterns
of belief, and the underlying ideologies in student writing:

> This section of the paper displays what I consider an excellent under-
> standing of the tensions between siblings and the mingling of love and
> anger that I recognize from my own experience as a brother and as a
> parent.

I know you offer a good deal of evidence, but the arguments for gun control here still appear rather superficial when I contrast them with those offered in class discussion last week.

Unconvincing. The scene just doesn't come alive for me, and I feel no sympathy for your uncle despite your extended description of the events.

The behaviors you describe as a way of poking fun at the overdressed couple in the elegant restaurant have a different effect on me. I see them as signs that the social background of these people has not given them the upper-class manners to enable them to "fit in." And I feel sorry for them. I'm not sure there is any way to reconcile our outlooks, though. If you wish to take my reaction into account, you might drop the exaggerated details in the last two sentences of the third paragraph. I say this tentatively, realizing that it is these sentences that most pleased the other students in your group.

Judgments like these should not be the sole grounds for response and evaluation, but they can be an important element.

If we make plain in class discussion and in response to drafts what we consider a forceful argument, a moving example, and an intriguing insight as well as unpersuasive lines of reasoning and objectionable perspectives on gender and race, and if we give students an opportunity to respond to these expectations through revision, then we should feel free to employ them in evaluating a finished paper without fear that we are unduly constraining student expression.

Though the outline of this third paradigm has been sketchy, I believe it offers worthwhile alternatives for reading and evaluating student writing and for composition instruction. It is by no means an ideal solution and may in turn prove to contain its own repressions, though in ways different from its predecessors. As is so often the case, however, repression may become the impetus for further development.

Works Cited

Althusser, Louis. *Lenin and Philosophy and Other Essays*. Trans. Ben Brewster. London: NLB, 1971.

Anson, Chris M. "Response Styles and Ways of Knowing." In *Writing and Response: Theory, Practice, and Research*. Ed. Chris M. Anson. Urbana, IL: NCTE, 1989, 332–366.

———, ed. *Writing and Response: Theory, Practice, and Research*, Urbana, IL: NCTE, 1989.

Barritt, Loren, Patricia L. Stock, and Francelia Clark. "Researching Practice: Evaluating Assessment Essays." *CCC* (1986): 315–327.

Belsey, Catherine. *Critical Practice*. London: Routledge, 1980.

Bernhardt, Stephen A. "Applying a Functional Model of Language in the Writing

Classroom." In *Functional Approaches to Writing: Research Perspectives*. Ed. Barbara Couture. Norwood, NJ: Ablex, 1986, 186–198.

Bourdieu, Pierre. *Distinction: A Social Critique of the Judgment of Taste*. Tr. Richard Nice. Cambridge: Harvard University Press, 1984.

Brannon, Lil, and C. H. Knoblauch. "On Students' Rights to Their Own Texts: A Model of Teacher Response." *CCC* 33 (1982): 157–166.

Couture, Barbara. "Effective Ideation in Written Text: A Functional Approach to Clarity and Exigence." In *Functional Approaches to Writing: Research Perspectives*. Ed. Barbara Couture. Norwood, NJ: Ablex, 1986, 69–92.

Decker, Randall E., and Robert A. Schwegler. *Patterns of Exposition 12*. Glenview, IL: Scott, Foresman/Little, Brown, 1990.

Diederich, Paul B. *Measuring Growth in English*. Urbana, IL: NCTE, 1974.

Dijk, Teun A. Van, and Walter Kintsch. *Strategies of Discourse Comprehension*. Orlando: Academic, 1983.

Fish, Stanley. *Is There a Text in This Class?* Cambridge: Harvard, University Press, 1980.

Freedman, Sarah Warshauer. *Response to Student Writing*. Urbana, IL: NCTE, 1987.

———. "The Registers of Student and Professional Expository Writing: Influences on Teacher's Response." In *New Directions in Composition Research*. Eds. Richard Beach and Lillian S. Bridwell. New York: Guilford, 1984, 334–347.

Fuller, David. "A Curious Case of Our Responding Habits: What Do We Respond to and Why?" *Journal of Advanced Composition* 8 (1988): 88–96.

Gere, Anne Ruggles. "Empirical Research in Composition." In *Perspectives on Research and Scholarship in Composition*. Eds. Ben W. McClelland and Timothy R. Donovan. New York: MLA, 1985, 110–124.

———. "Written Composition: Toward a Theory of Evaluation." *College English* 42 (1980): 44–58.

Griffin, C. W. "Theory of Responding to Student Writing: The State of the Art." *CCC* 33 (1982): 296–301.

Halliday, M. A. K. *Language as Social Semiotic*. Baltimore: University Park Press, 1978.

Harker, W. John. "Literary Theory and the Reading Process: A Meeting of Perspectives." *Written Communication* 4 (1987): 235–252.

Hilgers, Thomas L. "Toward a Taxonomy of Beginning Writers' Evaluative Statements on Written Compositions." *Written Communication* 1 (1984): 365–384.

Hillocks, George, Jr. *Research on Written Composition*. Urbana, IL: National Conference on Research in English, 1986.

Hirsch, E. D., Jr. *Validity in Interpretation*. New Haven: Yale University Press, 1967.

Holub, Robert C. *Reception Theory: A Critical Introduction*. London: Methuen, 1984.

Horvath, Brooke K. "The Components of Written Response: A Practical Synthesis of Current Views." *Rhetoric Review* 2 (1984): 136–156.

Knoblauch, C. H., and Lil Brannon. *Rhetorical Traditions and the Teaching of Writing*. Portsmouth, NH: Boynton/Cook, 1984.

Kucer, Stephen L. "The Making of Meaning: Reading and Writing as Parallel Processes." *Written Communication* 2 (1985): 317–336.

McCormick, Kathleen, Gary Waller, and Linda Flower. *Reading Texts: Reading, Responding, Writing*. Lexington, MA: Heath, 1987.

Macdonell, Diane. *Theories of Discourse: An Introduction.* Oxford: Blackwell, 1986.

Murray, Donald M. "Teaching the Other Self: The Writer's First Reader." *CCC* 33 (1982): 140–147.

Newkirk, Thomas. "The First Five Minutes: Setting the Agenda in a Writing Conference." In *Writing and Response: Theory, Practice, and Research.* Ed. Chris M. Anson. Urbana, IL: NCTE, 1989, 317–331.

Nystrand, Martin. "A Social-Interactive Model of Writing." *Written Communication* 6 (1989): 66–85.

———. "Sharing Words: The Effects of Readers on Developing Writers." *Written Communication* 7 (1990): 3–24.

———. *The Structure of Written Communication: Studies in Reciprocity between Writers and Readers.* Orlando: Academic Press, 1986.

Odell, Lee. "Defining and Assessing Competence in Writing." In *The Nature and Measurement of Competency in English.* Ed. Charles R. Cooper. Urbana, IL: NCTE, 1981, 95–138.

Onore, Cynthia. "The Student, the Teacher, and the Text: Negotiating Meanings through Response and Revision." In *Writing and Response: Theory, Practice, and Research.* Ed. Chris M. Anson. Urbana, IL: NCTE, 1989, 231–260.

Phelps, Louise Wetherbee. "Images of Student Writing: The Deep Structure of Teacher Response." In *Writing and Response: Theory, Practice, and Research.* Ed. Chris M. Anson. Urbana, IL: NCTE, 1989, 37–67.

Probst, Robert E. "Transactional Theory and Response to Student Writing." In *Writing and Response: Theory, Practice, and Research.* Ed. Chris M. Anson. Urbana, IL: NCTE, 1989.

Purves, Alan C. "The Teacher as Reader: An Anatomy." *College English* 46 (1984): 259–265.

Resnick, Stephen A., and Richard D. Wolff. *Knowledge and Class: A Marxian of Political Economy.* Chicago: University of Chicago Press, 1987.

Roth, Robert G. "The Evolving Audience: Alternatives to Audience Accommodation." *CCC* 38 (1987): 47–55.

Schwegler, Robert A. "Discourse Theory and the Reading of Student Texts." Paper delivered at New Directions in Communication Research, University of New Hampshire, 1986.

Sloan, Gary. "The Perils of Paper Grading." *English Journal* 66 (1977): 33–36.

Smith, Barbara Herrnstein. "Contingencies of Value." In *Canons.* Ed. Robert von Hallberg. Chicago: University of Chicago Press. 5–39.

Sommers, Nancy. "Responding to Student Writing." *CCC* 33 (1982): 148–156.

Wells, Susan. "Jurgen Habermas, Communicative Competence, and the Teaching of Technical Discourse." In *Theory in the Classroom.* Ed. Cary Nelson. Urbana, IL: University of Illinois Press, 1986. 245–269.

White, Edward M. "Holisticism." *CCC* 35 (1984): 400–409.

14

Reading Basic Writing: Alternatives to a Pedagogy of Accommodation

SUSAN WALL
Northeastern University

NICHOLAS COLES
University of Pittsburgh

At the bedrock of my thinking about this is the sense that language is power, and that, as Simone Weil says, those who suffer from injustice most are the least able to articulate their suffering; and that the silent majority, if released into language, would not be content with a perpetuation of the conditions which have betrayed them. But this notion hangs on a special conception of what it means to be released into language: not simply learning the jargon of an elite, fitting unexceptionably into the status quo, but learning that language can be used as a means of changing reality.

—ADRIENNE RICH
"Teaching Language in Open Admissions"

Every time a student sits down to write for us, he has to invent the university for the occasion—invent the university, that is, or a branch of it, like history or anthropology or economics or English. The student has to learn to speak our language, to speak as we do, to try on the peculiar ways of knowing, selecting, evaluating, reporting, concluding, and arguing that define the discourse of our community.

—DAVID BARTHOLOMAE
"Inventing the University"

Adrienne Rich's conviction that "language is power" is at the bedrock of the thinking of all those who write about Basic Writing in ways we want to consider here as "political." For example, in our second epigraph, David

Bartholomae privileges the language of the university precisely because he regards it as intellectually and socially powerful. Bartholomae, in fact, places the quotation from Rich above as the epigraph to his article on the legacy of Mina Shaughnessy, "Released into Language," in which he explicitly modifies Rich's "special conception" of what it means for marginalized students to be released into language:

> I think that the styles and projects of academic discourse can be exciting, creative, and liberating, even at the point at which they confine students to work that is, at least for undergraduates, ours and not theirs, and even to the degree to which that writing does not "change reality" or reshape the university and its disciplines. There are reasons, I believe, for students to learn to work within our community that are more important and more powerful than the dream of preserving their freedom. (84)

Clearly Bartholomae is skeptical of what he treats as Rich's utopian project: the language into which students are to be released must be "ours, and not theirs."

Rich and Bartholomae are two of the teachers from whom we have learned most about working with basic writers in humane and politically responsible ways. They, together with others such as Mina Shaughnessy, Patricia Bizzell, and Mike Rose, have moved us well beyond those reductive analyses that would locate basic writers' difficulties in their heads, in undeveloped cognitive processes, or in a simple ignorance of the codes of Standard English. They have enabled us to perceive our students in the contexts of their social and political situation as college students, within what many experience as a clash of cultures. And Shaughnessy and Bartholomae in particular have taught us a method we have come to regard as enacting a political stance, a habit of close and respectful attention to the actual texts of basic writers, to what they are saying and doing and attempting to get said and done. How then do we come to terms with what appears to be a radical divergence in the political bearings and epistemological assumptions of the pedagogies implied by the headnotes from Rich and Bartholomae above?

One way to construct this difference would be to say that we, in Composition in the 1980s, have redefined as "discourse" what we once scorned as "jargon." Certainly there were problems with the term "jargon," with its suggestion of uselessness and emptiness, together with the necessary implication of some other, cleaner language operating elsewhere, beyond the trammels of jargon. "Discourse," in part because participation in it seems inescapable, appears as a more neutral term to indicate language in use in specific contexts, and it allows us to shed the contentious 1960s sense of "elite" in favor of the apparently neutral notion of a "discourse community," whose operations determine what counts as knowledge within a particular profession, or branch of it. On the basis of these redefinitions, it could be said that we (again a generalized "we," in Composition, in the 1980s) became comfortable saying that what is needed by those students Rich and Bartholomae are talking about here (Open Admissions, non-traditional, basic, or underprepared students) is to learn the discourse conventions of the academic community. It is because this formulation still represents the most broadly persuasive current response to basic writers' difficulties that we want here to interrogate its politics: if Rich's call is for a pedagogy of liberation, is Bartholomae's, then, a pedagogy of accommodation? What alternatives to this dichotomy are represented in their work and that of others that suggest different ways of imagining the political possibilities of Basic Writing pedagogy?

David Bartholomae

We begin with the work of Bartholomae because it has been highly influential in the development of intellectually challenging, discourse-based courses for basic writers, and also because, as participants in the team of teachers at the University of Pittsburgh who implemented and revised these courses, we know the work and its implications well.

Bartholomae's recent work is most commonly cited in support of a pedagogy for basic writers that proceeds by demystifying the features of academic discourse in order to induct students into the language-using practices of the academy (Rose, "Remedial Writing"; Kogen). In fact, in "Inventing the University," Bartholomae attributes the call for such a pedagogy to Patricia Bizzell, author of such articles as "College Composition: Initiation into the Academic Discourse Community." Bizzell ascribes basic writers' problems to "their unfamiliarity with the academic discourse community, combined, perhaps, with such limited experience outside their native discourse communities that they are unaware that there is such a thing as a discourse community with conventions to be mastered" ("Cognition" 230). While Bartholomae does not criticize Bizzell either for her reification of "discourse community" or for her apparent assumption that basic writers are unaware of language differences, neither does he take up the call in precisely her terms.

"One response" to Bizzell's definition of the problem, Bartholomae observes, "would be to determine just what the community's discourse conventions are, so that these conventions could be written out, demystified, and taught in our classrooms . . ." ("Inventing" 147). This is the approach we see taken, for example, by Myra Kogen in "The Conventions of Expository Writing." Citing Bartholomae as one of her authorities, she sets out to "understand exactly what the conventions of argument in academic discourse really are" (26–27). The attempt, however, yields only the standard injunc-tions—the need for connection, generalization, support, audience aware-ness, a tone of reasonableness, etc.—familiar from traditional rhetorics and

handbooks. Bartholomae refuses a project that would define a set of discourse
conventions whose mastery would somehow lead to good academic writing.
Instead, he proposes "to examine the essays written by basic writers—their
approximations of academic discourse—to determine more clearly where
their problems lie. If we look at their writing, and if we look at it in the
context of other student writing, we can better see the points of discord
that arise when students try to write their way into the university"
("Inventing" 147). This second response is Bartholomae's characteristic
method, to look at specific examples of student work in order to understand
not only our expectations but the struggles that students do in fact go
through in attempting to meet them.

Here is how Bartholomae represents that struggle in "Inventing the
University":

> The student has to appropriate (or be appropriated by) a specialized
> discourse, and he has to do this as though he were easily and comfortably
> one with his audience, as though he were a member of the academy or
> an historian or an anthropologist or an economist; he has to invent the
> university by assembling and mimicking its language while finding some
> compromise between idiosyncracy, a personal history, on the one hand,
> and the requirements of convention, the history of a discipline, on the
> other. He must learn to speak our language. (135)

While Bizzell speaks of "our language" in terms of a set of discourse
conventions to be "mastered," Bartholomae defines the issue as one of
establishing a rhetorical stance—which immediately introduces conflict and
mediation, rather than simply socialization, as the problem the student
faces. He focuses on authority as a function of performance, as something
students must attempt to do even before they can do it well. And when we
pay attention to actual performances of students at work, we cannot predict
entirely the result, since that performance as he imagines it must necessarily
include, in a dialectical relationship to convention, the "idiosyncratic" contribution of the individual writer and his or her history.

What Bartholomae sees in these performances is a record of "appropriation," and appropriation is always a risky process since it can go either
way: "The student has to appropriate (or be appropriated by) a specialized
discourse. . . ." We would add, however, that it makes a world of difference
which way it goes. If the parentheses are dropped, the process of appropriation can be seen not as a one-way progression through successive
approximations to mastery of academic discourse, but as a political struggle
in which the student's identity as a student is at stake, a struggle between
"a personal history" and "the history of a discipline." It seems to us, then,
that the linguistic outcomes of this struggle cannot so confidently be labeled
"our language," as in, "He must learn to speak our language." What
troubles us about this formulation of the problem is the way in which it can

be, and in fact is now being, appropriated by those educators who want to argue for an unambiguously accommodationist Basic Writing pedagogy, a return to a new set of "basics," the conventions of academic discourse "written out, 'demystified,' and taught in our classrooms."

"Inventing the University" lends itself to such a reading, despite Bartholomae's desire to refrain from writing out the features of the discourse. In an often-quoted passage, he characterizes "our language," the language of the academy in which students are assumed to be seeking membership, in these terms:

> What our beginning students need to learn is to extend themselves by successive approximations into the *common* places, *set* phrases, *rituals* and *gestures*, *habits* of mind, *tricks* of persuasion, *obligatory* conclusions, and *necessary* connections that determine the "what might be said" and constitute knowledge within the various branches of our academic community. (146)

We emphasize the italicized terms to highlight the way in which, as Joseph Harris has noted, in this essay "the view of discourse at the university shifts subtly from the dynamic to the fixed—from something that a writer must continually reinvent to something that has already been invented, a language that 'we' have access to but that many of our students do not." Through this shift, Harris argues, "The university becomes 'our community,' its various and competing discourses become 'our language,' and the possibility of a kind of discursive free-for-all is quickly rephrased in more familiar terms of us and them, insiders and outsiders" (13).[1]

This distinction between "insiders" and "outsiders" is a key metaphor in Bartholomae's representation of the student's relation to the university, and it conditions his readings of the student essays that provide the central demonstration of his theory. He sees students trying to gain admittance, by their writing, to "the closed world of the academy." The writers in his examples are imagined as trying to "win themselves status as members of what is taken to be some more privileged group" (153). We can see this to be literally the case if we consider the rhetorical context in which these essays were written: these texts are placement exams, writings explicitly designed to determine the students' place in the academy, or at least in one or other of its hierarchy of writing courses. This is one of the most restrictive and, at the same time, least well defined rhetorical situations we put students into. Placement essays at the University of Pittsburgh are composed during the summer before their authors encounter the context of the academy or any of its disciplines, before they engage with a particular discourse that they must struggle with and against. This is why they must invent the university: They are literally trying to write their way into it. Their difficulties are not those of students who must struggle to appropriate or be appropriated by the discourse of a community they have already entered. There is a problem, therefore, in letting these essays stand for what student writers must generally learn to do and particularly, for our purposes here, what it means to be underprepared to do it.

To witness the drama of underprepared students engaged fully in university work we must look elsewhere in Bartholomae's work, particularly at "Facts, Artifacts and Counterfacts," "Teaching Basic Writing: An Alternative to Basic Skills," and "Writing on the Margins." In these essays he explores the paradox implicit in the metaphor, "Inventing the University": if the university is to be invented by students through their interventions in it, and specifically by their work as readers and writers, it cannot also be represented as already fully constituted by the operations of our discourse. To the contrary, the academy in the articles mentioned above comes to represent a community that emerges through the interactions of students, teachers, and texts, all now inside the university and participants in its discourse, albeit participants of unequal power.

Thus "Facts, Artifacts, and Counterfacts," co-authored with Anthony Petrosky, the title essay for the book that represents the basic reading and writing curriculum at the University of Pittsburgh, begins and ends with a significant shift in metaphor, from "outside/inside" to "margins/mainstream"—a division that locates the Basic Writing student, however tenuously, in the university. The goal of the curriculum, "is to enable these marginal students to participate in the academic project . . . and to demonstrate to them, and to the university, that such participation is possible" (38).

This insistence on the student's role as a participant in the production of academic knowledge becomes in "Facts, Artifacts" more than a matter of reimagining the education of the individual student. What we notice here is Bartholomae's willingness to talk about the development of this pedagogy in explicitly political terms. Quoting Jonathan Culler's claim that the factors that determine whose readings matter are ones that help "one to question the institutional forces and practices that institute the normal by marking or excluding the deviant" (6), Bartholomae goes on to enact his own increasingly critical reading of the "normal" discourse of the university as he and Petrosky describe what students in most disciplines are typically asked to write:

There . . . is a way of studying psychology by learning to report on textbook accounts or classroom lectures on the work of the profession. But there is also a way of learning psychology by learning to write like a psychologist—by learning, that is, to assemble materials, study them, and speak of them within the terms and structures of that discipline. In his four years of college education, the student gets plenty of the former but precious little of the latter. He writes many reports but carries out few projects. (38–39)

This critical stance is directly related to the political context of the authors' struggle within their university to establish the Basic Reading and Writing course and indeed to demonstrate that basic writers belong in a university in a course taken for full credit. In positioning themselves against the way that academic discourse is traditionally taught, Bartholomae and Petrosky are frank about the political risks of their introductory curriculum, that students "will not 'get' the canonical interpretations preserved by the disciplines, nor will they invent that work on their own" (38). But they insist nevertheless that the risk is worth taking, not only for the student but because the Basic Reading and Writing course, by positioning the student as a participant in academic discourse, stands for what the undergraduate curriculum ought to be.

Bartholomae and Petrosky set out, then, to create an alternative language to talk about the needs and potential of underprepared students, and they do so out of a running critique of the available discourses of remediation, "pushing against" the terms of those languages: reading comprehension as "getting the main idea," writing as a technology of topic sentences and "basic skills." They counterpose to these reduced versions of academic work terms and methods drawn from the discourses of reading research, critical theory, and "epistemic" writing pedagogies represented by, for example, William Coles and Ann Berthoff. This movement among and critical juxtaposition of competing discourses not only marks their own project, it also drives the pedagogy that they offer their students in Basic Reading and Writing. "[G]rowth takes place not through the acquisition of general rules but through the writer's learning to see his language in relation to the languages around him, and through such perception, to test and experiment with that language" ("Teaching Basic Writing" 85).

In Basic Reading and Writing, students are explicitly invited to "test and experiment" not only with their own language but also with the language of the academy, and to draw conclusions about its power and its limitations. In his own scholarship, Bartholomae has increasingly addressed himself to that same project. Whereas Bizzell and others who advocate an academic discourse pedagogy sound very comfortable as "masters" of the "native" tongue into which they would initiate students, he pursues the implications of Shaughnessy's startling claim that we can "see the difficulties of so-called remedial students as the difficulties of all writers, writ large" (*Errors* 293). This formulation is usually read as a universal statement about writing, taken to mean that the "difficulty" lies in the tension between any established discourse and the needs and abilities of the individual writer. But Bartholomae develops a more context-specific meaning of difficulty, as produced in part by an academic discourse that is itself seen as problematic.

One implication he develops from Shaughnessy's dictum is that our personal histories as academic writers should afford us a critical perspective on our discourse. From this point of view it is less easy to divide the participants in academic projects, into insiders and outsiders. In "Writing on the Margins" Bartholomae writes that Basic Writing students "are *in* college (or somewhere on the margins of the university)" (67). But at the same time he pushes against his metaphor, questioning what it means to be "on the margins." If the university officially places some students on the margins (in remedial courses), that position is a representation (perhaps in its most dramatic and telling form) of the position of every writer" (70). Any form of academic discourse "defines a center that puts some on the margins" (72). The simple dichotomy of value and privilege — us at the center, them on the margins — breaks down. The margin begins to be redefined as a vantage point from which the authoritative discourses at the center can be critiqued. In an explicit rejection of Shaughnessy's distinction between the "perverse" style of the basic writer and the "genuine" style of the professional academic, Bartholomae suggests that "the most perverse thing we do is allow some (including ourselves) to believe that the language of the university is genuine" (72).

This is the perversity of the argument for a pedagogy of initiation into academic discourse, of the notion that "there is such a thing as a discourse community" (Bizzell, "Cognition" 230) to be initiated into, and of the belief that it is constituted by conventions such as that "there is a tacit agreement that we live in a world of reason" (Kogen 32).[2] To the extent that such a belief constructs the academy as an isolated discursive utopia, it justifies the common connotation of the adjective "academic": irrelevant, moot, out of touch with ordinary life. And it exposes the fallacy of all appeals to a common discourse, "our language": such constructions always lead back to the particular practices of the persons arguing for them in their particular context.

The apparent perversity of Bartholomae's discourse lies in the difficulty of reconciling a dictum like "He must learn to speak our language" with the position he ascribes to successful Basic Writing students: [T]hey have learned (and perhaps in a way that their 'mainstream' counterparts cannot) that successful readers and writers actively seek out the margins and aggressively poise themselves in a hesitant and tenuous relationship to the language and methods of the university" ("Facts" 41). It is possible, however, to imagine such a reconciliation by reading the reference to "our language" in the first quotation as defined by the version of "success" offered by the second: "our language" understood as the language of running critique and revision of conventional academic discourse. Thus read, Bartholomae's pedagogy seems to require a deliberate tension between students' language and methods and the language and methods of the university. Yet, in part because he works with single sets of papers and in part because he rarely moves beyond texts to contexts (the classroom or beyond), this interaction, this attainment of a consciously marginal and critical stance, remains more a promise of his pedagogy than anything he demonstrates in his work to date.

What remains least developed in Bartholomae's pedagogy, as we reflect on our own relation to it over the years, is the role and status of the literate practices and cultural forms that students bring with them to their academic experience. His readings of student texts and the pedagogy that he derives from them seem to rest on a rather thin conception of student culture, of the material of their lives as this can be brought to bear on the development of a critical academic stance: their languages are described (from a point of view that seems fully at the "center") as "idiosyncratic" (less discursively determined than ours?) and their histories are said to be "personal" (as distinct from social, political, and economic) ("Inventing" 135). "Idiosyncratic" and "personal" are terms that make it possible to imagine Basic Writing students who find it "exciting, creative, and liberating" to do work that is "ours not theirs," and to do it "even to the degree to which that writing does not 'change reality' or reshape the university and its disciplines" ("Released" 84). But it is difficult for us to imagine students who might write to "change reality" (as Rich would have it) or to "reshape the university and its disciplines" (as Bartholomae's later work suggests) without also imagining that such motives might spring from their political and cultural situations both on the margins of the academy and in the other contexts in which they live and work.

"Interactionist" Pedagogies

We want now to examine other accounts by teachers and theorists of Basic Writing who, like Bartholomae, define advanced literacy instruction as a site of discursive conflict. While many of these accounts owe no particular conceptual debt to Bartholomae, we are reading them as extending the political possibilities of the pedagogy he proposes by foregrounding the struggle over discourse in the Basic Writing classroom as an interaction among cultures rather than a matter of finding a "compromise" between academic language and "idiosyncrasy, a personal history" ("Inventing" 135).

We do not, in considering these pedagogies together here, suggest that they comprise any single method. Nor can they be represented by one dominant figure, although it will be obvious that they owe much to two traditions: Marxism, especially as it informs the work of Paulo Freire; and ethnography, especially the work of Shirley Brice Heath. But if these pedagogies cannot be reduced to a single methodology, they do share certain epistemological and political assumptions about how advanced literacy develops. The relationship between a student's discourse and that of the academy is seen as dialectical, a two-way process of interaction that will, if it succeeds, necessarily involve teachers and students in the re-formation of both discourses.

The initial goal of these pedagogies is stated by Judith Goleman as a "Dialogical awareness of language differences ... [that] precedes the possibility of choice among those languages. [Dialogical awareness] ends the predetermined experience of a language and the conceptual world it frames and begins the process by which one actively chooses one's orientation among languages and the conceptual worlds they frame" ("The Dialogic Imagination" 135–136). A common methodological approach is, therefore, to create what Kenneth Burke calls "perspectives by incongruity"—setting alongside the dominant discourses in the academy others, such as the discourse of family or community, in order to invite critical reflections on the relations of language and power, and to begin to set the conditions for choice.

Because such metadiscursive consciousness requires constant reflection on everyday life and language, courses that make it the goal of instruction necessarily include the material of students' cultures as a subject of inquiry in the course. The method is both "dialogic"—in that it proceeds by dialogue between and among participants in the class and the texts and discourses honored by the academy—and, in some cases, specifically "ethnographic" in that it invites students and teachers to investigate the uses of literacy in differing social contexts, including circumstances of unequal power.

The ethnographic version of this juxtaposition of discourses turns students (and sometimes teachers) into researchers of various language contexts, comparing and contrasting them "by a two-way manipulation of knowledge from community to school and from school to community" (Heath 321). Thus Heath describes children becoming "participant observers" of language-using in contexts such as their homes, the youth club, or the pool hall; Nina Wallerstein invites students to bring artifacts and documents (such as union newspapers) to class for discussion; Nancy Martin and Peter Medway describe how children research history by interviewing people in their communities who have lived through the period they are studying; Goleman designs a course in which "students study speech acts in their everyday lives and connect them to concepts in their reading" ("Getting There" 49); and Suzy Groden, Eleanor Kutz, and Vivian Zamel teach beginning college writers from diverse backgrounds to "engage in ethnographic research on language use as a foundation for their college work" (132).

The role of the teachers in such courses, as Heath defines it, is "to help their students learn to see their daily actions in new terms: as the recording of events, discovering of patterns, and figuring out of options in making decisions.... Within class work the stress [is] on making linkages between how the students learned information in their daily lives, and ways they could talk about these ways of knowing at a 'meta' level" (339). These metaphors of "bridging" or "linkages between" cultures recast the conventional relationship of student culture to academic discourse, since they imply that teachers must learn from what students already know. Student culture is assumed to be the basis for further learning and not something to be traded in as part of the price of initiation. As one teacher quoted by Heath puts it, "the goal of learning from students is for us to know what they have, not to tell us what they lack" (314).

In pursuing these investigations of language, the pedagogies we are discussing often show the influence of Freire's "generative themes," topics central to the lives and cultures of the students. In some cases these themes are chosen by the instructors, who draw on prior experience to assume the importance to students of such topics as "work" (Shor; Coles and Wall). In other cases, generative themes evolve out of class dialogue. Nan Elsasser's female students at the College of the Bahamas, for example, engaged in associative exercises responding to words such as "sex," "home," and "work," chose "marriage" as a generative theme, and then defined key subtopics like "housework, divorce, sexuality, and domestic violence" (Fiore and Elsasser 91–93). Similarly, Linda Findlay and Valerie Faith, drawing not only on Freire but on the concept of "keywords" as developed by Sylvia Ashton-Warner in *Teacher* and Raymond Williams in *Keywords*, began by soliciting as "a linguistic object for reflection" their students' words for "key areas of knowledge or life" that they wanted to "open up." Analysis of the students' "relation to those themes" formed the basis of their pedagogical method (67–69).

This foregrounding of the material of students' lives implies a rejection of the split between subjective and objective knowledge that has traditionally informed the epistemology of college writing instruction, a dichotomy in which the role of the student's personal knowledge is restricted (if it is recognized at all) to the first-person narrative written as a point of entry into a hierarchy of increasingly impersonal academic discourse. The interactionist theorists we are considering here revise this traditional understanding of the role of the learner in the production of knowledge by defining that process as one that is simultaneously personal and social, subjective and objective, regardless of the genre of writing involved. They argue (explicitly or in their representations of writing contexts) that academic discourse of any kind is a product of all participants in it, even the most marginalized, and so is shaped by what they bring to it—their beliefs, their experiences, their culture. Thus academic knowledge is to be understood and represented in literacy instruction (as Freire has argued) as both subjective, the work of individual writers and speakers, and objective, the product of their collective dialogue, within the classroom and between the classroom and the larger social context.

To thus foreground dialogue in the construction of meaning entails two corollary assumptions about the epistemology of writing instruction understood as a political process. One is "that all knowledge is partial, since the perspective (e.g., cultural, ideological, temporal, spatial, etc.) of the knower necessarily defines, and therefore limits, the view of the object. In establishing meaning, dialogue is necessary for people to compensate for the limitations imposed by any single perspective ..." (Findlay and Faith 73). The other is that since the knowledge that academic discourse constructs is established by the dialogue of any of its participants, admitting new kinds of participants necessarily alters academic discourse and the knowledge it produces. We mystify this historical process, then, if we define personal

knowledge as something the student—or the teacher—leaves behind in
order to participate in the discourse of the academy.

If we take seriously the role of the learner in the making of knowledge,
then it is essential for us as teachers to be reflexive about the shaping
power of our own experiences as learners, particularly where the traditional
language of the schools has come to seem "natural" to those of us whose
home environments have fostered congruent literacy practices (Heath
266–267). For the same reason, we value in the work of our profession
forms of academic discourse that do not dichotomize theory and experience
but instead make a central place for stories about teaching and learning that
call the partiality of our own knowledge into question while building upon
the experiences of others. We are thinking here, for example, of works representing learners' dialogues (e.g., Coles; Heath; Medway; Martin); offering
case studies (Salvatori; Wall; Coles and Wall); locating theory in the context
of specific pieces of student writing (Bartholomae; Goleman, "Getting There";
Fiore and Elsasser; Coles); weaving autobiography with observation and
analysis (Rose, *Lives*; Rich; Heath; Bartholomae, "Wanderings"); in nearly
all cases writing anecdotally about how the authors' pedagogies were developed in dialogue with students and colleagues.

An interactionist pedagogy also, we feel, implies a need for more critical
reflection about choices of form for student writing, with particular sensitivity
to how such forms, understood as ways of knowing, relate to the political
situation of the marginalized student. A starting place would be to turn, as
John Clifford suggests, to feminist and other poststructural forms of literacy
discourse to sharpen our critical perspective:

> [T]he conventions of the typical academic, deductive essay as it appears
> in countless handbooks can be seen . . . as ideologically committed: the
> confident thesis statement and the logical arrangement of concrete evi-
> dence is, in fact, a specific way of asserting that the world is best
> understood in this way, that knowledge can be demonstrated in this
> unproblematic form, that the self can be authentic within these set
> confines. . . . [For such reasons] the dominant academic essay is not
> geared to please those who stand on the margins, those who, like
> feminists and Marxists, often feel alienated and displaced by the
> academy's "normal" discourse. (35–36)

Pamela Annas, for example, in "Style as Politics: A Feminist Approach to
the Teaching of Writing," sets against the "defended, linear, 'objective'"
discourse of the academy a language that is "sensual, contextual, and
committed" (360). She argues that features that have been regarded as
weaknesses in women's writing in fact mark its strengths: "an emphasis on
the particular, the contextual, the narrative, the imagistic, what Meridel
LeSueur has called circular rather than linear writing; and the different
content and conclusions that emerge as women write from a specific reality

as women" (371). An accommodationist Basic Writing pedagogy necessarily ignores the issues raised by Clifford and Annas; students may be permitted to begin a course by writing from their own cultural experiences, but they still end with forms of writing (the debate for a fictitious audience, the library research report, the "objective" critical essay) that mystify the role that students' experiences and choices play in the dialogical shaping of knowledge.

Many interactionist teachers of Basic Writing do, however, recognize the need to provide alternative forms for student projects that go beyond the boundaries of the typical academic assignment. In addition to writing up dialogues and oral histories based on ethnographic research, students have been asked to create videotapes and public-service radio spots (Wallerstein), to write long autobiographies illustrating some generative theme (Bartholomae and Petrosky; Coles and Wall), and even, in the case of Elsasser's students to co-author an "Open Letter to Bahamian Men" arguing for a set of "recommendations" to change their social/political relationships in marriage. (Actually published in the island's newspapers, this last example is particularly Freirean in its attempt to act upon society, not just to analyze it or what others have said about it.) These examples represent a movement toward a more diverse repertoire of discursive forms in order that the result of a dialogical pedagogy will be, in Goleman's words, "not the substitution of one bounded language for another" ("The Dialogic Imagination" 141) but rather the student's ability to transcend the belief that language must be unitary, that she must choose among multiple languages because only one can be "right."

Joseph Harris proposes the metaphor of "polyphony" to represent such a goal for students in college writing courses: "an awareness of and pleasure in the various competing discourses that make up their own" (17). Here, pleasure is contingent upon the way that "awareness" confers a kind of metadiscursive control, the ability to orchestrate these "overlapping" languages the way the composer of polyphony stands beyond any single voice in the music to weave them into harmonies in which dissonances add interest and complexity but are usually resolved. What the metaphor of polyphony does not acknowledge, however, is the political issue of how such resolution is achieved—or the possibility of unresolved dissonance or even subjection. Bizzell, for example, has recently expressed skepticism about pedagogies that go no further than teaching students to analyze the multiplicity of discourses that shape their own: "Stopping the argument at this point, I fear, means leaving out of consideration the cultural and political forces whereby one discourse asserts power over another ..." ("Foundationalism" 38–39). Her critique recognizes the struggle basic writers face in their encounters with the discourses of the academy. But we would also argue that the discourse of any writer is multiply determined and hence, potentially conflictual, an assumption implicit in the quotation Harris includes from Mary Louisse Pratt: "*People* and groups are constituted not by single unified belief systems, but by competing self-contradictory ones."[3] In the final section of our discussion we want to take up this problem of dissonance further, to look at studies that recognize competition and contradiction within and among discourses in student writing and their social contexts and treat these as signs of a struggle that requires an explicitly political analysis.

A place to begin such an analysis would be with the following redefinition of literacy by Stanley Aronowitz:

> The real issue for the "functionally" literate is whether they can decode the messages of media culture, counter official interpretations of social, economic, and political reality; whether they feel capable of critically evaluating events, or, indeed, of intervening in them. If we understand literacy as the ability of individuals and groups to locate themselves in history, to see themselves as social actors able to debate their collective futures, then the key obstacle to literacy is the sweeping privatization and pessimism that has come to pervade private life.[4]

Kyle Fiore and Nan Elsasser illustrate the connection between privatization and illiteracy as they describe the writing of the Bahamian women whom Elsasser taught in a course based on Freire: "Often, Freire says, students unaware of the connections between their own lives and society personalize their problems" (89). Because of this, they "analyze problems using concrete knowledge drawn from experience. They argue by anecdote" (93–94). At issue here is sole reliance on the personal and private, without the ability either to gain new perspective on the personal by wider reading or to use the personal to challenge that reading. Eventually we see these women "combine information gained from discussions and reading with their personal knowledge to create a solid argument by crisp, focused examples" (98). Fiore and Elsasser imply that these connections happened because of a context in which the women learned from one another and from their readings that the forms of oppression that each was experiencing in marriage were not hers alone, that other women had shared similar experiences and were coming to analyze them in new and more powerful ways. We see, in other words, no accounting for the change in these writers' ability to relate experiences to concepts ("examples to main points") apart from the significant change in their political consciousness, brought about in part by their dialogues in class and with the texts they were reading.

In a similar vein, Linda Findlay and Valerie Faith describe teaching students who also dichotomized the public and the private, believing that academic discourse had to be "objective" in the sense of neutral, arbitrary, and exclusive of personal attitudes and experiences. Where Findlay and Faith go beyond the analysis of Fiore and Elsasser is in their argument that one source of these students' privatization was the form of traditional academic discourse that in the past they had been encouraged to learn: "It was in writing, not in some general discussion about their place in society, that the students . . . sensed the gulf between their own thought and the language taught them by their culture, especially the academic jargon they learned to produce for success in school" (77). Their enactments of academic language—vague terms, heavy nominalization, the passive voice—are read politically as representing a "deep alienation from major cultural institutions": "[O]ne major form this alienation takes is a kind of illiteracy" (80—81).

Findlay and Faith's analysis allows us to see why becoming literate is a political struggle for all participants and not simply a teacher-initiated act of "empowerment." While they document significant change in their students' consciousness, it was a change that, in Freire's terms, did not go directly from "naive" to critical thinking but instead had to pass through a "super-stitious" phase of fear and resistance, since "their growing sense of the oppressiveness of the cultural institutions—to which their language was so closely related—made it a frightening thing to admit either that you were a victim of that system, or worse yet, an aspiring participant in it" (78). Their students continued to write poorly and to resist writing until they were able to reconceive their relationship to the institution of the university, to see that academic discourse is, like all language, socially produced, and that knowing this, they could have a role in reshaping it.

While we find Findlay and Faith's analysis of their students' difficulties astute, we are critical of the generally "liberationist" expectations they share with many other Freirean teachers. As Bartholomae and Petrosky argue, the outcome of teaching students to explore rhetorical relationships among discourses cannot be simply represented as either an accommodation to or a liberation from any particular discourse. "To move between languages," they say,

is not like shedding skin or changing clothes or replacing one tape with another in a cassette player. It is neither a matter of taking native abilities and refining them nor a matter of replacing ignorance with wisdom. Both of these designs imply pedagogies that we felt the need to push against when we began thinking about our course. There are liberation pedagogies to restore students to their "natural" voices and there are, to use Freire's terms, "banking pedagogies," which deposit true knowledge in minds that are otherwise empty. Our experience with basic readers and writers has taught us that the change that takes place can never be so complete or total, and the process can never be so easy, since, as [George] Steiner suggests, it calls into play "needs of privacy and territoriality vital to our identity." And if this is generally true for all language users, it is dramatically and sometimes violently true for our students. ("Facts" 7)

Thus, the development of advanced literacy may often entail not success
stories but what Bartholomae calls "chronicles of loss, violence, and compromise" ("Inventing" 145). And even in accounts that point to significant
achievement, the outcome for the student may be ambiguous, partial,
conflicted, and frequently unpredictable.

We see this illustrated in Goleman's essay, "Getting There: A Freshman
Course in Social Dialectics." There she demonstrates the self-censorship of
a student's voice in a paper that used Peter Farb's book *Word Play* to
analyze a speech situation involving the writer and her boss. The paper
created a lively class debate because while the body of the text "uses Farb
to explain her experience in a way [students] called 'personal' (and in a way
we would call dialogical)" (55), its ending seems to give all the credit for
new and powerful insights to Farb:

[T]he truth is, if Farb hadn't just given me a new insight into speech
situation and a few of its strategies such as the norms when interacting
with an authority figure, and different tones and approachs which totally
change speech situation, I probably would have done exactly what [my
boss] asked me to do. Unfortunately, there are many other people who
have overlooked these speech patterns are still being manipulated by
conversations, now maybe you won't be one of them." (53)

Goleman echoes Bartholomae when she reads this "self-effacing" conclusion
in terms of what he calls the Basic Writing student's "hesitant and tenuous
relationship" to the voices of academic authority, and she argues that such
students must be helped to become self-conscious of themselves as authors
and of "voice" and "authority" as "social practices." But, like Giroux, she
insists that authority in academic writing develops in ways that are inseparable from a critical knowledge of and sense of authority over one's own life
(55–56). From this standpoint, the unevenness of a student text that
appends a moralizing and self-effacing conclusion to an astute political
analysis of a social context can be read not merely as unfamiliarity with
academic discourse but as evidence of the uneven growth of critical consciousness: "To know this is to know something about the vicissitudes of
writing in relation to the vicissitudes of our own complex, inconsistent
subjectivity" (55). And from this standpoint, too (her essay implies), a
pedagogy that ignores the situation of the writer in history and her dialectical
relationship to the concept of literacy will invite reductive writing, "for to
deny the overdetermined and contradictory nature of our writing, our
lives, and thus, our writing about our lives, is to teach a simplified concept
whose practical application is bound to be confusing and can only discourage
further understanding" (56).

Many studies of interactionist teaching similarly acknowledge the complex
relationship between a writer's history and her struggle with advanced

literacy. Some, like Goleman's, focus on the difficulty basic writers experience with specific academic tasks. These would include the case studies by Mariolina Salvatori, Wall, and Coles in *Facts, Artifacts and Counterfacts*, which textually document student's uneven accomplishments in their efforts to move "against the authoritative institutional languages which threaten to structure their discourse for them" (Coles 196). While they represent students leading class discussions, learning to "talk back" to authoritative texts, and defining the value of advanced literacy for themselves, they also chronicle moments of confusion, of students losing their sense of authority, of miscommunication between students and teachers, of opportunities lost.

Other studies connect accounts of the struggles of basic writers more explicitly to the cultural codes of class, gender, and ethnicity. We think here of Lynn Troyka's insistence that teachers must establish classroom contexts that recognize the cultural assumptions of nontraditional students (like the man who would share his writing with his wife but not his co-workers, who might think it was "too well-written") (260–261); of Rich's unsentimental account of why students in Open Admissions programs will fail unless they trust that teachers will not simply continue to represent the dominant culture that has used language and literature "against them" (63); of our experiences with working-class adults, whose resistance to our requests that they think critically about their ideologies of "work" surfaced as ambivalence, confusion, or contradiction in their texts (Coles and Wall 311–312); and of Rose, who demonstrates (with his own story as well as those of other students) how difficult it is for learners "on the boundary" even to begin academic readings or assignments that violate their belief systems or ask that they question those in authority (*Lives* 177–193). Studies such as these lead us to share Rose's conclusion that what is needed is teaching that will invite people "truly to engage each other at the point where cultures and classes intersect" (137).[5]

Incoherence, overabstraction, overdependence upon anecdotal narrative, "moralizing" conclusions, empty jargon, self-contradiction, a hesitant "voice," silence: we read these features of Basic Writing as produced within the interaction, in classrooms, of multiple, competing discourses. These textual disturbances cannot be "remediated" by skills-based instruction, nor can they be resolved through a process of initiation into the conventions of "the academic discourse community." As long as academic discourse presents itself as the language of powerful "insiders" who require that students abandon their culture to join the "club," students will perceive academic culture as impersonal and alienating—as, in fact, merely "academic"—and their attempts to imitate it will reproduce the academic illiteracy that keeps them on the margins. Advanced literacy requires learners to adopt a stance that will allow them to see and to change their relationship to language, including the language of the academy; but the language of the academy itself will have to be redefined as multiple and changeable if we and our students are to have a hand in "inventing" it.

Notes

1. The division of participants into insiders and outsiders has become a staple metaphor in "social-contextual" discussions of academic literacy. Bizzell calls basic writers "outlanders" ("What Happens" 294) and likens them to "travelers[s] to an unfamiliar country" who must learn the language and attempt to "go native" ("Cognition" 238). Mike Rose, in a book that enacts an extraordinary sensitivity to the cultural diversity of both students and academic work, nevertheless falls back on the same formulation (*Lives* 142). Possibly the metaphor comes into the discourse of these writers by way of Mina Shaughnessy—acknowledged by Rose, Bizzell, and Bartholomae as a source and inspiration—who speaks of CUNY's "severely under-prepared" Open Admissions students as "true outsiders ... as if they had come, you might say, from another country" (*Errors* 3). It is worth noting, however, that she is here registering her own and her colleagues sense of shock in their initial encounter with the work of basic writers. Her more seasoned and characteristic view recognizes "the saving preparedness of these same students as thinking and speaking young adults to begin the hard work of learning in college" (274). This is a perspective that is particularly difficult to achieve if one's view is framed by the metaphor of insiders and outsiders.

2. In her recent essays Bizzell has considerably revised her position, arguing that "academic discourse is not presumed to be fixed in some final form, but rather to be reshaped constantly as people use it to do intellectual work together. Academic discourse is thus not presumed to be an authoritarian set of rules to which students must submit, but a changing practice that they have the chance of influencing even as it influences them" ("Foundationalism" 45). And yet, even here, Bizzell argues that students must first "go native": "Mastery of academic discourse must begin with socialization to the community's ways" through "imitation of experienced practitioners, such as their professors" (53).

3. Mary Louise Pratt, "Interpretive Strategies/Strategic Interpretations: On Anglo-American Reader Response Criticism," *Boundary* (11.1—2, Fall/Winter 1982—1983): 228; quoted in Harris 19, our emphasis.

4. Stanley Aronowitz, "Why Should Johnny Read?" *Village Voice Literary Supplement* (May 7, 1985): 13; quoted in Goleman, "Getting There" 49.

5. Recent works by Marilyn Cooper, Marjorie Roemer, and Geoffrey Chase have offered similar cultural/political analyses of the struggles of mainstream students, suggesting again the wisdom of Shaughnessy's dictum that the struggles of basic writers are the struggles of all writers "writ large." But as both Chase and Bartholomae suggest, what sets apart these mainstream writers is their consciousness of choice and control: "Perhaps what an experienced writer has that an inexperienced writer lacks is a consciousness of ... appropriation, particularly as that consciousness is manifested in the style on the page—in its record of push and above ..." ("Writing" 72—73).

Works Cited

Annas, Pamela. "Style as Politics: A Feminist Approach to the Teaching of Writing." *College English* 47.4 (1985): 360—371.

Ashton-Warner, Sylvia. *Teacher*. London: Virago, 1980.

Bartholomae, David. "Inventing the University." In *When a Writer Can't Write and Other Composing Process Problems*. Ed. Mike Rose. New York: Guilford, 1985, 134—165.

————. "Released into Language: Error, Expectations, and the Legacy of Mina Shaughnessy." In *The Territory of Language: Linguistics, Stylistics, and the Teaching of Composition.* Ed. Donald A. McQuade. Carbondale: Southern Illionois University Press, 1986, 65–88.

————. "Teaching Basic Writing: An Alternative to Basic Skills." *Journal of Basic Writing* 2.2 (1979): 85–109.

————. "Wandering: Misreadings, Miswritings, Misunderstandings." In *Only Connect: Uniting Reading and Writing.* Ed. Thomas Newkirk. Portsmouth, NH: Boynton/Cook, 1986, 89–118.

————. "Writing on the Margins: The Concept of Literacy in Higher Education." In *Sourcebook for Basic Writing Teachers.* Ed. Theresa Enos. New York: Random House, 1987, 63–83.

Bartholomae, David, and Anthony R. Petrosky. *Facts, Artifacts, and Counterfacts: Theory and Method for a Reading and Writing Course.* Portsmouth, NH: Boynton/Cook, 1986.

Bizzell, Patricia. "Cognition, Convention, and Certainty: What We Need to Know About Writing." *Pre/Text* 3 (1982): 213–244.

————. "College Composition: Initiation into the Academic Discourse Community." *Curriculum Inquiry* 12 (1982): 191–207.

————. "Foundationalism and Anti-Foundationalism in Composition Studies." *Pre/Text* 7 (1987): 37–56.

————. "What Happens When Basic Writers Come to College." *CCC* 37.3 (1986): 294–301.

Chase, Geoffrey. "Accommodation, Resistance and the Politics of Student Writing." *CCC* 39.1 (1988): 13–22.

Clifford, John. "Burke and the Tradition of Democratic Schooling." In *Audits of Meaning: A Festschrift in Honor of Ann E. Berthoff.* Ed. Louise Z. Smith. Portsmouth, NH: Boynton/Cook, 1988, 29–40.

Coles, Nicholas. "Empowering Revision." In *Facts, Artifacts, and Counterfacts: Theory and Method for a Reading and Writing Courses.* Eds. David Bartholomae and Anthony R. Petrosky. Portsmouth, NH: Boynton/Cook, 1986, 167–198.

Coles, Nicholas, and Susan V. Wall. "Conflict and Power in the Reader Responses of Adult Basic Writers." *College English* 49 (1987): 298–314.

Cooper, Marilyn. "Unhappy Consciousness in First-Year English." In *Writing as Social Action.* Marilyn M. Cooper and Michael Holzman. Portsmouth, NH: Boynton/ Cook, 1989.

Enos, Theresa, ed. *Sourcebook for Basic Writing Teachers.* New York: Random House, 1987.

Finlay, Linda Shaw, and Valerie Faith. "Illiteracy and Alienation in American Colleges: Is Paulo Freire's Pedagogy Relevant?" In *Freire for the Classroom: A Sourcebook for Liberatory Teaching.* Ed. Ira Shor. Portsmouth, NH: Boynton/ Cook, 1987, 63–86.

Fiore, Kyle, and Nan Elsasser, "'Strangers No More': A Liberatory Literacy Curriculum." *College English* 44 (1982): 115–128.

Goleman, Judith. "The Dialogic Imagination: Something More Than We've Been Taught." In *Only Connect: Uniting Reading and Writing.* Ed. Thomas Newkirk. Portsmouth, NH: Boynton/Cook, 1986, 131–141.

————. "Getting There: A Freshman Course in Social Dialectics." *Journal of Education* 169, 3 (1987): 48–57.

Groden, Susan, Eleanor Kutz, and Vivian Zamel. "Students as Ethnographers:

Investigating Language Use as a Way to Learn to Use Language." *The Writing Instructor* 1987.

Harris, Joseph. "The Idea of Community in the Study of Writing." *CCC* 40.1 (1989): 11–22.

Heath, Shirley Brice. *Ways with Words: Language, Life, and Work in Communities and Classrooms.* Cambridge: Cambridge University Press, 1983.

Kogen, Myra. "The Conventions of Expository Writing." *Journal of Basic Writing* 5.1 (1986): 24–37.

Martin, Nancy et al. *Writing and Learning Across the Curriculum, 11–16.* School Council Publications, 1976.

Medway, Peter. *Finding a Language: Autonomy and Learning in School.* London: Writers and Readers, 1980.

Rich, Adrienne. "Teaching Language in Open Admissions." In *On Lies, Secrets, and Silence: Selected Prose, 1966–1978.* New York: Norton, 1979, 51–68.

Roemer, Marjorie Godlin. "Which Reader's Response?" *College English* 49 (1987): 911–921.

Rose, Mike. *Lives on the Boundary: The Struggles and Achievements of America's Underprepared.* New York: Macmillan, 1989.

———. "Remedial Writing Courses: A Critique and a Proposal." *College English* 45 (1983): 109–128.

Salvatori, Mariolina. "The Dialogical Nature of Basic Reading and Writing." In *Facts, Artifacts, and Counterfacts: Theory and Method for a Reading and Writing Course.* Eds. David Bartholomae and Anthony R. Petrosky. Portsmouth, NH: Boynton/Cook, 1986, 137–164.

Shaughnessy, Mina. "Basic Writing." In *Teaching Composition: Ten Bibliographic Essays.* Ed. Gary Tate. Fort Worth: Texas-Christian University Press, 1976, 137–168.

———. *Errors and Expectations: A Guide for the Teacher of Basic Writing.* New York: Oxford University Press, 1977.

Shor, Ira. *Critical Teaching and Everyday Life.* Boston: South End Press, 1980.

Troyka, Lynn Quitman. "Perspectives on Legacies and Literacies in the 1980's." *CCC* 33 (1982): 252–261.

Wall, Susan. "Writing, Reading and Authority: A Case Study." In *Facts, Artifacts, and Counterfacts; Theory and Method for a Reading and Writing Course.* Eds. David Bartholomae and Anthony R. Petrosky, Portsmouth, NH: Boynton/Cook, 1986, 105–136.

Wallerstein, Nina. "Problem-Posing Education: Freire's Method for Transformation." In *Freire for the Classroom.* Ed. Ira Shor. Portsmouth, NH: Boynton/Cook, 1987, 33–44.

Williams, Raymond. *Keywords: A Vocabulary of Culture and Society.* New York: Oxford University Press, 1973.

15

Considerations for American Freireistas

VICTOR VILLANUEVA, JR.
Northern Arizona University

Reflections

Mami whispered in one ear: "Learn English. Teach it to us. That's how you'll get ahead."

Dad whispered in the other: "Be careful, Papi. They need to keep us stupid."

Papi won the Merriam-Webster spelling-bee championship in 1964 but was not accepted by the college-prep parochial school. He had learned. But he was still slotted for a trade. He went to one of Bedford-Stuyvesant's public schools — Hamilton Voc-Tech: foundry, carpentry, architectural drafting. He would rather read. He dropped out.

His GED in Vietnam. He went without question. Took the government at its word. The government counted on words — commie or country, coward or traitor or hero.

After Vietnam, reenlistment: the first baby under way, a sense that a GED wouldn't account for much. To Korea. He sees Korean President Pak declare martial law, train tanks on his citizenry, announce that the military will relax when the people vote for his reelection. American GIs, there to protect democracy, continue business as usual. Back in the World, few know. He starts to wonder how such big events could so successfully be kept secret from so many.

America apologizes to the Vietnam vet. He goes to community college. Does well. Transfers to Big State. Low tuition for the Vietnam vet.

At Big State he stumbles. Less a matter of brains than not knowing the rules, especially the unwritten, unstated ones. Not even the most helpful professor could explain the rules. She could teach him how to read theory and research; she could have him rewrite and rethink until there was clarity; but she could not understand the depth of his not understanding.

Working in the library mail room. Daedalus. The words "Puerto Ricans" on the cover. It had been a long time since he was part of the Puerto Rican community. He reads about retirement-aged Puerto Rican men descending to janitors after all the years at labor. Dad—who put so much stock in dignity—was mopping blood from hospital floors. He and Mami lived nearby, far from Puerto Ricans.

The student reads about middle-aged Puerto Rican women doing menial service jobs. Mami had once proudly claimed her position as keypunch operator with the New York Stock Exchange. She had slowed. Eventually down to nurse's aide, cleaning bile; then a clerk at a motel. He reads about Puerto Rican boys dropping out of high school at a rate approaching 80 percent. Something systemic is at work.

Graduate school. One of his students is a grocery checker at the local market. The checker boasts a new BMW. The graduate-student teacher hands the checker food stamps, then steals the grocery cart to get groceries home. This isn't how he believed things would be. Things seem to be getting harder as he gathers more credentials.

"Politics" takes on new meaning. More than Democrats and Republicans. More than intrigues in the workplace: he "played politics" in the Army; academics play politics. He was thinking more and more about politics as the way people get sorted.

For a very short time he is in charge of Big State's basic-writing program. No surprise, really. Good politics. Despite denials from those who know better, he had been typecast: the minority for the minority-sensitive job. The best-qualified: a brown slum kid, performing research on what happens to minorities in college writing classrooms, willing to perform an administrative job for student-assistant pay. For them, qualified "affirmative action" without hard commitments or great cash outlays. For him, the matter of typecasting, but also an opportunity to claim a curriculum. For both, good politics.

He was discovering Paulo Freire's politics. Freire fit with what he knew. But his cadre of Freireistas, his coworkers, would not read Freire as he had. Politics for most was exposing inequity, revealing what everyone already saw was unfair. Student teachers told of the suburbs, the college. Students told of the ghetto or migrants' quarters. Neither teacher nor student talked of how one group comes to be from ghettos as a matter of course and another comes to be from suburbs. Still, the basic writers had been heard for one or two academic quarters. This was worth something, a kind of politics.

He returns from a job interview to find a memo announcing his replacement for the coming year. He had not been consulted. This, too, was politics.

He has gained access but not much power. He abides by rules his co-workers don't even recognize as rules, rules of a system created by, peopled by, serviced by, and changed by, members of cultures and classes and histories much different from his own; systems created and maintained by those whose memories do not include having been colonized. He is often taken aback by how his co-workers think: worldviews radically different from his own. Yet he struggles to join in the conversation with the privileged whose senses of decency compel them to seek equity for those who have been traditionally excluded from the mainstream of society and from the academic tributary. Sometimes he thinks he's heard.

Speculations

This chapter presents a case for a classroom composition course that confronts tradition with change. There is a degree of acceptance among us all, no matter how critical we might be, of traditions and national-cultural norms, an acceptance that not only must be considered but can be exploited in promoting changes in the systems that sort us in particular ways. Yet mine will not be a radical view, in an orthodox Marxist sense, though it will be a view that aims at something more than relativism or pluralism. I will seek to mediate between the two prevalent trends among American Freireistas today: 1) the trend to reduce politics to discussions of the different cultures and histories found in the classroom, and 2) the trend to convert the classroom into a political arena that aims at pointing out injustices and instigating change. I will argue that history and culture alone do not make for a political sensibility, that such a view is reductive of the complex combinations of cultures and histories in American minorities, and that multiculturalism alone can be deceptive, in that it suggest a friendly pluralism that does not exist outside the classroom. As for the overtly political freshman composition classroom, I will present research that will suggest that a counterhegemonic politic is not likely to be received by the very students to whom such a politic would be directed. I will argue that to achieve a pedagogy that aims at more than mere reform we must begin by acknowledging the unlikelihood of dramatic revolutionary change in the most immediate future. I will argue that less dramatic but no less revolutionary change might come about by our becoming more aware of the workings of hegemony. We can turn to advantage the ways hegemony exploits traditions and the ways hegemony allows for change, ultimately making for changes that go beyond those allowed by the current hegemony.

Freire has become generally well known. We know that his pedagogy begins with private, lived experience. Past events affect how present and future events are read. Present events affect readings of the past. These personal accounts become generalized. In generalizing personal events, we find that they are not value-free, cannot be apolitical, are never not affected by and affecting our conduct as citizens of the various communities we travel within and through. We discover that we are constantly in dialectical relationships with our environments. For Freire, the more we are aware of the dialectic the more we can affect changes in our selves and in our environments. Freire's method is to make possible a "problematizing [of] . . . existential situations" (*Cultural Action* 18). We know this. It's basic Freire.

But it is unlikely that we would all know a phrase like "problematizing existential situations" in quite the same ways. The "problematic" suggests the systemic; the "existential" suggests the individual. We are familiar with the existential: the philosophical affirmation of individual freedom. We are, I think, less familiar with the problematic as a bit of neo-Marxian jargon.

The term "problematic" is attributed to Louis Althusser. It concerns the questioning of explicit and implicit messages contained within a theoretical framework, the questioning of deeply rooted assumptions. In terms of a social framework, Althusser believes we are not normally able to problematize. We walk about with a false consciousness, believing as real what has been created by those in charge. False consciousness is then passed on through what Althusser terms "interpellation" an unintentional reproduction that has us occupy certain positions that have already been determined by the needs of the greater system. For Althusser, there is no individual freedom, really.

Educational theorists and critics of both the political left and the political right have come to agree that reproduction is an essential function of education, according to Aronowitz and Giroux. The conservative, given to an overriding belief in individual will, denies a current systemic design that reproduces an historically set, hierarchical sociopolitical structure in which women and minorities are disproportionately relegated to the bottom. The structuralist Marxists (and others of the left, particularly orthodox Marxists) minimize the degree to which individual will can affect changes to the structure. Freire apparently accepts notions of false consciousness and interpellation. But he cannot deny individual will. Freire is caught between Althusser's structuralism and his own tendency toward utopian humanism.

The apparent contradiction in juxtaposing the problematic with the existential can be mediated, however, by way of Antonio Gramsci's particular brand of Marxism, especially his notion of hegemony. According to Perry Anderson, a historian of Western Marxism, Althusser's starting point in conceptualizing ideology and education was "overtly derived from Gramsci" (78). But Althusser, drawn to scientism, would remove the subjective in Gramsci. Yet it is the subjective, the roles individuals play in forming structures, that has Anderson consider Gramsci "the greatest and least typical" of Western Marxist thinkers (67). His contribution to Western Marxism, to sociopolitical theory in general, concerns *hegemony*, a concept that had him consider the roles of different kinds of intellectuals, the social and political dimensions of education, and the existence of mediate ideologies that make for historical blocs in which certain classes rule and other classes serve by a kind of consensus.

Briefly put, hegemony represents the ways in which ruling classes affect a society's moral and intellectual leadership so as to have the rulers' interests appear the interests of other social groups. That is, the dominant classes exploit commonalities between their ideologies and the ideologies of other classes. As a result, those in what Gramsci calls subaltern positions see themselves as serving their own interests. And they are, to some extent. They also see that they are serving the interests of the dominant classes, but self-interest overrides. The middle-level manager in a large corporation or the "owner" of a local franchise might know she is employed, that she is working for another, but through money-market shares, stock options, and the like she is able to play the part of a boss, while supplementing the interests of her bosses. Subalterns, then, cooperate in their own exploitation. We are subject to coercion only insofar as the dominant classes exert their power over the institutions that serve as transmitters or moral and intellectual codes: religion, education, mass media. Hegemony otherwise operates through consent, through what Foucault has called "discourse practices," although Gramsci does not reduce all knowing to the discursive.

What is most significant about hegemony for the argument I am presenting here is hegemony's accommodation of contradiction. Since hegemony is a network woven with the threads of both the official and the popular, consisting of the ideologies of the dominated and the dominant, it is permeable. Contradictions slip through. We are given to what Gramsci calls a "contrary consciousness," given to accepting the ideologies that serve the dominant, and equally given to the possibility of criticism. Hegemony contains the possibility for counterhegemony.

To appreciate the one, we must know the other, however. Cultural literacy of the type advanced by E. D. Hirsch, for example, plainly reproduces the hegemony; it does not prevent criticism, but neither does it encourage it. Freire's critical literacy at the sites of recent revolutions is directed almost exclusively at encouraging criticism, at countering hegemony. There, Freire must focus on having the previously dominated discard the elements of their ideologies that had served their oppressors. But here, in America, where revolution moves slowly; here, in the American college composition classroom, where our interchanges with students are relatively short—four or five hours a week, ten to fifteen weeks, perhaps as long as a year or two; here, counterhegemony cannot be easily sold.

Observations

In a recent research study I observed a talented, Freire-trained teacher, freed from usual curricular or institutional constraints, still get caught in the current hegemony, despite his apparent awareness of hegemony's workings.[1] I have seen his students, overtly caught in institutional and state apparatus, not resist hegemony, despite experiences that made it apparent they were oppressed. I have observed something of the fulfillment of an American Freireista's fantasy and have seen its limitations. Floyd taught writing in the Writer's Project of a Midwestern, not-for-profit private school aimed exclusively at low-income adolescents and young adults who had been locked out of traditional public schools but wanted back in. During the two semesters we observed, the Writer's Project was exclusively black one semester, and black with one white student the next. The executive director of the program was concerned mainly with latching onto philanthropic groups and garnering grants, so Floyed enjoyed pedagogical and theoretical freedom.

Floyd is a black poet of some note in the Midwest. His poetry is overtly political, radical, though he claims not to be Marxist or black nationalist. He has been to much of Africa, has taken part in the literacy campaign in Nicaragua and the campaign in Grenada, has met with Freire in Grenada. He works at the Writer's Project and teaches political science at the community college. He grew up in the neighborhood where the Project is located, went to the same schools as his students, saw the schools and the neighborhood deteriorate. He had been to the city's state university, a campus surrounded on three sides by the large black community, yet having relatively few blacks enrolled. He had seen his world as the Third World: colonialism at the heart of the heart of the Empire.

In class, Floyd talked of history and culture. He said that the idea of black progress was deceptive. Blacks had not simply risen from slavery; they were ancient peoples, once great. He told of Christopher Columbus's diary describing black Africans returning home from what Columbus had not yet discovered. Floyd played Charlie Byrd on his ghetto blaster: "You Wear the Crown." A line says, "Imhotep was you and me." Floyd showed that there were black cultures and black history before there were black Americans.

Floyd spoke not only of history and culture but also of ideology. He told students that as members of the Writer's Project they were meeting something of a cultural imperative. He said that lower- and middle-income blacks are members of a culture of oppressed people. He suggested that they would have to think of themselves as such. He outlined four preconditions for "the true progress of oppressed people":

1. the creation of history;
2. the raising of a mass consciousness to oppression;
3. the refusal of the people to accept oppression;
4. the rising of the conscious intellectual.

He would explain the preconditions only briefly, even though he recounted them often. He would not elaborate with me, either.

Yet as I see it, Floyd had superimposed a cultural concern on a class-structural model, discussing culture in classlike terms. Some of the precedent would come from Freire. Freire does not work out class distinctions, but does suggest that the transformation that the critically conscious, newly literate adult is to generate is the transformation of the class system, since those we call the marginalized are not in the margins of class but are within the structure—at the bottom. In Freire's words:

They are not "beings outside of"; they are "beings for another." Therefore the solution to their problem is not to become "beings inside of,"
but men freeing themselves; for, in reality, they are not marginal to the
structure, but oppressed men within it. Alienated men, they cannot
overcome their dependency by "incorporation" into the very structure
responsible for their dependency. There is no other road to humaniz-
ation—theirs as well as everyone else's—but authentic transformation of
the dehumanizing structure. (*Cultural Action* 11)

The "dehumanizing structure" in our society is not exclusive to class in
terms of prestige, socioeconomics, or workers and capitalists, however. The
class system in this country, as in others, coexists with a caste system, as
John Ogbu details, a system in which birth ascription cannot be transcended
in the same way one can leave the lower class and arrive at the middle,
itself a difficult enough task.[2] Consider, for example, the case of Lauro
Cavazos, the present Secretary of Education. Despite his being a sixth-
generation Texan and a university president—a longtime American and
longtime member of the middle class—his greatest qualification for the
post of Secretary was clearly his being an otherwise qualified Hispanic.
Despite having met all the conditions for assimilation, Cavazos must still be
a hyphenated American. Jesse Jackson was the "black candidate," but
Dukakis was not the "ethnic immigrant candidate," DuPont not the "upper-
class, bourgeois" candidate. It is possible (though difficult) to move from
one class to another; it is not now possible to become free of one's place in
a caste, the castes here consisting of racial minorities and Hispanics, those
whose histories tell of colonization and slavery.

Floyd apparently believed that the processes by which castelike systems
can be changed are much the same as the processes necessary for changing
class structures. Three of the four elements in Floyd's scheme explain the
dynamics of class,[3] the fourth looks to the individual within castes. "The
creation of history" is likened to "class formation," which tells of how
groups come together over time, historically. This is something more than
culture in the usual anthropological sense. It is not enough to recognize
and make explicit our cultures. We need to recognize cultures in the
context of other cultures, since none of us can be monocultural here.
Mexican-Americans may have a culture in common with many Mexicans,
say, but they also have a culture in common with fellow Americans. Their
relation to the Mexican can become antagonistic when they favor the
American, as in a Richard Rodriguez; the Mexican-American nationalist
would have a different relation to the American. Puerto Ricans may be
"Hispanics," yet our history in general and our history as it pertains to the
United States is very different from the histories of both the Mexican-
American and the Mexican. Newyorquinos are also Puerto Ricans, but we
are in many ways culturally closer to blacks than to Mexicans. Histories,

not readily available, needing to be re-created, tell of the formation of a class of Mexican-Americans, and they tell of the class of the Puerto Ricans of the Island, and they tell of the Puerto Ricans of *el bloque*. Hispanics all, yet different in their ways, their histories, their relations to other Americans, whose cultures and histories they also share to a great extent. Culture alone provides only a partial picture.

The second element in Floyd's kind of class structure is class consciousness. It's achieved when a class recognizes its ideologies. Gramsci tells of folklore containing "official culture" and "popular culture" (Cirese 212–247). Hegemony is both indigenous and externally imposed. This gets complicated for American minorities. I grew up eating rice and beans and thinking Teddy Roosevelt was great, never considering that one of the things that made him great was his subjugation of my ancestors. Now I consider the reasons why Puerto Ricans remain the most disadvantaged of American Hispanics (Conklin and Lourie 17), while I continue to enjoy the stories and myths of Teddy Roosevelt (liking the Teddy of *Arsenic and Old Lace* best). Minorities in particular cannot accommodate the ideological contraries we carry until we can recognize that we contain cultural multitudes that are sometimes opposed. Terms like African-American, Asian-American, Mexican-American can tell of a pluralism. They can also tell of an antagonism between cultures.

Class struggle concerns conflict. It concerns the point in which, in Floyd's terms, the oppressed refuse to put up with oppression. Floyd has his students take part in an antiapartheid rally, a gesture at political action, a gesture at extending students' senses of racial oppression beyond this country.

The extension of racial awareness leads to the fourth element in Floyd's scheme: the creation of the conscious intellectual. This is explicitly Gramscian. Gramsci writes of the organic intellectual who would be the voice of the oppressed class of which she is a part. This is not Floyd's role. As a teacher attached to teaching institutions, Floyd could be seen as the traditional intellectual rather than the organic. The students at the Writer's Project, according to Floyd, were potentially those conscious intellectuals. In his words,

> So for oppressed people to make progress, people like you are necessary. You have an important role. You're like the fuse on the dynamite. If you don't go anywhere, the people don't go anywhere. So the propaganda I'm laying out to you this morning is that if you change your self, you will change the people and in fact change the world, because you're influential. You can talk. You can write. People listen to you frequently. . . . You are leaders of a sort.

His students could be conscious intellectuals because they are discursive, says Floyd. The power of the conscious intellectual is in discourse: talking, writing, people listening. For Floyd, as for Freire, as for Gramsci, as for Marx, a "revolutionary act [is] an act of criticism with an eye to the practical" (Wilkie 233). The project's participants were to see themselves as *griots*, Floyd said, oral historians, "young installments in a long train of people who can tell the stories of black people and how we see the world."

In this, Floyd echoed the black nationalism of Marcus Garvey, whom Cornel West has labeled a "proto-Gramscian" (20). Gramsci had thought that a collective black sensibility might be necessary for black Americans to effect change, this by "giving the African continent a mythic function as the common fatherland of all the negro peoples" (21). Floyd had talked to the students about histories and cultures, ideologies and changes. He had raised their senses of worth. And he did introduce students to the word. His method of teaching composition, however, tended to fall on the side of tradition. He distrusted conventional writing-process pedagogy, even after attending the Bay Area's writing project. He would have good reason. Hegemony can operate by promoting the ruling classes' ideologies as universal. Process approaches to writing instruction are universal. They have given rise to cognitive explanations of writing, the cognitive sciences also given to universality. Cognitive explanations rendered basic writers, most often members of minority groups, cognitively dysfunctional.[4] When the cognitive extended to the social, what emerged was Thomas Farrell's claim that black youth reside in oral cultures, followed by the assertion that as long as those from oral cultures remain oral they would be incapable of reaching Piaget's level of formal operations, the ability to form abstract concepts.

Floyd was explicitly aware of Farrell's oral-culture hypothesis. To this, add Floyd's skepticism concerning just how much of the nuts-and-bolts of writing could be learned through process approaches, the skeptism common among those who first encounter process approaches about the apparent assumption that the skills of writing already exist or will come about through a kind of alchemy.[5] Floyd had an assistant manage drills-for-skills workbooks with his students. Yet he did not completely dismiss writing-as-process. There were drafts and discussions about drafts. But there was no talk in writing-process jargon: no talk of heuristics, brainstorming, clustering. Floyd would not speak of prewriting. He spoke, rather, of art following function, a kind of Aristotelian idea of having something to say then finding the appropriate artistic garb with which to adorn that something. The art was most often poetry for Floyd (although he would have guest artists from other genres address the Writers' Project, including a nationally known black cartoonist). The function he most envisioned for his students' art was structural change. A recognition of the need to instigate structural change would produce writing, apparently.

And some of his students had produced art. One claimed not to go to bed until he had written in his journal. His journal was not a diary. In class he reads "The Fatal Disease of Illiteracy," a poem. It tells of the powerlessness in a father who cannot read to his children. Another student, a car thief, a twenty-year-old high school sophomore, writes a poem about the struggle of writing. A couple of lines read, "Get to it and to it/Till I get it right." Revision was not a stage or dimension; it was the imperative for effectiveness. To watch Floyd move those he moved was inspiring.

He had introduced the word and he spoke of the world, yet he was not likely to move those who were not already predisposed to his worldview. His method of persuasion would obstruct such a move. His method was explicitly propaganda. He said so. Floyd would impart what he knew. Although Freire in the field would also impart, Freire the theorist would not. "In the liberating moment," says Freire, "we must try to convince the students and on the other hand we must respect them, not impose ideas on them" (Shor and Freire 33, 46). For all that was valid — even necessary — in what Floyd had said, there was no dialectic in his class. The hegemonic and counterhegemonic were not allowed evaluation.

So myths prevailed, for the most part. Those students who saw the hope of black peoples in religion, wrote of salvation through prayer and devotion, of future good in suffering now. Those who followed the tenets of nonviolent protest wrote of the steady progress black folks have known since the struggles of Martin Luther King. Those who believed in simple, undirected oppostion wrote of "blue-eyed devils." The students had not been politically affected in the manner Floyd had apparently intended.

Hegemony was more pervasive than Floyd had allowed. Freire notes that one who is not of the mainstream, whom he calls "alienated man," is "[i]rresistibly attracted by the life style of the director society; alienated man is a nostalgic man, never truly committed to his world" (*Cultural Action* 2). Although Freire seems to censure this alienated man, I believe the minority is predisposed to this kind of alienation. Victims of oppression tend to be enamored of their oppressors. Consider the great numbers of minorities who make careers in the military service, for example. This cannot be accounted for solely on the basis of economic security. We would have our Americanism recognized and acknowledged. Oppressor and oppressed have histories, cultures, ideologies, traditions in common. This is the tug inherent in hegemony.

Floyd's student were in the Writer's Project because they held some traditional national-cultural beliefs. They were in school to fulfill a dream, a longtime American dream of success through education. They were not in school to have their dreams destroyed. They would naturally resist any such attempt. Floyd's students could reason that no matter how slight their chances of getting into college or the middle class, they did have chances, maybe better than most. Floyd had said they were special, after all, that they were leaders, world changers. Floyd had himself made it through college, was a teacher, a published poet, a world traveler to pan-African conferences. In the students' eyes, Floyd made a better model of the bootstrap mentality than he made a model of the revolution. They said so.

He was "bad. You know. He got no-tay-rye-eh-tee. I mean with the bad rags and the ride and like that. You hear what I'm sayin'?"

It's not as if the students had no collective sense, did not see class difference and caste. According to Signithia Fordham, blacks simply have no reason to assume that the collectivity is a necessary precondition for success. Our current hegemony in the schools sanctions individual achievement. Individuals have gone farther than the race. All castelike minorities have their successful individuals—big stars, successful business-men, prominent politicians. The impetus for a radical collective is not readily apparent.

How could a collectivity gathered for revolution be appealing to ado-lescents seeking access, after all? Floyd might have seen revolution as consciousness-raising, as the demystification of otherwise mysterious class and cultural forces, but the word "revolution" nevertheless conjures up frightening pictures: not acts of criticism, but acts of violence, undertaken when there is nothing left to lose. Yet there are things left to lose here. There is still pie. Enough blacks gets through at least the class system to prove that there are still gains to be had. As far as Floyd's students could see—as far as American society-in-general is concerned—the gains for blacks and other minorities are getting better. More of those who have been traditionally excluded are gaining access. But the basic inequities remain. Reyes and Halcon report, drawing from Census Bureau figures, that there are just over 7,000 Hispanics who hold PhDs in America in the last years of the 1980s, up from an estimate in 1970 of less than 100 (though this last estimate was restricted to Chicanos). This is an impressive increase. Yet Reyes and Halcon also note that Hispanics comprise only 2.1 percent of all doctorates. Numbers go up; percentages still tell of the need for radical change.

Gramsci writes of "passive revolution." The term refers to revolutionary changes in the popular ideology or in the movement within the class structure that quiets voices of discontent without concomitant changes in the interests being served by the hegemony. This is the stuff of affirmative-action mandates, of task forces, commissions, and committees. The degree of progress being realized by minorities in this country at this time assures things will remain the same. Both the "progress" and its lack, the increasing numbers of successful minorities (who remain minorities despite success) and the concomitant growth of ghettos and *barrios*, or the increase in homeless families, are there to be seen. Individual achievement is sold as the betterment of society through the progress of a collection of indi-viduals. Such progress undermines Floyd's zeal, negates Floyd's call to arms. One successful figure—Floyd—espousing the students' abilities for success, is not likely to persuade those students that a revolutionary con-sciousness is a better definition of success than the possibility for individual fame or fortune.

Application

Floyd offered a worldview that if appreciated and acted upon could bring about change, could be liberatory in the purest, purist Freireian sense, freeing both oppressed and oppressor, as Freire would have it (*Pedagogy* 28). But Floyd had not affected a revolutionary consciousness in his students, at least not that could be seen, not at the time. More importantly, he had not prepared them for what they themselves desired—literacy of the kind that leads to certification, access to high school, maybe to college, the middle class. Note Freire:

> Both the traditional and the liberating educator do not have the right to deny the students' goals for technical training or for job credentials. Neither can they deny the technical aspects of education. There is a realistic need for technical expertise which education from a traditional or a liberatory perspective must speak to. Also, the students' need for technical training in order to qualify for jobs is a realistic demand on the educator. (Shor and Freire 68)

In Freire's terms, we can further revolutionary change better by being directive of the processes the students will undergo during the short time we come in contact with them than by our attempts at being directive of the students themselves (Shor and Freire 68). We can be about the task "of orienting . . . toward the future and of orienting critical knowledge toward this future so as to lay the foundations for it" (Lefebvre 75). The direction is not only contained in the present; it is contained in the past, not only in historical events but in assumed truths of the past: myths, ideologies, traditions.

Hegemony exploits traditions. The American Freireista can at least provide a way for students to discover those traditions that are in need of change. We can have students discover the traditions that form the foundations of the academy while simultaneously promoting and instigating change in the ideologies that shape the academy. Tradition and change for changes in tradition.

This can be accomplished structurally. My co-worker Dolores Schriner, along with others (including myself), have altered a freshman composition program so as to have the program contain a dialectical relationship between tradition and change.[6] We have developed a syllabus aimed at fostering a critical consciousness in freshman composition classrooms that include traditional students as well as newcomers, mainly Hispanic and Native American newcomers.

Part of the new syllabus grew out of an earlier experiment in which basic-writing students read *Child of the Dark*, the diary of Carolina Maria deJesus. The diary tells of a barely literate *mulata* in the *favelas* of Brazil, a woman who displayed the conflicts castelike minorities confront: survival, poverty and pride, resentment of and envy of those who have more, suffering indignity while trying to transcend the causes of the indignities. My aim in using the book was to have basic-writing students recognize that troubles are not unique to them; they share a common bond with the world's poor, particularly the poor of color. Problems can be systemic. Further, since deJesus's writing is not sophisticated, the students gained confidence in voicing responses to what they were reading. The problem with the experiment was, however, that though the students might have gotten a new look at the world, they had not looked at the academic community.

The new experiment introduced the dialectic by introducing the canon. What we developed was a syllabus of tradition and change, of changing worldviews. Students read the tradition — Hemingway. Hemingway is male superiority, somewhat critical of the State, but in the main pleased with "common sense" (and I mean Gramsci's "common sense": the popular ideology). There is room for criticism of Hemingway from the most radical student and from the conservative. After reading and discussing Hemingway, students read Buchi Emecheta, a book called *Double Yoke*. They read the story of a black African woman trying to get through different value systems, cultures, ways of viewing the world, juxtaposing village tradition against Western-style traditional education, trying to transcend her culture's atti- tudes, attitudes not much different from those of Western cultures. The idea here is of the same vein as that in using *Child of the Dark* — but now set in contrast to a traditional worldview and a traditional text from the American college canon.

To tie this reading to the students' past experiences, so as to have them problematize the existential within the academy, the students are asked to write in assignments that follow a set series about conflicts they have had to confront, and to consider the sources of those conflicts. Borrowing from Henry Giroux's adaptation of resistance theory, students are asked to consider in their writing the degrees to which they can or do resist, oppose, or accommodate conflicts. Bound student autobiographies become the third book in the course, an idea introduced by Bartholomae and and Petrosky, an idea also mentioned by Ira Shor. Students are eventually asked to generalize about their experiences. They are introduced to the rudiments of concept formation, an important skill for students and conscious intellectuals. Anecdotes and data being gathered by Schriner tell us the syllabus is working.

This particular syllabus is not the central issue, however. We will change books. I think of Ayn Rand against John Steinbeck or Louis L'Amour against Leslie Marmon Silko, though I would rather a DeJesus or Emecheta, thereby underscoring the systemic and downplaying a focus on any one American minority group. More than particular texts or a particular syllabus, however, is the recognition that institutional constraints are far broader than the demands of a local faculty, chair, or university president. We — all of us — abide by the greater constraints contained in hegemony. A dialectic between tradition and change might not immediately relinquish or overturn tradition. (Such is not likely in one semester in a college classroom, anyway.) But the dialectic might have students know the tradition critically, not only to acquire the literate, academic culture but to recognize their often antagonistic relationships to it. A dialectic between tradition and change would provide the means for access, acknowledge the political, the while avoiding propaganda. What results might not the have the bite of a Floyd-like Freirean perspective, might not give us the same sense of satisfaction we might get in imparting a vision of truth, but it will have our students and ourselves take part in "the Wrangle of the Market Place" (Burke 23). It might have us all recognize our world, the marketplace, as necessitating a wrangle, not just a simple climb.

Notes

1. My observations of Floyd were carried out following the ethnographer's naturalistic-observation techniques: three observers, each with notebook and video and audio recordings. The research had been funded by two grants provided by the University of Missouri-Kansas City. More important, it was conducted with the help of anthropologist Jeff Longhoffer, and the assistance of Marge Stephens, a graduate assistant and friend. Our intention had been to document students' literacy progress, particularly since Floyd believed his students were from an oral culture but did not accept Thomas Farrell's cognitive deficit-correlative, in which those from an oral culture are seen as cognitively inferior to literates. The research failed, as far as we were concerned, because Floyd never ventured into literate discourse, the writing consisting of song lyrics, raps, and poems, all hybrid discourse forms, written but relying on the oral. We filed a report. But our discussions after filing began to center more and more on Floyd, as this chapter demonstrates.

2. John Ogbu distinguishes the castelike from immigrant minorities, and distinguishes both the castelike and the immigrant from autonomous minorities. The immigrant minority is clear. Even if she maintains her ethnicity—as, say, Italians often do—the qualities ascribed to her ethnicity are not such that she would be necessarily excluded from the mainstream. The autonomous are those who are subject to ethnic or religious distinctiveness yet manage to accommodate the mainstream, even if not assimilate. Ogbu cites American Jews and Mormons as instances of autonomous minorities. The castelike are those who are regarded primarily on the basis of some particular birth ascription—in this country, race or a particular ethnicity (e.g., Hispanics). I believe, however, that we can further refine the concept of castelike minorities by looking to the common feature in their histories—colonization or colonization's commodified form, slavery. The autonomous minority holds no such memory in this country. There is no national memory of long-term subjugation of the autonomous minority or the immigrant, as there is of the Puerto Rican, the Mexican, the American Indian, the black. Looking to colonization makes an important distinction not contained in race alone. For example, East Indians are considered black by the British but not by Americans. India was a British colony, not an American colony. The American East Indian is simply another immigrant. Race alone is not the distinctive factor. Race and a history of subservience to those who remain dominant makes for the castelike minority.

3. For a comprehensive discussion on various theories of class structure see Erik Olin Wright's *Classes*.

4. I am here thinking of Frank D'Angelo and Andrea Lunsford, particularly because their views found such wide acceptance among compositionists for some time. Yet they were not alone; cognitive-deficit theories abound in other fields as well.

5. Martha Kolln, for example, wishes to reassert the need for instruction in traditional grammar and mechanics, arguing that no magical transformation will take place in student writing without this knowledge. And Lisa Delpit recently criticized process approaches to writing instruction on the grounds that students themselves perceive the need for specific instruction in grammar and mechanics. She also points out that black students in particular do not perceive of student-centered approaches as a means of instruction in the first place.

6. The research at Northern Arizona University is being supported by a three-year Ford Foundation Grant. Dolores Schriner has been in charge of the basic-writing component. (There is also a writing-across-the-disciplines component.) Among her assistants were myself, William Grabe, Deirdre Mahoney, and a score of graduate students. Throughout, we have consulted with and been visited by Suzanne Benally, David Bartholomae, Patricia Bizzell, Donaldo Macedo, and Anthony Petrosky, all of whom can find their influences reflected in the curriculum.

Works Cited

Althusser, Louis. *For Marx*. New York: Vintage, 1969.

———. *Lenin and Philosophy and Other Essays*. Trans. Ben Brewster. New York: Monthly Review Press, 1971.

Anderson, Perry. *Considerations of Western Marxism*. 1976. London: Verso, 1979.

Aranowitz, Stanley, and Henry Giroux. *Education Under Seige: The Conservative, Liberal, and Radical Debate Over Schooling*. South Hadley, MA: Bergin and Garvey, 1985.

Bartholomae, David. "Inventing the University." In *When a Writer Can't Write*. Ed. Mike Rose. New York: Guilford, 1985, 134–165.

Bartholomae, David, and Anthony Petrosky. *Facts, Artifacts, and Counterfacts: Theory and Method for a Reading and Writing Course*. Portsmouth, NH: Boynton/Cook, 1986.

———. *Ways of Reading: An Anthology for Writers*. New York: St. Martin's, 1987.

Bonilla, Frank, and Ricardo Campos. "A Wealth of Poor: Puerto Ricans in the New Economic Order." *Daedelus* (2): 134–176.

Burke, Kenneth. *A Rhetoric of Motives*. Berkeley: University of California Press, 1969.

Cirese, Alberta Maria. "Popular Culture: Gramsci's Observations on Folklore." In *Approaches to Gramsci*. Ed. Anne Showstack Sassoon. London: Writers and Readers, 1982.

Conklin, Nancy Faires, and Margaret A. Lourie. *A Host of Tongues: Language Communities in the United States*. New York: The Free Press, 1983.

D'Angelo, Frank. "Literacy and Cognition: A Developmental Perspective." In *Literacy for Life: The Demand for Reading and Writing*. Eds. R. W. Bailey and R. M. Fosheim. New York: MLA, 1983.

deJesus, Carolina Maria. *Child of the Dark: The Diary of Carolina Maria deJesus*. Trans. David S. Clair. New York: E. P. Dutton, 1962.

Delpit, Lisa D. "The Silenced Dialogue: Power and Pedagogy in Educating Other People's Children. *Harvard Education Review* 58 (1988): 280–298.

Emecheta, Buchi. *Double Yoke.* New York: Braziller, 1982.

Farrell, Thomas J. "IQ and Standard English." *CCC* 34 (1983): 470–484.

Flores, Juan, John Attinasi, and Pedro Pedraza, Jr. *"La Carreta Made a U-Turn:* Puerto Rican Language and Culture in the United States." *Daedalus* 2 (1981): 193–217.

Fordham, Signithia. "Racelessness as a Factor in Black Students' School Success: Pragmatic Strategy or Pyrrhic Victory?" *Harvard Education Review* 58 (1988): 54–84.

Freire, Paulo. *Cultural Action for Freedom.* Cambridge: *Harvard Educational Review* and Center for the Study of Development and Social Change, 1970.

———. *Pedagogy of the Oppressed.* New York: Continuum, 1982.

Giroux, Henry. *Theory and Resistance in Education: A Pedagogy for the Opposition.* London: Heinemann, 1983.

Gramsci, Antonio. *Selections from the Prison Notebooks.* Ed. and Trans. Quiten Hoare and Geoffrey Nowell Smith. New York: International, 1971.

Kolln, Martha. "Closing the Books on Alchemy." *CCC* 32 (1981): 139–151.

Lefebvre, Henri. "Toward a Leftist Cultural Politics: Remarks Occasioned by the Centenary of Marx's Death." Trans. David Reifman. In *Marxism and the Interpretation of Culture.* Eds. Cary Nelson and Lawrence Grossberg. Urbana: University of Illinois Press, 1988.

Lunsford, Andrea. "Cognitive Development and the Basic Writer." *College English* 41 (1979): 38–46.

Nelson, Cary, and Lawrence Grossberg, eds. *Marxism and the Interpretation of Culture.* Urbana: University of Illinois Press, 1988.

Ogbu, John U. *Minority Education and Caste: The American System in Cross-Cultural Perspective.* New York: Academic, 1978.

Reyes, Maria de la Luz, and John J. Halcon. "Racism in Academia: The Old Wolf Revisited." *Harvard Education Review* 58 (1988): 299–314.

Sassoon, Anne Showstack, ed. *Approaches to Gramsci.* London: Writers and Readers, 1982.

Shor, Ira, and Paulo Freire. *A Pedagogy for Liberation: Dialogues on Transforming Education.* South Hadley, MA: Bergin & Harvey, 1987.

Stavrianos, L. S. *Global Rift: The Third World Comes of Age.* New York: Morrow, 1981.

West, Cornel. "Marxist Theory and the Specificity of Afro-American Oppression." In *Marxism and the Interpretation of Culture.* Eds. Cary Nelson and Lawrence Grossberg. Urbana: University of Illinois Press, 1988.

Wilkie, Richard W. "Karl Marx on Rhetoric." *Philosophy and Rhetoric* 9 (1976): 232–246.

Wright, Erik Olin. *Classes.* London, Verso, 1985.

16

Public Opinion
and Teaching Writing

ANNE RUGGLES GERE
University of Michigan

Ask members of the general public if they favor teaching writing and, I'll
wager, the answer will be an unambiguous "yes." Writing may not occupy
the same sphere as apple pie and motherhood, but it has a central place in
American values. Desire to instruct their young in "readin', ritin', and
'rithmatic" motivated our ancestors to tax themselves to establish and
maintain public schools, and current school-tax rates testify to the public's
continuing veneration for the trinity of R's. Occasional taxpayer revolts
such as California's Proposition 13 and local defeats of referenda for school
funding punctuate the otherwise common assent of the public to supporting
an increasingly expensive public education in which writing plays a central
part.

Public support for writing instruction in higher education has been
equally enthusiastic. Tax-supported state colleges and universities typically
house large writing programs, and public figures — both on campus and in
the state house — underline the importance of writing instruction to undergraduate education. Enthusiasm for writing instruction does not always
translate into adequate support, as evidenced by the large number of part-
time and/or temporary instructors employed to teach writing in higher
education, a clear violation of the recent *Statement of Principles and
Standards for the Postsecondary Teaching of Writing*. As many English
department chairs have noted (and the MLA Job List confirms), however,
it is often easier to persuade a dean to allocate a position in composition
than in other areas of English Studies.

But ask members of the general public what they mean by "teaching
writing" and ambiguities emerge immediately. What, in the public view, is
writing, and what does it mean to teach it? In his *Contested Truths*, Daniel
Rodgers argues that the meanings of keywords in American politics have
been and remain objects of dissent, that they are continually remade,
repudiated, and fought over. Rather than the bedrock of political discourse,

263

these words provide the site for shifts and reversals, contests and dis-
cordancies. He asserts: "The keywords, the metaphors, the self-evident
truths of our politics have mattered too deeply for us to use them in any
but contested ways" (16). "Teaching writing" attained keyword status in
public discourse about education during the early history of this country
and remains a key term today, but like keywords in politics, it is the object
of dissent. Accordingly, I propose to examine public attitudes toward
teaching writing by delineating its contested meanings rather than searching
for a single meaning or a common theme.

Contested meanings for "teaching writing" manifest themselves in the
several definitions commonly applied to the term. Snippets of everyday
conversation reveal some of the multiple meanings assigned to "teaching
writing." The response of a retired schoolteacher to her friend provides one
example. When the friend reported that her son had just published a book
on writing, the teacher responded "Oh, that's wonderful. Has he improved
on the Snapping Turtle Method of writing the letter 'a'"? The business
executive who met an English teacher at a cocktail party provides another.
In response to learning the teacher's field, the executive exploded, "Well I
certainly wish you people would teach students how to write. You should
see what some of my employees produce. They can't even spell." The
attorney who testified at a schoolboard meeting about the district's writing
program provides yet another example. Rising to complain that the writing
program did not address the most pressing issues, the attorney asserted, "I
want students here to learn to make an argument, to produce writing that
will convince someone of something." Handwriting, usage, and rhetoric—
these meanings jostle one another as members of the general public talk
about teaching writing.

Sounding public opinion is, as pollsters attest, a complex task, and
available techniques work best with questions that yield to yes/no responses.
If the issue were simply one of learning whether the public favors teaching
writing, a quick survey would provide an answer, but understanding the
embedded contradictions that surround "teaching writing" requires examination of the discourse surrounding the term. In particular, the popular
press provides ample displays of language used to describe "teaching writing."
Not surprisingly, teaching writing has been discussed in the popular press
for at least a century, but the meaning of the term "teaching writing" has
been contested throughout the discussion.

The language surrounding "teaching writing" in the popular press reflects
the multiple meanings society assigns to this term. The relationship between
society and its popular press is a complex one shaped by many elements.
Although we do not usually think of the popular press as "controlled,"
scholars in journalism demonstrate that the "media in the United States are
obviously constrained in many different ways by many different forces"
(Nord 11). In particular, political and economic factors contribute to what
appears in the popular press. As John Trimbur explains elsewhere in this

volume, the "literacy crisis" is a recurring phenomenon in this country, and I argue that recent discussion of "teaching writing" reflects the interaction of the popular press with the society that supports its publication. Accordingly, this chapter views popular press publications as an expression of public opinion about teaching writing.

Headings in the *Reader's Guide to Periodical Literature* suggest dimensions of the contest surrounding "teaching writing." The first volume (1890–1899), like the most recent one, lists articles on teaching writing under the main heading of "English language, composition." This combination of words suggests multiple meanings that are elaborated in subheadings such as "composition and exercises," "idioms, corrections, errors," "misuse by foreigners," "orthography and spelling," "rhetoric," and "study and teaching." The term "teaching writing" exists not as a separate entity but as part of language or usage emerging most clearly under the subheadings "composition and exercises" and "study and teaching." (In the 1890–1899 volume of *Reader's Guide* the "rhetoric" heading refers readers to "composition and exercises.") For the 1890–1899 period, articles such as "Essay Correcting—Can It Be Made a Joy Forever?" and "Scientific Basis for Composition" cluster under "composition and exercises," while titles such as "Growing Illiteracy of American Boys" and "Teaching of English Grammar" appear under "study and teaching." Flanking these are titles such as "Shall and Will" and "English Historical Grammar." These titles imply multiple meanings for teaching writing.

Frank Luther Mott's history of American magazines indicates that *The Atlantic* and *Science* numbered among popular press publications in the 1890s, enjoying a proportionately wider readership than they do today. Accordingly, we can conclude, following the principle that popular journalism reflects popular ideas, that the contested meanings expressed by articles published in these magazines expressed public opinion about teaching writing at that time. Examination of two such articles, "Scientific Basis for Composition" and "English Historical Grammar" illustrates the complexities of this contest. "English Historical Grammar," published in *The Atlantic* in 1898, argues that rather than the source of "a standard of correctness . . . which may separate us from the vulgar who know not grammar" (99) grammar is a subject "as scientific as any of the sciences now studied in the universities" (105). Author Mark Liddell dismisses several misconceptions about grammar and concludes by urging that it be taught in schools and "furnish a field for original scientific work in university teaching" (107).

While Liddell asserts that "the written word, then, is not an essential part of language" (99) and that "study of grammar" will not "make us think more clearly and write better" (107), Charles Douglas, author of "The Scientific Basis for Composition," claims that language and composition are inextricably bound. Douglas asserts that one cannot understand composition without "investigating both the nature and process of handling both thought and language" (149). Douglas delineates thought into concept, judgment, and argument and then describes language as having progressed to "its present high state of efficiency as an instrument for the spoken and written expression of thought" (150). Principles of grammar, according to Douglas, have their basis in intellectual processes, and he urges that "logic" and "dialectic" be employed in composition classes. Douglas responds to the cry that "composition as it is taught in the schools is a failure" (150) with the recommendation that teachers introduce language study. Public opinion, to the extent that it is represented in these two articles, simultaneously weds and separates "teaching writing" and language study.

Evidence from other areas of the culture supports the view that "teaching writing" serves as the site for debate about the relationship between language and composition. The club movement, which extended across the country and included a sizable proportion of the population during the late nineteenth century, manifested a version of this contested view. Literary clubs popular on college campuses as well as study groups and women's clubs established in most cities and towns frequently required members to write papers and read them to the club. This self-sponsored composing can be described as an extra-academic form of "teaching writing." The "critic," a regular officer of these clubs, took responsibility for identifying faults of usage, mispronounced words, and improper use of idioms as well as rhetorical issues such as persuasiveness and appeal. To be sure, the critics' corrections reflect a more prescriptive view of language study than the one Liddell proposes, but by connecting usage and evaluation of the effectiveness of an argument, the critic embodied a contested set of meanings for "teaching writing."

While contested meanings for the term endure across the decades, we can identify periods when "teaching writing" plays a more prominent role in the public mind. Similar to the recurring cycles of literacy crisis that John Trimbur describes, these periods identify themselves by the amount of attention given to teaching writing in the popular press. These periodic outpourings on the teaching of writing provide a good indicator of public opinion about writing instruction.

The most recent outcry of public concern about teaching writing can be traced to the 1975 publication of *Newsweek*'s "Why Johnny Can't Write." Although *Time*'s "Bonehead English" appeared the year before, "Why Johnny Can't Write" heralds the beginning of a lengthy discussion of teaching writing in the popular press. Building on the popular appeal of Rudolf Flesch's *Why Johnny Can't Read*, this cover story defines teaching writing in terms of crisis. The opening paragraph reads:

> If your children are attending college, the chances are that when they graduate they will be unable to write ordinary, expository English with any real degree of structure and lucidity. If they are in high school and planning to attend college, the chances are less than even that they will be able to write English at the minimal college level when they get

there. If they are not planning to attend college, their skills in writing English may not even qualify them for secretarial or clerical work. And if they are attending elementary school, they are almost certainly not being given the kind of required reading material, much less writing instruction that might make it possible for them eventually to write comprehensible English. Willy-nilly, the U.S. educational system is spawning a generation of semiliterates. (58)

The visual presentation of the article combines with author Merrill Sheils' use of direct address and litany of inadequacies to implicate (and alarm) parents. Spread above the one-inch-high and two-page-wide *Why Johnny Can't Write* are four examples (in 12-point type) of flawed student writing. Two photographs, one of children passively watching television and another of a child reaching toward a book shelf, complete the visual frame. This introduction and presentation suggest that the article might answer the title's question and propose solutions for anxious parents to implement.

Instead, after elaborating on the enormity of the problem by citing evidence from declining scores on reading tests, the SAT, and the National Assessment of Educational Progress; from Marshall McLuhan's claim that "literary culture is through"; from Mario Pei's assertion that academia is controlled by those who preach "that one form of language is as good as another"; and from an executive's lament that "errors we once found common in applications from high school graduates are now cropping up in forms from people with four-year college degrees," Sheils changes the terms of the argument. She acknowledges that the writing skills of Americans have never been remarkable, but the "new illiteracy" is dismaying because "writing ability among even the best-educated young people seems to have fallen so far so fast" (59). In making this move, Sheils sets teaching writing to all students against teaching writing at places such as Berkeley, Michigan State, Temple, and Harvard (the sources of her "massive" evidence). "Teaching writing" thus provides the site for a contest between democracy and special privilege. Readers are left to wonder whether teaching writing is a concern for all students at all levels or only for those at a handful of relatively elite colleges.

Although Sheils casts the crisis in terms of an elite population, she paints its sources with a much wider brush. Television, with its encourage- ment of passivity, receives a large share of blame. Sheils also cites increased workloads that lead teachers to assign less writing, and then she goes on to excoriate a new emphasis on "creativity" in English classrooms, structural linguistics, *Webster's Third International Dictionary*, CCC's "Students' Right to Their Own Language," and the preparation English teachers receive, particularly in schools of education.

Contests of meaning abound in this litany and throughout the article. In drawing much of her evidence for declining writing abilities from standard- ized test scores, Sheils suggests that teaching writing means preparing students to do well on standardized tests. Yet, short-answer tests (the usual format for standardized tests) are cited as part of the problem in current writing instruction. Sheils emphasizes the connection between thinking and writing, but gives considerable attention to avoiding errors in modification, agreement, reference, and parallelism. That is, she inveighs against students who are unable to organize their thoughts in writing, but a prominent box in the article features a list of errors and how to avoid them. Sheils thereby sets avoidance of sentence-level error against power of thought. Having cited teachers' increased workload as one cause of declining writing skills, Sheils turns around and urges that teachers increase their workload by assigning more writing.

Steady and thoughtful reading is offered as a solution to problems in writing because "students who cannot read with true comprehension will never learn to write well" (59). A little later in the article, however, Sheils heaps praise upon Phillips Academy, where "the traditional four years of required English courses have been thrown out altogether and replaced with a school-wide requirement for competence in reading and writing. Every student ... must take the course until he passes it" (62). Presumably the student who passes in the first or second year will be excused from the reading that would have been part of the old four-year requirement. Television comes in for its share of drubbing as Sheils condemns the passivity it engenders in young viewers. Even though she cites passivity as a problem and urges that students take a more active part in their learning, she opposes "creativity" in the English classroom because "the creative school discourages insistence on grammar, structure and style" (60). Creativity thus contests with structure as an element in teaching writing. The training of writing teachers emerges as another source of the problem, and Sheils takes particular pleasure in condemning schools of education for failing to produce effective teachers. Yet, one of the solutions Sheils touts most highly is the Bay Area Writing Project (BAWP), a teacher-training program at Berkeley's School of Education.

This reading of "Why Johnny Can't Write" reveals the extent to which "teaching writing" serves as the site of contested meanings. Do multiple-choice tests pose a problem or identify one? What is the relationship between errors in usage and the quality of thought? If composition teachers are already overburdened, how can we ask more of them? If writers need to read more, how does eliminating English courses improve writing? Is it structure or creativity that we seek in our writing classes? Are schools of education part of the problem or part of the solution? These and other questions swirl throughout the *Newsweek* article. I point to these conflicted meanings, not to find fault with Sheils (although she deserves censure for her misrepresentation of structural linguistics), but to demonstrate how contested meanings pervade public opinion about teaching writing. Just as words like "the people," "government," and "the state" serve as sites of contest rather than of unified meanings, so "teaching writing" provides a locus for conflicting public views. Sheils merely reflects, and reflects well, the depth of public conflict about "teaching writing."

Subsequent articles in the popular press bear out the pervasiveness of these contested meanings. In the years before 1975, little on "teaching writing" appeared in the popular press. To be sure, professional journals carried articles on the subject regularly, but the popular press said nothing about teaching writing. *Time* (circulation 4,720,159) sounded the first alarm in 1974 with its "Bonehead English," claiming that among college freshman the "percentage of incompetent writers has risen in recent years" (106). This brief (1½-column) article introduced many of the themes (declining SAT scores, the negative influences of television, and inadequate high school instruction) that Sheils later developed, but *Newsweek* (circulation 3,181,187) ensconced "teaching writing" in the popular press.

In 1977 *Time* took a more optimistic posture with "Teaching Thinking on Paper." To be sure, the article begins with the obligatory summary of problems: "The symptoms are woefully familiar to college instructors everywhere. Nonsensical sentences. Disjointed paragraphs. Wandering structure. Recklessly dangling participles" (74). (Interestingly, sentence fragments do not make the list of symptoms.) Having limited the problem of writing instruction to the college level, the article proceeds to offer Professor A. D. Van Nostrand's "functional writing" as a solution.

Optimistic though it is, "Teaching Thinking on Paper" juggles its own set of contradictions. Having defined the problem in terms of syntactic and structural features such as modifiers and paragraphing, the article quotes Van Nostrand, who, echoing the *Newsweek* article, asserts that "the problem is not so much that Johnny can't parse a sentence as that he can't think" (74). Van Nostrand's "functional English" requires students to consider the audience and purpose, to write as if they had "a contract with the reader" (74). Rhetorical considerations of audience and purpose for writing contend with structural features such as "nonsensical sentences", "recklessly dangling participles" etc. in the space inhabited by "teaching writing."

U.S. News and World Report (circulation 2,287,061) added its voice to the discussion in 1979 with an editorial piece titled "Due Dismay about Our Language." Here the complaint centers on "an explosive increase in the number of writers and speakers who can't be bothered about meanings of words, singulars and plurals of nouns, tenses and moods of verbs, the right places to put punctuation or ways to arrange sentences to show what goes with what" (102). The solution centers on one Bill Gold, a journalist who fields "foul balls" of usage. Gold's usage campaign extends to *Webster's Third International Dictionary* because it "makes no attempt to be an authority on correct usage" (102). English teachers, one-third of whom have been found "unfit to teach their subject" (102) — although the nature of the unfitness is neither explained nor documented in any way — also come in for their share of blame. These two "truths" about the state of writing instruction contest each other, but an added dimension of dissent appears when author Marvin Stone goes on to complain about "the kind of writing that results from confused thinking and thus promotes further such thinking" (102). By so doing, Stone restates the contest between error and thinking that appeared in "Why Johnny Can't Write." Here the contest raises the question of whether writing errors result from or contribute to confused thinking.

The year 1981 might be cited as the high-water mark of this round of public interest in "teaching writing." *Family Circle*, (circulation 6,247,058), *Reader's Digest*, (circulation 16,250,000), and *Better Homes and Gardens* (circulation 8,012,035) all published articles on the subject. To put these figures in perspective, the current population of the United States is over 243 million, there were over 173 million potential voters for the 1986 election, some 110 million of these registered to vote, and over 79 million of these actually voted. In other words, the readership of an article about "teaching writing" in 1981 equals 30 million, or slightly less than half the number of people who voted in the 1986 election.

The *Family Circle* article (which was reprinted in *Reader's Digest*) took an approach almost identical to that of "Why Johnny Can't Write." Samples of flawed student writing deck the top margin and the first sentences (printed in much larger type than the rest of the article) reads: "Too many young Americans can't compose a simple paragraph—or even write well enough to hold a basic job. Here's why—and what you can do to help your children improve this important skill." The alarmist tone continues in the first paragraph with the revelation that "15 percent of America's young people are 'functionally illiterate,' which means they cannot read—or write—well enough to function at a minimal level in society" (99). Causes cited include television, the "Bad Period" of liberalizing in schools, the trend toward short-answer tests, lack of teacher training in writing, and the large teacher load. Solutions include the National Writing Project, renewed emphasis on the three R's, and parental involvement. This last solution receives the most attention. In addition to an exhortation to ask questions about the amount of writing assigned, the way writing is evaluated, and the extent of writing across the curriculum, the article features a box with ten suggestions for parents to help improve their children's writing.

Although it purports to give parents a clear message, this article, like its peers in the popular press, situates "teaching writing" on contested ground. The Bad Period is characterized as replacing goals of clarity and coherence with creativity and self-expression, but the boxed suggestions emphasize creative approaches such as writing on walls, writing captions, keeping a journal, writing stories, creating scripts, writing directions, and describing sensations. Nothing of "clarity" or "coherence" appears in the list. As was true in the *Newsweek* article, the enormous teacher load is detailed as part of the explanation for writing problems, but a few paragraphs later parents are exhorted to demand that their children write more, which would, presumably, increase the teacher load. Another familiar contest appears as author Brandt faults machine-scored tests for "juvenile writing delinquency" (100) and observes that the SAT is and observes itself machine-scored. Brandt notes the irony of documenting the writing crisis with SAT scores while faulting machine-scored tests for decreased writing abilities among students, but the contested meanings stand. Brandt asserts that students don't get enough practice in writing, but acknowledges that "Americans in general are doing less writing" (101). This contest between demanding more writing of students at the same time that society decreases its own writing remains unaddressed. Parents intent on following this article's injunctions must conclude that "teaching writing" should emphasize clarity/coherence and creativity/self-expression; that writing teachers are overworked and that they should be expected to do more; that SATs provide a good measure of writing abilities and that machine-scored tests like SATs contribute to writing problems; that it is important for students to learn to write and that society does not value writing.

"New Approaches to Teaching Youngsters How to Write," the *Better Homes and Gardens* article of the same year, moves away from the alarmist position of the *Family Circle/Reader's Digest* article to take a more upbeat perspective. In answer to the question of whether students' writing abilities have improved in recent years, author Dan Kaercher states: "Reports are more optimistic today than they were in the mid-1970s when an NAEP study indicated students' writing abilities had dropped significantly since the late 1960s" (21). But there is still a problem. NAEP results show that "More youngsters are able to write with minimal competence, but fewer youngsters excel in writing" (32). The solution lies not in grammar drills but in training teachers through programs like the National Writing Project, in writing practice that can be gained by balancing reading with writing, in writing across the curriculum, in giving more time to writing, in redesigning textbooks, and in replacing short-answer tests with essays.

Although many contemporary composition instructors might view the positions taken in this article as more "enlightened" than others in the popular press, this article shares with its peers a contested view of what it means to teach writing. The central argument of the article, that the process of writing should be emphasized, stands in opposition to the recommendation that writing should be tested because tests emphasize the product, not the process of writing. Implementing the recommendation that writing be balanced with reading requires reducing the amount of reading students do, yet the author identifies lack of reading as one of the reasons for students' problems in writing. In advocating writing across the curriculum Kaercher acknowledges that teachers in other disciplines may resent being required to teach writing, but he ignores his own earlier point that effective writing instructors need training and implies that anyone can teach writing. Among the proposals for reducing the teachers' load is using lay readers. While this may be a good suggestion, it contradicts Kaercher's claim that teaching writing involves more than "putting red marks all over the page" (33). Even when viewed from a relatively enlightened position, then, "teaching writing" serves as the site of contests about process and product, reading and writing, instructors' need for specialized training, and effective evaluation.

In 1983, *Parents Magazine* (circulation 1,721,816) featured an article that picked up on the *Better Homes and Gardens* theme of emphasizing process rather than product. Titled "A Revolution in Writing," this article locates the revolution in the work of the National Writing Project, not in computers or back-to-the-basics movements. Author Francis Roberts claims that NWP training enables teachers to "shift from the old role of paper grader to editor, adviser, and fellow writer" (52). Citing research claims that "the teaching of formal grammar, if divorced from the process of writing, has little or no effect on the writing ability of students" (52–53), Roberts goes on to claim that working directly with students on their writing is more effective than red-penciling errors.

In the remainder of the article, Roberts offers parents ways they can help their children learn to write. These ways include reading aloud, conversation, sharing drafts, preserving children's papers, allowing for uneven progress in writing development, and advocating an updated writing program in the school. As did the author of the *Better Homes and Gardens* article, Roberts includes the address of the NWP, urging parents to write for materials and information. This shift from teachers to parents highlights another contest of meaning. Is teaching writing the province of the school or the home? Are teachers or parents charged with major responsibility? Another contest of meaning is inherent in the central assumption of this article. Roberts bases his claim for revolution on the work of the "small band of reformers" (52) associated with the NWP. Important and influential though the NWP has been, Roberts notes that "the federal funds that helped launch the National Writing Project are fast disappearing" (33), which raises questions about the long-term health of this revolution. More-over, the best estimates indicate that fewer than 15 percent of the teachers in this country had participated in the NWP by 1983 (Gere 30), raising questions about how realistic it is to describe the NWP as a panacea for problems in teaching writing.

Although not about the teaching of writing per se, another 1983 publication lends further perspective on the contest of meanings surrounding the term. This conversation with Professor Hugh Kenner titled "Writing Is an Abnormal Act in Today's Electronic World" appeared in *U.S. News and World Report*. (circulation 2,287,061). It takes a much less alarmist view of the crisis in writing. Kenner asserts, "While I do not applaud the decline in writing, I do think it's possible to exaggerate the dangers" (81). Kenner goes on to urge that schools "stop pretending that writing is a perfectly natural act, like breathing" (80) and to note the services (such as describing famous people whom we can now see on television or in photographs) that writing no longer provides.

Attention of the public press has moved away from teaching writing in recent years. Except for an article titled "Do You Have the 'Write' Stuff?" published by *Seventeen* (circulation 1,853,314) in 1985, the popular press did not give attention to the topic between 1983 and 1987. The *Seventeen* article offers advice to students writing college-application essays and includes its own set of contested meanings about writing, such as be original but not too original, be sincere but add humor, and avoid generalizing but convey your feelings about what you've done. Written by a teacher of English, this advice embodies the same conflicts that mark other discussions of teaching writing in the popular press.

The sense of crisis and urgency seems to have passed by the late 1980's and with it the contested meanings for "teaching writing." Both of the articles published in 1987 take a positive and optimistic view of writing instruction. *Time's* "Great Human Power or Magic" describes the Bread Loaf program to train teachers of writing from rural schools. This article emphasizes that students "write well when they have information to communicate" and accordingly recommends that stories told by elderly people, observations about science projects, and letters to students in other schools be part of the writing program. "Great Human Power or Magic" also explains the computer network (BreadNet) that enables students from rural schools in places as distant as Alaska and North Carolina to write to and for one another. Alternative views of writing instruction are dismissed with an instructor's comment that "We have nothing against skill-and-drill curricula except they don't work." Teaching writing is portrayed as creating "real situations" in which students write.

Similarly, *U.S. News & World Report's* "Kids Can Learn to Write — and Enjoy It" advocates that students choose their own topics for writing. Roy Peter Clark, the writing instructor interviewed in this article, speaks against using writing as punishment, against sentence diagramming, and against traditional methods of simply assigning writing and correcting mistakes when writing is handed in. In addition, the article contains a boxed list of suggestions for parents. The list, very similar to that in the *Reader's Digest* article, includes taking dictation from children, encouraging children to keep diaries, reading aloud, and discussing television stories. But unlike the *Reader's Digest* article, this one contains no contested meaning for "teaching writing."

It would be tempting to see the decade between 1975 and 1985 as a neat curve of rising and falling action with the contest of meanings for "teaching writing" fading away as an increasingly enlightened population came to a consensus on the meaning of the term. But a more accurate reading of the situation suggests that the contest of meanings for "teaching writing" will emerge when the topic once again receives a flurry of attention from the popular press. People in this country feel too strongly about "teaching writing" to leave it uncontested.

In addition, publicly contested meanings for "teaching writing" reflect

the multiple meanings professionals assign to the same term. As the pages
of our journals reveal, we who take composition studies as our academic
specialty do not agree on a single meaning for "teaching writing." The
advice we give, the observations we make, the categories we establish all
attest to the diverse meanings we assign to the term. John Simon's account
of professionals participating in a "panel discussion for high school teachers
of English about ways of teaching students how to write" (12) demonstrates
the contested meanings "teaching writing" has for professionals. Simon
summarizes the discussion this way:

> In short, the teachers were told that creative writing could be taught,
> and that it couldn't be. All writing should be based on personal experi-
> ences and be highly self-expressive: it should also imitate the classics
> and not be self-expressive at all. There should be much reading aloud,
> perhaps coupled with singing and dancing; there should be less talk
> and more writing. Kids should be taught writing by way of living,
> lusting and loving; grand existential strategies should be strictly
> avoided, and kids should learn to think, explicate texts, and do research.
> Above all, kids should be allowed to use their own jargon, dialect, lingo;
> above all, kids should be taught through imitation of superb writers how
> to transcend their own lingo, dialect, jargon. (18)

The popular press clearly has no monopoly on conflicted meanings for
"teaching writing." Professionals in composition instruction embrace as
various a set of meanings as does the general public reflected in the
popular press. The term cannot be reduced to a single definition or set of
definitions. Rather, it serves as the site for a contest of meanings.

This contest of meanings indicates the great significance that people in
the United States attach to "teaching writing." Perhaps this significance
derives from a sense of the political importance of writing in a democracy
or perhaps it derives from a feeling that success in our economic system
requires writing ability or perhaps it derives from some entirely different
set of concerns. Whatever its reasons, the general public values "teaching
writing" too highly to limit it to a single meaning. That the popular press
reflects this contest of meanings is, then, entirely appropriate. The form of
representation employed by the popular press is, however, problematic.

All of the public press articles considered here contain, as we have seen,
conflicting views on writing instruction, but none of the articles acknowledges
these contested meanings. Rather, the articles tend to invoke the language
of crisis and describe the sources of the problem—television, allocation of
resources, linguistic theories, and educational programs—in terms of large
and seemingly monolithic forces. By employing discourse at this level of
abstraction, these articles blur the various meanings attached to "teaching
writing," and the possibility for thoughtful consideration of these meanings
is considerably reduced. Readers of the popular press find it difficult to talk

about the contested meanings of "teaching writing" because those contended terms are not made explicit. It is not surprising, then, that suggestions for action are designated for the private sphere inhabited by parents and children. As long the contested meanings of "teaching writing" remain buried under the hyperbole of crisis and large causes, substantive public community conversations about these meanings or about possible action remain impossible. Bringing the contested meanings for "teaching writing" into direct focus in the popular press would be the first step toward creating the ground for collective action designed to improve writing instruction in our schools and colleges.

Works Cited

Brandt, Anthony. "Why Kids Can't Write." *Reader's Digest* 118 (April 1981): 99–102.

Douglas, Charles. "The Scientific Basis of Composition." *Science* 22 (September 15, 1893): 149–150.

Dyer, Joyce. "Do You Have the 'Write' Stuff?" *Seventeen* 44 (November 1985): 154+.

Kaercher, Dan. "New Approaches to Teaching Youngsters How to Write." *Better Homes and Gardens* 59 (November 1978): 21–25.

Liddell, Mark. "English Historical Grammar." *The Atlantic* 82 (July 1898): 98–107.

Ludtke, Melissa. "Great Human Power or Magic." *Time* 119 (September 14, 1987): 76.

Nord, David Paul. "First Steps Toward a Theory of Press Control." *Journalism History* 4 (Spring 1977): 8–13.

Roberts, Francis. "A Revolution in Writing." *Parents* 58 (October 1983): 52–54.

Rodgers, Daniel. *Contested Truths: Keywords in American Politics Since Independence.* New York: Basic, 1987.

Sheils, Merrill. "Why Johnny Can't Write." *Newsweek* 92 (December 8, 1975): 58–65.

Simon, John. "The Language." *Esquire* 87 (June 1977): 12+.

Statement of Principles and Standards for the Postsecondary Teaching of Writing. Conference on College Composition and Communication. Urbana, IL: NCTE, 1989.

Stone, Marvin, "Bonehead English." *Time* 106 (November 11, 1974): 106

————. "A Conversation with Hugh Kenner: Writing Is an Abnormal Act in Today's Electronic World." *U.S. News and World Report* 90 (February 14, 1983): 80–81.

————. "A Conversation with Roy Peter Clark: Kids Can Learn to Write—and Enjoy It." *U.S. News and World Report* 91 (August 6, 1987): 68.

————. "Due Dismay about Our Language." *U.S. News and World Report.* 86 (April 23, 1979): 102.

————. "Teaching Thinking on Paper." *Time* 109 (April 18, 1977): 74.

17

Literacy and the
Discourse of Crisis

JOHN TRIMBUR
Worcester Polytechnic Institute

Since *Newsweek*'s "Why Johnny Can't Write" issue appeared on December 8, 1975, the idea of a national literacy crisis has become a fixture in the popular consciousness. The resonance of the two terms — "literacy" and "crisis" — has taken on a certain formulaic, self-explanatory quality. Just to utter the phrase is to perform the act, putting literacy in crisis by releasing diffuse but widely shared anxieties about deteriorating educational standards, drops in test scores, the permissiveness of the 1960s, black English, the effects of television and video games, John Dewey and progressive education, and the failure to compete economically with the Japanese. The rhetorical power of the phrase "literacy crisis" resides in its ability to condense a broad range of cultural, social, political, and economic tensions into one central image.

Writing teachers and writing-program administrators have not been immune to the rhetorical power of this widely heralded literacy crisis. If anything, the idea of a literacy crisis has been taken for granted as a handy rationale to offer department chairs, deans, faculty committees, and external grant-funding agencies. The very words "literacy crisis" have become a ritual invocation that justifies our activities and shapes our self-images. We like to think that we writing teachers, theorists, researchers, and program administrators (unlike our colleagues in literature) are going about society's business, doing what parents, the public, and the employers of our graduates want done — to teach our students how to read and write or, as employer surveys often put it, how to "communicate effectively."

There is little question that writing programs and composition studies have been direct beneficiaries of the current literacy crisis. Many colleges and universities that dropped freshman composition requirements in the 1960s have reinstated them. There has been a proliferation of new courses in technical, business, scientific, and legal writing, new writing-across-the-curriculum programs, new writing requirements in the junior year — in short, a new awareness of and institutional commitment to the importance

277

of writing in undergraduate education. In the flurry of activity it has taken
to launch new courses and programs, however, we have not stopped often
enough to ask what we are subscribing to when we say the magic words
"literacy crisis," what we are taking for granted. The purpose of this
chapter is to investigate the cultural and political meanings of a discourse
that puts literacy in crisis.

The *Newsweek* article "Why Johnny Can't Write" offers a useful starting
place to look at the rhetorical strategies that have articulated the literacy
crisis. The article begins by speaking directly to parents:

> If your children are attending college, the chances are that when they
> graduate, they will be unable to write ordinary, expository English with
> any real degree of structure and lucidity. If they are in high school and
> planning to attend college, the chances are less than even that they will
> be able to write English at the minimal college level when they get
> there. (58)

Forget for a moment the methodological difficulties of determining exactly
what a "minimal college level" of literacy might be. Forget, too, how recent
work on the discipline-specific genres of academic discourse calls into
question the possibility of formulating any general model of "ordinary,
expository English." Notice instead the alarmist tone and the appeal to
parental anxieties. What *Newsweek* writer Merrill Sheils taps into are the
anxieties arising from a particular historical conjuncture during the Carter
years of the mid-1970s—a time of energy crisis, declining productivity and
"stagflation," the Iran hostage crisis, diminished expectations, and increased
competition for jobs and college admission.

Sheils constructs a scenario of worried parents concerned not about the
public good and how to provide a decent education for all children but
about their private interests and how to secure a competitive edge for their
children. Confronting the beleaguered parental figure in Sheils's scenario
are a range of stock characters: the "permissive" or radical teacher, the
"progressive" school system experimenting with the child, affirmative-action
and equal-opportunity programs that "favor" minorities and lower standards,
college admission committees scrutinizing SAT scores and class rank, prospective employers who repeatedly find that recent graduates can't read
and write well or "communicate effectively." Lurking just below the surface
of Sheils's scenario, however, more powerful because it is not articulated
explicitly, is the ongoing crisis of the middle class, the threat of downward
mobility to baby boomers and their children as the bubble of postwar
prosperity and American global hegemony burst in the 1970s.

The discourse of the literacy crisis of the mid-1970s offered middle-class
parents an explanation of what was troubling them, a reason for the perceived
uncertainty about their children's futures. For the middle class, the crisis
of literacy standards appeared to deprive the schools of a fundamental

measure to rank students in a meritocratic order, to certify the success of *their* children, and to legitimate the unequal outcomes of the others—the minorities, the poor, and the working class. As Sheils stages it, the literacy crisis of the mid-1970s registers a crisis of confidence in which public education no longer seems to be linked directly to individual success and economic well-being. But instead of fostering a critical examination of the connection among schooled literacy, upward mobility, and national prosperity—the constellation of popular beliefs the historian Harvey Graff has labeled the "literacy myth"—the prevailing discourse of crisis reinvests mythic powers in literacy, calling upon literacy standards to shore up a faltering meritocracy.

The final paragraph of "Why Johnny Can't Write" explains how this is to be done:

> The point is that there have to be some fixed rules, however tedious, if the codes of human communication are to remain decipherable. If the written language is placed at the mercy of every new colloquialism and if every fresh dialect demands and gets equal sway, then we will soon find ourselves back in Babel. In America . . . there are too many people intent on being masters of their language and too few willing to be its servants. (65)

Sheils couches her "point" here in terms of a call for standard English as the proper arbiter of language practice and literacy instruction, an argument *for* an authoritative version of written English and *against* the incursion of colloquialism and dialect. Sheils's goal is a reaffirmation of linguistic norms in order to regularize and regulate communication, to halt the slide into a pluralistic, polyphonic English. This argument, of course, rehashes an old debate about the nature of language that goes back at least to the eighteenth century, with advocates of a final, fixed version on one side and advocates of an organic, developing version on the other—correctness versus usage. The danger Sheils refers to, however, is not and never has been that of reverting "back to Babel." The threat is not that of linguistic chaos but of blurring the lines between "us" and "them," between what Sheils so revealingly calls "masters" and "servants."

At stake in Sheils's discourse of crisis is not whether students read and write better or worse than they did twenty or fifty years ago, but whether literacy can still draw lines of social distinction, mark status, and rank students in a meritocratic order. The literacy crisis *Newsweek* announced in the mid-1970s is only a continuation of an ongoing discourse that has repeatedly put literacy in crisis since the mid-nineteenth century. This discourse is not concerned primarily with student performances, declining standards, or increased social demand for reading and writing. Rather, the discourse of literacy crises engages deep-seated cultural anxieties and attempts to resolve them magically, by regulating the production and use of literacy and by drawing lines between standard English and popular vernaculars, "masters" and "servants." My argument is that middle-class anxieties about loss of status and downward mobility have repeatedly been displaced and refigured in the realm of language practices and literacy education. For the middle class, literacy appears to go into crisis precisely because of the faith they have invested in schooled literacy as the surest means of upward mobility and individual success, a form of cultural capital that separates their children from those of the working class and the poor.

Historiography of Literacy Crises

The key text that informs my argument is a passage from the Italian Marxist Antonio Gramsci. What Gramsci says in the following lines advances our understanding of literacy crises more than all of the alarmist rhetoric that has accumulated since "Why Johnny Can't Write" appeared:

> Each time that in one way or another the question of language comes to the fore, that signifies that a series of other problems is about to emerge, the formation and enlarging of the ruling class, the necessity to establish more "intimate" and sure relations between ruling groups and the national popular masses, that is the reorganization of cultural hegemony. (quoted in Giroux 1)

Literacy crises, as I will show, have served as strategic sites for what Gramsci calls the "reorganization of cultural hegemony." Cultural hegemony is a term Gramsci uses to describe two interrelated processes—the consolidation of political authority by the state through consent rather than coercion, and the establishment of the leadership of one particular class or political group in relation to other classes and political groups. As Gramsci suggests, literacy crises play out in symbolic form the relations between "ruling groups" and the "popular masses," as well as the aspirations of the middle class to intellectual, moral, and political leadership. Cultural hegemony is rarely imposed from above. It has to be negotiated locally in the practices and procedures of everyday life, naturalized as a matter of what we take to be common sense. The negotiation of cultural hegemony, that is, involves a double making: the hegemonic representations articulated by the dominant culture must also, as Stuart Hall puts it, "foster forms of consciousness which accept a position of subordination" (59).

From this perspective, the discourse that creates a crisis in literacy cannot be understood apart from the rise of mass public schooling and the establishment of a meritocratic educational order. Literacy crises have been instrumental in both the appropriation of literacy by the institutions of public schooling and the naturalization of schooled literacy as a moral and cognitive measure of the individual. Inspired by middle-class aspirations, the discourse of literacy crises portrays the schooled literacy of public education simultaneously as an arena of equal opportunity for all who wish to enter and as an explanation of the success or failure of individuals in class society.

To see literacy crises as negotiations of cultural hegemony means, for one thing, that we cannot dismiss them, as leftists sometimes do, simply as hoaxes, manufactured events, plots by the ruling class and its house intellectuals. While the reasons given to establish the reality of literacy crises — the connection, say, between illiteracy and crime in the nineteenth century or the decline of test scores in the twentieth—do not hold up well to empirical scrutiny, these reasons nonetheless constitute necessary and enabling fictions that inscribe motives in educational policy and practice. To say that literacy crises are ideological events does not mean that they simply purvey forms of false consciousness that disguise the "real" interests of the ruling class in the name of the general public interest. Rather, literacy crises are attempts to resolve in imaginary ways actual tensions, anxieties, and contradictions. To think of literacy crises as ideological events is to think rhetorically — to see literacy crises conjuncturally, as strategic pretexts for educational and cultural change that renegotiate the terms of cultural hegemony, the relations between classes and groups, and the meaning and use of literacy.

This perspective on literacy crises, moreover, differs markedly from the prevailing accounts offered to explain what causes literacy to go into crisis. The historiography of literacy crises in American history remains in a rudimentary and impressionistic phase. Those who write about literacy crises do not agree on what causes them, how many there have been, or even how we should define literacy. Nonetheless, for our purposes here, we can distinguish two representations of literacy crises, two ways of telling the story.

The first explanation asserts that literacy crises occur when the ability to read and write actually and demonstrably declines. The second holds that literacy crises result not from deteriorating performances but from heightened expectations and increased social and economic demand for reading and writing. The first explanation employs a narrative that tells of the decline of literacy; the second, a narrative that tells of its progress. Each has shaped the discourse of literacy crises in important ways, and each, as we will see, has done more to restrict our understanding than to illuminate it.

The Narrative of Literacy's Decline

In "Why Johnny Can't Write," *Newsweek* reporter Sheils tells the story of literacy in decline, a narrative strategy shared by a wide range of commentators, from Allan Bloom and E. D. Hirsch, Jr., to Edwin Newman and John Simon. We can find earlier instances of this policing of language during the 1950s in books such as *Why Johnny Can't Read* and *Educational*

Wastelands, but the decline narrative goes back much further into the American past. There are signs of it, for example, as early as the 1830s and 1840s, in what Dennis Baron calls "linguistic insecurity." Linguistic insecurity was a persistent theme in the nineteenth century that resulted, on the one hand, from nationalist sentiment to overcome cultural dependence on England by affirming the value of American English and, on the other, from the representation of linguistic propriety as a mark of class, status, and social position, necessary for self-improvement and upward mobility. Throughout the nineteenth century, the middle class worried about the state of American English, about the coarsening effects of the frontier, regional dialects, and urban immigrant masses, about the correctness and propriety of their own speech habits and forms of written expression. By the 1890s, as E. L. Godkin's "The Illiteracy of American Boys" indicates, the decline theory had become a popular preoccupation. "I meet every day with men whom we call educated," Godkin writes, "who do not seem to care how they speak or how they write." Not only is the language of the educated in decline, but, as Godkin asserts, a "dialect is being formed today under our very noses in New York, which bears only a faint resemblance to English" (2).

Godkin's article on the "growing illiteracy" of those entering college takes as its starting point what is offered as empirical evidence of deteriorating educational standards—the entrance examinations read by the Harvard Committee on Composition and Rhetoric, of which Godkin was a member. The Harvard Report issued by the committee in 1893 caused a scandal about the preparation of secondary students in writing and initiated a now familiar tradition of articulating a literacy crisis by presenting test results to shock the public and the educational community. Since the 1890s, we can see literacy crises produced, as it were, by the extension of standardized testing: during World War I with the first widescale intelligence testing of Army recruits, again during World War II with further mass testing, and most recently in the notorious decline of SAT scores from 1963 to 1980.

Test results, of course, possess a kind of facticity that appears to put them above question and beyond interpretation. They appear, that is, to offer self-evident accounts of literacy crises—of deteriorating educational standards and declining student performances. It is a mistake, however, to assume, as advocates of the decline theory do, that test scores speak for themselves. We might, for example, read the Harvard Report of 1893 not as the result of the deplorable preparation of entering freshmen but, as Susan Miller does in this volume, as the response of an antidemocratic and elitist Old Guard to the admission of "new" students drawn from what Godkin calls the "unliterary" and "illiterate" families of the new middle class. By Miller's account, the Harvard Report registers the renegotiation of higher education's traditional mission of preparing a liberally educated elite from the best families for careers in the law, medicine, the ministry, and public service into that of training white-collar workers, professionals, and technical experts to staff the ranks of an emerging corporate order.

Along the same lines, critics such as Ira Shor, Richard Ohmann, and Andrew Sledd have offered readings of the declining test scores of the 1960s and 1970s that contest their self-evident status as proof that literacy is in decline. Shor argues that the decline of SAT scores, which were especially (and disturbingly) pronounced among the highest-achieving students, resulted from a "performance strike," an expression of disenchantment with schooling, a sign of the wider alienation of American youth from mainstream values and of their recognition that an increasingly "over-educated" society could not provide jobs commensurate with individuals' levels of academic attainment. Ohmann points out that despite the drop in SAT scores (which, after all, do not contain a writing sample), other test scores from the 1970s such as the National Assessment of Educational Progress reveal limited, if uneven, gains in writing skills. Sledd asserts that the decline of SAT scores can be accounted for by reference not to a literacy crisis but to a "demographic bulge," in which more students from large families, who typically perform at levels below those of students from small families, were taking the SATs in the 1970s. Once the family size of the test takers dropped in the early 1980s, the test scores corrected themselves and started to rise. Finally, in the one case I know of where there are large-scale comparative data, Robert J. Connors and Andrea Lunsford have replicated the research of John C. Hodges, author of the *Harbrace College Handbook*, who in 1939 analyzed patterns of error marked on 20,000 student themes. Connors and Lunsford found that students make about the same number of errors, if somewhat different ones, as they did fifty years ago.

My point here is not to disprove the literacy crisis of the mid-1970s but to separate its discourse from the empirical evidence it has relied upon. As Shor, Ohmann, and Sledd argue, we can read the test results to tell the story not of a "decline in literacy" but of "an *increase* in equality and social justice" (Ohmann 233) — a sign of the expansion of educational opportunity in the late 1960s and early 1970s for women, minorities, and working-class students who had formerly been excluded from higher education. And from this perspective, alarmism about declining test scores and educational standards can be seen not just as a pretext to return to the basics and restore order, discipline, and morality to the schools. It also registers anxiety that the meritocracy itself has broken down. The discourse of literacy in crisis is not simply a nostalgic longing for a golden age of American education, but an antidemocratic attack on the educational reforms of the 1960s and 1970s, an offensive to stop affirmative-action, remedial, and equal-opportunity programs in higher education and to firm up the meritocracy in order to consolidate the privileges of middle-class and upper middle-class students.

The Narrative of Literacy's Progress

It is easy enough to read the narrative of literacy's decline as a reaction
not against threatened standards but rather against different, more democratic standards. There is, however, another explanation of literacy crises
that appears to be more plausible. In "The Nature of Literacy: An Historical
Explanation," Daniel P. Resnick and Lauren B. Resnick argue that it is not
low achievement but increased cultural expectations that promote concern
about literacy standards. Robin Varnum has used this argument to claim
that the history of literacy crises tells the story not of declining standards
but of progress. With each successive crisis, she says, "a new and higher
standard of literacy had come generally to be accepted" (153). Economic
and technological development led to a current standard of literacy that is
"vastly more sophisticated than those concepts which were current in 1880
or 1920" (160). Moreover, for Varnum, literacy crises demonstrate not the
failure but the success of American education: "in the reform movements
which have resulted from each crisis, American educators have continuously
been successful in meeting the challenge of raised expectations" (148).

Now there is, to be sure, some truth in the Resnick-Varnum narrative of
progress. As the Resnicks point out, literacy no longer means just the
ability to sign one's name, as it did in the seventeenth or eighteenth
century, or the ability to decode written passages without considering
comprehension, as it did in many nineteenth-century common schools.
Varnum shows that the concept of literacy was indeed enlarged during
World War I, when the general intelligence tests administered to Army
recruits required the ability to comprehend what was read. During World
War II, the fear of propaganda and what communications advocate Lennox
Grey called "the advanced illiteracy that makes dupes of facile but uncritical
readers" raised the standard of literacy to include the ability to analyze
assumptions and draw inferences from written texts.

By this account, literacy crises take place when a cultural lag occurs,
when literacy practices and literacy education have not quite caught up to
increased expectations and heightened demand. Literacy crises result, that
is, from the progressive imperatives of public policy, economic development,
technological and scientific innovation. This explanation of literacy crises,
moreover, underwrites the way a sector of business and government—
"new-age" postindustrial managers, technocratic futurists, and manpower
allocators—has described the need for increased literacy standards and a
more highly trained and trainable workforce as the economy shifts from an
industrial assembly line to a new high-tech service and information economy.
In this view, a heightened demand for literacy is linked to job performance,
productivity, and the need to improve the competitive position of the
United States in the world market. Postindustrial politicians are more
likely to explain why the United States has lost its competitive edge by
citing the presumed, if highly questionable, correlation between productivity
and universal literacy rates in Japan than by citing standardized test scores.

The point to make here is that the increased demand for literacy and the raised expectations about literacy standards are not as innocent or as uniformly progressive as the Resnicks and Varnum suggest. Varnum's account of literacy crises portrays literacy as a neutral technology that changes meaning and gains greater sophistication in response to modernizing trends and progressive socioeconomic pressures. My argument is that literacy and its crises are always interested, always articulated in a relation to power and the negotiation of cultural hegemony. By translating the increased demand for literacy as the inevitable result of economic and technological progress, Varnum leaves out the ways in which "raised expectations" express political interests and social tensions. To cite an obvious example, the literacy tests adopted as a requirement for suffrage by Connecticut in 1855 and Massachusetts in 1857 resulted not from so-called heightened standards of literacy but from a heightened desire to exclude Irish Catholics from political participation. Similarly, the use of literacy tests in the post-Reconstruction South was part of a wider consolidation of white supremacy and a Jim Crow regime.

There is no question that a major shift is going on in the American economy. The commodification and computerization of information can be seen in the widespread use of data processing, marketing research, and computer simulations. Information is entering and transforming the means of production to an unprecedented degree. But it is unclear whether these changes mean that higher levels of literacy are actually required for job performance when nine new jobs are created for cashiers and checkout clerks to each one for computer programmers.

The "raised expectations" about literacy currently held by policymakers do not simply reflect wider changes in the economy. These expectations also articulate new relations to a changing workforce. According to a recent study conducted by the Hudson Institute for the Labor Department, lower birth rates among whites compared with other groups of Americans, combined with immigration from Asia and Latin America, are producing telling demographic changes in the workforce. By the year 2000, the study estimates, 80 percent of the people entering the workforce will be women, blacks, Hispanics, or immigrants. For policymakers, literacy appears to be a key tool to socialize these new workers to the discipline of the workplace and to guarantee productivity. As Kenneth Levine's study of employers' use of literacy tests as screening devices for prospective employees suggests, literacy may not be directly related to the type of occupation or job skills demanded of these new workers. Instead, as Levine argues, literacy serves as a kind of "proxy" to assess cooperativeness, reliability, and trainability.

Marcienne S. Mattleman and Joe Torsella claim that the social costs of illiteracy have reached "frightening dimensions," prompted not only by the "billions of dollars" illiteracy costs the economy in "unemployment, under-employment, and diminished worker productivity" but, more tellingly, by a "social landscape of crime, drug abuse, and hopelessness" in which illiteracy is embedded. Their argument, however, speaks more to the persistent effects of Reaganomics and the turning of the United States into a "double-peaked" society of rich and poor than to a crisis in literacy. Rather, literacy appears both as a social explanation that individualizes oppression by blaming the victim and as a tool to incorporate all the "other Americas"—the poor, blacks, Hispanics, new Asian immigrants—into a monolingual body politic.

Transformations of Literacy

What I hope to have suggested so far is that literacy crises are always strategic: They perform certain kinds of ideological work by giving a name to and thereby mastering (rhetorically if not actually) cultural anxieties released by demographic shifts, changes in the means of production, new relations and conflicts between classes and groups of people, and reconfigurations of cultural hegemony. By representing literacy in crisis, the discourse of literacy externalizes these deeper structural changes and shifts in the political balance of power and refigures them in the problem of language and education—of learning how to read and write.

The story of literacy crises I want to tell emphasizes the ideological work performed by the schooling of literacy—the appropriation and regulation of the multiple popular literacies that flourished before the common-school movement and the institution of mass public education in the mid-nineteenth century. Literacy crises can best be understood not in terms of student performance or social demand but in terms of the transformations of literacy enacted by the common-school crusade of 1840 to 1870 and the rise of progressive education from 1890 to 1920. During these two periods of school reform—against a backdrop of massive and rapid social change, industrialization, immigration, urbanization, and class strife—common-school advocates and progressive educators, in different ways, represented schooled literacy as a means of ameliorating class antagonisms, equalizing economic opportunity, and ensuring social cohesion and political integration. By incorporating literacy into the institutions of schooling, the common-school movement established, and progressive education refined, a discursive apparatus to regulate the production of literacy and to measure its outcomes.

The primary effect of the schooling of literacy has been to equate literacy with educational practices, to identify reading and writing as a set of discrete skills and subskills students acquire as they move from grade level to grade level, the necessary foundation of a student's ongoing education. But it is precisely because we have so thoroughly naturalized literacy as a fundamental outcome of schooling that we need to look more closely at how schooling has transformed literacy and defined its cultural meanings.

During the eighteenth and early nineteenth centuries, two apparently contradictory attitudes toward literacy vied for influence among ruling

elites in the Anglo-American world. On the one hand, republican spokesmen
in America argued that literacy was a key component of nation building and
a responsibility of the state. Schooled literacy was seen as a social necessity,
not an individual right—a means of overcoming regionalism and securing
the loyalty of citizens to the central state. As Samuel Harmon Smith wrote
in 1798, "it is the duty of the nation to superintend and even coerce the
education of children, and . . . high considerations of expediency not only
justify, but dictate the establishment of a system which shall place under a
control, independent of, and superior to, parental authority, the education
of children" (quoted in Soltow and Stevens 47–48). In this regard, Benjamin
Rush, one of the early leading advocates of public education, was even
more blunt: "Let our pupil be taught that he does not belong to himself,
but that he is public property" (quoted in Spring 83). On the other hand, in
England, Tories also say literacy in social and political terms, but ironically
their anxieties developed because the popular masses had indeed learned
to read and, to a lesser extent, to write. In the shadow of the French
Revolution, British commentator Vicesimus Knox observed gloomily in
1793 that the "lowest of the people can read." Political debates once
confined to the propertied classes, Knox complained, have now spread to
the "cottages, the manufactory, and lowest resorts of plebeian carousel.
Great changes in the public mind are produced by this diffusion; and such
changes must produce public innovation" (quoted in Laquer 195).

Tories such as Knox linked literacy to Jacobinism, religious dissent, and
working-class radicalism. While such explicitly reactionary sentiments were
rarely expressed so overtly in the United States, the codes that made it a
crime for slaves to learn to read and write reveal the recognition by North
American slaveowners and their northern sympathizers of the subversive
powers of literacy. It is noteworthy that the last of the prohibitions on
literacy was made into law in 1835, just after Nat Turner's rebellion, at a
time when white fears of slave revolts had reached a peak of intensity.

An episode from Frederick Douglass's autobiography offers a clarifying
case in point of the ideological construction of literacy in the antebellum
South. When Douglass's master ordered his wife to stop teaching Douglass
to read, the slaveowner made it clear what was at stake:

"If you teach that nigger (speaking of myself) how to read, there would
be no keeping him. It would forever unfit him to be a slave. He would
at once become unmanageable, and of no value to his master. As to
himself, it could do him no good, but a great deal of harm. It would
make him discontented and unhappy." (36)

For Douglass, however, the master's opposition to his learning to read and
write came as a "new and special revelation, explaining dark and mysterious
things. . . . I now understood what had been to me a most perplexing
difficulty—to wit, the white man's power to enslave the black man" (36).

Despite the threat of punishment or of being sold, slaves continued clandestinely to learn to read and write, for religious reasons and as an act of political resistance. The acquisition of literacy enabled slaves to circumvent their masters' control in important ways. Literate slaves wrote passes for themselves and for fellow slaves to visit relatives and friends on nearby plantations or to escape to the North. Slaves such as Douglass and Harriet Jacobs first learned of the abolitionist movement by reading newspapers and pamphlets, and they used the literacy they had acquired to forge a public voice for African-Americans through slave narratives and antislavery writings. Historians' estimates of literacy among slaves range from 5 to 27 percent (Finkelstein 138, n. 50), and these figures testify to the persistent struggle of African-Americans to assert their identity, to create free spaces within an oppressive slaveholding order, and to influence public opinion against slavery.

Among free whites, before the establishment of mass public education, upwards of 80 percent of the men and a somewhat lesser percentage of women could read and write on at least a rudimentary level. This popular literacy was transmitted as frequently through the family or from master to apprentice as through schooling. Unlike the literacy of the common schools, popular literacy in the eighteenth and early nineteenth centuries was largely a local phenomenon, embedded in the everyday life, practical affairs, and political activities of family, workplace, and community. For the white male population of merchants, farmers, mechanics, and artisans, literacy was tied inextricably to the democratic aspirations of the new nation. Jacksonian Democrats, the International Workingmen's Association, and organizations of mechanics and artisans viewed literacy as a means of alerting victims of inequality and injustice to the evils of the aristocrats and monopolists. Literacy offered a weapon to defend democratic principles, a means to curb the power of the state and to attack the elitism of existing educational institutions. Broadsides, ballads, newspapers, political and religious tracts, books, and almanacs circulated widely in the early nineteenth century—enlarging the public sphere of civil society. As Shirley Brice Heath notes, the "writing of reports of opinion and events and how-to accounts was viewed as the responsibility of all citizens across social classes and roles.... In the new republic, literacy was both a Christian and a patriotic duty" (28). Rooted in the everyday life of ordinary people, popular literacy in the early nineteenth century belonged to civil society, not to the state. It was a tool for organizing and maintaining the voluntary associations Tocqueville found so uniquely characteristic of American aspirations, a part of a wider democratic culture.

This popular literacy, moreover, contrasts sharply with the literacy instruction provided through private and public schools during the same period. Throughout the eighteenth and nineteenth centuries, educators were exremely reluctant to teach writing as well as reading, especially to poor and working-class students. This was due in part to the scarcity of quills, ink, and paper in early American schools, but there were also ideological pressures that restricted literacy education to reading. One was the legacy of the Protestant Reformation and its view of literacy as a matter of religious training and reading the Bible. The English evangelical educational reformer Hannah More wrote that her "plan of instruction" for the poor "is extremely simple and limited. They learn, on weekdays, such coarse works as may fit them for servants. *I allow of no writing for the poor.* My object is not to make them fanatics, but to train up the lower classes in habits of industry and piety" (quoted in Soltow and Stevens 13, my emphasis). It was one thing for the poor to learn to read the Bible and religious tracts. Writing was more threatening to the ruling elite because it provided the populace with a means to voice their own interests and to participate more widely in public and political life. In England, the Anglican-run public schools of the early nineteenth century only gradually added writing to the curriculum, and then only in response to the fact that working-class youth were already learning to write in Sunday schools and the indigenous private schools that grew up in working-class communities. In the United States, the private and public schools of the eighteenth and nineteenth centuries remained under religious influence, and writing instruction was largely confined to copying exercises, penmanship, and memorization drills.

The neglect of writing instruction must be seen, however, not just as a repression of individual and collective expression. It was also part of a reorientation of individuals and groups toward literacy through schooling. What early nineteenth-century forms of literacy instruction in America and England suggest is that evangelical reformers such as Hannah More and advocates for Lancasterian monitorial schools, which provided the dominant model of instructing the urban poor in the first half of the nineteenth century, grasped the idea that literacy posed a threat to political stability, as Tories and slaveholders had concluded. But more important, they began to see that literacy, or more specifically the control of it, could serve as a means to discipline and regulate habits and character.

The Common-School Movement

Horace Mann's crusade for a system of publicly supported common schools demonstrates the extent to which schooling transformed literacy from a tool of participation in public life into an instrument of social control. For the coalition of reformers and industrialists Mann skillfully brought together in the 1840s, schooled literacy represented an investment in human capital. The pervasive drills of nineteenth-century schools, in which teachers assumed managerial rather than pedagogical roles, taught not only grammar and mechanical correctness but also how to accept supervision, follow directions, and concentrate on tedious and repetitive tasks. But if the routines of schooling embodied the work rhythms of an emerging capitalist order, the common schools did not simply impose a new regime of industrial discipline. As industrial capitalism took hold and the spread of the factory system transformed society, the schooling of literacy in the common schools provided a strategic site for the renegotiation of cultural hegemony.

According to Mann, universal public education offered the "balance wheel of the social machinery." The purpose of schooled literacy, as one advocate put it, was to enable the poor "to look upon the distinctions of society without envy" and to be "taught to understand that they are open to him as well as to others and to respect them for this reason" (quoted in Curti 93). Mann's vision of the common school as an egalitarian corrective to the "domination of capital and the servility of labor" finally collided with the stubborn facts of increasing capital accumulation and class stratification, but the ideology of equal opportunity offered, as it were, an imaginary relationship to the actual conditions of a transformed social order. As formerly independent producers turned into wage laborers and a permanent proletariat, the farmers, artisans, and mechanics who had constituted the middling classes of the colonial and early national periods looked to the common schools as their best chance to avoid proletarianization, to join the newly formed middle classes, and to recoup their threatened status through hard work, intelligence, and entrepreneurial drive. As the "middle" in middle class was redefined by larger social forces — no longer an equilibrium between the extremes of the wealthy and the poor but rather an upwardly mobile strata — Americans increasingly came to identify their hopes and aspirations with the free schools and a system of universal public education.

The rise of the common-school movement, then, must be seen in light of wider, complicated changes in the class structure of American society, and especially in the context of the cultural anxieties of the new middle classes. The common schools certainly represent an important experiment in democratic education, but they also signal a critical transformation of the cultural meaning of literacy. The "linguistic insecurity" of the mid-nineteenth century — manifested in the growing emphasis on grammar instruction, the proliferation of self-help manuals teaching proper speech and writing, the public discussion of the "state" of American English, and the formation of local literary societies — served to put literacy in crisis by identifying linguistic propriety with social status and redefining literacy as a token of middle-class respectability. The popular literacy of the early nineteenth century was a democratic tool, a literary and intellectual resource to know one's rights, to defend against monopolies and special interests, and to resist unjust and illegitimate authority. By midcentury, however, the extension of education through the common school appropriated the popular cultural force of literacy, domesticating and channeling it into controlled and regulated practices. "The major goal of mass schooling," Jenny Cook-Gumperz writes, "was thus to control literacy, not to promote it; to control both the forms of expression and the behavior which accompany the move into literacy" (28).

Thus, schooled literacy emerged in the mid-nineteenth century as both a means to regulate popular literacy and a social marker to divide the literate from the illiterate, the worthy poor from the unworthy, "us" from "them." A moral consensus took root that transformed the popular activities of reading and writing into schooled practices and a kind of cultural capital, the possession of which signified an individual's assimilation into mainstream middle-class culture. Literacy increasingly came to be seen not as a practical tool for everyday affairs or an intellectual resource against injustice but as a measure of the person. By the 1840s, prison officials and educators noted that the prison population had a higher rate of illiteracy than the general population, and throughout the nineteenth century reformers linked illiteracy to crime and poverty. Illiteracy no longer meant simply the inability to read and write but was refigured as the cause of idleness, intemperance, and improvidence—a measure and mark of moral failure.

Progressive Education and the
Reorientation of Reading and Writing

One of the ironies of late nineteenth-century America is that the widespread availability of affordable reading matter—made possible by cost-reducing innovations in publishing, transportation, and marketing—only raised the level of cultural anxiety about literacy. The publishing boom, as Burton J. Bledstein notes, not only disseminated the printed word on an unprecedented scale, it also served "to encourage confusion and frustration that gave way to self-doubt and mistrust" (78). Vice societies, social hygienists, and educators warned the public about the dangers of unregulated reading material, and increasingly librarians, teachers, and public spokespersons were expected to help middle-class Americans distinguish wholesome from degenerate reading material. The emergence of what we call the "reading public" takes place through a process of social atomization, whereby readers are constructed as isolated and private consumers, dependent on the judgment of professional writers, reviewers, librarians, and educators to regulate their reading habits. Unlike earlier forms of popular literacy that enlarged the public sphere of discourse and extended opportunities to participate in public life, by the late nineteenth century a reorientation of literacy practices had occurred that privatized the act of reading and recast readers as clients whose primary obligation was to trust the judgment of experts and professionals.

This growing reliance on professionals was also enacted within the schools and led to the second major transformation of schooled literacy. By the early twentieth century, with the rise of progressive education, the introduction of a professional bureaucracy produced significant changes in the organization and nature of public education. Progressive educators developed a standardized curriculum, plans of instruction, and testing systems that made the evaluation of skills and the measurement of abilities possible. With the development of ability and intelligence testing in the early part of the century, schools increasingly became what Joel Spring calls a "sorting machine" to rank students and certify outcomes. As comprehensive high schools spread and the leaving age of compulsory schooling was raised, universal mass education gained in social power as the preeminent legitimating agency of an individual's success and the arbiter of attainment. The democratic ideology of the common school—where all students had studied the same curriculum—gave way to ability grouping in elementary schools and tracking in middle schools and high schools, overseen by counselors and testing experts. The "student-centered" approach of progressive education promised greater flexibility in curriculum as well as the instruction needed to handle the influx of working-class immigrants into public secondary education. In practice, however, it produced not greater equality but greater stratification between classes and ethnic groups. The Superintendent of Schools in Cleveland offered a typical argument for educational stratification in 1910:

> It is obvious that the educational needs of children in a district where the streets are well paved and clean, where the homes are spacious and surrounded by lawns and trees, where the language of the child's playfellows is pure, and where life in general is permeated with the spirit and ideals of America—it is obvious that the educational needs of such a child are radically different from those of a child who lives in a foreign and tenement section. (quoted in Bowles and Gintis 192)

As Cook-Gumperz argues, "the transformation of literacy from a moral virtue into a cognitive skill is the key to the twentieth century changes in the ideology of literacy" (37). Reading and writing, of all the measurable skills, appeared to offer the surest means to evaluate and rank student aptitude and performance. As the psychometric testing paradigm lent a scientific authority to the reforms of progressive education, educators began to represent literacy as a decontextualized set of skills developed through a uniform and universal process that mirrored deeper cognitive abilities and that could be measured by neutral and objective testing mechanisms with national norms. In this way, not only was literacy redefined as a unitary standardized abstraction instead of variable concrete practices, but students were also refigured, no longer simply as moral subjects but now as accounting units and batteries of test scores. Unlike earlier pluralistic forms of popular literacy, where the value of reading and writing had resided in their actual uses, literacy acquired a kind of exchange value that represented measurable cognitive abilities. If the common-school movement moralized literacy into a form of cultural capital that divided middle-class from working-class students, progressive education converted this cultural capital into the form of credentials.

It should not be surprising, then, that the literacy crisis of 1890 to 1920 articulated middle-class anxieties released by the emergence of a credentialed society. The transformation of entrepreneurial capitalism into the present corporate order produced not only massive industrialization, increased proletarianization, and heightened class conflict. As the monopolies absorbed small-scale producers, there occurred a shift of the middle classes from self-employed operators of family-owned businesses and enterprises to salaried employees, the white-collar workers of the huge, vertically integrated corporations. In contrast to the entrepreneurial boom times in the latter half of the nineteenth century, when the middle classes aspired to rise from rags to riches on the strength of frugality, practical knowledge, and small-scale capital investment, the corporate order of the twentieth century elaborated complex hierarchical bureaucracies, creating thousands of clerical, advertising, sales, bookkeeping, middle-level management, and low-level supervisory positions. At the same time, professional associations of lawyers, doctors, dentists, and engineers sought to regularize standards of training in professional schools, leading to the institution of national boards and accrediting agencies to certify the credentials of individual practitioners in their respective fields.

With these broad social changes, the middle class turned from petty proprietors into a professional-managerial stratum within the corporate order. The literacy crisis of 1890 to 1920, like the crisis of the 1840s, concentrated middle-class fears of loss of status, downward mobility, and the prospect of sinking into the working class or urban poor. These fears, moreover, led the middle classes to identify their private interests with an increasingly stratified and meritocratic order in education. Redefined as a cognitive instead of a moral measure of the individual, literacy was simultaneously reaffirmed as the middle classes' primary hope of upward mobility, social status, and respectability—a cultural marker to divide them and their credentials from the poor and the working class below.

Conclusion

My argument is that the discourse that puts literacy in crisis during the mid-nineteenth century and again at the turn of the century is a discourse about the ongoing crisis of the middle class. Fear of downward mobility and loss of status has repeatedly been displaced and refigured as a fear of the alien and the other—whether Irish Catholics in the 1840s, southern and eastern Europeans in the 1890s, or Hispanics and Asians in the 1980s— repeatedly linking middle-class anxieties to nativist sentiments, such as the current new-right campaign to make English the official language, and the backlash against affirmative-action, equal-opportunity, and open-admissions programs in higher education.

Left-wing critics such as Shor, Ohmann, and Sledd have effectively exposed prevailing representations of the current literacy crisis. This is important work but it should not obscure the fact that literacy *is* in crisis in contemporary America and, as I have tried to show here, has been repeatedly in the past. However, it is not deteriorating educational standards or the needs of a new high-tech postindustrial economy that have put literacy in crisis but the appropriation of literacy by a stratified educational apparatus and the wider meritocratic order of a credentialed society. Part of the ideological work performed by the discourse of crisis has been the privatization of literacy—the representation of reading and writing not as means of enlarging the public sphere of discourse and political participation but as personal credentials, forms of cultural capital, and articulations of a wider ideology of possessive individualism. What is posed, finally, by the literacy crisis of the mid-1970s is the fate of American democracy and of the capacity of its citizens to think in terms not of private interests but of the public good.

In an era of diminished expectations, persistent economic anxiety, and a restricted political discourse, imagination and political courage are required if literacy is to be re-represented as an intellectual resource against injustice, a means to ensure democratic participation in public life. As writing teachers, theorists, researchers, and program administrators, we are already deeply implicated in the reward system, division of labor, and meritocratic order that have privatized literacy. Our own academic positions are authorized by the hegemony of expertise that legitimates a stratified and antidemocratic educational system. It is now time for us to contest the prevailing representations of literacy and the systems of tracking in secondary schools and of selective admissions in higher education that literacy measures, regulates, and certifies. To counter the growing privatization of education, we need to revive the movement of the late 1960s and early 1970s to democratize higher education through open admissions to *all* colleges and universities, free tuition, and a livable student stipend.

Works Cited

Baron, Dennis. *Grammar and Good Taste: Reforming the American Language.* New Haven: Yale University Press, 1982.

Berger, Joseph. "After Work, Many Now Go to School." *New York Times* (September 8, 1988): A27.

Bledstein, Burton J. *The Culture of Professionalism: The Middle Class and the Development of Higher Education in America.* New York: Norton, 1976.

Bowles, Samuel, and Herbert Gintis. *Schooling in Capitalist America: Educational Reform and the Contradictions of Economic Life.* New York: Basic Books, 1976.

Connors, Robert J., and Andrea A. Lunsford. "Frequency of Errors in Current College Writing, or Ma and Pa Kettle Do Research." *CCC* 39.4 (1988): 395–409.

Cook-Gumperz, Jenny. "Literacy and Schooling: An Unchanging Equation?" In *The Social Construction of Literacy.* Ed. Jenny Cook-Gumperz. Cambridge: Cambridge University Press, 1986, 16–44.

Curti, Merle. *The Social Ideas of American Educators.* Totowa, NJ: Littlefield Adams, 1968.

Douglass, Frederick. *Narrative of the Life of Frederick Douglass*. 1845. Garden City: Dolphin, 1963.

Finkelstein, Barbara. "Reading, Writing, and the Acquisition of Identity in the United States: 1790–1860." In *Regulated Children/Liberated Children: Education in Psychohistorical Perspective*. Ed. Barbara Finkelstein. New York: Psychohistory Press, 1979, 114–139.

Giroux, Henry A. "Literacy and the Pedagogy of Political Empowerment." In Introduction to Paulo Freire and Donaldo Macedo, *Literacy: Reading the Word and the World*. So. Hadley, MA: Bergin and Garvey, 1987, 1–27.

Godkin, E. L. "The Illiteracy of American Boys." *Educational Review* 8 (1897): 1–9.

Graff, Harvey. *The Literacy Myth: Literacy and Social Structure in a Nineteenth-Century City*. New York: Academic Press, 1979.

Hall, Stuart. "The Problem of Ideology—Marxism Without Guarantees." In *Marx One Hundred Years On*. Ed. Betty Matthews. London: Lawrence and Wishart, 1983, 57–85.

Heath, Shirley Brice. "Toward an Ethnohistory of Writing in American Education." In *Variation in Writing: Functional and Linguistic Cultural Differences*. Ed. Marcia Whiteman. Baltimore: Lawrence Erlbaum, 1981, 25–45.

Laquer, Thomas. "Working Class Demand and the Growth of English Elementary Education, 1750–1850." In *Schooling and Society: Studies in the History of Education*. Ed. Lawrence Stone. Baltimore: Johns Hopkins University Press, 1976, 192–205.

Levine, Kenneth. *The Social Context of Literacy*. London: Routledge and Kegan Paul, 1986.

Mattleman, Marcienne S., and Joe Torsella. "The Shame—and Costs—of Illiteracy." *New York Times* (September 13, 1986): A25.

Ohmann, Richard. *Politics of Letters*. Middletown, CT: Wesleyan University Press, 1987.

Resnick, Daniel P., and Lauren B. Resnick. "The Nature of Literacy: An Historical Explanation." *Harvard Educational Review* 47.3 (1977): 370–385.

Sheils, Merrill. "Why Johnny Can't Write." *Newsweek* 92 (December 8, 1975): 58–65.

Shor, Ira. *Culture Wars: School and Society in the Conservative Restoration, 1969–84*. Boston: Routledge and Kegan Paul, 1986.

Sledd, Andrew. "Readin' and Riotin': The Politics of Literacy." *College English* 50.5 (1988): 496–508.

Soltow, Lee, and Edward Stevens. *The Rise of Literacy and the Common School in the United States: A Socio-Economic Analysis to 1870*. Chicago: University of Chicago Press, 1981.

Spring, Joel. "The Evolving Political Structure of American Schooling." In *The Public School Monopoly: A Critical Analysis of Education and the State in American Society*. Ed. Robert Everhart. Cambridge: Ballinger, 1982, 77–108.

18

Observations on Literacy: Gender, Race, and Class

MICHAEL HOLZMAN

There follow some observations about literacy in the United States and an attempt to use those observations as a basis for an argument about the place of literacy in our society. More exactly, this is a consideration of the role of illiterate adults in our society and the concept of literacy as part of the ideological structure of that society. It could be said that the public debate about the plight of illiterate adults is—in part—a way of avoiding discussing racism, specifically the prejudice against the descendents of Afro-American slaves. In the final analysis this prejudice and its structural manifestation as "the underclass" has become a seemingly essential characteristic of our country. In the same way, the very term "underclass" helps us avoid a direct confrontation with racism. The underclass is not a late twentieth-century equivalent of the "lumpen proletariat," some "reserve army" of labor. Composed as it typically is of black people—young men dying young, women on welfare alone with their children—it has as its essential economic function precisely not to add to the labor force. Meaningful considerations of illiteracy, then, must take place in the context of an analysis of our prejudices in regard to race and gender.

When we consider the issue of illiteracy in our society it is helpful to do so along two dimensions: the *literal* dimension, which is eventually the ideological; and the *symbolic* dimension, which is, ironically enough, also the real. Let us begin with the literal dimension. It is, of course, literally true that some adults cannot read and write. There is this situation. And there is an interpretation of this situation as a social "crisis," the literacy crisis. And yet, one thing does not necessarily imply the other. Some adults cannot read and write, but that is not what we mean by illiteracy or the illiteracy problem. The mere fact of illiteracy is not in itself a matter of social concern. A moment's reflection will tell us, for example, that there are people who cannot read who are not poor, and people who cannot read who are not oppressed as a consequence of their illiteracy. On the one hand, there are those whom we might term the physically illiterate, those who have lost the ability to read and write after suffering strokes or other injuries, or through blindness. There are also certain dyslexics who must make their way in the world without benefit of the written word. On the other hand, there are people who simply have not learned to read and yet have not been economically handicapped by this. There are inheritors of great wealth who do not read or write and there are many people, perhaps otherwise indistinguishable from other more or less illiterate beneficiaries of the schools, who have prosperous careers and whom we learn about when they seek adult literacy tuition, if they do seek it, for social or family, not economic, reasons.

Now you might say that the illiteracy of the blind is, as it were, figurative, the illiteracy of the wealthy a curiosity. And, of course, these illiteracies are not obscure at all. They are well known and the reader can surely add other, similar, categories to this list. But those already mentioned should suffice to illustrate the claim that an adult's inability to read and write is not necessarily related to specific social disadvantage—say, poverty. It is only that in many cases illiteracy "happens" to accompany poverty. Now, the point here is not to question the reality of the presumed strong statistical association between illiteracy and poverty; it is first to highlight the complexity of illiteracy as an issue and then to draw attention to certain aspects of illiteracy as a symbol. When then we turn our attention to a symbolic dimension of illiteracy, we find that in our society it stands not so much for ignorance as for the reality of powerlessness and domination. In the United States at the end of the twentieth century, illiteracy, like homelessness, is a way in which domination becomes visible. We think about illiteracy as a "problem" with a "solution": literacy. In the same way naming "homelessness" as a problem implies the solution of "homes" (not houses). But people usually are not homeless because of a lack of "homes". They are homeless because of complex interactions of personal circumstances and governmental policies and procedures—ultimately, because it is useful for them to be treated in this manner—useful if we wish the present structures of society to be maintained.

One might say the symbolic level is a way of thinking about inequity so as not to understand it. Discovering and denouncing a series of symbolic issues, *problems*, implies that there is an underlying *unproblematic* social reality merely marred by temporary aberrations—homelessness, illiteracy— that can and therefore will be eliminated, perhaps after the next election. The literal dimension of illiteracy is ideological in that it allows seemingly random individual facts to disguise structural inequities. The symbolic dimension is real as it becomes part of the structure of that which is, and appears as that which must be. However, when we consider illiteracy in its social context we are not speaking literally of the inability to decipher and inscribe the written language; nor are we speaking of one of many mysterious symbols that seeks to conceal the nonetheless evident inequities in our society. A consideration of the social context of illiteracy points to that structural manifestation of illiteracy that simultaneously is caused by the forces of domination and that also helps perpetuate the oppression of oppressed people, the "economically disadvantaged," that is, the poor.

It is useful to acknowledge that this association of poverty and illiteracy is neither causal nor necessary. It has not always been the case, nor, as we have just seen, is it universally the case today. In the quite recent past, enough people in this country were illiterate—particularly women—that the phenomenon could not be automatically associated with any particular social class below the very wealthy. And to run this argument a bit further, Harvey Graff's research into the etiology of these matters as they stood a few generations ago in Canada has demonstrated that comparative literacy was not an economically determining factor in that country as it made the transition from the Third to the First World. In a country without a significant black population, distinctions among white ethnicities, which were linked to class, were a much more powerful predictor of income level. Once we begin working along this line, we can find many more examples of the lack of correlation among literacy, economic success, and status. There are the contemporary village merchants in India with their hired scribes and there are their sisters in West African marketplaces. There was the European military ruling class of the High Middle Ages. In a certain early modern Jewish tradition, wealth and literacy were often connected only by marriage. If a sign of the ideological is that it appears to be "second nature," then the sheer naturalness of the link among status, economic success, and literacy in our society is an indication precisely of the contingent nature of this relationship.

In the United States today, illiteracy symbolizes that condition of "economic disadvantage" associated with the most oppressed people in our society. No one opening Kozol's *Illiterate America* did so thinking they were about to read about Scarsdale or La Jolla. Not all the economically disadvantaged are illiterate, not all illiterates are disadvantaged—it is not a "real" correspondence—but there is something to this association, something that may be illuminated if we bring another aspect of the literal dimension of illiteracy into the foreground. One of the earliest efforts to achieve universal adult literacy occurred in Sweden in the late seventeenth century (Johansson). The kind of literacy in question was that required to produce a signature and to read set texts. The motivating vehicle used was amusing and quite simple: No one who was not literate in this way could get married. The effort was a great success, which did not, however, have economic repercussions: Literate peasants are no less subjected to their landlords than their illiterate peers. A second example occurred during the Civil War following the Bolshevik Revolution when the first mass literacy campaign of this century was instituted by the Red Army among the peasant recruits pressed into service to replace the factory workers who had formed that army's original core (von Hagen). It seemed that the commissars were worried that the troops would be unable to read *Pravda*. A party that had come to power on the basis of its talent for organization and propaganda needed a literate army. All through the 1920s recurrent efforts were made to achieve this goal and then to extend that work to the civilian population. Nonetheless, full adult literacy was not reached until after World War II, that is, until a new generation had come of age. It is perhaps encouraging that Soviet military discipline was not as powerful a force for literacy as Lutheran marriage regulations. And yet the Red Army literacy campaigns (rather than the Swedish) have been the prototypes for all that have followed.

These literacy stories, the Swedish and the Soviet, might be about technique, the technique of encouraging the spread of literacy. As such, they are sufficiently fascinating. The Swedish Lutheran Church wanted people to read, but to read only certain texts, and to write, but to write only their signature attesting to their adherence to the doctrines set forth in those texts. The Red Army had slightly broader ambitions. Recruits had to read a variety of texts, texts changing with the military situation and shifts in the Party line. On the other hand, it was unnecessary for them to be able to write, although this, too, might be useful for military purposes, and by that date reading and writing were bound together conceptually. Pedagogy followed motive in both these cases. In Sweden, literacy tuition was the responsibility of the father of the house. In the Red Army, there were government and Party officials charged with fulfilling this function.

There are other instructive stories along these lines; however, the point at issue is not ethos but audience. The interests of the Church and those of the Party are equally totalizing in that each institution takes itself to be the communion of all believers, and for a national church and a ruling party that communion must necessarily include everyone within the domain. When belief is encoded in texts (rather than in sermons or ceremonies) illiteracy is unacceptable, subversive. The goal of education must then become effectively that of universal adult literacy (literacy as defined by the needs of the institution in question), and the efficiency of the means employed to achieve that goal are measured against that standard.

The United States has neither a national church based on the individual interpretation of common texts, nor a ruling party committed to the written word as a method of influence. Indeed, we appear to be without any hegemonic ideological vehicle analogous to these institutions. That does not mean that we are without ideology, not even that we are without a hegemonic ideology. It is simply that in this country there are many ideological transmitters that, in the first analysis, as it were, may differ markedly in their short-term goals and strategies. There is corporate America; there are the various religious institutions; there are the military and the universities; there are ethnic and ancestral organizations. Each of these interest groups has its own particular population and the sum of those populations is equal to a large proportion of the citizenry, perhaps even a majority, but it does not include everyone in the country. There are some people in this country, a rather large number, perhaps, whose faith is not required by the coalition of those central to its ideological and socioeconomic identity. Again, this is not an unusual situation. Even in periods and places where a single hegemonic ideology appeared to claim the allegiance of all inhabitants, some groups were accepted as being outside that circle. In early medieval Europe, one way of referring to minority groups that did not share in the dominant ideology was as "pagans," the country people who were not easily brought into the system of beliefs tied to capital and court. In this country today, where it has been said that economics itself is a sort of ideology, our pagans beyond the reach of capital and courts are called the underclass.

As was noted earlier, discussions of illiteracy in the United States usually assume that the illiterate are members of this group, that people fail to become literate as a consequence of underclass status, or that a consequence of illiteracy is assignment to that group, or both, recurrently. It is this situation—these assumptions—that attracts attention to the "literacy crisis." The concerns are not pedagogical. Reading theories are not, in themselves, the matter at issue. Nor is it the case that illiteracy, per se, is the issue. The focus of concern is the social immobility of members of the underclass; illiteracy is taken as important inasmuch as it is seen as contributing to this immobility. There are various layers of irony present in these assumptions, assumptions about the history of social mobility in the United States, assumptions about the relationship between class and race—for the degree of social mobility in this country has never been as great as that claimed in school textbooks, and the limited range of social mobility has rarely been faced. Social mobility has—need one say it?—rarely included blacks. A hyperbolic logic here would give a quick and polemical summary to these lines of thought by calling "underclass" an ideological euphemism for the descendents of slaves and the concern for their illiteracy a way of blaming the victims for their own oppression.

However, let us back away from that for a moment and attempt a seemingly contradictory argument that the essential characteristic of the underclass is not their poverty, color, ethnicity. Their essential characteristic is that they are economically superfluous. They are, to use the terminology invoked earlier, at once pagans without the law and, from an economic point of view, what might be called social luxuries—as odd as this might seem—the equivalent of an aristocracy or a space program.

Just here we probably need a brief discussion of this theory of economic superfluity. For example, there is a common belief that employment is linked to national prosperity, that the higher the percentage of employment, the more prosperous the country and the higher the profits of corporations, the profits of corporations in this argument being taken as equivalent to the national welfare. And yet during the Depression the profitability of big business had recovered to 1929 levels by 1936, while unemployment remained high—an odd fact. But again, once we begin to look for other, similarly odd stories, they multiply readily enough. Think of the lack of employment outside the home for middle-class women in the 1950s. Or, if one wishes to go further afield, think of the noneconomic activities of members of religious orders in places and periods when these have absorbed large parts of the population. (Or the classic English working class on the dole in Leeds and Sheffield—the price of the contemporary restructuring of the English economy.) Full employment is not necessarily an overriding societal goal; ideological forces or simply those of commerce can be sufficiently persuasive to insulate groups from active participation in the economy.

Even our own exemplary economy can tolerate, may require, economically superfluous groups, for better or worse, and for worse one of those is the underclass. Now something that follows immediately from this concept of an economically superfluous underclass is that it is not necessarily in the interest of the groups that dominate the economy to change the status of such an underclass. Beyond the ideological motives involved, there even may be some narrow economic justification for perpetuating this situation; the underclass acts in the economy like the space program or the military: a sector capable of absorbing otherwise disruptive production and expenditures. But there is a broader, more general, structural justification for our underclass, and that justification is ideological rather than economic. The cost of the underclass—and it may very well be a significant cost—is a cost borne for ideological reasons. Another hyperbolic summary: it is ideologically desirable to maintain this group in economic bondage.

There are a number of strands to this argument, a web that is too complicated to fully explore here, but some regions might be touched. One such region is that of intention. Many observers write as if the existence and nature of the underclass were the consequence of a failure of institutions to achieve their aims. But in cases where institutions fail more often than they succeed—and those institutions nonetheless survive—a law of parsimony, call it Holzman's razor, would state it to be more reasonable to say that these institutions had achieved implicit aims at the expense of those proclaimed. Our schools, for example, have many missions. They prepare some children for lives in factories and fast-food stores, others for lives designing or directing those factories and services. They are most often successful with this. It is reasonable, then, to believe that they have not failed in their mission in regard to the children of the underclass, that, in a manner of speaking, they have succeeded in this mission, also. Hence, we can say that children of the underclass are often educated into illiteracy to one degree or another, educated in this way among others into lives in the underclass.

Schools—this is a truism, is it not?—the schools exist in order to reproduce the structure of society. The society they produce includes a largely black underclass. As this has been the case over time and is a constant result of differing circumstances, it would be reasonable to say that schooling in this country is—by and large—structured so as to have that result. Literacy is a key factor in this. But the point is not illiteracy as an end in itself, but the concomitant economic superfluity of a particular segment of the population. Indeed, Graff would tell us that a shift in the equation concerning the variable "literacy" would not change its value, that the underclass would still exist and be exemplified by its most typical citizens, women who are black and poor. (The statistically "typical" illiterate, on the other hand, is white.)

A hierarchy logically requires some final level, some absolute zero of society: the Other. In religious societies, that space is filled by the pagan, the unbeliever. In a society where economics *is* ideology, that necessary Other, that social absolute zero, manifests at the intersection of the forces of domination: sexism, racism, class prejudice. Just as in traditional societies the Other is sufficiently necessary for the reproduction of the social structure that when absent it must be invented, as witches, perhaps, we as a society invent and perpetuate that dark Other, the underclass, and mark it well. We mark it as, among other things, illiterate.

This argument inverts the infrastructure/superstructure relationship traditional in critical thought. However, if the primary category is that of domination — manifesting now as sexism, now as racism or class prejudice — then it is the case that the economic relations in society come into play secondarily. Or, if we do not want to simplify matters to that extent, we might wish to speak of a dialectical tension among these categories. Be that as it may, at this point there seems to be no abstract economic rationale for sexism and racism. These modes of domination are simply characteristic givens of our society. Many things about America could change, and it would still be recognizable. Change these two and we would be in new territory.

When we speak of the problem of adult illiteracy, what we are actually grappling with is very specifically the illiteracy of those members of our society who are considered economically superfluous. Illiteracy in social terms, then, is simply an *inessential* attribute, a symbol, of this economic superfluity. Taken one person at a time, it is amenable to technical solution: Illiterate adults can learn to read. But the argument here is social, not individual. Carefully designed basic literacy programs do work; their students can achieve their goals. But such are the difficulties placed in their way that just 9 percent of those adults contacting literacy programs finally are able to spend a significant amount of time in them. What does it mean for an institution to fail to serve 91 percent of those it is presumably intended to help? And even if the administration of adult literacy programs could be reformed, teaching people how to read and write merely increases the number of people with those skills. It does not eliminate "illiteracy." As quickly as our adult literacy classes produce literate adults, our schools produce many more illiterate youth. And as literacy campaigns come and go and are not fundamental to our social structures, the forces resulting in the production of illiteracy, which are fundamental and which abide, will continue to provide a vast potential student population for adult literacy classes.

If adult basic education is our society's offer of a last chance for literacy, it is more reasonable to think of it as successfully functioning as a very strait gate indeed than as a system in need of tinkering. The present set of literacy education opportunities offer no realistic route out of the underclass for most of those held in that condition. Their failures — and their successes — are part of the way in which the underclass is maintained and reproduced. Not the most significant part, but a part, nonetheless, a part in which we, as specialists in the matter, have a special interest.

What then can we do? It is hardly reasonable to look to the English classroom for the solution to the issues of racism, sexism, and class domination that are at the root of the problem of the underclass. And yet, because the English classroom, K-12 as well as at the postsecondary level, is the place where the gatekeeping function of educators is most frequently exercised, it may also be a place where that function might be challenged. Some have argued that this is best accomplished by the teaching of "critical thinking," either as technique or as content. Certain advocates of "critical thinking" as a classroom technique seem to believe that the propaganda of the word is all-important, a belief easily acquired by those too familiar with the university lecture hall, too unfamiliar with the classrooms of P. S. 30, say, and those inhabited at night by adult literacy classes (except those definitionally atypical ones that they themselves have taught). The behavior of many critics who write about education is congruent with the existing structure, no matter what they might write in opposition to it. Whatever they say, and whatever their intentions, the effect of their writing and speeches is to position themselves as liberators, as more or less charismatic leaders, and it seems that charismatic leaders are always objectively in opposition to the liberation of those-to-be-led.

It is not so much what is taught in classrooms that needs to be changed — although that does need to be changed — but it is the way that schools function as hierarchical organizations that mold the larger hierarchical society, that needs to be changed. A more fundamental approach would be to consider how education takes place, rather than continuing to focus exclusively on curriculum and pedagogy. If the issue of adult illiteracy is a manifestation of social relationships — relationships mirrored and reproduced by the schools — a mode of education that is essentially nonhierarchical would be to the point. This mode would emphasize cooperative learning rather than individual competition, collaborative teaching rather than the teacher as martyr, star, and savior. Teachers, working together with technical experts as needed, would design, then operate schools specifically appropriate for the particular students who attend them. Assessment would be an aid to education rather than an impediment. These schools would be places where everyone learns as a matter of course. They would assume students to be fully individualized persons whose abilities are the foundation for their achievements. Relationships among the adults working in the school would be collegial, not hierarchical. They would model in the classroom that society that we might hope to achieve in other parts of our world.

For in education, as in politics, the most adequate justification for the means that we utilize is the humanity of those means themselves.

Works Cited

Graff, Harvey J. "Literacy, Jobs, and Industrialization: The Nineteenth Century." In *Literacy and Social Development in the West: A Reader*. Ed. H. J. Graff. Cambridge: Cambridge University Press, 1981.

Johansson, Egil. "The History of Literacy in Sweden." In *Literacy and Social Development in the West: A Reader*. Ed. H. J. Graff. Cambridge: Cambridge University Press, 1981.

von Hagen, Mark L. *The Red Army and the Revolution: The Politics of Culture and Enlightenment, 1917–1930*. Columbia University dissertation, 1984.

Contributors

James Berlin spent the first six years of his teaching career in elementary schools in Detroit and Flint. After suffering burnout, he earned a doctorate in Victorian literature from The University of Michigan. The demand for his specialty being nearly nonexistent, he took a position as an assistant professor of composition (not English) at Wichita State University. In 1978 he attended a year-long postdoctoral seminar in rhetoric with Richard Young at Carnegie-Mellon University. In 1981 he moved to the University of Cincinnati to be director of freshman English. In 1987 he began his present position as professor of English (at long last) at Purdue, where he teaches courses in rhetoric and composition and occasionally literary theory. Berlin comes by his politics honestly (as opposed to dishonestly), his paternal grandfather having been a part of the international workers' movement in Poland prior to World War I.

Richard Bullock lives in Yellow Springs, Ohio, with his wife, Barb, and their three sons. He is an associate professor of English at Wright State University in Dayton, where he directs the writing programs and occasionally teaches courses in nonfiction. His previous publications include *Seeing for Ourselves: Case Study Research by Teachers of Writing*, co-edited with Glenda Bissex (Heinemann, 1987).

Nick Coles is a professor in the English Department at the University of Pittsburgh, where he teaches and writes about composition, poetry, and working-class literature. He is the director of the Western Pennsylvania Writing Project, a university/school collaboration affiliated with the National Writing Project. A previous article on the politics of literacy instruction, "Conflict and Power in the Reader-Responses of Adult Basic Writers," also co-authored with Susan Wall, appeared in *College English* in 1987. Coles's most recent publication is an anthology of work-poetry, *Working Classics: Poems on Industrial Life*, co-edited with Peter Oresick (University of Illinois Press, 1990).

Robert J. Connors took his PhD from Ohio State University in 1980 and taught there and at Louisiana State University. In 1984, he moved to the University of New Hampshire, where he is currently an associate professor of English. He is the author of a number of articles on rhetorical history and theory, published in *CCC, CE, RR, FEN, TWI, JTWC, P and R, RSQ, QJS*, and others. With Lisa Ede and Andrea Lunsford, he co-edited *Essays on Classical Rhetoric and Modern Discourse.* He co-authored *The St. Martin's Handbook* with Andrea Lunsford and *The St. Martin's Guide to Teaching Writing* with Cheryl Glenn and edited the *Selected Essays of Edward P. J. Corbett.* In 1982, he was given the Richard Braddock Award by the CCCC for the article "The Rise and Fall of the Modes of Discourse," and in 1985 was co-recipient of the Mina P. Shaughnessy Award from MLA for *CRMD.* He is an anarcho-syndicalist, which fortunately no one understands.

Timothy R. Donovan is Associate Professor of English at Northeastern University in Boston. He is also Director of the Institute on Writing and Teaching at Martha's Vineyard. For many years he directed the freshman English program at Northeastern, and most recently was coordinator of its advanced writing program. He is co-editor of *Eight Approaches to Teaching Composition* (NCTE, 1980) and *Perspectives on Research and Scholarship in Composition* (MLA, 1985), and he has authored numerous articles on writing, pedagogy, and administration.

Elizabeth A. Flynn is co-editor, with Patrocinio Schweickart, of *Gender and Reading: Essays on Readers, Texts, and Contexts* and editor of the journal *Reader.* She has published articles on gender and language use in *College English, College Composition and Communication,* and elsewhere. She is currently focusing on chronicling the contributions of "foremothers" of composition studies. She also directs Michigan Tech's Institute for Research on Language and Learning and is a co-principal investigator of a grant funded by the National Science Foundation in support of Michigan Tech's Writing Across the Curriculum Program.

Toby Fulwiler was an alternate delegate for Eugene McCarthy from Wisconsin in 1968. Upon returning from Chicago, he burned his Democratic Party card. He never, however, actually burned his draft card—a nonevent about which he has mixed feelings. Now at the University of Vermont, his current political activities include growing tomatoes, riding motorcycles, and teaching writing.

Anne Ruggles Gere is Professor of English and Professor of Education at the University of Michigan, where she also serves as codirector of the PhD in English and Education. Her publications include *Writing Groups: History, Theory, and Implications, The Active Reader: Composing in Reading and Writing,* and *Into the Field: The Interdisciplinary Site of Composition Studies.*

Bruce Herzberg is Associate Professor of English and Director of the Freshman Communication Program at Bentley College, where he teaches composition, literature, and speech. He has also helped coordinate Bentley's writing-across-the-curriculum program and its business-communication program. He is co-author, with Patricia Bizzell, of *The Rhetorical Tradition* and the *Bedford Bibliography for Teachers of Writing*.

Michael Holzman is author of *Writing As Social Action* (Boynton/Cook, Heinemann, 1989), written with Marilyn Cooper and co-editor of an adult literacy resource book with Jane MacKillop entitled *The Gateway: Paths to Adult Learning* that will be available nationally in 1991.

Susan Miller is Professor of English and a faculty member in the University Writing Program and in Educational Studies at the University of Utah. She has written *The Written World: Reading and Writing in Social Contexts*, *Rescuing the Subject: A Critical Introduction to Rhetoric and the Writer*, and *Textual Carnivals: The Politics of Composition*. She teaches courses in writing, rhetorical and composition theory and history, cultural and literacy studies, and modern literary theory. In 1990–1991, she was a University Bennion Public Service Professor, focusing on linking academic and public literacy programs.

Thomas Newkirk teaches writing at the University of New Hampshire and just completed a four-year stint as Director of Composition. He has edited *Only Connect: Uniting Reading and Writing* (Boynton/Cook), *To Compose: Teaching Writing in High School and College* (Heinemann), and in 1989 he published *More than Stories: the Range of Children's Writing* (Heinemann). His chapter in this volume draws on his work in teacher research and his concern that such work is dismissed by an increasingly distant corps of academic researchers.

Richard Ohmann is professor of English at Wesleyan University. His most recent book, *Politics of Letters*, appeared in 1987 (Wesleyan University Press). He is a member of the board of *Radical Teacher* and Director of the Center for the Humanities at Wesleyan.

Louise Wetherbee Phelps is Professor of Writing and English at Syracuse University, where she has directed the Writing Program since 1986. Previously she taught at Cleveland State University and the University of Southern California. She has written *Composition as a Human Science: Contributions to the Self-Understanding of a Discipline* (Oxford, 1988) and, most recently, essays on interpreting student texts, planning a developmental writing curriculum, audience and authorship, and teachers' practical wisdom.

Because of her experiences as administrator, program designer, and teacher in a collaborative environment, her interests have turned to what she calls the "prosaics" of composition, involving the daily work and institutional settings of the academic study and teaching of writing. She is currently co-editing with Janet Emig a book on feminism in American composition and rhetoric.

Charles Schuster is an associate professor of English and director of the undergraduate and graduate rhetoric and composition programs at the University of Wisconsin—Milwaukee. A former director of the NCTE Commission on Composition, he has published a number of essays and reviews. His current projects—in addition to the next volume in this series—include a freshman rhetoric, *The Situated Writer*, and an anthology of readings, *Speculations*.

Robert A. Schwegler is an associate professor in the English Department at the University of Rhode Island. In addition to publishing several composition textbooks, he has authored or co-authored articles on readers' expectations for academic discourse, on gender and strategies of argument, and on forms of research writing. He is presently at work on a book-length project tentatively titled *A Theory of Evaluation*.

James Slevin is Professor of English and Chair of the English Department at Georgetown University, where he also directs the writing program. He has taught at Georgetown, Lincoln University, the University of Virginia, and Cornell University. He is currently a member of the CCCC Executive Committee and the NCTE College Section Steering Committee.

John Trimbur is Associate Professor of English in the Department of Humanities at Worcester Polytechnic Institute. He has published a number of articles on collaborative learning, writing theory, and cultural studies and is working on a textbook, *Reading and Writing Culture*, with Diana George.

Victor Villanueva, Jr., is an Assistant Professor of English at Northern Arizona University, where he teaches courses on rhetorical theory, composition theory, and the politics of literacy. His studies are principally on the interrelationships between ideology and language. Publications include "Whose Voice Is It Anyway: Rodriguez' Speech in Retrospect," which appeared in the *English Journal* (December 1987), and "*Solamente Ingles* and Hispanics" in *Not Only English: Affirming America's Multilingual Heritage* (edited by Harvey Daniels, published through the NCTE). He is a member of the NCTE Commission on Language and is the current chair of the NCTE Committee on Racism and Bias in the Teaching of English.

Susan Wall teaches English at Northeastern University, where she is Associate Director of the Institute on Writing and Teaching at Martha's Vineyard and coordinator of the M. A. Degree Program in Writing offered through the Institute. In addition to teacher education and basic writing, her interests include composition theory and case-study research.